D1602359

SIGNAL DETECTION THEORY
AND ROC ANALYSIS
IN PSYCHOLOGY AND DIAGNOSTICS
Collected Papers

SIGNAL DETECTION THEORY
AND ROC ANALYSIS
IN PSYCHOLOGY AND DIAGNOSTICS
Collected Papers

John A. Swets
BBN Corporation and
Harvard Medical School

LEA LAWRENCE ERLBAUM ASSOCIATES, PUBLISHERS
1996   Mahwah, New Jersey

Lawrence Erlbaum Associates, Inc., Publishers
10 Industrial Avenue
Mahwah, New Jersey 07430

Library of Congress Cataloging-in-Publication Data
Swets, John A., 1928–
    Signal detection theory and ROC analysis in psychology and
diagnostics : collected papers / John A. Swets.
        p. cm. — (Scientific psychology series)
    Includes bibliographical references and index.
    ISBN 0–8058–1834–0 (alk. paper)
    1. Signal detection (Psychology)   2. Perception.   3. Recognition
(Psychology)   4. Psychometrics.   5. Psychophysics.   6. Imaging
systems in medicine.   I. Title.   II. Series.
    BF237.S93 1995
    152.1—dc20   95-36337

Books published by Lawrence Erlbaum Associates are printed on acid-free paper, and their
bindings are chosen for strength and durability.

Printed in the United States of America

10 9 8 7 6 5 4 3 2 1

Contents

Preface

Signal detection theory, as developed in electrical engineering and based on statistical decision theory, was first applied to human sensory discrimination 40 years ago. The theoretical intent was to provide a valid model of the discrimination process and the methodological intent was to provide reliable measures of discrimination acuity in specific sensory tasks. The first studies in the psychology laboratory demonstrated that decision factors are fundamentally involved in even the simplest discrimination tasks. In a detection task, the observer decides how likely the presence of a signal must be before he or she will report that a signal is present rather than just noise. In a recognition task, in which a signal is known to be present, the observer decides how likely the presence of Signal A must be relative to Signal B in order to report A. In other words, the observer sets a decision criterion, or a response threshold, along a probabilistic decision variable. The immediate import of this finding was to undermine the venerable concept of a physiologically determined sensory threshold. The decision criterion is set intelligently in accordance with the observer's perception of the prior probabilities of the two possible stimuli and of the various benefits and costs of correct and incorrect responses. The first studies showed also that an analytical method of detection theory, called the relative operating characteristic (ROC), can isolate the effect of the placement of the decision criterion, which may be variable and idiosyncratic, so that a pure measure of intrinsic discrimination acuity is obtained. The model and methods were then used in other areas of psychology in which discrimination is central, including recognition memory, conceptual judgment, and animal learning.

For the past 20 years, ROC analysis has also been used to measure the discrimination acuity or inherent accuracy of a broad range of practical diagnostic systems. It was widely adopted by methodologists in the field of information retrieval, is increasingly used in weather forecasting, and is the generally preferred method in clinical medicine, primarily in radiology. Initial applications have been made also in nondestructive testing of materials, polygraph lie detection, aptitude testing, and survey research. The same need to neutralize variable decision criteria exists in each of these instances, but in these cases additional analysis of the decision criterion plays a basic role in going beyond accuracy to influence and measure the efficacy or utility of a diagnostic system. The decision criterion should be set in routine practice so it is appropriate to the probabilities and the benefits and costs that inhere in any specific diagnostic setting; it should be set as near optimally as possible in assessments of efficacy. The main methodological advances in ROC analysis in the past 20 years have been made in diagnostics and, for the most part, they await employment in the psychology laboratory.

This book attends to both themes, ROC analysis in the psychology laboratory and in practical diagnostic settings, and to their essential unity, by presenting 12 selected articles. The value of assembling them was suggested when one article in preparation in the mid 1980s turned into four separate ones. Together, those four articles give a unified, current statement of the concepts just mentioned: one shows that existing data across the range of discrimination tasks produce ROCs of a certain form; the second develops the implications of that form for theory and measures; the third treats issues in applying the methods and measures that arise in diagnostic settings; and the fourth discusses the science of setting an appropriate decision criterion. These four articles appear, however, in three different journals. Moreover, the seven papers chosen here to illustrate diagnostic applications were published in six diverse journals and a technical report. I appreciate the assurance of publisher Lawrence Erlbaum, senior editor Judith Amsel, and series editors Stephen Link and James Townsend, that the appearance of these materials in one place can be useful now. Introductions to the book and its three parts provide emphasis as well as orientation and attend to some common misconceptions.

The 12 articles appear here as chapters, with only minor corrections and some simplifications of titles, and they preserve the reference and notation styles of the respective journals; I thank the several publishers by whose permission they are reprinted. Some of them were written with colleagues, who are listed in the Acknowledgments with full chapter citations; I am much in their debt. I appreciate also the valuable contributions of several associates who served as advisors to applications in diagnostic fields; they are identified in the respective chapters. Research sponsors for the works in this book include the National Aeronautics and Space Administration, the Council on Library Resources, the Advanced Research Projects Agency of the Department of Defense, the National Cancer Institute, the Agency for Health Care Policy Research, the U. S. Department of Commerce, and the Science Development Program of Bolt Beranek and Newman Inc. (BBN), where the research was conducted. BBN has been a fine place to be for thirty-some years; it has provided a stimulating environment in which I could combine basic and applied research of my choice. Lisa Kennedy there helped with manuscript preparation.

I owe much to long-time colleagues in this line of research. They include Wilson Tanner, Jr., Theodore Birdsall, and David Green of The University of Michigan (the latter also at the Massachusetts Institute of Technology and BBN), and at BBN J. C. R. Licklider, Joseph Markowitz, Ronald Pickett, David Getty, and William Salter, and medical-school faculty members Charles Metz (University of Chicago), Carl D' Orsi (University of Massachusetts), and Robert Greenes, Barbara McNeil, and Steven Seltzer (Harvard Medical School). They have been mentors in many subjects and treasured friends.

Special thanks to my wife Mickey. Her constant support has helped make my work fun.

John A. Swets
Cambridge, Massachusetts

Acknowledgments

Chapter 1 originally appeared as: "The Relative Operating Characteristic in Psychology." *Science,* 1973, *182*(4116), 990–1000.

Chapter 2 originally appeared as: "Form of Empirical ROCs in Discrimination and Diagnostic Tasks: Implications For Theory and Measurement of Performance." *Psychological Bulletin,* 1986, *99*(2), 181–198.

Chapter 3 originally appeared as: "Indices of Discrimination or Diagnostic Accuracy: Their ROCs and Implied Models." *Psychological Bulletin,* 1986, *99*(1), 100–117.

Chapter 4 originally appeared as: "Measuring The Accuracy of Diagnostic Systems." *Science,* 1988, *240*(4857), 1285–1293.

Chapter 5 originally appeared as: "The Science of Choosing the Right Decision Threshold in High-Stakes Diagnostics." *American Psychologist,* 1992, *47*(4), 522–532.

Chapter 6 originally appeared as: "ROC Analysis Applied to the Evaluation of Medical Imaging Techniques." *Investigative Radiology,* 1979, *14*(2), 109–121.

Chapter 7's full citation is: Swets, J. A., Pickett, R. M., Whitehead, S. F., Getty, D. J., Schnur, J. A., Swets, J. B., and Freeman, B. A. "Assessment of Diagnostic Technologies." *Science,* 1979, *205*(4407), 753–759.

Chapter 8's full citation is: Swets, J. A., Getty, D. J., Pickett, R. M., D' Orsi, C. J., Seltzer, S. E., and McNeil, B. J. "Enhancing and Evaluating Diagnostic Accuracy." *Medical Decision Making,* 1991, *11*(1), 9–18.

Chapter 9 originally appeared as: "Effectiveness of Information Retrieval Methods." *American Documentation,* 1969, *20*(1), 72–89.

Chapter 10's full citation is: Humphreys, L. G., and Swets, J. A. "Comparison of Predictive Validities Measured with Biserial Correlations and ROCs of

Signal Detection Theory." *Journal of Applied Psychology,* 1991, *76*(2), 316–321.

Chapter 11's full citation is: Salter, W. J. and Swets, J. A. "Applications of Signal Detection Theory to Survey Research Methodology." Report No. 5785, 1984, Bolt Beranek and Newman Inc.

Chapter 12's full citation is: Getty, D. J., Swets, J. A., Pickett, R. M., and Gonthier, D. "System Operator Response to Warnings of Danger: A Laboratory Investigation of the Effects of Predictive Value of a Warning on Human Response Time." *Journal of Experimental Psychology: Applied,* 1995, *1*(1), 19–33.

Introduction

The focus of this book is on *detection* and *recognition* as fundamental tasks that underlie most complex behaviors. As defined here, they serve to distinguish between two alternative, confusable stimulus categories, which may be perceptual or cognitive categories in the psychology laboratory, or different states of the world in practical diagnostic tasks.

The task of detection is to determine whether a stimulus of a specified category (call it category A) is present or not; a "signal" is to be distinguished from a stimulus from category B, consisting of background interference, or "noise." The task of recognition is to determine whether a stimulus known to be present, as a signal, is a sample from signal category A or a signal category B. The task of *diagnosis* can be either a detection or recognition task, or both. For example, Is there something abnormal on this X-ray image, and, if so, does it represent a malignant or benign condition? In the laboratory, the objective is to measure the acuity with which organisms can make perceptual or cognitive distinctions. In diagnostics, the objective is to assess the acuity or accuracy of human observers and of devices, working by themselves or in combination.

As a result of applying experimentally the concepts of signal detection theory, present understanding of these tasks is that they involve two independent cognitive processes—one of *discrimination* and one of *decision*. A discrimination process assesses the degree to which the evidence in an observation favors the existence of a signal (versus noise alone) or of Signal A (versus signal B). A decision process determines how strong the evidence must be in favor of alternative A to make response A, and makes a choice of A (or B) after each observation depending on whether the requisite evidence is met. Strength of evidence lies along a probabilistic continuum, and the decision maker sets a cutoff along the continuum—a "decision criterion"—such that a strength of evidence greater than the criterion leads to a response of A and a strength lesser, to a response of B.

The observed behaviors in the tasks of interest need to be decomposed, so that the discrimination and decision processes can be evaluated independently. We need to measure the acuity of discrimination unaffected by the location of the decision criterion and vice versa. The emphasis has been on obtaining a pure measure of acuity, but in some instances the criterion is the center of attention. In diagnostic tasks, the placement of the decision criterion is a strong determinant of the efficacy, as opposed to the acuity, of a system.

This book's twelve chapters are organized into three parts. Part I, on "Theory, Data, and Measures," begins in Chapter 1 with a description of signal detection theory in its historical contexts of statistical theory, of detection theory as developed in the field of electronic communications, and of sensory or psychophysical theory in psychology. It shows how a decision process intervenes between stimulus and response in even the simplest discrimination tasks.

Chapter 1 also develops the concept of the receiver, or relative, operating characteristic (ROC) as a graphical means of separating the processes of discrimination and decision, and providing quantitative measures of their function. For specific stimulus categories A and B, the ROC graph is a plot of the proportion of A stimuli called A (y-axis) against the proportion of B stimuli called A (x-axis), as the decision criterion for responding A varies from strict (few stimuli called A) to lenient (most stimuli called A). The A and B categories often have a valence, such that A is "positive" and B is "negative," and so the y-axis is the proportion of true-positive responses (often called "hits") and the x-axis is the proportion of false-positive responses (often called "false alarms"). The ROC represents all four of the response proportions in a two-alternative task: the false-negative proportion and the true-negative proportion are the complements of the other two. (The "R" in ROC stood for "receiver" in the original application to electronic communications. A more general term seems appropriate as applications are made in other fields; the choice of "relative" is explained in Chapter 1.)

Chapter 2 portrays a representative sample of empirical ROCs from the psychology laboratory and from diagnostics and shows them to be basically constant in form, with variation in a single parameter. In Chapter 3, the ROC is seen to provide a touchstone to assess the validity of the many indices of discrimination acuity that have been proposed and used. The better known of the non-ROC indices are shown to imply ROCs having forms not observed in practice and these indices can be seen to give quantitative results that vary substantially while discrimination acuity, in fact, remains constant (and vice versa). In general, the various indices that can be shown to assume a threshold theory—a theory without a variable decision process—are invalidated. In diagnostics, these various indices correspond to the assumption that a diagnostic system has inherent a particular, fixed decision criterion, and, hence that it issues just a single pair of true- and false-positive proportions, which are taken to reflect the system's acuity of discrimination. In medicine, for example, it is common to describe a diagnostic system by its "sensitivity" (its single true-positive proportion) and "specificity" (the complement of its single false-positive proportion).

Part II, on "Accuracy and Efficacy of Diagnoses," focuses in Chapter 4 on accuracy and in Chapter 5 on efficacy. In this terminology, accuracy means discrimination acuity; the efficacy of a diagnostic system depends both on its inherent acuity and on how well its decision criterion is located. The usual objective is a system as acute as it can be made—by selection and training of the human decision maker and by the design of any device employed. ROC theory adds as a second objective the choice of a decision criterion that gives the best balance of true-positive and false-positive response proportions. Ideally, that balance will reflect for a given setting the prior probabilities of the two stimuli to be distinguished (sometimes called "base rates") and also the benefits and costs of correct and incorrect responses. Chapter 4 gives the acuities or accuracies of several representative diagnostic systems in clinical radiology, information retrieval, weather forecasting, polygraph lie detection, and aptitude testing. Chapter 5 develops the need and the theory for setting the optimal decision criterion, taking as examples testing for the human immunodeficiency virus (HIV) and detecting cracks in airplane wings.

In Part III, "Applications in Various Diagnostic Fields," seven chapters describe the ROC evaluation of diagnostic systems in five fields: radiology (three chapters), information retrieval, aptitude testing, survey research, and automated warning systems. In each case, the primary objective is a pure measure of acuity or accuracy, appropriate to the full range of possible placements of the decision criterion. In some cases, the great dependence of the value of the system on the choice of a decision criterion is explicit.

I
THEORY, DATA, AND MEASURES

The three chapters of Part I describe: (a) the origins of signal detection theory and ROC analysis in statistics and engineering and the relation of these concepts to historical concepts in psychophysics and psychology; (b) experimental data in the form of empirical ROCs that support signal detection theory and ROC analysis in psychology and diagnostics; and (c) the implications of those ROC data both for psychological theory and for the several measures of discrimination performance that have been used in psychology and in diagnostic fields.

Chapter 1 describes the relevant psychophysical theory beginning with Gustav Fechner in 1860. It acknowledges Louis Leon Thurstone's 1920s conception of the two stimulus categories to be distinguished as leading to two overlapping (bell-shaped) distributions on an observation variable. In Thurstone's theory, the two stimuli are symmetrical as far as distinguishing between them is concerned, and so a criterion is set on the observation variable where their distributions cross one another. This chapter goes on to show how H. Richard Blackwell in the 1950s extended the conception of the overlapping distributions from Thurstone's consideration of the "paired-comparison," or recognition, task (which Blackwell termed "two-alternative forced-choice") to the "yes-no," or detection, task. This extension was made in the interests of threshold theory, which detection theory replaces, but it was a step along the way, inasmuch as the yes-no task lies at the heart of signal detection theory and is the basis for the ROC. As the last piece of relevant history, this chapter shows how statistical theory developed by Jerzy Neyman and Egon Pearson in 1933, and extended by Abraham Wald in 1950, formed the basis for signal detection theory. In statistical theory, the two overlapping distributions are statistical hypotheses—a null hypothesis and an alternative. In classical hypothesis testing, a decision criterion is selected to yield some small probability of rejecting the null hypothesis when it is true (that is, of making a false-positive decision or Type I error)—usually .05 or .01. Similarly, Blackwell assumed a fixed sensory threshold that would lead to a negligible proportion of positive responses when only noise is present. In going from hypothesis testing to a broader class of statistical decisions, Wald made it clear that a decision criterion could be set anywhere along a decision variable. This was the same variable—the likelihood ratio—for any task and for any definition of the optimal criterion. (A detailed treatment of the statistical heritage of detection theory is given by Gigerenzer, G., and Murray, D. J., *Cognition as intuitive statistics*. Hillsdale, NJ: Lawrence Erlbaum Associates, 1987.)

Chapter 1 points up that the signal detection theory of interest here was developed in the early 1950s by Wesley Peterson and Theodore Birdsall, who were then graduate students in electrical engineering at the University of Michigan. Wilson Tanner and I, graduate students there in psychology, joined them in research and made the first application of the theory to human observers in a study of visual discrimination. Though unaware of Wald's work a few years earlier, Peterson and Birdsall also conceived of a decision criterion that could vary across the range of a decision variable that is the likelihood ratio. To show the consequences in performance of a variable criterion, they devised the ROC. The ROC shows, for a given discrimination acuity (and a given signal strength), how the true-positive proportion (TPP) varies with the false-positive proportion (FPP) as the criterion, or the observer's willingness to make the positive response, is varied. On ordinary arithmetic scales, the ROC extends from 0 to 1.0 on each scale, concave downward, that is, with decreasing slope. An ROC lying on the positive diagonal, with TPP = FPP, shows zero discrimination; an ROC following the left and upper borders, with TPP = 1 for all FPP, shows perfect discrimination. Statisticians sometimes remark that the ROC is simply the "power function" of statistical theory, but the two functions differ fundamentally. In fact, the power function—which shows how TPP increases with increasing signal strength for some selected, small, fixed FPP—is the century-old "psychometric function" of psychological theory.

Chapter 1 proceeds to describe computational procedures for the index of discrimination acuity called d', as popularized in the early applications of signal detection theory in psychology. This chapter anticipates the diminished value of d' suggested by the accumulating data. Specifically, it shows the theoretical ROC on a bivariate-normal graph, that is, on normal-deviate scales that provide a linear ROC. The measure d' is appropriate for ROCs of slope = 1, but empirical data show ROCs of other slopes, varying primarily between 0.5 and 1.0. This chapter mentions the area under the ROC as a "non-parametric" discrimination index appropriate to varying ROC slopes; it does not anticipate the later prominence of an area measure based on bivariate-normal distributions. Chapter 2 shows the robustness of the linear ROC on the binormal graph, by displaying dozens of empirical ROCs that are fitted well by a linear function, with varying slope. The appropriate index is termed A_z—the A for "area" and the "z" to connote the normal-deviate scales of the ROC plot. This index varies from .50 at chance performance to 1.0 at perfect performance. It is now the index of general choice in diagnostic applications of ROC theory and also should be, I suggest, in psychology.

The index of the decision criterion called β (beta) is also described in Chapter 1. It is defined as the criterion value on the likelihood-ratio decision variable and also as the slope of the tangent to the ROC (on ordinary arithmetic scales) at the point that is generated by the given criterion. In contrast to d', the index β has held up well in my opinion (but see Macmillan, N. A., and Creelman, C. D. Response bias: Characteristics of detection theory, threshold theory, and "nonparametric" indexes. *Psychological Bulletin,* 1990, *107*(3), 401–413). A strong point is that optimal decision criteria can be specified by β.

Chapter 1 concludes with a review of conclusions drawn from applications of the ROC in psychology, highlighting areas in which the ability to separate discrimination and decision processes led to revised psychological conceptions. An example is sensory vigilance, in which performance effects long thought to represent declines in discrimination acuity were found in most instances to represent a change in the placement of the decision criterion. Similarly, many established findings thought to represent effects of memory and forgetting in recognition tasks were shown to be effects of differences in the decision criterion.

The empirical ROCs of Chapter 2 sample the psychological topics of human visual detection, recognition memory for odors and for words, conceptual judgment, and animal learning. The chapter's ROCs from diagnostic applications include some from medical imaging, information retrieval, weather forecasting, aptitude testing, and polygraph lie detection. They demonstrate the use of the "rating" task to calculate ROCs based on the adoption of several decision criteria simultaneously, as opposed to successive adoption of single criteria in successive conditions of a yes-no task. The conclusion to be drawn from the survey of empirical ROCs is not that deviations from the linear binormal form never appear, but that the few deviant ROCs do not show any apparent pattern and hence do not support any other particular form. For practical purposes, the linear binormal ROC is apparently adequate and satisfactory and the discrimination index A_z is simple and generally useful. For conceptual calibration, it may help to know that A_z is theoretically equal to the percentage of correct responses in a paired-comparison, or two-alternative forced-choice, task. That is, an observer represented in a yes-no or rating task by an A_z = .80 will state correctly on 80% of the trials which of a pair of stimuli is signal (vs. noise) or Signal A (vs. Signal B).

Chapter 3 is fundamental to measurement of discrimination acuity. It shows that non-ROC indices of discrimination acuity drawn from a 2-by-2 table of stimulus and response are invalid. Included are the percentage of correct responses (that is, the overall percentage of correct positive and negative responses); the true-positive (or "hit") probability corrected for chance success (corrected in either of two ways); the measure of association called the Kappa statistic, used also as a measure of observer agreement; the correlation coefficient derived from 2-by-2 tables, called phi; and an index representing those developed in the field of weather forecasting, called the skill test. In addition to invalidity, these indices suffer from the inconvenience of not accounting for a variable decision criterion; their use assumes that the criterion placement on which they are based is fixed.

The percentage of correct responses is probably the index most difficult to give up. It seems close to the data, unencumbered by theoretical considerations. Yet, it is the easiest to dismiss, even on arithmetic grounds. And it can be shown to make strong theoretical assumptions, as strong as those made by d' and A_z. If empirical ROCs for given observers and tasks look anything like the ROCs shown in Chapter 2 to be representative, the percentage of correct responses will be a highly variable and undependable index of discrimination acuity for those observers and tasks.

To illustrate, the percentage of correct responses, P(C), varies substantially with the prior probabilities (or base rates) of the stimuli. Indeed, it may be defined as the prior probability of a positive stimulus, P(S+), times the conditional probability of a positive response given a positive stimulus, P(R+|S+)—hence, P(S+) P(R+|S+)—added to the product of the corresponding quantities for negative stimuli and responses, i.e., P(S−) (P(R−|S−). [The first conditional probability is the y-axis of the ROC function, earlier defined as TPP, and the second is the complement of the ROC's x-axis, FPP, that is, the true-negative proportion, TNP.] If the prior probabilities are extreme, say P(S+) = .90 and P(S−) = .10, an observer can achieve the higher number as P(C) by giving the same response (here R+) on every trial without attempting to discriminate. Two observers or diagnostic devices can give equal values of P(C) with the incorrect responses from one being almost all false-negative responses (misses) while those from the other are nearly all false-positive responses.

Other difficulties with P(C) can be seen by plotting the ROCs it implies. In general, for any index, one can plot in ROC space its isopleths for various values of the index—the isopleth being a curve connecting points at a given value of the index. The P(C) index, like all of the indices just mentioned as invalid, implies ROCs that are linear on ordinary arithmetic scales. Such ROCs are defined as "irregular," because they do not extend, in concave form (that is, with a smoothly decreasing slope), from the lower-left corner of the ROC graph to the upper-right corner. Instead they cross the axes of the graph at points other than 0 and 1. In so doing, they imply the occurrence of "singular" detection, that is, values of TPP greater than 0 for FPP = 0 and a value of TPP = 1 for values of FPP less than 1.

Moreover, the ROCs for P(C) vary widely in slope with variations in the prior probabilities, P(S+) and P(S−). Specifically, the ROC slope for P(C) is equal to [1 − P(S+)]/P(S+). Thus, the slope is very steep for P(S+) = 0.25 (i.e., slope = 3.0) and very shallow for P(S+) = 0.75 (i.e., slope = 0.33). But every point along lines of both slopes that intersect the negative diagonal at a given point are given the same value of P(C), equal to the ordinate value TPP at that point. Thus, all points along ROCs of any slope that intersect the negative diagonal at an ordinate or TPP value of 0.60, for example, are assigned that value of P(C), or 60%. That value of P(C) can correspond to any of the full range of possible A_z values, from chance to perfect performance. Indeed, some points along ROCs for P(C) will be beneath the positive diagonal and so performances at a level poorer than chance performance will be assigned a value of P(C) greater than 50%.

A distinction must be made between the use of P(C) in a one-observation, asymmetric (yes-no) task and in a two-observation, symmetric (paired-comparison or two-alternative forced-choice) task. In the former, the two stimulus alternatives have a polarity (for example, signal-noise, abnormal-normal, safe-dangerous, wanted-unwanted), and frequently have different prior probabilities, and hence the decision criterion can vary over a large range. In such a setting, P(C) is a poor index of acuity as just indicated. In the symmetric task, on the other hand, the prior probabilities are usually 50-50 and the choice is between alternatives with equal valence (signal in interval 1 or signal in interval 2, signal on the left or signal on the right, etc.), and hence the decision criterion is likely to be symmetric and stable. As mentioned earlier, P(C) in this task is theoretically equal to the area under the ROC, which is the measure of choice in the asymmetric, one-observation task. So P(C) is often appropriate in laboratory studies in which the forced-choice method can be used. The yes-no method is more natural and realistic in practical diagnostic situations.

Chapter 3 shows that three other existing indices of acuity yield ROCs very similar in form to that predicated on the index d′. These are the index η drawn from Luce's choice theory, the log-odds ratio, and Yule's Q index (which is the version for 2-by-2 tables of Goodman's and Kruskal's Gamma index). Like d′, they will be unreliable to the extent that linear binormal ROCs vary from a slope of 1. Unlike indices of the class previously mentioned and illustrated by P(C), which are usually drawn from a single 2-by-2 table and represent a single decision criterion or fixed threshold, the four measures just mentioned are consistent with signal detection theory and a variable decision criterion in the sense that they yield "regular" ROCs as just defined. These ROCs, however, do not represent the range of empirical ROCs in that they have a fixed slope (near 1) on a binormal graph. The conclusion drawn is that none of these indices should be used in preference to the area index A_z. As I indicated earlier, this conclusion is widely shared in medical evaluations, and to some degree in other diagnostic fields, but remains to be appreciated widely in the psychology laboratory.

As described in the Appendix, several computer programs are available for fitting empirical ROCs and for estimating their indices and standard errors.

1

The Relative Operating Characteristic in Psychology

Psychological measurements of an individual's ability to make fine discriminations are often plagued by biasing factors that enter as a covert discrimination is translated into an overt report about it.

Reliable, valid measures are desired of an individual's ability to make a great variety of sensory discriminations, along dimensions such as brightness, hue, loudness, pitch, and the intensive and various qualitative attributes of taste and smell and touch. Sometimes the focus is on the organism's capacity for discrimination, as when the functioning of the sense organs is under study. At other times, interest centers upon the discriminability of the alternatives, as when the measures are used in the development of a product such as color film or tea.

Also sought are accurate measures of more complex perceptual discriminations. How well do individuals judge relative size, distance, direction, time, and motion? How noticeable is a given road sign, and how distinguishable are the signs that employ different combinations of shape, color, and notation to convey different meanings?

Further, it is important to develop unbiased measures of cognitive discriminations, such as those related to memory and conceptual judgment. Psychologists ask people to distinguish objects they have seen before from objects they have not, perhaps nonsense syllables or advertisements; to tell from an article's title, descriptors, or abstract whether it is relevant or irrelevant to a particular need for scientific information; to say whether a given opinion is representative of source A or of source B; and so on.

The translation of covert discrimination into overt report is not direct and simple, according to psychological theory, either because the output of the discrimination process is not definite or because judgmental considerations can override that output. In any case, an inherent ambiguity makes an individual's report prone to influence by such factors as expectations and motivations or, more specifically, by such factors as probabilities and utilities. Thus: The immediate evidence may favor alternative A, but alternative B is more probable on the whole, so I'll more likely be correct if I report B. Again: The evidence may favor A, but the penalty for incorrectly reporting A is relatively large (or the reward for correctly reporting B is relatively large), so I'd be wise to report B.

That probabilities and utilities influence outcomes of the important discriminations people are called upon to make is perfectly clear—as when the clinician reads an x-ray, when the pilot emerges from a low ceiling, or when the Food and Drug administrator suspects that a product is harmful. Less clear, perhaps, is that these and similar biasing factors can play a large role in any discrimination problem, even those problems posed in the rarified atmosphere of the laboratory. A laboratory subject may have unrealistic notions about the prior probabilities of the two alternatives presented, or about the sequential probabilities in random sequences of alternatives. One subject may not mind failing to notice a very small difference and feel foolish asserting a difference when there is none, while another subject may strive to detect the smallest possible difference and accept errors of commission as simply part of the game.

One bothersome effect of the biasing factors, of course, is the variability they introduce. When biases vary out of control, then measurements vary for no apparent reason—from one subject to the next, from one day to the next, from one laboratory to the next. Worse, however, is the potential that biases contribute for misinterpretation. As I shall show, the effects of biasing factors on the report have often been viewed as properties of the discrimination process, with the result that incorrect conclusions have been drawn about the nature of perception and cognition and have been held for long periods.

Psychologists have sought for more than a century to devise measurement procedures that minimize the extent of bias, and, indeed, one procedure more than a century old is largely successful in this respect. The procedure is to present two alternatives at a time, with the assurance that one is A and the other is B, and to ask which is which. Under this scheme, probabilities and utilities are essentially symmetrical. However, it is often desirable, and sometimes necessary, to present just one alternative at a time. In these cases, one must let the biases play and then try to remove their effects by later analysis.

An analytical technique developed more recently does the trick fairly well. It distills and quantifies, collectively, the various factors that bias an individual's report and leaves a relatively pure measure of discrimination. It amounts, quite simply, to plotting the data in the form of what I call here the relative operating characteristic (ROC). The ROC is a curve whose overall location corresponds to a particular degree of discrimination, while the position of any point along the curve represents a particular degree of bias in the report. This provision for two independent measures contrasts the ROC with measurement techniques available earlier, in which discrimination and report bias are confounded in a single free parameter.

The ROC originated in the concept of the operating characteristic, as developed in the statistics of testing hypotheses. This concept was refined—transformed into the relative operating characteristic—in the context of electronic signal detection. I shall trace this development, but I shall first consider how psychology arrived at the point of being ready to accept the ROC. This entails mainly a consideration of psychophysics, a discipline whose beginnings laid the foundation of experimental and quantitative psychology.

After placing the ROC in historical perspective, I describe how to work with it. In speaking to certain practical questions, such as estimation procedures, I also try to indicate ways in which the ROC analysis falls short of perfectly accomplishing the tasks set for it. Last, I review a broad range of applications in psychology, emphasizing those outside of psychophysics, for example, in the study of vigilance, perception, and memory.

PSYCHOPHYSICS

One of the first people to tackle the problem of obtaining precise measures of discrimination was Gustav Theodor Fechner (1801 to 1887). Though a physicist, physiologist, doctor of medicine, poet, aestheticist, and satirist through 70 years of intellectual productivity, he aspired most consistently to be a philosopher. His aim was to overthrow materialism, and he conceived psychophysics to help in this aim by showing empirically the relationship between mind and body. He developed psychophysics as the measurement of attributes of sensation (intensity, quality, duration, extent) and the correlation of these measurements with physical measurements of the stimuli. His *Elemente der Psychophysik* was published in 1860 and translated into English to celebrate its centennial (*1*).

Fechner brought together and further developed what are still the basic psychophysical methods. He used them to measure both the just noticeable difference between two stimuli (otherwise called the difference limen or difference threshold) and the stimulus just noticeable (the absolute limen or threshold). Whereas he sought to obtain in this way the unit and the natural origin of the psychological continuum, I shall not be concerned here with scaling stimuli, but with absolute and difference measures as they are useful individually, depending on the problem. In current terminology, the absolute case is called "detection" and the difference case is called "recognition"; detection is the special case of recognition where one of the two stimuli to be discriminated is the null stimulus.

As Fechner put it, the first problem psychophysical methods confront is "the great variability of sensitivity due to individual differences, time, and innumerable internal and external conditions" (*1*, p. 44). As a matter of course, the methods do so by replication. Each stimulus value may be presented to each subject hundreds of times in order to obtain a relatively stable estimate of the proportion of positive responses. By a positive response, I mean either "yes, I recognize stimulus A [as opposed to B]," in the single-stimulus, or yes-no, forms of the various methods; or "stimulus A is greater than stimulus B," in what have come to be called the paired-comparison, or forced-choice, forms.

Fechner plotted the proportion of positive responses against a physical measure of stimulus strength or stimulus difference to get the psychometric function. This function ordinarily takes the form of an ogive, as shown in Fig. 1a. This form is consistent with a constant sensory effect of a given stimulus and a bell-shaped distribution over time of an assumed physiological threshold, as well as with a fixed physiological threshold and a bell-shaped distribution of the sensory effect of repetitions of a given stimulus (Fig. 1b). Fechner extracted one number from the psychometric function—either a measure of central tendency (usually the median) or a measure of dispersion (a transformation of the standard deviation)—to represent the keenness of discrimination, in particular, to designate the average magnitude of stimulus or stimulus difference needed to exceed the physiological threshold. This number was expressed in units of the physical measure and was taken as a stimulus threshold, which is a statistical construct, as contrasted with the hypothesized physiological threshold. The one number, unfortunately, particularly in the single-stimulus methods, is subject to wide varia-

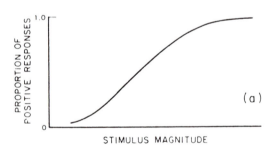

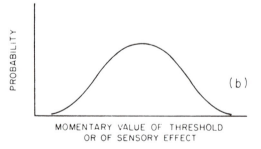

FIG. 1. (a) The psychometric function—the proportion of positive responses as a function of stimulus magnitude; (b) the mechanism assumed to underlie the psychometric function—a temporal variation either in a sensory threshold or in the sensory effect of a given stimulus (1).

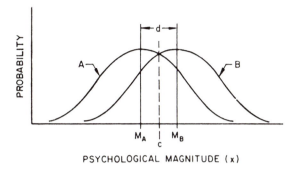

FIG. 2. Hypothetical distributions of the psychological magnitudes of
two confusable stimuli, *A* and *B* (2). The distance between their means,
d, can be inferred from the observer's judgments and is a measure of
discriminability. The dashed line, *c,* represents a symmetrical decision
criterion, in anticipation of the ROC analysis, which emphasizes a variable criterion.

tion with variation in the judgmental factors that intervene between discrimination and response.

Louis Leon Thurstone (1887 to 1955) made the next great advance in the study
of discrimination. Bringing the tradition of psychometrics together with psychophysics, he showed how Fechner's methods could be used to quantify psychological attributes of stimuli not readily susceptible to physical measurement—how
they could be used, for example, to assess the excellence of handwriting. Thurstone stressed the variable psychological magnitude (sensory effect) of repetitions
of a given stimulus and ignored the concept of a physiological threshold. He also
emphasized the importance of the paired-comparison procedure in reducing distor-
tions of response frequencies and concentrated on difference (recognition), as
opposed to absolute (detection), measurements.

Thurstone's approach to measuring discrimination was outlined in his basic
work in 1927 (2). His model begins with the assumption of overlapping distributions of the psychological magnitudes of two similar stimuli, shown in Fig. 2, the
starting point of every other model I consider here. The model proceeds with
some very specific assumptions (also characteristic of most of the more recent
models), including normality of the distributions, zero correlation between stimuli, and equal standard deviations. From the proportion of times stimulus B is
judged greater than stimulus A, along with a table of areas under the normal
curve, one determines the difference between the means of the two distributions.
This difference, denoted *d* in Fig. 2, is expressed in units of the standard deviation.

Thurstone could get by with the single parameter because he supposed, with
justification, that the paired-comparison procedure comes close to eliminating

judgmental biases. He assumed that subjective probabilities and utilities were symmetrical, that the observer would select B as his response whenever the psychological magnitude of stimulus B exceeded that of stimulus A, and vice versa.

This assumption of symmetry can be simply related to the essence of the ROC analysis, if one considers the implications of the assumption for the single-stimulus procedure. First, define the judgmental or response bias in terms of the decision criterion: the decision criterion is a cutoff point (c) along the axis of sensory effects (x) such that values of x above c lead to response B, while values of x below c lead to response A. Then note that Thurstone's assumption of symmetry is equivalent to assuming a decision criterion (represented by the dashed line in Fig. 2) located at the point where the two distributions cross. The ROC analysis, on the other hand, allows the observer to locate the decision criterion anywhere throughout the entire range of x and extracts a measure of discrimination, for example, the one I have denoted d in Thurstone's model, that is independent of the location of the criterion. The ROC technique thus salvages the single-stimulus procedure, in which a symmetrical or otherwise reliable criterion is highly unlikely. The ROC technique also yields a second measure, that of the location of the decision criterion.

The next step in psychophysics was taken in the 1940's and is typified in the work of H. Richard Blackwell (3). Blackwell advocated a procedure akin to the paired-comparison procedure, which he called the forced-choice procedure, but it is his application of some of Thurstone's thinking to the single-stimulus (yes-no) procedure that is of interest here.

Blackwell focused on the detection problem, in which one of the two stimuli considered is the null stimulus. By the time he began his work, however, developments in electronics and physiology had changed the conception of the null stimulus from being nothing, or a blank presentation, to being a stimulus in fact. In particular, the new view was that the variability inherent in the environment and in the observer—what we have come to call "noise"—would produce sensorineural activity that could be confused with the sensory effect of the stimulus to be detected. So one of Thurstone's (normal, uncorrelated, constant-variance) distributions, the one with the lower mean, could represent noise alone, while the other could represent noise plus "signal." Noise and signal effects can be plotted on the same axis because they are, by definition, qualitatively the same. The minimal background of noise is created by uncontrollable events outside and inside the observer; the level of noise can be raised by introducing a masking stimulus background—for example, an illuminated screen when the signal is a brief spot of light or a hissing sound when the signal is a brief tone.

Although Blackwell realized that noise could interfere with detection of the signal, he made a further assumption that essentially eliminated the possibility of noise being mistaken for a signal. He assumed the existence of a criterion for a positive response at a level such that the observer would rarely be misled by the noise into reporting a signal (see dashed line in Fig. 3). With such a criterion, fixed over time, the number of false-positive responses ("yes" responses to noise alone) that could be attributed to the noise, when it momentarily reached a high level, would be negligible. Such a criterion reminds one of the familiar rule in statistical testing for rejecting the null hypothesis at, say, the 1 percent level of confidence.

Blackwell acknowledged that biasing factors might favor a positive response, that the observer might say "yes" on some trials even though the sensory effect during the trial period failed to exceed the criterion (although he ignored the possibility that the observer might say "no" when the sensory effect did exceed the criterion). Blackwell assumed, however, that values of sensory effect below the fixed criterion were indistinguishable—as if this criterion were a physiological threshold—so that the observer could only be guessing that a signal was present when one of these values occurred and would then be correct only by chance. He therefore applied a correction for chance success, according to which the proportion of false-positive responses is taken as an index of the amount by which the proportion of correct-positive responses is inflated, so that by a subtractive procedure the proportion of "true" positive responses is obtained. A correction for chance success was used by others in sensory studies; indeed, it is familiar throughout psychology, having a long history in, for example, studies of recognition memory. In the form of the correction Blackwell adopted, the proportion of correct-positive responses minus the proportion of false-positive responses is divided by 1 minus the proportion of false-positive responses.

Given the proportion of so-called true responses for each stimulus magnitude,

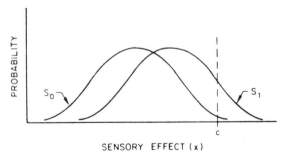

SENSORY EFFECT (x)

FIG. 3.   A possible revision of Thurstone's recognition model to represent detection. Sensory effect is assumed to vary according to the left-hand distribution when the null stimulus, S_0, or noise alone, is present and according to the right-hand distribution, S_1, when a given signal is added to the noise. The criterion for a positive response, c, is assumed to be fixed at such a point that it is rarely exceeded by noise alone, with no discrimination possible below that point; therefore, positive responses to the null stimulus can be considered random guesses (3).

it was a short step to plotting the psychometric function and taking the stimulus magnitude corresponding to a response proportion of 0.50 as the stimulus threshold, a one-parameter measure of discrimination.

It can be shown that use of the chance, or guessing, correction assumes that all psychometric functions based on raw proportions, whatever the proportion of guesses or false-positive responses, will correct to a single true curve, as represented in Fig. 4. To state it another way, the chance correction assumes statistical independence of false-positive and true-positive responses. The next pertinent development in psychophysics was the empirical finding that this assumption is not justified, a finding that served to discredit the notion of a fixed criterion for response (or a physiological threshold) located at the upper end of the noise distribution and to undermine the associated measure of discrimination.

Before turning to those empirical results, a few more words about the concept of the null stimulus. In the view of classical psychophysics, the observer should report his *sensations;* to base his reports on the *stimulus*—for example, to let stimulus probabilities and stimulus-response utilities affect the report—is to commit the "stimulus error." In that context, presentation of the null stimulus is a "catch trial": If the observer is caught in a false-positive response, he or she is admonished to pay better attention to the task. The null stimulus is presented infrequently, and the false-positive responses are not counted (4).

An opposing view, the so-called objective view, was advanced about the turn of the century, adopted by Thurstone and to a lesser extent by Blackwell, and embraced with a vengeance in the context of the ROC analysis. The observer is expected to commit the stimulus error. The probability of a false-positive response must then be carefully estimated, preferably on the basis of as many trials as the probability of a correct-positive response. Rather than subjecting these

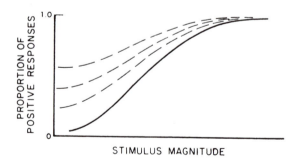

FIG. 4. The correction for chance success implies that psychometric functions obtained with different proportions of false-positive responses (dashed lines) will all correct to one "true" function (solid line). The correction simply normalizes any curve obtained, reducing to zero the proportion of positive responses made to zero stimulus magnitude.

proportions to the correction for chance, which assumes a decision criterion fixed at a particular value, the ROC analysis uses them to determine the location at that time of a variable criterion.

Substantive support for the ROC approach was supplied by three empirical studies conducted independently in the early 1950's by Moncrieff Smith and Edna A. Wilson, William A. Munson and John E. Karlin, and Wilson P. Tanner, Jr., and me. In each study, data were obtained from observers using different decision criteria in yes-no detection tasks (5).

Smith and Wilson, working at the Lincoln Laboratory of the Massachusetts Institute of Technology, were studying the gains in detection performance that were expected to accrue from using teams of observers rather than individual observers. The basis for the study was the assumption that temporal variations in the sensitivity of individuals are less than perfectly correlated, and therefore if one observer were momentarily insensitive another might detect the signal. In their analysis, Smith and Wilson varied the number of individual positive responses that they would take as representing a positive response by the team and noted corresponding differences in the numbers of false-positive responses issued by the team. Recognizing that the number of team false positives would depend also on individual tendencies toward false positives, they instructed some observers to be "conservative" and others to be "liberal" in deciding to report a signal; still others were to respond according to a four-category scale of certainty that a signal existed.

Munson and Karlin, at the Bell Telephone Laboratories, were examining some concepts derived from the communications theory developed by Claude Shannon of that same laboratory. Measuring the rate of information transmitted by their observers' detection judgments required a good estimate of the probability of a positive response to the null stimulus. Their data showed individual differences among their observers that they described by the terms "safe," "objective," and "risky."

Tanner and I, at the University of Michigan, had studied sensory psychology with Blackwell and were associated with the laboratory in which fellow graduate students Wesley W. Peterson and Theodore G. Birdsall were applying statistical decision theory to radar detection problems and were developing the ROC analysis. We encouraged our observers to vary the proportion of false positives from one group of trials to another by varying the a priori probability of signal presentation and the values and costs (in cents) associated with correct and incorrect "yes" and "no" responses. We also required observers to set several criteria simultaneously and report according to a rating scale.

The three sets of experiments—two in audition, one in vision—showed that the correction for chance did not map all psychometric functions, with different proportions of false-positive responses, onto the same curve. Stimulus thresholds decreased as false positives increased. Corrected, "true" proportions of positive responses at each signal level were highly correlated with proportions of false-positive responses. Evidently, the observers did not produce more positive responses by guessing, by responding "yes" to a random selection among indistinguishable sensory effects that fell beneath a fixed criterion or sensory threshold, but rather by setting a lower criterion. It was clearly courting trouble, then, to extract one of the traditional measures of discrimination without regard to the variable criterion.

At the same time, it was clear that means existed for calibrating any criterion an observer might adopt. What has come to be the preferred measure, the likelihood ratio, was proving useful in a related problem in the field of mathematical statistics. A brief review will give the highlights of that development.

STATISTICAL THEORY

The problem faced in testing statistical hypotheses, or in making statistical decisions, is usually represented pictorially in much the same way that Thurstone and Blackwell represented the discrimination problem. Figure 5 shows the familiar overlapping, bell-shaped distributions, here representing sampling distributions of test statistics. The left distribution represents the null hypothesis, H_0, and the right one represents an alternative hypothesis, H_1. H_0 might assert, for example, that the mean of a population, μ, is equal to some value, μ_0, while H_1 asserts that μ is equal to some other value, μ_1. On the basis of an observation x, one or the other of the hypotheses is accepted.

The construction of a statistical test is equivalent to dividing the x axis into

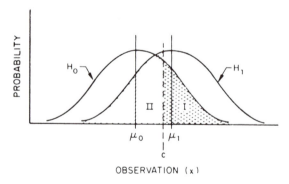

OBSERVATION (x)

FIG. 5. Population distributions in statistical theory: H_0, the null hypothesis, asserts that the population mean, μ, equals μ_0; H_1, an alternative hypothesis, asserts that $\mu = \mu_1$. The area under H_0 to the right of the decision criterion c represents the probability of a type I error; the area under H_1 to the left of c represents the probability of a type II error.

two regions; that is, setting a decision cutoff, or criterion (c), such that sample values of x less than c lead to acceptance of H_0 and sample values of x greater than c lead to acceptance of H_1. Where the criterion is set will determine the relative probabilities of the two possible types of errors: type I errors, which consist in accepting H_1 when H_0 is true, and type II errors, which consist in accepting H_0 when H_1 is true. In general, one wants to adjust these error probabilities in accordance with the relative costs of the two kinds of error, but must choose among several different rules for doing so.

General principles governing such rules were advanced by Jerzy Neyman and Egon Sharpe Pearson in 1933 (6). The particular rule associated with them, and the most familiar rule in statistics, is to fix the probability of a type I error arbitrarily (at a significance level, or confidence level, usually .05 or .01) and then to choose the criterion in such a way as to minimize the probability of a type II error. They showed that the best such test is defined in terms of the likelihood ratio, which is the ratio at any value of x of the ordinate of the H_1 distribution to the ordinate of the H_0 distribution. One accepts H_1 whenever the likelihood ratio exceeds some number c, where c is chosen to produce the desired probability of a type I error.

Ordinarily, instead of considering the probability of a type II error, the focus is on 1 minus that probability, or the probability of accepting H_1 when it is true, called the "power" of the test. Under the Neyman-Pearson rule, then, one fixes the probability of a type I error and chooses the likelihood ratio equal to c in order to maximize the power of the test. When H_0 is tested against several alternatives instead of just one, the power function of the test can be represented as in Fig. 6a. Note that this function is essentially the same as the psychometric function defined by Fechner and that the Neyman-Pearson decision rule was assumed in Blackwell's model.

The operating characteristic, as defined in statistics, is simply 1 minus the power function, as shown in Fig. 6b. The ROC is a graphic way of comparing two operating characteristics—the one just defined and another, rarely seen, if ever, that shows the variation in the probability of a type I error with a fixed probability of a type II error. The ROC gives the two types of errors equal status and shows how they covary as the criterion changes for any given difference between the means of the two hypotheses.

The advance in statistical decision theory that brings one to the present time, although probably understood by Neyman and Pearson, was made by Abraham Wald in the 1940's (7). Wald showed that several quite different decision rules—such as maximizing the proportion of correct decisions, maximizing the expected value of a decision, and maximizing the minimum payoff—are unified by means of the likelihood ratio. He made it clear that one construct would handle many of the decision rules an observer might adopt, as well as any of the many criteria that one of those rules might dictate.

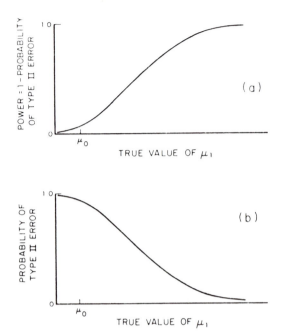

FIG. 6.   (a) The power function of a statistical test. (b) The inverse of the power function, the operating characteristic.

DETECTION THEORY

The detection of electromagnetic signals in the presence of noise was seen in the early 1940's to be a problem of testing statistical hypotheses. Noise alone was identified with the null hypothesis, H_0, while noise plus a signal was associated with the alternative hypothesis, H_1. The concern then for radar signals highlighted the importance of a variable decision criterion and the possibility of various decision rules. In the radar context, type I errors are "false alarms" and type II errors are "misses," and whereas both are pretty clearly bad in a defensive situation, their relative cost varies widely with different threats and available reactions to a threat.

The unification of several decision rules by the likelihood ratio was described in two presentations at the 1954 Symposium on Information Theory (sponsored by the Institute of Radio Engineers at the Massachusetts Institute of Technology) —one by David Van Meter and David Middleton of Harvard University and another by Wesley W. Peterson, Theodore G. Birdsall, and William C. Fox of the University of Michigan. Discussion following the coincidence revealed that the Harvard theorists had read Wald, while the Michigan theorists had developed the idea independently. It was this unification of several decision rules that established the generality of the ROC analysis.

The ROC analysis first appeared in the literature in the transactions of that symposium (in papers by the two groups of authors just mentioned and in a paper by Tanner and me), although Peterson and Birdsall had presented it a year earlier in a technical report (8). So it is fair to say, from the vantage point of psychology, that Peterson and Birdsall showed us how to plot the data.

The ROC is a plot of 1 minus the probability of a type II error (which equals "power" in statistics and the probability of a "hit" in the detection context) against the probability of a type I error (or "false alarm"), as the decision criterion varies, with the difference between the means of the two hypothetical distributions as the parameter. This difference between the distributions' means is essentially the d of Fig. 2 (representing Thurstone) and the $\mu_1 - \mu_0$ of Figs. 5 and 6 (representing statistical tests). When Peterson and Birdsall used normal distributions of equal variance, which they derived for certain kinds of signal and noise, they used the symbol d to denote the difference between the means in units of the variance. When Tanner and I assumed distributions of that form, we used the symbol d' to denote the difference between the means in units of the standard deviation ($d' = \sqrt{d}$). Other assumptions and no assumptions are possible, and require other notations, but the measure d' is the one used most often in psychology.

Figure 7 shows a family of ROC curves based on normal, equal-variance distributions (solid lines). Note that vertical and horizontal cuts through the curves yield the two kinds of operating characteristic mentioned earlier: the vertical cut gives the probability of a type II error for fixed probability of a type I error, the garden variety operating characteristic; the horizontal cut gives the unfamiliar reverse of that operating characteristic. It is because the ROC is a comparison of two operating characteristics that I use the term "relative" operating characteristic, according to a suggestion by Birdsall. Originally, serving to confuse the ROC and the OC (operating characteristic) in the detection context, the R stood for "receiver." That terminology stemmed from the broader perspective of communications, which views detection as part of the reception process. Sometimes, according to a suggestion by R. Duncan Luce, the ROC's footing in statistics is ignored in psychological usage and the ROC is called an "isosensitivity curve" (9). This term might be preferable except for the fact that the ROC is also applied to problem areas in psychology not usually thought of in terms of sensitivity (to memory, for example), and the proliferation of terms like "isomnemonic curve" obscures the identity of the single, underlying technique.

The ROC analysis thus gives a measure of discrimination that is independent of the location of the decision criterion and is presumably uncontaminated by the processes, such as expectation and motivation, that affect the response. At the same time, the ROC analysis provides a measure of the net effect of processes that influence response—specifically, the location of the decision criterion—at

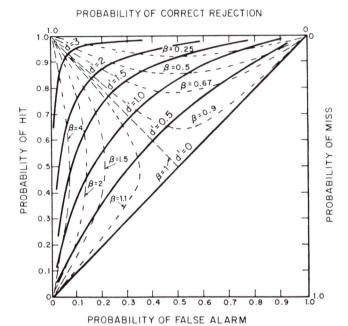

PROBABILITY OF CORRECT REJECTION

FIG. 7.   A family of theoretical ROC curves based on normal, equal-variance distributions, with the parameter d' (solid lines). Also shown is a family of theoretical isobias curves, with the parameter β (dashed lines). The quantities shown on the left and lower coordinates are the two quantities ordinarily used in ROC analysis; the quantities shown on the right and upper coordinates are added here to point out that they are complements of the other two, respectively.

any given time. This measure, called β in the ROC context, is the value of the likelihood ratio at which the criterion has to be set to yield a particular point on a given ROC curve. It can be shown that the measure β equals the slope at which the given ROC curve passes through that particular point. The dashed lines in Fig. 7 are curves of constant β, or isobias curves.

We will proceed shortly to consider some computational details. Note simply now that, if one assumes normal, equal-variance distributions, then certain response proportions plotted as a single point in the ROC space yield independent measures of discrimination (d') and extra-discrimination effects (β). Ordinarily, the decision criterion is manipulated from one group of trials to another, or a rating technique is used to the same effect, in order to obtain better definition of the curve.

In leaving this brief treatment of detection theory, I should observe that the theory has been developed to specify a variety of forms of ROC curves for various kinds of signals and noises and to specify ideal detection performance for various kinds of signals and noises. Although I do not treat the topic here, mathematical models of ideal observers—which show in the limit how d' or a similar measure varies with a physical measure of signal-to-noise ratio—have been used as normative models in sensory psychology, in an attempt to determine what sort of information the human observer extracts from the stimulus (10).

COMPUTATIONAL PROCEDURES

Data collected for a given location of the decision criterion yield a 2-by-2 contingency table of stimuli and responses. I refer to the stimuli as S_1 and S_2 in the recognition case, and as S_0 and S_1 in the detection case (where S_0 is the null stimulus); and, similarly, to the responses as R_1 and R_2 or R_0 and R_1. Although one of my major purposes is to relate the ROC analysis to a broad class of perceptual and cognitive discrimination problems, it will be simplest to use the terminology of the detection problem throughout the following discussion of computational procedures.

An example of a contingency table for the detection case is shown in Fig. 8. These frequency data give estimates of the conditional probability of a false alarm

$$P(R_1|S_0) = 10/100 = .10$$

and of the conditional probability of a hit

$$P(R_1|S_1) = 80/100 = .80$$

(The other two conditional probabilities implied by the table, "misses" and "correct rejections," are their complements.)

The straightforward way to calculate d' and β from these two probabilities is

	S_0	S_1
R_0	90	20
R_1	10	80
	100	100

FIG. 8. A contingency table of stimulus and response. The detection notation is used: S_0 for the null stimulus and S_1 for the stimulus to be detected; R_0 for the "no" response and R_1 for the "yes" response.

by means of a table of normal curve functions. The false-alarm probability of .10 indicates that the criterion is 1.28 standard deviations above the mean of the S_0 distribution, and the hit probability of .80 indicates that the criterion is 0.84 standard deviations below the mean of the S_1 distribution. The value of d' is the sum

$$1.28 + 0.84 = 2.12$$

The measure β is the ratio of the ordinate of the S_1 distribution to the ordinate of the S_0 distribution at the criterion setting

$$0.28/0.18 = 1.55$$

Tables that give d' and β directly for any pair of false alarm and hit proportions are also available (*11, 12*).

When data are available for several criterion locations, either because the observer varied his or her criterion from one group of trials to another or reported by means of a rating scale, one may use graphs to estimate d'. The theoretical curves of Fig. 7 are straight lines of unit slope when plotted on probability scales—that is, on coordinate scales that space linearly the normal deviates—as shown in Fig. 9. Thus, one can fit several points by a straight line of unit slope and get d', by subtracting the normal-deviate value corresponding to the hit proportion from the normal-deviate value corresponding to the false-alarm proportion, at any point along that line (*13*).

Not all data are fitted well by a straight line of unit slope, of course, and this fact presents a complication. A departure from linearity violates the normality assumption, and nonunit slope violates the equal-variance assumption; in fact, for normal distributions, the slope equals the ratio of the standard deviation of S_0 to the standard deviation of S_1. As it happens, the linearity condition is usually met, and the question is what to do about nonunit slope. It is apparent that the measure d' is everywhere different along a line of nonunit slope, and so does not provide the necessary invariance.

There are three or four ways to contend with this problem. A direct reaction is to use two parameters to represent the ROC curve; for example, (i) the difference between the means of the two supposedly normal distributions, with the standard deviation of the S_0 distribution as the unit, and (ii) the slope of the ROC. An alternative is to use a one-parameter description that ignores slope information; for example, the value of d' at the negative diagonal or the perpendicular distance from the center of the ROC space to the ROC curve, each of which enlists a unit based on the standard deviations of both distributions.

Another way to achieve a one-parameter representation is to assume distributions that predict nonunit slopes—specifically, distributions that predict how the slope will vary with the difference between the means. One can assume, for example, normal distributions with standard deviations that are constant fractions of the means (although then the decision axis cannot be monotonically related to

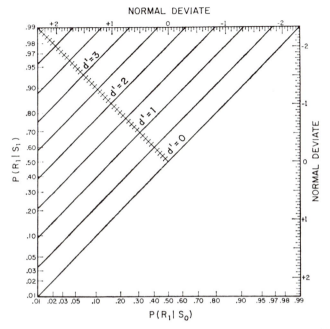

FIG. 9. The theoretical ROC curves of Fig. 7 plotted on probability scales (left and bottom) and on linear normal-deviate scales (top and right).

likelihood ratio). One might otherwise assume Poisson, exponential, gamma, or Rayleigh distributions, in each case distributions whose variances are direct functions of their means. This class of alternatives predicts slopes less than unity, slopes that decrease with increasing discrimination—a prediction reasonably in accord with data. In some discrimination tasks a rationale exists for selecting one of these distributions.

At the other extreme, one might want to assume nothing at all about the distributions underlying the ROC. The proportion of the area of the entire ROC space that lies beneath the ROC curve is a distribution-free measure of sensitivity. It is equal to the probability of a correct choice in a two-alternative, forced-choice task no matter what distributions exist. This and the other measures mentioned in the preceding paragraphs have been described in more detail elsewhere (10, 11, 14). The main point for present purposes is that, although the simple measure d' will not do the whole job, other measures of discrimination that are independent of report bias can be extracted from the ROC.

While on the subject of alternative measures of discrimination, let me note that measures of criterion location other than the likelihood ratio are also available. The distance in standard-deviation units from the mean of the S_0 distribution to the criterion location is one such measure, with certain advantages and disadvantages relative to the likelihood ratio (*15*). A nonparametric index of response bias is also available (*16*).

The fact that detection theory predicts ROC curves quite different in form from the ones that can be derived from the chance correction formula, with which the psychological detection theory was first compared, may be the reason that some investigators have tried to infer too much about underlying processes from the form of empirical ROC curves. The basic thought to keep in mind in this regard is that the ROC form reflects only the differences between the two underlying distributions; it does not imply anything about the form of the distributions individually. Indeed, most unimodal distributions will produce an ROC curve that is very nearly a straight line on probability scales; even a rectangular S_0 distribution and a ramp S_1 distribution lead to a linear ROC on those scales (*17*). Moreover, assumptions about the decision process enter in a critical way. Thus, for example, if the variance of the decision criterion is large, the slope of the linear ROC will approach unity, even if the standard deviation of S_1 is much larger than the standard deviation of S_0 (*18*). Again, with certain parameters assumed for the decision process, a two-state discrimination process can produce as smooth an ROC curve as that produced by a discrimination process that yields a continuous output (*19*). It may also be noted in this connection that the technique used to calculate an ROC curve from rating data is cumulative and therefore forces a monotonic, increasing curve.

When the ROC analysis was first devised, data points were fitted by eye, for lack of a known alternative, and this procedure is still probably adequate for many applications. However, several more objective estimation procedures have been devised (*20*). Significance tests for observed differences in d' have also been developed (*21*), and the sampling variability of the value of d' at the negative diagonal and of the area under the ROC curve have been examined (*22*).

APPLICATIONS

The ROC confers the ability to measure covert discriminations in single-stimulus tasks in a relatively pure form—to measure these discriminations, at least to first order, unconfounded by the biasing factors that tended to distort the overt report in the measurement procedures previously available. How has psychology profited?

Published studies in which the ROC has been used fall into a dozen or so substantive areas. In some of these areas the value has primarily been more reliable and valid measurements; I will treat those areas here only by reference. In other areas the ROC has led to substantially revised interpretations; I will discuss briefly a few examples: sensory functions, vigilance, perceptual selectivity, and memory.

The basic applications of the ROC to sensory processes have been presented in a collection of articles (*11*) and a systematic textbook (*10*). These volumes report studies of detection and recognition processes in several sensory modalities and support the following conclusions.

1) Empirical ROC curves can be reliably obtained by manipulating signal probability or the values and costs of the various stimulus-response outcomes; by verbal instructions to adopt, say, a "strict," "medium strict," "medium," "medium lax," or "lax" criterion; or by instructions to use those criteria simultaneously as the boundaries of rating categories.

2) Measures of sensitivity that do not isolate effects of changes in the decision criterion ignore a substantial source of variation.

3) The ROC analysis rescues an important test method, previously suspect because of its great susceptibility to biasing effects—the single-stimulus method.

4) Of sensitivity measures extant, only those associated with the ROC model give reasonably consistent results across yes-no, rating, and forced-choice procedures.

5) When the stimulus is measured in terms prescribed by detection theory, the functional relationship obtained between d' and stimulus magnitude is practically the same from one laboratory to another.

6) Some prominent conceptions of the sensory threshold are incorrect, and the theories and test methods that depend on them are invalid.

Vigilance is the practical detection problem—the observation period is long and signals occur infrequently. The first studies, around 1950, showed that the probability of a correct detection drops off noticeably in only a half hour or so of observation (*23*). What seemed at the time to be a rapid decrement in performance was surprising, for the subject was not asked to work very hard. Hundreds of studies conducted since, with a great variety of stimulus displays, have shown the same sort of decrement. They have examined a host of psychological, physiological, situational, and environmental variables thought to affect alertness, including work-rest cycle, intersignal interval, irrelevant stimulation, incentives, knowledge of results, introversion-extroversion, temperature, drugs, age, and sex (*24, 25*). At least five theories have been proposed to account for the apparent decrement in sensitivity (*26*).

In the early 1960s, several investigators, led by James P. Egan (*27*), began to question the assumption that a sensitivity decrement occurs in these vigilance tests. The ROC analysis makes it clear that the probability of a hit could decline without implying a decrease in sensitivity; if the proportion of false alarms also dropped, sensitivity might remain constant while the decision criterion changed. A progressively more conservative decision criterion might come about as the result of a decreasing expectation of signal occurrence (for example, when a naive subject experiences a high signal probability in training sessions and then a low signal probability in test sessions), or it might result from a motivational change (for example, if the perceived value of a hit were to decrease over time relative to the perceived cost of a false alarm).

The ROC analysis was quickly employed in some 30 studies of vigilance (28). What they add up to is that with almost all stimulus displays, including those used in the earliest experiments, the sole change over time is in the decision criterion. Sensitivity remains constant. Alertness, apparently, remains essentially constant. With a few stimulus displays—specifically, visual displays with undefined trials or with trials occurring at a rate greater than about one per second— changes in both d' and β are observed: sensitivity decreases and the criterion becomes more stringent. In short, a sensitivity decrement in vigilance tests is uncommon, and when it occurs it is smaller than originally supposed. The practical problem is training the observer to hold a constant decision criterion. One study has shown that the observer will hold a constant decision criterion if the values of correct responses and the costs of incorrect responses are well defined (29).

It was in the late 1940's that several theorists in the field of perception emphasized the perceiver's contribution to what he perceives, a contribution that stems from inner states such as needs, emotions, and values. They were dubbed "new look" theorists, and the term "old look" was then applied to the theorists, primarily Gestaltists, who concentrated on stimulus determinants and denied effects of experience.

Several experiments, most of them using words as stimuli, were purported to show perceptual selectivity. Differences in measured thresholds of different classes of words were attributed to mechanisms of perceptual vigilance, sensitization, and perceptual defense. However, most of these results were soon accounted for in terms of differences in the commonality of the words employed, the "word-frequency effect." At first, word frequency was viewed as affecting perception per se, as effecting a selective intake of information. Then much converging evidence showed instead that stimulus frequency affects the response system.

At the same time that differences in thresholds were examined, several experimenters sought to demonstrate subthreshold, or "subliminal," perception related to inner states of the observer. Several lines of criticism were applied to these experiments, including the criticism that many of the results showed only that discrimination was possible when identification was not, or that forced-choice thresholds are typically lower than yes-no thresholds.

The ROC analysis came into contact with developments in this area at many points. For one reason, many of the experiments used the correction for chance and the associated concept of threshold. For another reason, the notion of relative willingness to respond was put forth in connection with taboo-word experiments. The ROC analysis was used to explain that yes-no thresholds are higher than forced-choice thresholds because stringent yes-no criteria are encouraged and, of course, to suggest that the presumed threshold was actually a response criterion (30).

Granting that stimulus probability affects the response system, which brings one back to the old look, the question then addressed was whether the mechanism is a guessing process or a variable criterion. At the time, contradictions flew back and forth, and there was some doubt that the most familiar experimental paradigm can distinguish the two kinds of mechanism (*31*). After the most extensive analysis to date, including the results of a new experimental paradigm, Donald E. Broadbent argued quite persuasively that the mechanism is a variable criterion (*25*). His experimental results, incidentally, indicate that d' is *lower* for common words than for uncommon words.

In a recognition memory task, the subject is asked to say whether each of a series of items was presented before ("old") or not ("new"). Following Egan again (*10, 32*), one may refer to the picture of the two distributions and a variable criterion and identify the new items with the left-hand (noise) distribution and the old items with the right-hand (signal) distribution. The assumption is that all items fall along a continuum of memory strength, at a location affected by acquisition and forgetting. This identification should allow phenomena of memory to be separated from biases associated with the response.

Several presumed memory effects were early on shown by the ROC analysis to be response effects only: that is, d' remains constant, while β changes. One such effect is the better recall of more common words; in fact, here again there is evidence that d' is lower for common than for uncommon words (*25, 33*). A related finding is that familiar associations are no better recalled than unfamiliar ones when unbiased measures are used (*34*). The typical increasing rate of false-positive responses in a continuous recognition task has been shown to be a reflection of criterion change rather than a buildup of proactive interference (*35*). Various amounts of learning interpolated between acquisition and recall have an effect on β but not on d'; this result is contrary to the extinction hypothesis of retroactive inhibition and indicates that generalized response competition is responsible for the criterion change (*36*). Although changes in semantic or association context from acquisition to recall have been reported to reduce recognition accuracy, with the reduction explained in terms of multiple representations in memory, one study showed these changes to affect only the response process (*37*). Another study used the ROC to assert an equality of females and males in recognition memory, even though they may differ with respect to response bias (*38*).

Other memory studies show a change in both d' and β, thereby demonstrating that the ROC analysis is required. Meaningfulness in a paired-associate, short-term memory task was found to affect memory and response bias (*39*). In that study and in another (*40*), both d' and β were correlated with serial position. Finally, increasing the similarity of distracting items to target items raises the criterion while lowering d' (*41*). Two articles have reviewed many of these studies in more detail and have considered some of the theoretical issues involved (*15, 17*).

The ROC analysis has also been applied in the areas of attention (*25*), imagery

(42), learning (43), conceptual judgment (44), personality (45), reaction time (46), manual control (47), and speech (10). Rats, pigeons, goldfish, and monkeys have produced exceptionally neat ROC curves, by rating and yes-no responses, with variations in signal probability or with differential reinforcement (48). Lee B. Lusted has applied the ROC to medical decisions, particularly in radiology (49). An early finding in physiological psychology is that the amplitude of a particular component of evoked cortical potentials increases monotonically with increasing strictness of the decision criterion, whether the criterion is manipulated by varying the signal probability or by varying the values and costs of the possible stimulus-response outcomes. This component was always present when the observer correctly reported a signal to exist, but was never present when the response was a miss or a false alarm (50). The ROC has also been used to evaluate the effectiveness of information retrieval systems (51).

SUMMARY

The clinician looking, listening, or feeling for signs of a disease may far prefer a false alarm to a miss, particularly if the disease is serious and contagious. On the other hand, one may believe that the available therapy is marginally effective, expensive, and debilitating. The pilot seeing the landing lights only when they are a few yards away may decide that the plane is adequately aligned with the runway if alone and familiar with that plight. One may be more inclined to circle the field before another try at landing if there are many passengers or recent memory of another plane crashing under those circumstances. The Food and Drug administrator suspecting botulism in a canned food may not want to accept even a remote threat to the public health. But one may be less clearly biased if a recent false alarm has cost a canning company millions of dollars and left some damaged reputations. The making of almost any fine discrimination is beset with such considerations of probability and utility, which are extraneous and potentially confounding when one is attempting to measure the acuity of discrimination per se.

The ROC is an analytical technique, with origins in statistical decision theory and electronic detection theory, that quite effectively isolates the effects of the observer's response bias, or decision criterion, in the study of the discrimination behavior. This capability, pursued through a century of psychological testing, provides a relatively pure measure of the discriminability of different stimuli and of the capacity of organisms to discriminate. The ROC also treats quantitatively the response, or decision, aspects of choice behavior. The decision parameter can then be functionally related to the probabilities of the stimulus alternatives and to the utilities of the various stimulus-response pairs, or to the observer's expectations and motivations. In separating and quantifying discrimination and decision processes, the ROC promises a more reliable and valid solution to some practical problems and enhances our understanding of the perceptual and cognitive phenomena that depend directly on these fundamental processes. In several problem areas in psychology, effects that were supposed to reflect properties of the discrimination process have been shown by the ROC analysis to reflect instead properties of the decision process.

REFERENCES AND NOTES

1. G. T. Fechner, *Elemente der Psychophysik* (Breitkopf & Hartel, Leipzig, 1860). English translation of volume 1 by H. E. Adler, *Elements of Psychophysics,* D. H. Howes and E. G. Boring, Eds. (Holt, Rinehart & Winston, New York, 1966). Reviewed by J. A. Swets, *Science* **154,** 1532 (1966).
2. L. L. Thurstone, *Psychol. Rev.* **34,** 273 (1927); *Am. J. Psychol.* **38,** 368 (1927).
3. H. R. Blackwell, *J. Exp. Psychol.* **44,** 306 (1952); *J. Opt. Soc. Am.* **53,** 129 (1963).
4. E. G. Boring, *Am. J. Psychol.* **32,** 449 (1921).
5. M. Smith and E. A. Wilson, *Psychol. Monogr.* **67,** No. 9 (1953); W. A. Munson and J. E. Karlin, *J. Acoust. Soc. Am.* **26,** 542 (1954); W. P. Tanner, Jr., and J. A. Swets, *Psychol. Rev.* **61,** 401 (1954).
6. J. Neyman and E. S. Pearson, *Phil. Trans. Roy. Soc. London Ser. A. Math. Phys. Sci.* **231,** 289 (1933).
7. A. Wald, *Statistical Decision Functions* (Wiley, New York, 1950).
8. W. W. Peterson, T. G. Birdsall, W. C. Fox, *Trans. IRE Prof. Group Inf. Theory* **PGIT-4,** 171 (1954); D. Van Meter and D. Middleton, *ibid.,* p. 119; W. P. Tanner, Jr., and J. A. Swets, *ibid.,* p. 213; W. W. Peterson and T. G. Birdsall, *The Theory of Signal Detectability* (technical report No. 13, Electronic Defense Group, University of Michigan, Ann Arbor, 1953).
9. R. D. Luce, in *Handbook of Mathematical Psychology,* R. D. Luce, R. R. Bush, E. Galanter, Eds. (Wiley, New York, 1963), pp. 103–189.
10. D. M. Green and J. A. Swets, *Signal Detection Theory and Psychophysics* (Wiley, New York, 1966). A reprint of this book, with a supplementary bibliography of publications from 1967 to 1988 was published by Peninsula Publishing, Los Altos, CA, 1988.
11. J. A. Swets, Ed., *Signal Detection and Recognition by Human Observers* (Wiley, New York, 1964).
12. D. R. Freeman, *Tables of d' and β* (technical report No. APU 529/64, Applied Psychology Research Unit, Cambridge, England, 1964); L. Hochhaus, *Psychol. Bull.* **77,** 375 (1972).
13. Codex graph paper No. 41,453 runs from .01 to .99 on the probability scales, which is adequate for psychological applications, and gives the normal-deviate scales as well. Kueffel and Esser No. 47 8062 is the other probability-by-probability graph paper available; it is scaled from .0001 to .9999 and does not give the normal-deviate scales.
14. A. I. Schulman and R. R. Mitchell, *J. Acoust. Soc. Am.* **40,** 473 (1966); J. Markowitz and J. A. Swets, *Percept. Psychophys.* **2,** 91 (1967); B. C. Brookes, *J. Doc.* **24,** 41 (1968); S. E. Robertson, *ibid.* **25,** 1 (1969); *ibid.,* p. 93.
15. W. P. Banks, *Psychol. Bull.* **74,** 81 (1970).
16. W. Hodos, *ibid.,* p. 351; J. B. Grier, *ibid.* **75,** 424 (1971).
17. R. S. Lockhart and B. B. Murdock, Jr., *ibid.,* p. 100.
18. W. Wickelgren, *J. Math. Psychol.* **5,** 102 (1968).
19. D. Krantz, *Psychol. Rev.* **76,** 308 (1969).
20. J. C. Ogilvie and C. D. Creelman, *J. Math. Psychol.* **5,** 377 (1968); D. D. Dorfman and E. Alf, Jr., *Psychometrika* **33,** 117 (1968); *J. Math. Psychol.* **6,** 487 (1969); I. G. Abramson and H. Levitt, *ibid.,* p. 391; D. R. Grey and B. J. T. Morgan, *ibid.,* **9,** 128 (1972).
21. V. Gourevitch and E. Galanter, *Psychometrika* **32,** 25 (1967); L. A. Marascuilo, *ibid.,* **35,** 237 (1970).

22. I. Pollack and R. Hsieh, *Psychol. Bull.* **71**, 161 (1969).
23. N. H. Mackworth, "Research on the measurement of human performance" (Medical Research Council Special Report Series No. 268, His Majesty's Stationery Office, London, 1950).
24. D. N. Buckner and J. J. McGrath, Eds., *Vigilance: A Symposium* (McGraw-Hill, New York, 1963); J. F. Mackworth, *Vigilance and Habituation: A Neurophysiological Approach* (Penguin, Middlesex, England, 1969).
25. D. G. Broadbent, *Decision and Stress* (Academic Press, London, 1971).
26. J. P. Frankmann and J. A. Adams, *Psychol. Bull.* **59**, 257 (1962).
27. J. P. Egan, G. Z. Greenberg, A. I. Schulman, *J. Acoust. Soc. Am.* **33**, 993 (1961).
28. About half of these studies were published early enough to be discussed in reviews by Broadbent (*25*), by J. A. Swets and A. B. Kristofferson [*Annu. Rev. Psychol.* **21**, 339 (1970)], and by J. F. Mackworth [*Vigilance and Attention: A Signal Detection Approach* (Penguin, Middlesex, England, 1970)].
29. P. Lucas, *J. Acoust. Soc. Am.* **42**, 158 (1967).
30. J. A. Swets, W. P. Tanner, Jr., T. G. Birdsall, *The Evidence for a Decision-Making Theory of Visual Detection* (technical report No. 40, Electronic Defense Group, University of Michigan, Ann Arbor, 1955); I. Goldiamond, *Psychol. Bull.* **55**, 373 (1958); J. Pierce, *ibid.*, **60**, 391 (1963).
31. D. E. Broadbent, *Psychol. Rev.* **74**, 1 (1967); J. Catlin, *ibid.*, **76**, 504 (1969); L. H. Nakatani, *ibid.*, **77**, 574 (1970); M. Treisman, *ibid.*, **78**, 420 (1971); J. R. Frederiksen, *ibid.*, p. 409; L. H. Nakatani, *ibid.*, **80**, 195 (1973); J. Catlin, *ibid.*, p. 412.
32. J. P. Egan, *Recognition, Memory, and the Operating Characteristic* (technical note AFCRC-TN-58-51, Hearing and Communication Laboratory, Indiana University, Bloomington, 1958).
33. J. D. Ingleby, thesis, Cambridge University (1969).
34. D. McNicol and L. A. Ryder, *J. Exp. Psychol.* **90**, 81 (1971).
35. W. Donaldson and B. B. Murdock, Jr., *ibid.* **76**, 325 (1968).
36. W. P. Banks, *ibid.* **82**, 216 (1969).
37. F. DaPolito, D. Barker, J. Wiant, *Psychonomic Sci. Sect. Hum. Exp. Psychol.* **24**, 180 (1971).
38. M. Barr-Brown and M. J. White, *ibid.* **25**, 75 (1971).
39. G. A. Raser, *J. Exp. Psychol.* **84**, 173 (1970).
40. B. B. Murdock, Jr., *ibid.* **76** (Suppl. 4, part 2) 1 (1968).
41. G. Mandler, Z. Pearlstone, H. S. Koopmans, *J. Verb. Learning Verb. Behav.* **8**, 410 (1969).
42. S. J. Segal and V. Fusella, *J. Exp. Psychol.* **83**, 458 (1970); *Psychonomic. Sci. Sect. Hum. Exp. Psychol.* **24**, 55 (1971).
43. G. R. Grice, *Psychol. Rev.* **75**, 359 (1968).
44. Z. J. Ulehla, L. Canges, F. Wackwitz, *Psychonomic Sci. Sect. Hum. Exp. Psychol.* **8**, 221 (1967); *ibid.*, p. 223.
45. R. H. Price, *Psychol. Bull.* **66**, 55 (1966); W. C. Clark, *ibid.* **65**, 358 (1966).
46. R. Pike, *Psychol. Rev.* **80**, 53 (1973); R. G. Swensson, *Percept. Psychophys.* **12**(1A), 16 (1972).
47. H. S. Cohen and W. R. Ferrell, *IEEE Trans. Man-Mach. Syst.* **10**, 41 (1969).
48. D. S. Bough, *Science* **158**, 940 (1967); J. A. Nevin, in *Animal Psychophysics*, W. C. Stebbins, Ed. (Appleton-Century-Crofts, New York, 1970); D. Yager and I. Duncan, *Percept. Psychophys.* **9**(3B), 353 (1971); M. Terman and J. S. Terman, *ibid.* **11**(6), 428 (1972); A. A. Wright, *Vision Res.* **12**, 1447 (1972); B. M. Clopton, *J. Exp. Anal. Behav.* **17**, 473 (1972); T. F. Elsmore, *ibid.* **18**, 465 (1972); W. Hodos and J. C. Bonbright, Jr., *ibid.*, p. 471.
49. L. B. Lusted, *Science* **171**, 1217 (1971); *Introduction to Medical Decision-Making* (Thomas, Springfield, Ill., 1968); in *Computer Diagnosis and Diagnostic Methods*, J. A. Jacquez, Ed. (Thomas, Springfield, Ill., 1972).
50. D. Paul and S. Sutton, *Science* **177**, 362 (1972); K. C. Squires, S. A. Hillyard, P. H. Lindsay, *Percept. Psychophys.* **13**, 25 (1973).
51. J. A. Swets, *Science* **141**, 245 (1963); *Am. Doc.* **20**, 72 (1969), Chapter 9 in this volume.

2 Form of Empirical ROCs in Discrimination and Diagnostic Tasks

A companion chapter (Chapter 3) derives the form of the *relative* (or *receiver*) *operating characteristic* (ROC) that is algebraically implied by each of a dozen or so commonly used indices of discrimination accuracy, and identifies the models of the discrimination process that are implied by the main categories of those forms. In this chapter I present a broad sample of empirical ROCs for comparison with the theoretical forms. They are drawn from discrimination tasks used in the psychology of perception, learning, memory, and cognition, and from several practical fields in which a discrimination, or diagnosis, is made in the interest of prediction, selection, or corrective action. The fields included are medical imaging, information retrieval, weather forecasting, aptitude testing, and polygraph lie detection.

PRECÍS OF ROC FORM, INDICES, AND MODELS

ROC Form

The ROC, in a sentence, is a graph showing the conditional probability of choosing Alternative A when that alternative occurs (here denoted by h, for "hit") plotted against the conditional probability of choosing A when Alternative B occurs (here denoted by f, for "false alarm"). Both h and f increase as the tendency to choose Alternative A increases, or as the criterion for choosing A becomes more lenient.

The form of an ROC is best visualized on a "binormal" graph—a graph in which the usual probability coordinates are rescaled so that their corresponding normal-deviate values are linearly spaced, as in Figure 1. On such a graph, empirical ROCs are consistently fitted well by a straight line that varies in slope; the slopes are generally between 0.5 and 1.5, as indicated in Figure 1a by dashed lines. (Other details of the figure are discussed next.)

Indices and Models

The indices chapter (Chapter 3) shows that the form of predicted ROCs serves to sort common accuracy indices and their implied models into three categories.

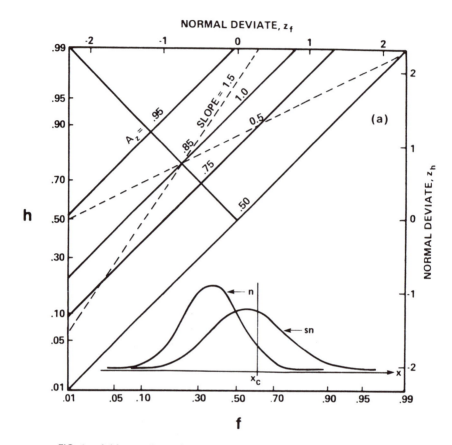

FIG. 1. A binormal graph, on which probabilities (left-hand and bottom axes) are scaled so that the corresponding normal-deviate values are linearly scaled (right-hand and top axes). a: the solid lines of slope = 1.0 represent relative operating characteristics (ROCs) consistent with the d' index. (The index values shown are of A_z, the area under the binormal ROC [on ordinary scales]. The dashed lines, of slope $\neq$ 1.0, represent ROCs consistent with the A_z index, which might arise from distributions of observations of "noise alone" [n] and "signal plus noise" [sn] of unequal variance, as illustrated at bottom right; the distributions shown are normal. The slopes of 0.5 and 1.5 bound almost all empirical ROCs. h = probability of a "hit"; f = probability of a "false alarm.") b: ROC's implied by the η, log odds ratio (LOR), and Yule's Q indices, with index values of η. (Logistic distributions of equal variance, as illustrated at bottom right, produce ROCs having the form of those implied algebraically by η, LOR, and Q.)

32

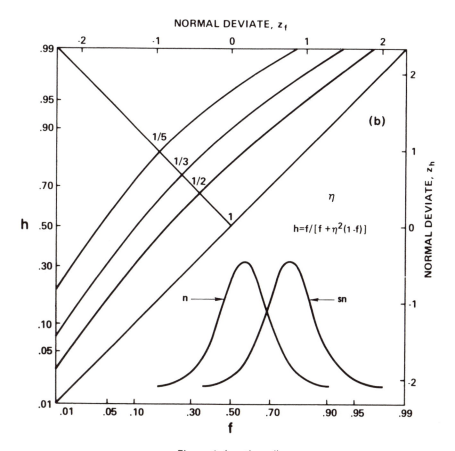

Figure 1. (continued)

The first category contains models and indices that predict linear, or effectively linear, binormal ROCs of slope = 1.0. The indices and models of the second category predict binormal ROCs that are distinctly curvilinear. Those in the third category predict, or permit, ROCs consistent with both the observed linearity and variable slope, and are thus preferred. Chapter 3 shows how indices in the first two categories are subject to considerable unreliability.

Indices in the first category include one of the several indices associated with signal detection theory, namely d' (Green & Swets, 1966/1988), and three indices nearly equivalent to d': Luce's (1959, 1963) η, the log-odds ratio (LOR; e.g., Goodman, 1970), and Yule's (1912) Q. The index d' predicts a linear ROC of slope = 1.0, as indicated by the solid lines in Figure 1a. The indices η, LOR, and Q imply a slightly curved ROC, as shown in Figure 1b, that is indistinguishable from a straight line of slope = 1.0 with ordinary amounts of data.

The model for d' is a *variable-criterion* model of the general sort considered in signal detection theory, but specifically one in which observations under each alternative have normal (Gaussian) distributions of equal variance. Two normal distributions (though with unequal variance) are shown at bottom right in Figure 1a, and are denoted n and sn for the "noise-alone" and "signal-plus-noise" alternatives. The criterion is symbolized in the figure by the vertical line, x_c; observations $x > x_c$ lead to the choice of sn and observations $x < x_c$ lead to the choice of n. A variable-criterion model consistent with η, LOR, and Q contains logistic distributions of equal variance, which are similar to the normal distribution, as shown at bottom right in Figure 1b.

The second category contains a variety of other common indices, including two versions of the "hit" probability corrected for chance success, here denoted by H_C and H'_C (where $H_C = [h - f]/[1 - f]$ and $H'_C = h - f$); percentage correct, PC; the kappa statistic, K, as a chance-corrected PC; and the fourfold point correlation coefficient, ϕ. The index H_c implies the curvilinear ROC of Figure 2a. The index H'_C leads to the curvilinear ROC of Figure 2b; as do PC and K when the alternatives to be discriminated are equally probable; and the ROC for ϕ for equal probabilities is practically indistinguishable from that of Figure 2b. For the last three indices, unequal probabilities tilt the ROC away from symmetry about the minor diagonal.

The index H_C implies a *high-threshold* model and H'_C, PC, and ϕ imply a *double-threshold* model. In detection-theory terms, threshold models are based on uniform distributions, as shown in Figures 2a and 2b.

The third category contains a few nearly equivalent indices, including the perpendicular distance from the origin of the binormal ROC graph to the ROC, but perhaps the most common is the area under an ROC (on ordinary scales) that is assumed to be linear on a binormal graph, denoted A_z. The index A_z is consistent with a linear (binormal) ROC having a slope in the range of slopes found empirically. Swets and Pickett (1982) discuss the indices in this category and list a revised version of Dorfman and Alf's (1969) computer program for estimating A_z. Illustrative values of A_z are shown in Figure 1a; its values range from .50 at the positive diagonal, representing chance performance, to 1.00 for perfect discrimination. This index is equivalent to the percentage of correct responses made in a two-alternative, forced-choice test, that is, when a random draw from each of the sn and n distributions is compared on each trial (Green & Swets, 1966/1988).

The index A_z is associated with a variable-criterion model in which the underlying distributions can have unequal variances, as illustrated by the normal distributions at bottom right in Figure 1a. It should be noted that A_z does not assume normal distributions, but rather any form of distribution that can be transformed monotonically to the normal distribution. Thus A_z, and the binormal assumption more generally, make a particular assumption about the (observable) functional form of the ROC, and not about the (usually unobservable) forms of

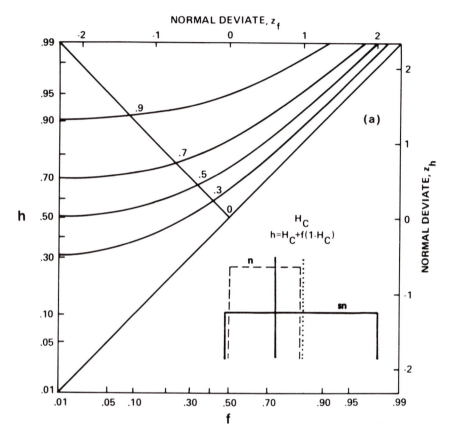

FIG. 2. a: Theoretical relative operating characteristics (ROCs) of the high-threshold model on a binormal graph, labeled by the index associated with that model, H_C. (The uniform distributions show some observations of "signal plus noise" [sn] and none of "noise alone" [n] to exceed a high threshold symbolized by the dotted line; the solid vertical line connotes a variable criterion according to which, in this drawing, about one-third of the observations below the threshold lead to the choice of the sn alternative. h = probability of a "hit"; f = probability of a "false alarm.") b: Theoretical ROCs of the double-threshold model on a binormal graph, labeled by one of the indices associated with that model, H'_C. (The uniform distributions of n and sn are related to two thresholds [dotted lines]; in this illustration, a variable criterion [solid vertical line] is set so that about one-third of the observations falling between the thresholds lead to the choice of the sn alternative.)

35

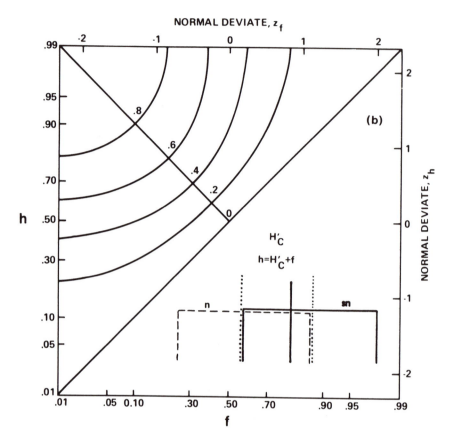

Figure 2. (continued)

the underlying distributions. As discussed elsewhere, the forms of the underlying distributions imply a particular form of ROC, but, when the distributions are continuous (as in Figure 1) as opposed to uniform (as in Figure 2), the converse is not true. In general, the ROC reflects the difference between two distributions rather than the distributions themselves, and any monotonic transformation applied to two underlying distributions will result in the same ROC (Egan, 1975; Swets, Tanner, & Birdsall, 1961). Simply as a convenient convention, A_z is parameterized in terms of an effective pair of normal distributions, and then the binormal ROC slope consistent with A_z is equal to the ratio of standard deviations, σ_n/σ_{sn}.[1]

---

[1]The unequal-variance model presents a problem for theory in that the observation or decision axis (labeled x in Figure 1a) is not monotonic with the likelihood ratio, that is, with the ratio of the

Scope and Procedure of This Article

The indices of the three categories delineated are the main ones used in experimental psychology and in practical fields like those mentioned previously. They include not only indices devised in one or more fields but essentially all measures of statistical association, inasmuch as the latter (for 2×2 tables) are usually functions either of the cross-product ratio (i.e., *ad/bc,* where those letters symbolize the cell entries)—as are η, LOR, and Q—or of the correlation coefficient, ϕ, which depends also on the marginal frequencies of the table (Bishop, Fienberg, & Holland, 1975).

After a few notes on the way ROCs for individual observers are obtained and then combined into average or typical ROCs, I present the sample of empirical ROCs selected for this chapter. In the four practical fields other than medical imaging, they are illustrative of the only sets of ROCs of which I am aware. In that field and in experimental psychology, the main selection criterion was that they be based on a sufficient number of trials to show relatively little variability, in order to give a good look at their form. A second criterion, applied to ROCs in psychology, was that they represent the various types of discrimination tasks used in psychological experiments. As far as I know, no empirical ROCs support a form other than the one inferred here.

For the several ROCs shown, the interest lies first in the adequacy of a linear fit and then in the slope of the line. The goodness of fit is reported when available, that is, when the data have been submitted to a computer program, such as that described by Dorfman and Alf (1969), that makes a chi-square test of a maximum-likelihood estimation of a linear fit. The slope is reported in every case, as measured graphically from a visual fit when an objective fit was not made. The question of whether some pattern exists in the variation of slope that is observed is discussed briefly in a closing section.

All of the ROCs that follow are presented as being effectively linear and not in the least suggestive of one of the curvilinear forms of Figure 2. The visual effect is compelling enough, I believe, to permit us to forgo a statistical comparison of each empirical ROC with each theoretical ROC.

Notes on Data Collection and Combination

The direct way to trace out an ROC is to have an observer adopt a different decision criterion, or response bias, from one group of trials to another, and so

---

ordinate of the *sn* distribution to the ordinate of the *n* distribution; in particular, the likelihood ratio is > 1.0 at both ends of this axis. As noted earlier (Laming, 1973; Swets, Tanner, & Birdsall, 1961), this model requires adding a substantive psychological assumption to the structure of statistical decision theory. One would prefer a better way to handle binormal ROC slopes unequal to 1.0, and better ways exist for certain fixed slopes (see Chapter 3), but the unequal-variance model seems to be the best available for treating variable slopes. The aberrations that occur in ROCs, if the decision is based on *x* rather than the likelihood ratio of *x,* are usually small and at the edges of the graph.

obtain several different points (Tanner & Swets, 1954). A more efficient way is to have the observer use a rating scale—say, a five-category scale of confidence that a particular alternative is the correct one—in a single group of trials (Swets et al., 1961). The procedure for obtaining simultaneously a number of different ROC points (one fewer point than the number of categories) from rating data is detailed by Green and Swets (1966/1988). In brief, one assumes in analysis that observations that lead to responses of the highest category of confidence are those that meet the strictest decision criterion being used, and that observations leading to responses of either of the two highest categories are those that meet the next strictest criterion, and so on, cumulatively (when the lowest category is finally included, the ROC point calculated in the uninformative $h = f = 1.0$). Most of the data I present were obtained by some version of the rating-scale technique.

It is often desirable to portray a composite ROC based on several observers. Macmillan and Kaplan (1985) have published a general analysis of ways to obtain composite ROCs and support the pooling of rating data. Most of the ROCs I present are based on such a pooling.

EMPIRICAL ROCS IN EXPERIMENTAL PSYCHOLOGY

The empirical ROCs displayed here are drawn from a range of tasks studied in experimental psychology—tasks focused on sensory functions or perception, memory, learning, and conceptual judgment.

Vision

The first rating ROCs obtained are shown in Figure 3 (Swets, Tanner, & Birdsall, 1955, 1961). Four observers used a 6-category rating scale for a signal that was a flash of a spot of light, and made nearly 1,200 observations. The figure is reproduced from Dorfman and Alf (1969); a later version of their program (Swets & Pickett, 1982) indicates that the probabilities associated with the chi-square tests of the linear fits are approximately .70, .05, .40, and .60 for the four observers, respectively, and that the group chi-square is not statistically significant ($>.25$). The four binormal slopes are 0.71, 0.74, 0.72, and 0.89.

Recognition Memory—Words

Some results of Egan's (1958) extension of the ROC to memory for words are reproduced in Figure 4. Subjects were given either one or two presentations of a list of 100 words and were later asked to rate their confidence (7-category scale) that each of a list of 200 words was on the first list; the 200-word list contained all of the words on the 100-word list. The labels on the graph's axes are the probabilities that "old" words (ordinate) and "new" words (abscissa) are said to

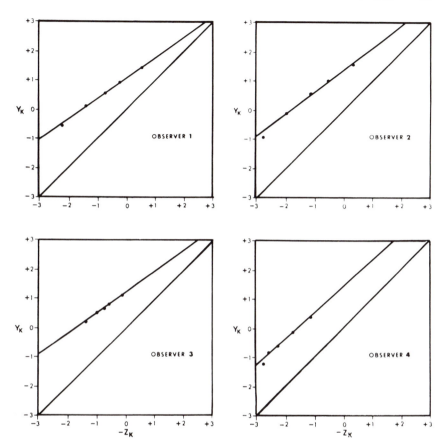

FIG. 3.   Relative operating characteristics (ROCs) for 4 observers in a vision experiment. (Y_κ = normal-deviate value corresponding to the conditional probability of a "hit." $-Z_\kappa$ = normal-deviate value corresponding to the conditional probability of a "false alarm." From "Maximum Likelihood Estimation of Parameters of Signal-Detection Theory and Determination of Confidence Intervals—Rating Method Data" by D. D. Dorfman and E. Alf, Jr., 1969, *Journal of Mathematical Psychology, 6,* p. 492. Copyright 1969 by Academic Press. Reprinted by permission.)

be "old." The bottom ROC gives the combined result for the middle 50% of the 16 subjects given one presentation; the top ROC shows the same thing, but for two presentations. The binormal slopes of the two lines are 0.67 and 0.71.

Recognition Memory—Odors

Fifteen subjects of Rabin and Cain (1984) were exposed to 20 odors and were tested with those 20 embedded in a set of 40. They used a 10-category rating

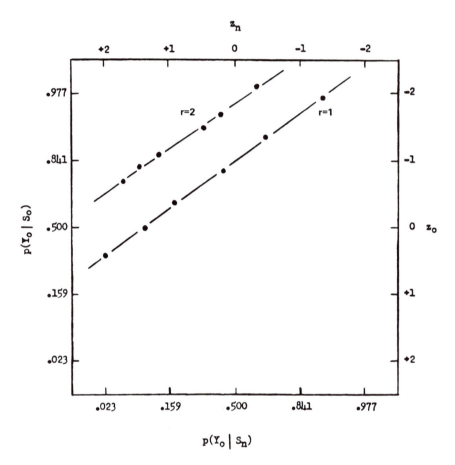

FIG. 4. Two relative operating characteristics (ROCs), each based on 8 subjects, in an experiment on recognition memory for words. (r = number of repetitions of the list of "old" stimuli. S_n = presentation of a "new" stimulus. S_o = presentation of an "old" stimulus. Y_o = a "yes" response to an "old" stimulus, indicating that an old stimulus was called old. z_n = normal-deviate value corresponding to the conditional probability of a "false alarm," $P[Y_o|S_n]$. z_o = normal-deviate value corresponding to the conditional probability of a "hit," $p[Y_o|S_o]$. From "Recognition Memory and the Operating Characteristic" by J. P. Egan, 1958, Technical Note, Indiana University, Hearing and Communication Laboratory, following p. 28. Reprinted by permission.)

scale and were tested after intervals of 10 min, 1 day, and 7 days—each time with a different set of 20 new odors. The pooled results are reproduced in Figure 5. The bottom two ROCs have slopes very near 1.0; the top ROC has a slope of about 1.1.

Animal Learning

Blough (1967) reinforced pigeons for pecking at a single wavelength and measured their (lower) rates of responding to nearby wavelengths. These response

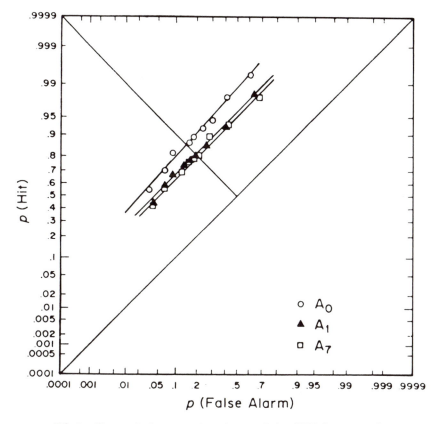

FIG. 5. Three relative operating characteristics (ROCs) representing 15 subjects at three retention intervals, in an experiment on recognition memory for odors. (A_0, A_1, and A_7 = Group A, a group tested at all three intervals: 0 = 10 min; 1 = 1 day; and 7 = 7 days. From "Odor Recognition: Familiarity, Identifiability, and Encoding Consistency" by M. D. Rabin and W. S. Cain, 1984, *Journal of Experimental Psychology: Learning, Memory, and Cognition, 10,* p. 320. Copyright 1984 by the American Psychological Association. Reprinted by permission.)

rates indicated the pigeons' certainty that the reinforced stimulus (signal) was present. Figure 6 shows quite good linear fits in the bottom two panels, for two birds, with slopes ranging mainly between 0.5 and 1.0 (with one at about 0.33).

Conceptual Judgment

Lee (1963) devised a discrimination task to make the observational continuum external to the observer, but we can view it as a cognitive task. Specifically, a dot

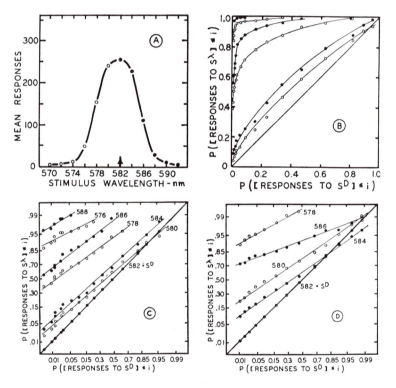

FIG. 6. Relative operating characteristics (ROCs) from 2 pigeons in an experiment on stimulus generalization along a continuum of wavelength of light. (Data from 28 sessions. Panel A shows the generalization gradient to several unreinforced wavelengths [S^] around 582 nm, the reinforced wavelength [S^D]; Panel B shows the ROCs on ordinary scales, of the six stimuli nearest 582 nm, for 1 bird. Those ROCs are shown on a binormal graph in [C], and the ROCs of a second bird are shown in [D]. Axes in [B], [C], and [D] represent relative frequencies that a given number [i] of responses or fewer were made to the stimulus in question. From "Stimulus Generalization as Signal Detection in Pigeons" by D. S. Blough, 1967, *Science, 158,* p. 941. Copyright 1967 by the American Association for the Advancement of Science. Reprinted by permission.)

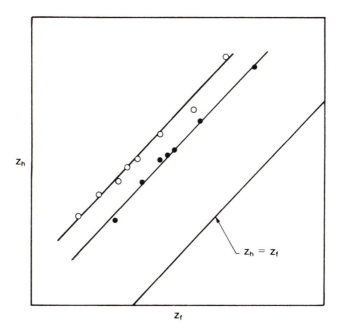

FIG. 7.   Relative operating characteristics (ROCs) for 2 observers in an experiment on conceptual judgment. (z_f = normal-deviate value corresponding to the conditional probability of a "false alarm." z_h = normal-deviate value corresponding to the conditional probability of a "hit." From "Choosing Among Confusably Distributed Stimuli With Specified Likelihood Ratios" by W. Lee, 1963, *Perceptual and Motor Skills, 16,* p. 230. Copyright 1963 by Southern Universities Press. Adapted by permission.)

was presented somewhere along the long dimension of a plain file card. The experimenter located two normal distributions along this dimension (not visible to the observer), randomly chose one on each trial, and then randomly chose a point from it to present to the observer. Information about the distributions was made available to the subject by means of feedback after each trial as to the source distribution of the point on that trial. In short, the subject was to build up an impression of experimental distributions similar to the picture at bottom right in Figure 1a (though Lee's distributions were of equal variance). The ROCs for two observers, based on an 8-category scale, are reproduced in Figure 7. Their slopes are about 1.05.

ROCS FROM PRACTICAL FIELDS

Considered next are illustrative ROC data from the fields of medical diagnosis (specifically, medical imaging), information retrieval, weather forecasting, aptitude testing, and polygraph lie detection. As in the previous section, the straight-line fit and the range of binormal slopes are of principal interest. Values of A_z are mentioned here when comparisons within a given field are of interest. Chapter 4 shows how well diagnostic systems of various kinds perform, and examines the relative ease and difficulty of obtaining good estimates of accuracy in different fields.

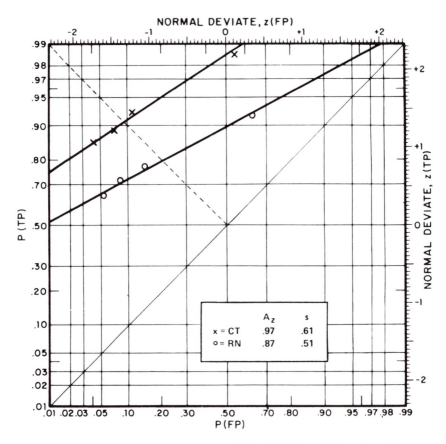

FIG. 8. Relative operating characteristics (ROCs), each based on 6 observers, representing two image modalities in clinical medicine. (CT = computed tomography; RN = radionuclide scans. FP = false-positive response, or "false alarm." TP = true-positive response, or "hit." A_z = the area under the ROC plotted on ordinary scales. s = slope of the binormal ROC. From "Assessment of Diagnostic Technologies" by J. A. Swets, R. M. Pickett, S. F. Whitehead, D. J. Getty, J. A. Schnur, J. B. Swets, and B. A. Freeman, *Science, 205,* p. 757. Copyright 1979 by the American Association for the Advancement of Science. Reprinted by permission.)

Medical Imaging

The ROCs shown in Figure 8 were obtained in an evaluation of computed tomography (CT) and radionuclide scans (RN) in the detection of brain lesions (Swets et al., 1979). One hundred thirty-six cases of patients subjected to both imaging modalities were interpreted by 12 radiologists (6 CT specialists and 6 RN specialists). The cases were selected on the basis of having adequate truth data (histological confirmation of 84 abnormal cases and 8-month follow-up of 52 normal cases) and to provide appropriate representation of lesion types and locations.

The ROCs shown were obtained via a 5-category rating scale of probability of abnormality. Each ROC is based on the pooled rating data of six radiologists. This method of combining data was defended on the grounds that the ROCs obtained from individual readers were fitted well by straight lines (chi-square analysis yielded $p > .20$ for 11 of the 12 readers) and showed little variation across readers in accuracy (A_z from .96 to .98 for CT and from .83 to .89 for RN). Both the pooling of rating data and the averages of A_z yielded $A_z = .97$ for CT and $A_z = .87$ for RN. Individual slopes averaged 0.70 for CT (range from 0.49 to 1.04), compared with the pooled slope of 0.61, and 0.52 for RN (range from 0.37 to 0.68), compared with the pooled slope of 0.51.

Figure 9 shows an ROC representing 10 cytotechnologists who viewed approximately 6,000 individual cell photomicrographs to discriminate between abnormal and normal cells in screening for cervical cancer (Bacus et al., 1984). True cell class was based on full case information and consensus among other cytotechnologists and pathologists. The observers classified the cells relative to 18 categories of both type and severity of abnormality; the experimenter ordered those categories according to the likelihood of abnormality to obtain the 17-point ROC shown. The relevant indices are $A_z = .87$, slope = 1.33. Computer-based, automated evaluation of the same slides—based on a multivariate Gaussian classification scheme and standard measurements of area, density, color, shape, and texture—yielded a very similar ROC, with $A_z = .90$ and slope = 1.21 (Bacus, 1982). (A review of medical studies reporting ROCs that were available at the time was given by Swets, 1979, who found values of A_z generally between .85 and .95; see Chapter 6).

Information Retrieval

Three major studies of information retrieval conducted in the mid-1960s were analyzed shortly thereafter in ROC terms (see Chapter 9). They were conducted at Harvard University (Salton & Lesk, 1966), at Cranfield, England (Cleverdon & Keen, 1966), and at Arthur D. Little, Inc. (Giuliano & Jones, 1966). The first and third studies were of computer-based systems; the second was of a traditional, manual library system. The computer system in the first study, for each query,

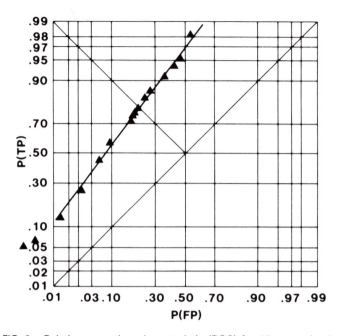

FIG. 9. Relative operating characteristic (ROC) for 10 cytotechnologists screening slides for evidence of disease. (From "Malignant Cell Detection and Cervical Cancer Screening" by J. W. Bacus, E. L. Wiley, W. Galbraith, P. N. Marshall, G. D. Wilbanks, and R. S. Weinstein, 1984, *Analytical and Quantitative Cytology, 6,* p. 125. Copyright 1984 by The International Academy of Cytology. Reprinted by permission.)

examined every word of every document in a given collection, either of the full text or just the abstract; made associations of words in the document with words in the query by various techniques (word-stem match, synonym recognition, statistical word-word associations, etc.); and calculated the relevance of each document to the query. The ROCs were obtained by choosing various decision criteria (rating categories) on this relevance scale. Actual relevance and nonrelevance were determined by a panel of judges.

Figure 10 shows the results of six retrieval methods (as indicated in the figure) applied to one of the collections of documents used in the first study. For each method, 35 queries were directed to a collection of 82 documents. The six lines, fitted by eye, are reproduced on the full plot at the bottom of the figure. For present purposes, note that straight lines give a quite good fit (a possible staircase effect might be due to the small number of relevant documents per query) and that the slopes vary slightly from 1.0 (approximately 0.85 to 1.0). The scale along the negative diagonals in the graphs is of the accuracy index d' (which is

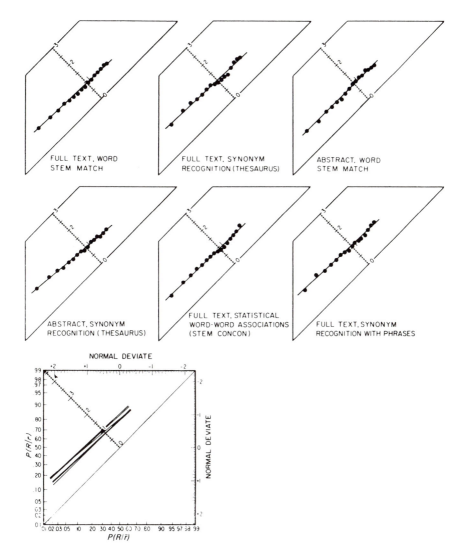

FIG. 10. Relative operating characteristics (ROCs) representing six methods of information retrieval. (The 6 fitted lines of the upper panels are also shown in the bottom panel. $\bar{r}$ = the presentation of an irrelevant document. R = the response of "relevant." r = the presentation of a relevant document. From "Effectiveness of Information Retrieval Methods," by J. A. Swets, 1969, *American Documentation, 20,* p. 79. Copyright 1969 by John Wiley and Sons, Inc. Reprinted by permission.)

suitable when the slope is 1.0). The six methods are seen to vary little about $d' = 1.0$, which corresponds to $A_z = .76$.

Other document collections and retrieval methods used in the three studies showed linear fits as good or better than those in Figure 10. All of them showed a similarly small effect of method within a given collection. Slopes typically range from about 1.0 to 1.3. Values of A_z range from .76 to .96 in the Harvard study, from .83 to .91 in the Cranfield study, and from .87 to .93 in the Arthur D. Little, Inc. study. (Overall, five of the six major conditions across studies produced values of A_z that are almost uniformly spread between .85 and .95.)

Weather Forecasting

Mason (1982) published some 20 ROCs for forecasting various types of weather, of which 6 are shown in Figure 11. They are all based on the probability reports generally issued by forecasters (usually in 13 categories for rain, and in smaller numbers of categories for other weather events). Whether the weather event in question actually occurred or not was determined according to procedures established in the weather forecasting field.

Figure 11a shows an ROC for rain based on some 17,000 reports at Chicago. The linear fit is very good; slope $= 0.97$, $A_z = .85$. Fits based on about 3,000 reports of individual forecasters were almost as good. Figure 11b refers to prediction of a minimum temperature $<28°F$ near Albuquerque; slope $= 1.38$, $A_z = .89$. Figure 11c refers to predictions of one or more tornadoes in areas delineated by the Severe Storms Forecast Center in Kansas City; based on about 90 reports, slope $= 0.70$, $A_z = .77$. (These figures are based on data published earlier by A. Murphy, who was instrumental in the move to probability forecasting, and R. L. Winkler [Murphy, 1977; Murphy & Winkler, 1977a, 1977b].) Figure 11d shows ROCs for fog-risk forecasts at the Canberra, Australia, airport issued 24, 18, or 12 hours earlier than the specified time, and based on over 300 reports. The A_z rises from .72 to .76 to .81 as the time shortens; the corresponding slopes are 1.27, 1.22, and 1.0. (Mason's further analyses show A_z values for rain ranging across locations from .74 to .89. Predicting lightning and fog gave an A_z of about .75; predicting temperatures within intervals and tornadoes showed an A_z of about .70. So, the range over-all is approximately .70 to .90.)

Aptitude Testing

Historically, aptitude tests have predicted a continuous variable, principally graded school performance or rated job performance. In this case the product-moment correlation coefficient serves well as an index of the test's performance—that is, of its validity as a predictor—that is based on all available information.

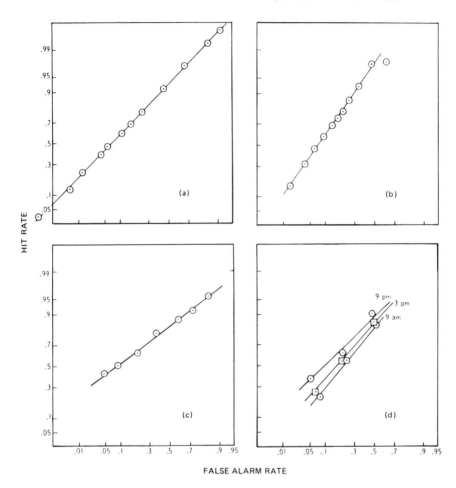

FIG. 11. Relative operating characteristics (ROCs) for weather fore-casting. (a: rain; b: minimum temperature; c: tornadoes; and d: fog. From "A Model for Assessment of Weather Forecasts" by I. Mason, 1982, *Australian Meteorological Magazine, 30,* pp. 296, 297, 299. Copyright 1982 by the Australian Government Publishing Service. Reprinted by permission.)

However, the predicted variable may be binary, as when students working under individually paced instruction complete the course or not, or when the rating of workers reduces to whether or not they can do the job well enough to stay on it, and then the accuracy of the test's discrimination is of interest. An accuracy index can serve as an alternate measure of validity.

To simulate such a binary outcome, I have analyzed data (kindly supplied to

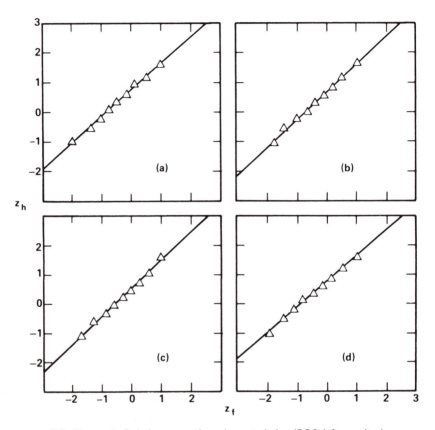

FIG. 12. a–d: Relative operating characteristics (ROCs) for aptitude tests predicting performance in four Navy schools. (Analysis of data supplied by the Navy Personnel Research and Development Center.)

me by the Navy Personnel Research and Development Center) with a cut-score for success in a course of instruction set arbitrarily at the 50th percentile of the distribution of final grades. Nine ROC points were generated by taking deciles of aptitude-test scores.

Figure 12 shows the ability of the Armed Forces Qualification Test to predict such "pass-fail" performance in four Navy schools: (a) quartermaster, (b) signalman, (c) electrician's mate, and (d) mess management. The slopes vary from 0.86 to 0.96, and the values of A_z vary from .66 to .72. Based on a few hundreds of students, the linear fits are good: chi-square analysis of 12 linear fits (based on three different cut scores of final grades) gave probabilities ranging from .13 to

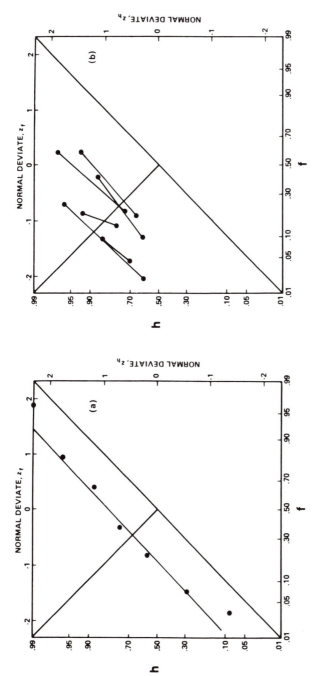

FIG. 13. Relative operating characteristics (ROCs) for polygraph lie detection. a: for 6 examiners in a laboratory study. (h = probability of a "hit"; f = probability of a false alarm. Based on data from an unpublished doctoral thesis by J. J Szucko summarized by Szucko & Kleinmuntz, 1981.) b: 2-point ROCs, derived from experiments using positive, negative, and inconclusive categories, conducted in 6 laboratories. (Based on data summarized by Saxe, Dougherty, & Cross, 1985.)

51

.98.[2] The other applications of the ROC to aptitude testing are given in Chapter 10.

Polygraph Lie Detection

The literature contains about 10 studies of the accuracy of polygraph lie detection in each of two main classes: field studies and laboratory, or analogue, studies. The former include various crimes and compare the polygraph examiners' decisions with judicial outcomes, panel decisions, or confessions. The latter are based on mock or role-playing crimes, so they have an advantage in the surety of "ground truth" and a disadvantage in the severity of the consequences. The field studies have been reviewed in the context of a detection-theory analysis by Ben-Shakhar, Lieblich, and Bar-Hillel (1982); both classes of studies were reviewed in an analysis for the federal Office of Technology Assessment (Saxe, Dougherty, & Cross, 1985).

One of the laboratory studies yielded a 7-point ROC; six of them can be analyzed (as I have) to provide 2-point ROCs, by virtue of including an "inconclusive" category along with "deception" and "no deception" categories. The field studies each yielded a single point in ROC space. Figure 13a shows the one full ROC available. In a study made by Szucko and Kleinmuntz (1981), 15 subjects carried out a mock crime and 15 did not. Their polygraph records were examined by six interpreters who judged the likelihood of deception, in response to each of three questions, on an 8-category scale. The six individual ROCs ranged in A_z from approximately .65 to .75; the pooled ROC shown has an A_z of about .75 and a slope of about 0.95. The straight-line fit is not good at the ends, which might result from the combination of a relatively low A_z and a small number of observations (45). Though, of course, not evidence for linear binormal ROCs, Figure 13b shows 2-point ROCs from six other laboratory studies. For them, A_z ranges from about .80 to .95 and the slopes range (with one exception) from about 0.75 to 1.3.

POSSIBLE PATTERN OF SLOPE VARIATION

My concern for empirical (binormal) ROC slopes has been to show that they vary considerably, enough to introduce considerable unreliability if they are assumed,

---

[2]I should note that these values of A_z are depressed, as raw correlation coefficients on the same sample would be, because they are computed only on the candidates selected to take the course. In correlational terms, the effect is one of "restriction of range" of the two variables. Similarly, in discrimination terms, the spectrum of abilities considered is restricted by the lack of course data on unselected candidates, so that discrimination within the sample considered is more difficult. A

by using a given index, to be fixed at some particular value. The question may then arise whether the observed slope variation has some pattern and whether some account of that pattern can be given. I believe that a partial pattern can be discerned and that some relevant theory exists, and so a few remarks on the topic may be heuristic.

In the original development of the signal detection theory that gave rise to the ROC (Peterson, Birdsall, & Fox, 1954), it was assumed that a signal is added at times to background noise to produce a distribution of observations of signal plus noise having a higher mean value than the distribution of observations of noise alone. Then, if the signal adds a constant, the two distributions would have the same variance. Given that the binormal ROC slope under the normal (Gaussian) model equals the ratio of standard deviations, σ_n/σ_{sn}, the ROC slope would be 1.0 in this case. The signal was assumed in theory to add a constant to the noise when all of its appropriate parameters—such as frequency, phase, amplitude, starting time, and duration—are fixed and known to the observer; this signal is "specified exactly" in the theory's terms.

If, on the other hand, one or more of the signal's parameters varies at random from one occurrence to another, the signal is only "specified statistically," and adds additional variance to that of the noise. Distributions other than the normal (e.g., exponential, Rayleigh) can be adduced to treat this case, or the normal model can be retained with the assumption that $\sigma_{sn} > \sigma_n$ and, therefore, that the ROC slope is <1.0 (Green & Swets, 1966/1988). Consistent with such a theory, early work on human sensory processes was taken to indicate slopes near 1.0 for pure-tone signals, specifiable as sine waves, and slopes <1.0 for auditory signals that are samples of white noise, visual signals that are flashes of white light, and other signals in which certain parameters (e.g., frequency or phase) are not specified exactly. The ROCs shown above for white visual signals have slopes mostly around 0.70.[3]

The first binormal slopes noted as quite consistently >1.0 are the ones for information retrieval, which range mostly from 1.0 to 1.3, as mentioned above.

---

correction for restriction of range is usually made for correlation coefficients, and a larger study of Navy data of the sort described here showed median uncorrected and corrected coefficients of .43 and .73, respectively (Swanson, 1979). I have not addressed the question of a similar correction for the A_z index, but Gray, Begg, and Greenes (1984) have provided an approach to the problem.

[3]The idea that uncertainty about the signal adds variance to the *sn* distribution, beyond that of the *n* distribution, might suggest that binormal slopes < 1.0 will usually be observed whenever a brief signal is added to a continuous noise background, because the observer will usually have some uncertainty about at least the location of the signal in time or space. A related suggestion would be that slopes near 1.0 will result when the two alternatives to be discriminated are alike with respect to most of their physical characteristics (e.g., both are brief tones, or lights, or samples of noise, and vary along a single dimension, such as frequency or amplitude). D. R. J. Laming and A. Craig (personal communications, 1985) have advanced this distinction as providing a good summary of existing data from sensory tasks.

This result seems reasonable, inasmuch as the "signals" are then relevant documents and these signals are not in any sense added to "noise," or irrelevant documents. In this case, two separate kinds of stimuli, with some common properties, are presented individually, rather than being mixed in a single presentation—in effect, signals are presented without noise. We can suppose that the few documents relevant to a given query are less variable than the host of documents irrelevant to that query—that, in terms of the normal model, $\sigma_s < \sigma_n$. The situation is similar in aptitude testing. Those passing courses are not added to, or mixed with, those failing courses in a single presentation; the slopes <1.0 for aptitude tests are consistent with the finding that those passing are more variable (considering here only individuals meeting the test's criterion score).

Beyond this point, though, the picture seems unclear. Why, in medical images, have we seen slopes <1.0 for brain tumors (on average, 0.50 to 0.60) and >1.0 for abnormal tissue cells (on average, 1.2 to 1.3)? Or why do data show "old" words to be more variable than "new" words (slopes near 0.70)? In the recognition of "old" and "new" odors, the present data show nearly equal variance (slopes near 1.0). Again, some weather events have shown slopes definitely <1.0, and others, slopes clearly >1.0.

In the net, several puzzles remain, and support at least the present use of an area index such as A_z. And, indeed, evidence suggests that different individuals can produce ROCs of different slopes under the same signal and noise conditions (e.g., Green & Swets, 1966/1988).[4]

CONCLUSIONS

Empirical ROCs drawn from experimental psychology and several practical fields, representing available discrimination data, are fitted well on a binormal

---

[4]The present approach assumes that every point on an empirical ROC represents an observer or system operating at a constant accuracy, but there may be cases in which that assumption does not hold. For example, a human observer in a "yes-no" task might discriminate with greater accuracy at a lenient decision criterion, if that criterion is adopted because the prior probability of a "signal" is high, than at a strict criterion, if that criterion is adopted because the signal probability is low; a possible mechanism for this effect is that the signal is better defined when presented relatively often (Markowitz & Swets, 1967). Knowing when the assumption of constancy holds and when it does not requires a knowledge of the distributions underlying the ROC. Thus, knowledge that the distributions are of equal variance would indicate varying accuracy when a binormal slope $\neq 1$ is obtained. Unfortunately, evidence about the distributions tends to exist—for example, in machine-based systems for information retrieval or medical diagnosis, or in aptitude testing—when there is little reason to doubt the assumption of constant accuracy. In general, the working assumption of constant accuracy seems preferable to using an index that leads to the conclusion of inconstancy for all binormal ROC slopes other than the single slope that it implies. Moreover, the rating-scale technique is relatively insensitive to variables that might affect accuracy differently at different decision criteria—for example, prior probability of signal, and rewards and penalties for correct and incorrect responses.

graph by straight lines of varying slope. This robust finding supports the use of the accuracy index A_z. It also supports the validity of a particular variable-criterion model of the discrimination process, one incorporating distributions of unequal variance. The indices d', η, LOR, and Q imply binormal ROCs that are linear or nearly linear but with a fixed slope $= 1.0$, and hence they do not agree sufficiently well with the data. By the same token, variable-criterion models that assume equal-variance distributions, which have been associated with d' and η and can be associated with LOR and Q, are of limited validity and utility. Several other common indices—including the chance-corrected hit probabilities, H_C and H'_C; percentage correct, PC; the kappa statistic, K; and the correlation coefficient, ϕ—imply binormal ROCs that are distinctly curvilinear and diverge considerably from the data. Therefore, their corresponding models, which are members of the class of threshold models, are invalid. The unreliability of the various indices that misrepresent empirical ROC form can be substantial: Index values can vary from low to high, by $>100\%$, when, in fact, accuracy is constant (see Chapter 3).

DISCUSSION

Signal detection theory was originally developed as a mathematical theory for the process of detecting radar signals (Peterson et al., 1954), but was soon found useful in understanding the behavior of human observers of simple visual and auditory signals (Tanner & Swets, 1954; Tanner, Swets, & Green, 1956). The general applicability of the theory to human discrimination was indicated by its ability to treat empirical findings in recognition memory (Egan, 1958). Its applicability to humans, and to devices that aid or supplant humans, in practical discrimination or diagnostic tasks was suggested by analyses of information-retrieval systems (Swets, 1963, 1969, see Chapter 9). The common denominator in these tasks is, first, an observation process that lends varying degrees of assurance about the occurrence of the alternatives to be discriminated and, second, a desire to assign those varying degrees to one or the other alternative in some reasonable way.

In experimental psychology, the process of discrimination is of interest in its own right: Is it governed by a fixed, physiologically determined threshold or is it adaptive, via a variable decision criterion, to different conditions of expectancy and motivation? Consistent support for the latter process unifies psychological conceptions of a broad range of behaviors and indicates the extensive role of cognitive factors in discrimination tasks. Also, in experimental psychology, the way in which discrimination acuity or capacity varies with independent variables can reveal something substantive about the nature of the particular mechanism of discrimination—be it perceptual, memorial, or cognitive. In practical fields, more emphasis is placed on the absolute level of discrimination acuity that is evidenced, which is of substantive interest in decisions about using, and attempting to improve on, a given technique or system for diagnosis (Swets & Pickett, 1982).

The bonus that the appropriate detection-theory model carries along is the ability it provides, via the ROC, to obtain a relatively pure index of discrimination capacity—one largely independent of the decision criterion or choice tendency—and also an index of the decision criterion that is operative in any given instance. Experimental psychology and practical fields thereby gain a valid and reliable index of discrimination capacity. Psychology, especially, acquires an ability to determine whether various variables that effect a change in performance do so by affecting discrimination acuity or the decision criterion (Chapter 1). An example here is the finding that the declining hit rate observed in perceptual vigilance experiments is often the result of an increasingly strict criterion rather than of decreasing sensitivity (Parasuraman, 1984).

Practical fields need a criterion-free index of discrimination capacity when the criterion used with a given system varies widely over the different settings in which that system is used, and for which it is being evaluated. Thus, for example, the strictness of the criterion used with a particular imaging system in clinical medicine can be quite different in screening and referral settings, and the criterion used with a weather forecasting system will differ from one geographical region to another and from one user of forecast information to another.

Practical fields, moreover, acquire an ability from the ROC to assess the efficacy of a diagnostic system for a specific setting. In a given setting, one is fundamentally concerned with some measure of the system's utility, for example, its expected value or payoff, as determined by the probabilities of the various outcomes of the decision and by the benefits and costs of those outcomes. For specific settings in which the probabilities, benefits, and costs are stable and can be estimated, the emphasis is more on the payoff associated with a particular point on the ROC—that is, with a particular decision criterion—than on an index of the locus of all ROC points. For any of several decision rules that seek to maximize one or another quantity related to utility, one can calculate the optimal decision criterion, or operating point on the ROC (Green & Swets, 1966/1988; Swets & Pickett, 1982; Swets & Swets, 1979). And then, usually, the system can be adjusted to operate at or near that criterion or point. Because the binormal slopes of empirical ROCs vary widely from one instance to another, in a manner so far not predictable, both the calculation of, and adjustment to, the optimal criterion depend on having the empirical ROC in hand.

REFERENCES

Bacus, J. W. (1982). *Application of digital image processing techniques to cytology automation* (Tech. Rep.) Chicago: Rush Presbyterian-St. Luke's Medical Center, Medical Automation Research Unit.

Bacus, J. W., Wiley, E. L., Galbraith, W., Marshall, P. N., Wilbanks, G. D., & Weinstein, R. S. (1984). Malignant cell detection and cervical cancer screening. *Analytical and Quantitative Cytology, 6*, 121–130.

Ben-Shakhar, G., Lieblich, I., & Bar-Hillel, Y. (1982). An evaluation of polygraphers' judgments: A review from a decision theoretic perspective. *Journal of Applied Psychology, 67*, 701–713.

Bishop, Y. M. M., Fienberg, S. E., & Holland, P. W. (1975). *Discrete multivariate analysis: Theory and practice.* Cambridge, MA: MIT Press.

Blough, D. S. (1967). Stimulus generalization as signal detection in pigeons. *Science, 158,* 940–941.

Cleverdon, C., & Keen, M. (1966). *Factors determining the performance of indexing systems: Test results* (Vol. 2). Cranfield, England: Association of Special Libraries and Information Bureau.

Dorfman, D. D., & Alf, E., Jr. (1969). Maximum likelihood estimation of parameters of signal-detection theory and determination of confidence intervals—rating method data. *Journal of Mathematical Psychology, 6,* 487–496.

Egan, J. P. (1958). *Recognition memory and the operating characteristic* (Technical Note). Indianapolis: Indiana University, Hearing and Communication Laboratory.

Egan, J. P. (1975). *Signal detection theory and ROC analysis.* New York: Academic Press.

Giuliano, V. E., & Jones, P. E. (1966). *Study and test of a methodology for laboratory evaluation of message retrieval systems* (Interim Rep. No. ESD-TR-66-405). Cambridge, MA: Arthur D. Little.

Goodman, L. A. (1970). The multivariate analysis of qualitative data: Interactions among multiple classifications. *Journal of the American Statistical Association, 45,* 226–256.

Gray, R., Begg, C. B., & Greenes, R. A. (1984). Construction of receiver operating characteristic curves when disease verification is subject to selection bias. *Medical Decision Making, 4,* 151–164.

Green, D. M., & Swets, J. A. (1966). *Signal detection theory and psychophysics* New York: Wiley. (Reprinted, 1988, Los Altos, CA: Peninsula.)

Laming, D. (1973). *Mathematical psychology.* London: Academic Press.

Lee, W. (1963). Choosing among confusably distributed stimuli with specified likelihood ratios. *Perceptual and Motor Skills, 16,* 445–467.

Luce, R. D. (1959). *Individual choice behavior.* New York: Wiley.

Luce, R. D. (1963). Detection and recognition. In R. D. Luce, R. R. Bush, & E. Galanter (Eds.), *Handbook of mathematical psychology* (pp. 103–189). New York: Wiley.

Macmillan, N. A., & Kaplan, H. L. (1985). Detection theory analysis of group data: Estimating sensitivity from average hit and false-alarm rates. *Psychological Bulletin, 98,* 185–199.

Markowitz, J., & Swets, J. A. (1967). Factors affecting the slope of empirical ROC curves: Comparison of binary and rating response. *Perception & Psychophysics, 2,* 91–100.

Mason, I. (1982). A model for assessment of weather forecasts. *Australian Meteorological Magazine, 30,* 291–303.

Murphy, A. H. (1977). The value of climatological, categorical and probabilistic forecasts in the cost-loss ratio situation. *Monthly Weather Review, 105,* 803–816.

Murphy, A. H., & Winkler, R. L. (1977a). Reliability of subjective probability forecasts of precipitation and temperature. *Journal of the Royal Statistical Society, 26c,* 41–47.

Murphy, A. H., & Winkler, R. L. (1977b). Probabilistic tornado forecasts: Some experimental results. *Preprints, Tenth Conference on Severe Local Storms* (pp. 403–409). Omaha, NE: American Meteorological Society.

Parasuraman, R. (1984). Sustained attention in detection and discrimination. In R. Parasuraman & R. Davies (Eds.), *Varieties of attention* (pp. 243–272). New York: Academic Press.

Peterson, W. W., Birdsall, T. G., & Fox, W. C. (1954). The theory of signal detectability. *Transactions of the IRE Professional Group on Information Theory, 4,* 171–212. (Reprinted in R. D. Luce, R. R. Bush, & E. Galanter (Eds.). (1963). *Readings in mathematical psychology* (pp. 167–211). New York: Wiley.

Rabin, M. D., & Cain, W. S. (1984). Odor recognition: Familiarity, identifiability, and encoding consistency. *Journal of Experimental Psychology: Learning, Memory, and Cognition, 10,* 316–325.

Salton, G., & Lesk, M. (1966). *Information storage and retrieval* (Scientific Rep. No. 11). Ithaca, NY: Cornell University, Department of Computer Science.

Saxe, L., Dougherty, D., & Cross, T. (1985). The validity of polygraph testing. *American Psychologist, 40,* 355–366.

Swanson, L. (1979). Armed services vocational aptitude battery, Forms 6 and 7: Validation against school performance in Navy enlisted schools (July 1976–February 1978) (Tech. Rep. No. 80-1). San Diego, CA: Navy Personnel Research and Development Center.

Swets, J. A. (1963). Information retrieval systems. *Science, 141,* 245–250.

Swets, J. A. (1969). Effectiveness of information retrieval methods. *American Documentation, 20,* 72–89. (Chapter 9 in this volume.)

Swets, J. A. (1973). The relative operating characteristic in psychology. *Science, 182,* 990–1000. (Chapter 1 in this volume.)

Swets, J. A. (1979). ROC analysis applied to the evaluation of medical imaging techniques. *Investigative Radiology, 14,* 109–121. (Chapter 6 in this volume.)

Swets, J. A. (1986). Indices of discrimination or diagnostic accuracy: Their ROCs and implied models. *Psychological Bulletin, 99,* 100–117. (Chapter 3 this volume.)

Swets, J. A., & Pickett, R. M. (1982). *Evaluation of diagnostic systems: Methods from signal detection theory.* New York: Academic Press.

Swets, J. A., Pickett, R. M., Whitehead, S. F., Getty, D. J., Schnur, J. A., Swets, J. B., & Freeman, B. A. (1979). Assessment of diagnostic technologies. *Science, 205,* 753–759. (Chapter 7 in this volume.)

Swets, J. A., & Swets, J. B. (1979). ROC approach to cost-benefit analysis. *IEEE Proceedings of the Sixth Conference on Computer Applications in Radiology* (pp. 203–206). Newport Beach, California. (Reprinted in K. L. Ripley & A. Murray [Eds.], *Introduction to automated arrhythmia detection* [pp. 57–60]. New York: IEEE Computer Society Press, 1980)

Swets, J. A., Tanner, W. P., Jr., & Birdsall, T. G. (1955). *The evidence for a decision-making theory of visual detection* (Tech. Rep. No. 40). Ann Arbor: University of Michigan, Electronic Defense Group.

Swets, J. A., Tanner, W. P., Jr., & Birdsall, T. G. (1961). Decision processes in perception. *Psychological Review, 68,* 301–340.

Szucko, J. J., & Kleinmuntz, B. (1981). Statistical versus clinical lie detection. *American Psychologist, 36,* 488–496.

Tanner, W. P., Jr., & Swets, J. A. (1954). A decision-making theory of visual detection. *Psychological Review, 61,* 401–409.

Tanner, W. P., Jr., Swets, J. A., & Green, D. M. (1956). *Some general properties of the hearing mechanism* (Tech. Rep. No. 30). Ann Arbor: University of Michigan, Electronic Defense Group.

Yule, G. U. (1912). On the methods of measuring association between two attributes. *Journal of the Royal Statistical Society, 75,* 579–642.

3

Indices of Discrimination or Diagnostic Accuracy

Subjects in experiments on perception, learning, memory, and cognition are often required to make a series of fine discriminations. In a common method, a single stimulus is presented on each trial and the subject indicates which of two similar stimuli it is, or from which of two similar categories of stimuli it was drawn. In addition, in several practical settings, professional diagnosticians and prognosticators must say time and again which of two conditions, confusable at the moment of decision, exists or will exist. Among them are physicians, non-destructive testers, product inspectors, process-plant supervisors, weather forecasters, mineralogists, stockbrokers, librarians, survey researchers, and admissions officers. There is interest in knowing both how accurately the experimental subjects and professionals perform and how accurately their various tools perform, and a dozen or more indices of discrimination accuracy are in common use. In this chapter I cover a way of discriminating among those indices that permits sifting the ones that are valid and reliable from the ones that are not. This proposed touchstone for indices is the *relative* (or *receiver*) *operating characteristic* (ROC).

In this chapter I argue that there is no model-free approach to confusion data, and specify the models implied by several common indices. Many of the points I make may be familiar to experimental psychologists from previous discussions of signal detection theory, but they are generalized now to provide a theoretical overview of questions usually addressed heuristically, and with uneven success. The package is presented as a useful contribution to other fields and to those who have avoided the indices of detection theory in favor of indices presumed to make fewer or weaker assumptions.

The path of this chapter is not simple and quick, but the outcome is quite manageable. A half-dozen indices imply threshold models, which are clearly at odds with existing data. These indices are hence subject to unnecessary unreliability (instability, imprecision), and so, as a mnemonic device, might be given a near-failing grade of "D." Four indices are consistent with variable-criterion models, which are in much better agreement with the data. However, they assume as fixed a certain parameter that the data tell us must be free, and hence they may be given a "C." Lastly, a few indices drawn from the class of variable-criterion models accommodate the free parameter mentioned. They are the best available, but because improvements might still be made, they could be given a "B."

With the single-stimulus method, in which either Alternative A or Alternative B is presented, analysis of data in terms of the ROC can provide a relatively pure index of discrimination capacity, or accuracy. In particular, an ROC index may be largely unaffected by the discriminator's criterion for choosing, say, Alternative A (or, as in the terminology of the threshold models, by the discriminator's bias toward the choice of A). Data show that the decision criterion (or response bias) is necessarily involved in the single-stimulus method, and varies both from one person to another and within a person over time. It, and its variation, will confound indices of accuracy unless steps are taken to isolate it.

The ROC is a graph of the functional relation between the proportion of times that Alternative A is chosen when it occurs and the proportion of times that Alternative A is chosen when Alternative B occurs—as the decision criterion or response bias varies. In signal detection theory, the first quantity is termed the *hit rate* and the second, the *false-alarm rate*. (Also indicating the frequent asymmetry between Alternatives A and B are the corresponding terms "true-positive ratio" and "false-positive ratio.") The two quantities in question vary together from low to high as the criterion for choosing Alternative A is made more lenient (or the bias toward the choice of A becomes stronger)—and, thus, for any particular degree of accuracy, an ROC curve is traced from left to right and low to high. Figure 1 shows an example implied by a particular model (discussed in the section on *Equal-variance, normal PDFs*). In general, an index of discrimination that specifies the locus of such a curve, rather than a single point on it, reflects all possible decision criteria or response biases, and hence is independent of any one (see, e.g., chapter 1 in this volume).

Many accuracy indices are calculated from a single ROC point, in disregard of the full curve that results from variation in the decision criterion or in the response bias. However, I suggest here that a candidate index may be evaluated by plotting the family of ROCs that it implies. Strictly, one plots the isopleths, at various values of the index, on the ROC graph. An isopleth, or curve connecting points at which the index has a constant value, is the ROC implied by the index for that value. The gist of this chapter is that an index is valid, and is likely to be reliable, only if its implied ROCs have the same form as the empirical ROCs found for the discrimination problem (observer, task, setting) in question.

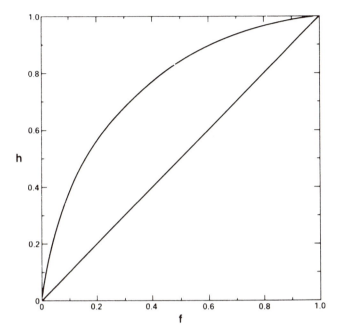

FIG. 1. An illustrative ROC (relative operating characteristic), showing the conditional probability of a hit (h) as a function of that of a false
alarm (f), as the decision criterion varies.

Fine structure is added to that theme because an index's ROCs can reveal
several of its properties. They may show, for example, that the index violates a
basic measurement purpose by giving the same value to better-than-chance and
poorer-than-chance performances. They can disclose that the index depends on
factors irrelevant to discrimination per se, not only the observer's tendency to
choose one or the other alternative, but also the relative frequency of occurrence
of the two alternatives. Further, ROCs may show that two apparently different
indices are practically the same.

Principally, an index's ROCs can identify certain fundamental assumptions
that use of the index makes about the nature of the discrimination process. In
effect, they specify the model implied by the index for that process. One example
of an assumption or model is that the representations (observations or samples) of
the alternatives on which choices are based have just a few values (or states). The
opposing assumption is that the values of representations vary continuously over
a wide range. A second example is that certain states of the representations,
bounded by a fixed threshold, lead directly to the choice of a given alternative.
The opposing assumption is that the observer can choose which values will lead
to which choice, or can relocate a decision criterion at will. A final example is

that the basic statistics of the variable representations are the same across all tasks and discriminators. The opposing assumption is that those statistics can vary in some specified manner.

One might imagine that different models are appropriate for different tasks or observers. However, the working hypothesis is advanced here that all discrimination data will agree best with a model that includes: (a) continuous representations of the alternatives, (b) a decision criterion controlled by the observer, and (c) a particular free parameter of the statistics of the representation values; namely, the relative variance of the distributions of representation values that are associated with the two alternatives. If this hypothesis is true, then using an index that implies another model requires specific justification, conceivably on some pragmatic basis.

My plan is first to set forth the formal description of discrimination performance in the 2×2 contingency table, or confusion matrix, and to define various accuracy indices in terms of the quantities in that table. Then I review ROC theory; I discuss general ways of generating ROCs of various forms for the class of continuous, variable-criterion models; the ROCs of four indices consistent with such a model, with fixed and equal variances of the two distributions, are presented in that context. Third, I present the ROCs for six indices that imply one or another threshold model and discuss these models. Fourth, I review ROC practice; I point to illustrative empirical ROCs from several areas of psychology and from other fields, shown in a companion chapter (Chapter 2), and summarize their general features. Lastly, I point out the implications of empirical ROCs for the validity of the various models, and review indices that are appropriate to the form of empirical ROCs.

FORMAL DESCRIPTION OF DISCRIMINATION PERFORMANCE

For present purposes, the relevant data from a two-alternative, single-stimulus discrimination task are fully contained in a 2×2 contingency table (Table 1). Occurrences of the two alternatives are denoted by A and B and the corresponding choices are denoted by $\tilde{A}$ and $\tilde{B}$. The cell entries (a, b, c, and d) indicate the frequencies of the four possible conjunctions of occurrence and choice. The column sums give the frequencies of occurrences and the row sums give the frequencies of choices. The total sample size (N) appears as the overall sum.

The relative frequency of a conjunction can be taken as an estimate of the *joint* probability of its two elements: for example, a/N is an estimate of $P(A \cdot \tilde{A})$. Dividing a cell frequency by its column sum yields a ratio that is an estimate of a *conditional* probability, specifically, the probability of a choice conditional on an occurrence. For example, $a/(a + c)$ is an estimate of $P(\tilde{A}|A)$. The latter proba-

TABLE 1
Formal Description of Discrimination Performance

Choice	Occurrence		Sum of row frequencies
	A	B	
$\bar{A}$	a	b	a + b
$\bar{B}$	c	d	c + d
Sum of column frequencies	a + c	b + d	N = a + b + c + d

bility and $b/(b + d)$, or $P(\bar{A}|B)$, contain all of the information in the table, because the other two conditional probabilities are their complements.

As I mentioned, the two probabilities just listed are the coordinates of the ROC graph. Given that the two alternatives are often the presence and absence of something (e.g., a weak spot of light or a weak tone in an experiment on sensory capacity—and disease, rain, or oil, in practice), the terms *hit* and *false alarm* are often used, and I use h and f to stand for these conditional probabilities. Another variable of importance is the probability of occurrence of Alternative A ("something" or "signal"), namely $(a = c)/N$, here denoted by s.

DEFINITIONS OF VARIOUS INDICES

Tables 2 and 3 define illustrative indices as proposed in various fields, first in terms of the frequencies of the 2 × 2 table (Table 1) and then in terms of the two or three main probabilities derived from them: h, f, and (in some cases) s. The derivations of the second definition of each index are not given here, but in general are obtained by substitution according to equalities of the following sort: $a/(a + c) = h$, $(a + c)/N = s$, $a = hsN$; $b/(b + d) = f$, $(b + d)/N = 1 - s$, and $b = f(1 - s)N$. Tables 2 and 3 also give the formulas for the ROCs that may be obtained by rearranging the (second) definitions in terms of h, f, and (in some cases) s. I examine later the forms of the ROC specified by these formulas.

Table 2 lists six indices that imply fixed-threshold models. Table 3 lists four indices that are consistent with variable-criterion models that have fixed distributional parameters, that is, equal variances. The indices identified in this article as preferred to either kind just mentioned are defined later, after the form of empirical ROCs is adduced.

Consider first Table 2. The first two indices listed are forms of "corrected hit probability." Both indices focus on h, but attempt to correct it for any spurious component that may be induced by a tendency toward false alarms, which is

TABLE 2
Definitions and ROC Formulas for Indices That Imply
a Threshold Model

Index name and symbol	Definitions and ROC formulas
1. Corrected hit probability, H_c	$H_c = [a/(a + c)] - [b/(b + d)]/[1 - [b/(b + d)]]$
	$= (h - f)/(1 - f)$
	$h = H_c + f(1 - H_c)$
2. Corrected hit probability, H'_c	$H'_c = (ad - bc)/(a + c)(b + d)$
	$= h - f$
	$h = H_c + f$
3. Proportion correct, PC	$PC = (a + d)/N$
	$= (1 - s)(1 - f) + sh$
	$h = [PC - (1 - s)(1 - f)]/s$
4. Skill test, Z	$Z = 4(ad - bc)/N^2$
	$= 4s(1 - s)(h - f)$
	$h = f + [Z/4s(1 - s)]$
5. Kappa statistic, K	$K = \dfrac{2(ad - bc)}{2(ad - bc) + N(b + c)}$
	$= \dfrac{2s(1 - s)[h - f]}{(1 - 2s)[hs + f(1 - s)] + s}$
	$h = \dfrac{f(1 - s)[1 - (1 - K)(1 - 2s)] + sK}{s[1 + (1 - K)(1 - 2s)}$
6. Phi coefficient, ϕ	$\phi = (ad - bc)/[(a + c)(b + d)(a + b)(c + d)]^{1/2}$
	$= \dfrac{[(1 - s)s]^{1/2} [h - f]}{[\{sh + (1 - s)f\}\{1 - [sh + (1 - s)f]\}]^{1/2}}$
	$h = \{\phi^2 + 2(1 - s)(1 - \phi^2)f$
	$+ \phi[\phi^2 + 4(1 - s)(1 - f)/s]^{1/2}\}/\{2[(1 - s) + s\phi^2]\}$

Note. ROC = relative operating characteristic. The numbers 1–6 order these equations in sequence with those presented in the text. The first two equations for each index are different, but equivalent, definitions; the third equation is the ROC formula for that index.

TABLE 3
Definitions and ROC Formulas for Indices
Consistent With a Variable-Criterion Model

Index name and symbol	Definition and ROC formula
7. Detectability, d'	$d' = z_{b/(b+d)} - z_{a/(a+c)}$
	$= z_f - z_h$
	$z_h = z_f - d'$
8. Choice-theory measure, η	$\eta = (bc/ad)^{1/2}$
	$= \{[f(1 - h)]/[h(1 - f)]\}^{1/2}$
	$h = f/[f + \eta^2(1 - f)]$
9. Log odds ratio, LOR	$\text{LOR} = ln(ad/bc)$
	$= ln[h(1 - f)/f(1 - h)]$
	$h = f/[f + e^{-\text{LOR}}(1 - f)]$
10. Yule's Q	$Q = (ad - bc)/(ad + bc)$
	$= (h - f)/(h - 2fh + f)$
	$h = f\left/\left[f + \dfrac{1 - Q}{1 + Q}(1 - f)\right]\right.$

Note. ROC = relative operating characteristic. The numbers 7–10 order these equations in sequence with those presented in the text. The first two equations for each index are different, but equivalent, definitions; the third equation is the ROC formula for that index.

estimated by f. The first index, designated H_c, subtracts f from h, and then divides by $(1 - f)$ to normalize the range of the corrected value (e.g., Blackwell, 1963; Fisk & Schneider, 1984). It has been used primarily in studies of sensory functions. The second, H'_c, corrects simply by subtracting f from h (e.g., Gillund & Shiffrin, 1984; Woodworth, 1938). In psychology this index is associated primarily with studies of recognition memory, and it is also prominent in weather forecasting (e.g., Hanssen & Kuipers, 1965) and medical diagnosis (e.g., Galen & Gambino, 1975; Youden, 1950).

"Percentage correct" is the name usually given the overall percentage of correct choices of either alternative. It is listed in Table 2 in the more convenient form of "proportion correct" (PC). Proposed at least a century ago (Finley, 1884) to evaluate the accuracy of tornado prediction, it is still popular in many fields, including weather forecasting (e.g., Brier & Allen, 1952; Ramage, 1982) and medical diagnosis; in fact, in medical diagnosis, it is often taken as synonymous with accuracy (see Metz, 1978).

Probability that Alt A was chosen

A contemporary of Finley (Gilbert, 1885) pointed out the dependency of PC on s and, indeed, the fact that PC could be as high as s or $(1 - s)$ by chance, without discrimination. Now, in weather forecasting, indices that measure the extent to which discrimination exceeds chance performance are generally called *skill scores*. An example is given by the index designated Z (Woodcock, 1976) listed in the table. As shown later, a higher value of h relative to f must be achieved to attain a given value of Z as s departs from the symmetrical .50. Several other indices proposed in weather forecasting have been analyzed in ROC terms by Mason (1982), including indices proposed by Heidke (1926), Vernon (1953), Appleman (1959), Schrank (1960), Bermowitz and Zurndorfer (1979), and Rousseau (1980).

A statistic used as a measure of observer agreement in clinical medicine (Landis & Koch, 1977), called the kappa statistic (K), is another form of chance-corrected counterpart to PC, and is listed fifth in Table 2.

The final index considered in Table 2 is another measure of association in statistics. Phi, equal to $(\chi^2/N)^{1/2}$, is called the fourfold point coefficient and the root-mean-square contingency (Hays, 1973). It (or its square) has been used as a discrimination accuracy index in experimental psychology (Wellman, 1977; see also Nelson, 1984), weather forecasting (Pickup, 1982); and nondestructive testing (see Swets, 1983a, 1983b).

Table 3 lists four indices that have been, or can be, associated with variable-criterion models. They are all consistent with the assumption (as will be seen later) that the distributions of observation values stemming from the two alternatives to be discriminated are of equal variance—a restrictive assumption not supported by data.

The first index listed is the first index defined in the psychological application of signal detection theory, the detectability index d' (Tanner & Swets, 1954). It is defined in terms of integrals of normal (Gaussian) distributions and is given in terms of the normal deviate, or z score; d' is the z score corresponding to f minus the z score corresponding to h.

The next index, η, is defined in Luce's (1959, 1963) general theory of choice. Both η and the next measure, the log odds ratio (LOR), are similar to d', but depend on logistic, rather than normal or Gaussian, distributions (thus permitting an explicit writing of the ROC function, as shown).

The LOR was described by Goodman (1970) and is used extensively in biostatistics (see Gart, 1971). The odds are those of a correct choice (ad) relative to an incorrect choice (bc). As the two ROC equations show, $\eta^2 = e^{-\text{LOR}}$.

Lastly, the measure Q was defined by Yule (1912). For two alternatives, Goodman and Kruskal's (1954) gamma measure is equal to Q. It was recently proposed as an accuracy index in psychology by Nelson (1984). Nelson contrasted PC, (see Table 2), d', and Q, and advocated Q over d' primarily on the basis that it was thought to make weaker assumptions. As I show later, and as Table 3 indicates by the common form of the ROC formulas for η, LOR, and Q, the latter index is also consistent with (though it need not assume) logistic distributions in detection theory.[1]

ROC THEORY

Basic Model

The ROC graph was designed in the context of the theory of signal detectability by Peterson, Birdsall, and Fox (1954) to provide an index of accuracy consistent with their basic model of the detection process. They saw the detection task as one of discriminating occurrences of "signal plus noise" (*sn*) from occurrences of "noise alone" (*n*). Given that noise is a random variable, the two alternatives can be considered as statistical hypotheses.

The theory of statistical decision, or of testing statistical hypotheses (e.g., Wald, 1950), is the basis for a model that provides an accuracy index that is independent both of the probability of occurrence of the two alternatives (*s* and 1 − *s*) and of the discriminator's tendency to favor the choice of one or the other alternative. Neither variable, the detection theorists suggested, is usefully or properly regarded as part of the process of discrimination per se and neither should therefore influence an index of discrimination capacity or accuracy. Because they are variables, an accuracy index tacitly dependent on them would be imprecise at best. An accuracy index that incorporated an explicit and monitored dependence on them would imply a model of the choice process as well as of the discrimination process and would need to be validated by data.

The detection-theory model is depicted in Figure 2. The horizontal axis is akin to the decision variable of statistical theory: The variable x is a measure of the strength of the observation, or the magnitude of a sample statistic. The vertical axis is probability density. The left-hand distribution is the probability density function (PDF) of x for n, analogous to the null hypothesis, H_0. The right-hand distribution is the PDF for *sn*, analogous to the other hypothesis under test, H_1. The degree of overlap of the two distributions determines the confusability of the two alternatives, reflected in the figure by the difference between the distribution means, and denoted by θ. Thurstone (1927) called these distributions "discriminal dispersions" in psychometric theory: They acknowledge the idea that repre-

---

[1]In treating the related indices Q, η, and LOR (Table 3) as well as ϕ (Table 2), I essentially include almost all standard measures of association as derived in statistical theory. Bishop, Fienberg, and Holland (1975) point out that in 2×2 tables, almost all such measures reduce either to functions of the cross-product ratio (and are independent of marginal totals), as are Q, η, and LOR, or to functions of the correlation coefficient (and are sensitive to marginal totals), as in ϕ. The kappa statistic (Table 2) is a measure of agreement described by Cohen (1960) as a special case of association for larger tables, and as essentially equivalent to association in 2×2 tables (again, sensitive to marginal totals).

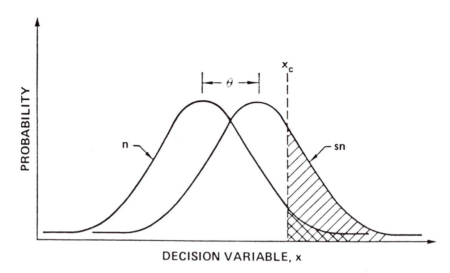

FIG. 2. Detection-theory model of the discrimination process (see text). (x: a measure of the strength of the observation; n: the distribution of observations [or probability density function] that arises from the noise-alone events; sn: same, but for the signal-plus-noise event; x_c: a critical value of x; and θ: the difference between the means of the two distributions.)

sentations of a given alternative, either psychologically in perception or cognition or more generally as samples of any kind, vary from one occurrence of the alternative to another, and can be considered to lie along a single dimension.[2]

A critical value of x, or the detection criterion (x_c), separates the values of x that lead to the choice of sn (i.e., $x \geq x_c$) from those that lead to the choice of n (i.e., $x < x_c$). The particular value of x_c selected depends in theory on the probability s and on the benefits and costs of the four possible choice outcomes.

The area under the sn distribution to the right of x_c (hatched) equals the probability h, and the area under the n distribution to the right of x_c (cross-hatched) equals f. The ROC is traced from left to right on the graph of h versus f as x_c moves from right to left. This graph and an illustrative ROC are shown in Figure 1. The ROC shown in Figure 1 is that indicated by the specific model and specific discriminability portrayed in Figure 2: namely, Gaussian or normal distributions of equal variance separated by a particular value of θ. Larger θs lead to ROCs that are higher on the graph, and vice versa. Discrimination accuracy is at the chance level when the ROC follows the positive diagonal (the distributions

---

[2]Multidimensional representations can be mapped onto the single dimension of likelihood ratio, the ratio of the ordinate of the PDF for sn to the ordinate of the PDF for n (Green & Swets, 1966/1974; Peterson, Birdsall, & Fox, 1954).

overlap completely), and is perfect when the ROC follows the left-hand and top axes (the distributions do not overlap at all). Appropriate indices are discussed later, but note that accuracy independent of the criterion for choice can be indexed either by a theoretical parameter related to the PDFs that might underlie an ROC, such as θ, or by some other measure of the locus of the ROC, perhaps one empirically based, such as the proportion of the graph's area lying beneath the ROC.

ROC theory as applied in psychology is discussed in detail elsewhere (Green & Swets, 1966/1988; Chapter 1 in this volume), and its applications in other fields have also been summarized (Swets & Green, 1978). Note that within the framework of detection theory, ROCs can be generated in two main ways. (a) One can assume PDFs, on the decision variable, of one or another specific form. As indicated previously, the PDF form determines the ROC form. (b) One can assume some ROC form directly, without recourse to PDFs, as specified by an algebraic formula that relates h to f. Relevant examples in each category are described next.

ROCs Generated by PDFs

Equal-variance, normal PDFs. The equal-variance, normal PDFs of Figure 2 were the first considered in detection theory, and represent a signal with all of its parameters (i.e., frequency, phase, amplitude, starting time, and duration) exactly known by the observer. The corresponding accuracy index was taken as

$$d' = (m_{sn} - m_n)/\sigma_n. \tag{11}$$

which expresses the difference between the means (m) of the two PDFs in terms of the standard deviation (square root of variance) of the PDF for the n (or, equivalently, for the sn) alternative. Figure 3a shows illustrative ROCs for equal-variance, normal PDFs; as in later figures, the form of the PDFs is shown in the inset at lower right.

Equal-variance, logistic PDFs. The logistic PDF is similar to the normal (Gaussian) PDF (e.g., Bush, 1963; Laming, 1973), and logistic PDFs of equal variance for n and sn yield ROCs similar to those of equal-variance, normal PDFs (Luce, 1963). Figure 3b shows such PDFs and illustrative ROCs. Compared with the normal PDF, the logistic PDF is slightly taller, narrower through the midsection, and wider at the tails. The accuracy index shown, η, is that defined in Luce's choice theory (Equation 8, Table 3).

As indicated, the LOR index, though defined outside of detection theory and the concept of the ROC, is based on the logistic distribution (and, in detection theory, would be derived from equal-variance, logistic PDFs), and yields ROCs identical in form to those of η as shown in Figure 3b. I show later, when discussing algebraically defined ROCs, that Q, also defined without regard to the

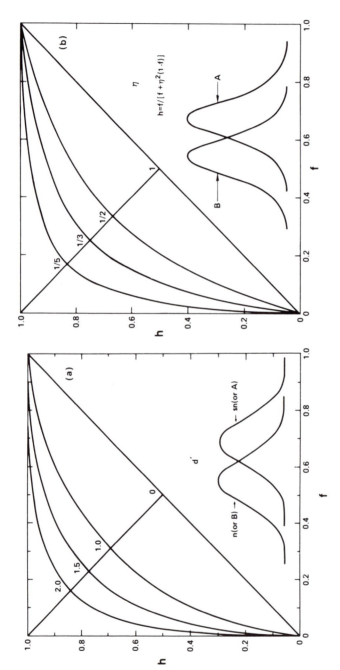

FIG. 3. a: relative operating characteristics (ROCs) for equal-variance, normal proba-bility distributions. b: ROCs for equal-variance, logistic probability distributions. (h: conditional probability of a hit; f: conditional probability of a false alarm; n: the distri-bution of observations [or probability density function] that arises from the noise-alone event; sn: same, but for the signal-plus-noise event; A and B: more general designations of the two events; d': an accuracy index based on equal-variance, normal distributions; and η: an accuracy index based on equal-variance, logistic distributions.)

ROC concept or underlying distributions, yields ROCs identical to those of η and LOR. Their ROC formulas, as noted in Table 3 (Equations 8–10), are of the same form. The ROCs of the LOR and Q, with representative index values, are shown in Figure 4.

ROCs on a binormal graph. The use of a different scale on the axes of the ROC graph is convenient for fitting empirical ROCs and for comparing theoretical ROCs. The scale used most often is one on which the spacing of the probabilities is transformed so that their corresponding normal deviates, or z scores, are linearly spaced. A graph with such a scale on both axes is called a *binormal* graph. On such a graph, ROCs for constant d' are straight lines with slope of 1, as Figure 5a shows (Peterson et al., 1954).

Logistic PDFs yield straight-line ROCs on what Birdsall (1966) called a "lor-lor" graph, where, as with the LOR index, *lor* stands for the natural logarithm of the odds ratio. However, given the similarity of the normal and logistic ROCs apparent in Figure 3, one would suspect that logistic-based ROCs are not far from straight lines on a binormal graph. Following Birdsall (1966), logistic ROCs (with the values of η shown in Figure 3) are shown on a binormal graph in Figure 5b, where a slight bow can be seen. Figures 3 and 5 indicate that the logistic and normal forms of ROC could be distinguished in data only with exceptionally reliable data, based on a large number of observations, and could not be distinguished for most practical purposes.

Unequal-variance, normal PDFs. The early detection experiments with human observers produced some ROCs like those of Figure 3, but most were not symmetrical about the negative diagonal; they rose more steeply from the origin and then bent more sharply toward the upper corner. This effect at first seemed to be more pronounced in data as the signal strength was increased, that is, for progressively higher ROCs (Swets, Tanner, & Birdsall, 1961). Such ROCs would arise from normal PDFs having a larger variance for sn than for n, and such that the difference in variance increased with $(m_{sn} - m_n)$. ROCs based on a mean-to-sigma ratio of 4.0 (i.e., assuming $[m_{sn} - m_n]/[\sigma_{sn} - \sigma_n] = \Delta m/\Delta\sigma = 4.0$) agreed reasonably well with the early data (Green & Swets, 1966/1988).

Illustrative ROCs based on that ratio, and illustrative PDFs, are shown on ordinary scales in Figure 6a. On a binormal graph, ROCs with a fixed mean-to-sigma ratio are straight lines with a progressively shallower slope as they rise on the graph, as shown in Figure 6b. Given that such ROCs cannot be indexed by d' (Equation 11), because d' is not constant along them, Figure 6 shows Δm as an index, which was an early attempt to handle ROCs consistent with unequal-variance, normal distributions. The definition of Δm is analogous to d',

$$\Delta m = (m_{sn} - m_n)/\sigma_n, \tag{12}$$

and can be used along with the slope of an empirical ROC in a two-parameter description of data (Green & Swets, 1966/1988).

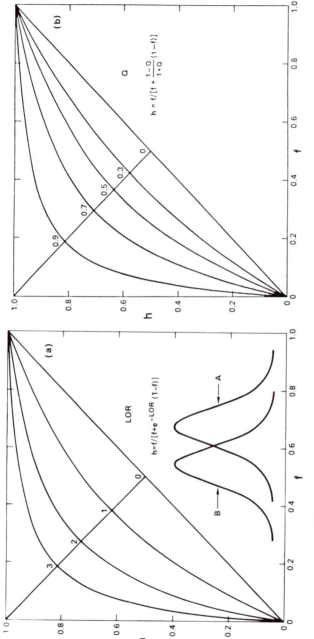

FIG. 4. a: relative operating characteristics (ROCs) for the log odds ratio (LOR) index. b: ROCs for Yule's Q index. (h: conditional probability of a hit; f: conditional probability of a false alarm; A and B: distributions of observations [or probability density functions] that arise from the two possible events; and LOR and Q: accuracy indices that correspond in detection theory to equal-variance, logistic distributions.)

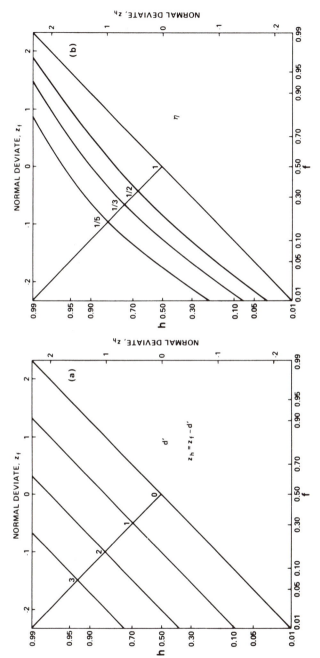

FIG. 5. a: relative operating characteristics (ROCs) for equal-variance, normal distributions on a binormal graph. b: ROCs for equal-variance, logistic distributions on a binormal graph. (h: conditional probability of a hit; f: conditional probability of a false alarm; z_h, and z_f: normal-deviate values of h and f; d′: an accuracy index based on equal-variance, normal distributions; and η: an accuracy index based on equal variance, logistic distributions.)

73

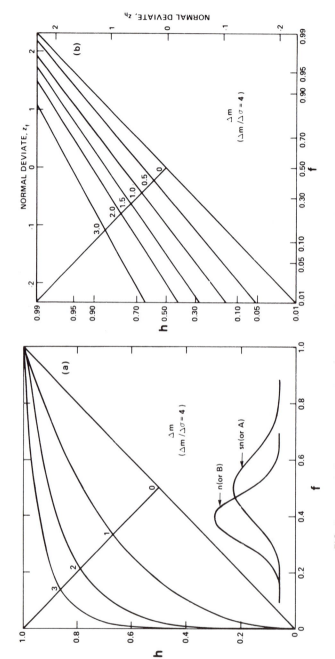

FIG. 6. a: relative operating characteristics (ROCs) for unequal-variance, normal probability distributions, with a mean-to-sigma ratio of 4.0 on ordinary scales. b: the same ROCs but on a binormal graph. (h: conditional probability of a hit; f: conditional probability of a false alarm; n (or B) and sn (or A): distributions of observations [or probability density functions] that arise from the two events; Δm: an accuracy index based on unequal-variance, normal distributions; m: the mean of a distribution; and σ: the standard deviation of a distribution.)

Other PDFs for asymmetrical ROCs.   Though unequal-variance, normal (or logistic) ROCs cannot be indexed by a single quantity unless some further assumption is made, such as that the mean-to-sigma ratio is fixed, some other forms of PDF give rise to ROCs similar to those of Figure 6, and can be indexed by a quantity that is constant along a given ROC without concern for relative variances. Some of these were defined in detection theory as suitable for a signal having one or more parameters (e.g., phase) known only statistically to an observer (Peterson et al., 1954). Included are the Rayleigh PDF (Jeffress, 1964), chi-square and noncentral chi-square PDFs (Birdsall & Lamphiear, 1960), and exponential PDFs (Green & Swets, 1966/1988).

Algebraic ROCs

Power ROC.   ROCs having the general pattern of those in Figure 6 are specified by the formula for a power function: $h = f^k$, where $k < 1$ (Egan, Greenberg, & Schulman, 1961). A few power curves are shown in Figure 7a, which indicates how the value of k can serve as an accuracy index. The PDFs inset, which produce power ROCs, are exponentials (Green & Swets, 1966 /1988). These ROCs, of course, are straight lines on log-log scales. Again, however, they are quite close to straight lines on normal-normal scales, as Figure 7b shows.

Conic ROCs.   Arcs of circles, ellipses, parabolas, and hyperbolas can serve as algebraically specified ROCs (Birdsall, 1966). Of these, the hyperbola is singled out here, for reasons stated next.

Algebraic ROCs and Related PDFs

As mentioned previously, exponential PDFs generate power ROCs, though these ROCs are simply identified directly by their algebraic formula. In the same vein, Birdsall (1966) observed that logistic PDFs generate ROCs that are rectangular hyperbolas. Thus, the ROC specified by the equation for a hyperbola was shown in Figures 3b and 4a, and both η (Equation 8) and LOR (Equation 9) are associated with hyperbolas. Not originally derived from logistic PDFs (nor dependent on them), but implying hyperbolic ROCs, is the index Q (Equation 10). I show that LOR, η, and Q specify hyperbolic ROCs in the Appendix.

RELATION OF d', η, LOR, AND Q

The indices η, LOR, and Q are related by the following equations defining LOR and Q in terms of η:

$$LOR = ln(1/\eta^2), \tag{13}$$

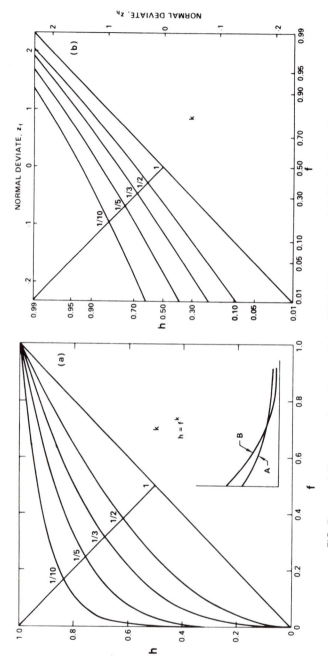

FIG. 7. a: relative operating characteristics (ROCs) for exponential distributions, in the form of a power function, on ordinary scales, b: the same ROCs on a binormal graph. (h: conditional probability of a hit; f: conditional probability of a false alarm; A and B: distributions of observations [or probability density functions] that arise from the two events; and k: an accuracy index based on exponential distributions.)

and

$$Q = (1 - \eta^2)/(1 + \eta^2). \tag{14}$$

As developed by C. E. Metz (personal communication, 1984), there is a one-to-one correspondence between those three indices and the value of d' taken at the negative diagonal of the ROC graph, termed d'_e. Following Luce's (1963) derivation of

$$\eta \approx \exp[-(2/\pi)^{1/2}d'_e], \tag{15}$$

and Equations 13 and 14, we have

$$\text{LOR} \approx 2(2/\pi)^{1/2}d'_e, \tag{16}$$

and

$$Q \approx \tanh[(2/\pi)^{1/2}d'_e]. \tag{17}$$

These approximations can be shown to be quite good for $d'_e < 2$ and can be extended by a correction term to higher values. They are reasonably good for a fairly substantial range of ROC points centered at the negative diagonal; for example, they are good to within 2% for ROC points having f values within $\pm$ .10 of its value at the negative diagonal. The need for approximate equations stems from the nature of the definition of d', but corresponding values of the four indices, according to exact relations, could be tabled. The key exact relation is

$$\eta = \{1/[\Phi(d'_e/2)]\} - 1. \tag{18}$$

To review a bit of history, Luce (1963) showed that η corresponds to a distance between the means of logistic PDFs in signal detection theory, via the relation $\eta = \exp[-(\Delta m)/2]$, where Δm is defined as in Equation 12. The logistic function was demonstrated to be "very similar" to the normal function (Bush, 1963, p. 448; Laming, 1973, p. 23), differing at most by "less than two parts in a hundred" (Luce, 1959, p. 55). The ROCs of η were observed to have "substantially the same" form as those of d' (Luce, 1963, p. 131). Ogilvie and Creelman (1968) observed that LOR is approximately 1.64 times d'_e. C. E. Metz and I. B. Mason (independent personal communications, 1984) pointed out that LOR and Q are transformations of η. Edwards (1963) had shown that measures of association drawn from a 2×2 table that are independent of the marginal frequencies should logically be some function of the cross ratio, that is, η^2; he specifically qualified LOR and Q (and disqualified ϕ, defined in Equation 6). Birdsall (1966) showed that logistic PDFs generate hyperbolic ROCs.

Birdsall (1966) pointed out that hyperbolic ROCs are difficult to distinguish from the ROCs of d' in a figure reproduced here as Figure 8a. It shows an equal-variance, normal ROC as a curve ($d' \approx 1.5$), along with selected points from the hyperbolic ROC that fits it best. As he put it, "If one's definition of 'close' means 'as points appear when plotted on linear [scales],' then these two [PDFs] yield ROC curves that are quite close" (1966, p. 178).

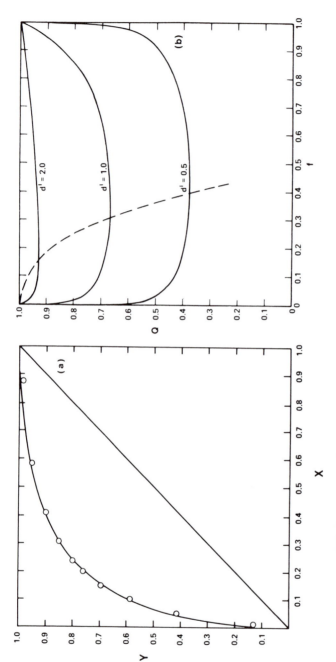

FIG. 8. a: comparison of a hyperbolic relative operating characteristic (ROC), as generated by equal-variance, logistic probability distributions (open circles) and an ROC based on equal-variance, normal probability distributions (curve). (Reproduced from Birdsall, 1966.) b: Q as a function of f for three values of d' (solid lines) and the contour of values of f at the negative diagonal of the ROC graph (broken line). (Y: conditional probability of a hit; X or f: conditional probability of a false alarm; Q: an accuracy index that corresponds in detection theory to equal-variance, logistic distributions; and d': an accuracy index based on equal-variance, normal distributions.)

Birdsall observed, however, that as a second-order effect, η, LOR, and Q do diverge from d' at the edges of the plot. Ordinarily, too few observations are made to define such extreme probabilities with adequate reliability, but that may not always be the case. So let us examine some representative values of Q and d' for values of $f < .10$. Figure 8b shows Q as a function of f for three values of d' (solid lines). Between $f = .01$ and .10, the value of Q for constant d' varies by about 4% for $d' = 2.0$, 17% for $d' = 1.0$, and 26% for $d' = 0.5$. At such values of f, especially at low index values, Q and d' cannot be used interchangeably.[3]

Figure 8b also helps demonstrate a point made earlier. It shows the contour of values of f taken at the negative diagonal of the ROC graph for various ROCs (broken line). It can be seen that Q (and, hence, LOR and η) vary by only a few percent from d' over a range of f of 0.20 or more, centered about the negative diagonal. This graph, then, supports the statement that the approximations given above for the correspondence of η, LOR, and Q to d'_e are quite good for a fairly large range of off-diagonal ROC points.

In summary, ROC analysis shows that the four indices have a kinship in theory and indicates that under most conditions, they would lead to the same conclusions in practice. Surely an advocacy of one over another is considerably enlightened by a comparison of their ROCs. That is particularly true for Nelson's recent advocacy of Q for research on "feeling of knowing," inasmuch as researchers in that field have acknowledged the problems of the variable decision criterion (Nelson, 1984, pp. 117–119, 121–122, 125–126).

Note also that the same or similar conclusions that would usually be indicated by the four indices may be faulty because of the straitjacket these indices put on the form of a ROC. For example, consider that if the top curve of Figure 6b represented an observed ROC, calculated values of d' would vary by about 100% along that curve (from about 2.7 at the left to about 1.3 at the right), and would vary by about 20%–25% in a range of $f \pm .10$ about the negative diagonal, where $f = .14$ (i.e., from about 2.0 at $f = .04$ to about 2.5 at $f = .24$); all of which is unnecessary error of measurement.

CONCEPT OF THE REGULAR ROC

In making the transition from indices associated with the class of continuous, variable-criterion models to those associated with threshold models, it will be

---

[3]I. B. Mason (personal communication, 1985) pointed out the importance of the divergence of Q and d' in weather forecasting, where the usual decision variable, posterior probability, serves to expand the left side of the graph as compared with Figure 8b. That expanded region is of detailed interest in the field, in which a distinction is made routinely among posterior probabilities of 0, .02, and .05 (see, e.g., Murphy, 1977).

helpful to have in mind the concept of the "regular" ROC. Almost any form of ROC can be generated within signal detection theory: even the forms implied by threshold models, as we shall see, follow from assuming rectangular PDFs. However, what can be thought of as canonical, or classic, detection theory contains an assumption that leads to regular ROCs. This assumption is that any value of the observation or decision variable can arise from either alternative (n or sn); in other words, that noise is thoroughly noise, perturbing observation values throughout their range.

Given enough observations, this assumption implies that $f = 0$ will be attained only when $h = 0$, and that $h = 1$ will be attained only when $f = 1$. A regular ROC is thus interior to the unit-square ROC graph (ordinary scales) except at the chance points ($f = 0$, $h = 0$) and ($f = 1$, $h = 1$). Nonregular ROCs are those permitting "singular" detection, that is, ROC points having $h > 0$ for $f = 0$ or $h = 1$ for $f < 1$. On ordinary scales, such ROCs will cross the left-hand axis above the lower left-hand corner or the top axis short of the upper right-hand corner. The theoretical ROCs seen so far are regular; the theoretical ROCs seen next are nonregular. Data, as I show elsewhere (Chapter 2) and characterize here, yield regular ROCs.[4]

INDICES IMPLYING A THRESHOLD MODEL

The six indices remaining to be considered, those in Table 2 that were anticipated to imply a threshold model, can be handled with fewer subtleties than the four from Table 3 discussed previously. For one thing, their ROCs look very different from the ones already discussed, so that contrast is easy. For another, because their ROCs all look very different from data, I do not go to great lengths to compare and contrast them with each other. One of these indices implies a high-threshold model; the other five imply a double-threshold model.

Note first that the ROC formulas for the first five indices in Table 2 show h as a linear function of f. Hence, their ROCs will be straight lines on *ordinary* scales. Thus they are nonregular. The ROCs of the sixth index listed are nearly straight and are also nonregular. For the most part, the models implied by these indices assume that observation values have just two or three states. Such models might include underlying PDFs that are truncated or, alternatively, a threshold on the observation variable, such that values on a given side of the threshold are indis-

---

[4]I borrow "regular" from Birdsall (1966) who meant something slightly more specific by it. His definition is essentially the same as Egan's (1975) definition of a "proper" ROC. A *proper* ROC is based on likelihood ratio as the decision variable (see Footnote 2). Such an ROC will have two other properties of a regular ROC: (a) It will be complete; that is, for each value of the horizontal axis there is one value of the vertical axis; (b) It will be convex; that is, it will be on or above the line segments connecting any two points the discriminator can produce. In general, these ROCs will have a monotonically decreasing slope from the point (0, 0) to the point (1, 1).

tinguishable from each other. I present the six ROCs next, followed by a brief characterization of the models.

Corrected Hit Probability H_c

The ROC's for H_C, the first of the two chance-corrected versions of h, are shown in Figure 9a. They were derived by Tanner and Swets (1954) as representing both the particular correction and the so-called high-threshold model advocated, for example, by Blackwell (1963). They intersect the left-hand axis and the upper right-hand corner. Craig (1979) reported that an index used to assess inspector accuracy in industrial monitoring also leads to the ROC of the high-threshold model.

Corrected Hit Probability, H'_C

The ROCs for H'_C, the simpler chance-corrected version of h, appear in Figure 9b. They were first drawn by Egan (See Green & Swets, 1966/1988). They cross both the left-hand and upper axis. Craig (1979) pointed out that the non-parametric measure of the area beneath an ROC that is constructed by connecting a single observed point and the corners (0, 0) and (1, 1), a special case of the general area measure discussed by Green and Swets (1966/1988), also leads to the theoretical ROC of the double-threshold model.

Percentage (Proportion) Correct, PC

The ROCs for PC are shown in Figure 10a. The three values of s included (.25, .50, .75) indicate the strong dependence of PC on that variable. For $s = .50$, these ROCs have the same form as those of H'_C, as Macmillan and Kaplan also showed (1985).

In general, the slope of the ROCs for PC is $(1 - s)/s$. The ROCs of different slope rotate about their intersection with the negative diagonal. All points along an ROC that intersects the negative diagonal at a given point are assigned the same index value, which is equal to the value of h at the negative diagonal. The reader might note, for example, the broad locus of ROC points assigned PC = .70, at the three values of s shown: thus, at $f = .40$, h could be 1.0, .80, or .73; at $f = .10$, h could be .63, .50, or .10. For values of $s \neq .5$, some ROCs will cross the positive diagonal, with the result that some better-than-chance performances are given the same index value as some poorer-than-chance performances.

Skill Test Z

ROCs for the index Z, calculated by Mason (1982), are shown in Figure 10b. They have the same form as those of H'_C and of PC for $s = .5$. As the curves for

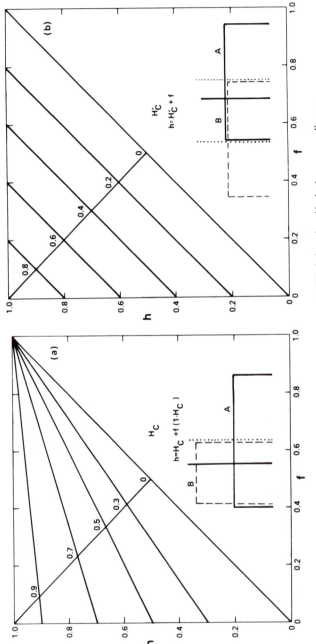

FIG. 9. a: relative operating characteristics (ROCs) for the H_C index on ordinary scales. b: ROCs for the H'_C index on ordinary scales. (h: conditional probability of a hit; f: conditional probability of a false alarm; A and B: distributions of observations that arise from the two events; H_C: an accuracy index that implies a high-threshold model; and H'_C: an accuracy index that implies a double-threshold model.)

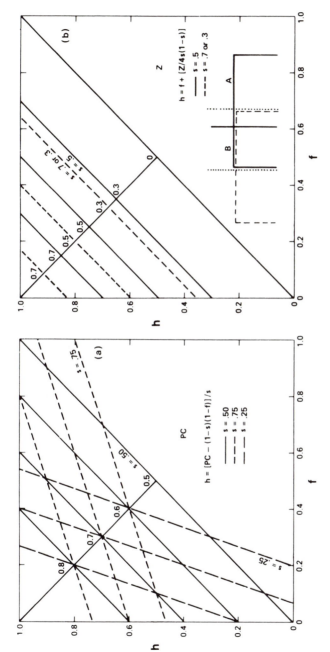

FIG. 10. a: relative operating characteristics (ROCs) for the PC index on ordinary scales. b: ROCs for the Z index on ordinary scales, (*h*: conditional probability of a hit; *f*: conditional probability of a false alarm; *s*: probability of occurrence of one event; *A* and *B*: distributions of observations that arise from the two events; PC: the accuracy index that is the percentage of correct responses; and Z: an accuracy index, as defined in the figure, used in weather forecasting.)

83

$s = .70$ and $.30$ show, Z depends on s in that better performance in terms of h and f is required to achieve a given index value if the probabilities of the two alternatives differ.

Kappa Statistic, K

The use of K was suggested as a possible accuracy index by G. Koch (personal communication, 1984), and my calculations of its ROCs are shown in Figure 11a. Again, slopes of 1 occur for $s = .50$, and, indeed, for $s = .50$, $K = H'_C$. As with PC, the slope varies with s. All points on the upper three ROCs yield the same value of K (.50) and so do all points on the lower three ROCs (.20).

Phi Coefficient, ϕ

In Figure 11b, it can be seen that ROCs for ϕ (discussed by Swets, 1983a, 1983b) share with H'_C, Z, and K the intersection of both axes other than at the corners. They differ in having a slight curvature. Only the ROCs for $s = .5$ are shown; as with PC and K, ROCs for ϕ tilt away from symmetry about the negative diagonal for other values of s. N. Macmillan (personal communication, 1985) pointed out that a nonparametric area index based on a single observed ROC point, as proposed by Pollack and Norman (1964), denoted A', yields ROCs that closely resemble those of ϕ for $s = .5$ (see their Figure 2 or Macmillan and Kaplan's [1985] Figure 11). C. E. Metz (personal communication, 1985) observed that both of these ROCs are arcs of an ellipse.

Threshold Models

As mentioned previously, the model for H_C is a high-threshold (two-state) model. As indicated in the inset to Figure 9a, representations of Alternative A (distributed according to the solid line) may fall above or below the threshold (shown as a dotted vertical line). The threshold is "high" in that it is never exceeded by representations of Alternative B (distributed according to the dashed line, slightly offset). Values above the threshold are indistinguishable from one another, as are values beneath it. The value of h at threshold, that is, at $f = 0$, is the "true" h and is inflated according to a chance mechanism when $f > 0$. That is, the observer who desires a higher h than that given at $f = 0$ must respond "Alternative A" to a random selection of values of the decision variable x that fall beneath the threshold. One may picture such an observer in detection-theory terms as setting a decision criterion somewhere beneath the threshold; the solid vertical line represents a criterion set so that about one-third of the observations beneath the threshold receive the "Alternative A" response. Of course, the x-axis in this picture is not a continuum; the probabilities associated with the subareas of the rectangles can be viewed as massed at appropriate points along the x-axis.

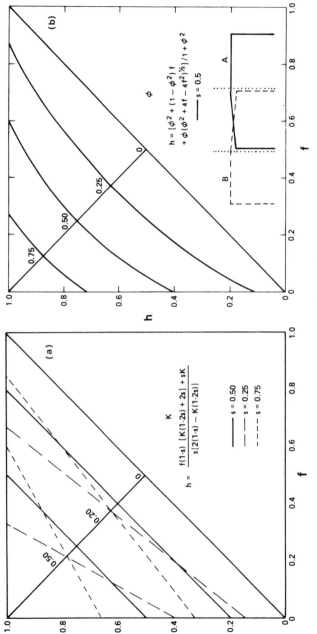

FIG. 11. a: relative operating characteristics (ROCs) for the kappa index on ordinary scales. b: ROCs for the ϕ index on ordinary scales. (h: conditional probability of a hit; f: conditional probability of a false alarm; s: probability of occurrence of one event; A and B: distributions of observations that arise from the two events; K: the accuracy index supplied by the kappa statistic; and ϕ: the accuracy index supplied by the phi coefficient.)

85

A double-threshold model is implied by H'_c, PC, Z, K, and ϕ. All but ϕ correspond to a three-state model: Two thresholds define three categories of representations of the alternatives such that the values within each category are indistinguishable (Swets, 1961). This model can be related to uniform PDFs as in Figures 9b and 10b. Some representations, arising only from A, are above a high threshold (dotted vertical line on right) and lead correctly to the choice of A; others, arising only from B, are beneath a low threshold (dotted vertical line on left) and lead correctly to the choice of B. Representations in a third category arise from A or B, fall between the two thresholds, lead to either choice, and are correct or incorrect strictly by chance. In detection-theory terms, the solid vertical line represents a decision criterion that assigns about one-third of the indeterminate representations to Alternative A. (Again, however, the x-axis is not a continuum.) The model for ϕ is similar, but the representations in the middle category are distinguishable from each other to a slight degree (see Fig. 11b, inset) and thus permit slightly better than chance behavior. The ROCs in Figures 9–11 (for $s = .5$) are symmetrical about the negative diagonal, as they would be for symmetrically placed thresholds, and as implied by the various indices. More detailed discussions of the models (except that of ϕ) are given by Green and Swets (1966/1988).

EMPIRICAL ROCS AND SUITABLE INDICES

Characterization of Empirical ROCs

Chapter 2 in this volume includes a large number of empirical ROCs drawn from psychological experiments on sensory capacity, memory, cognition, and learning, as well as from other fields, including aptitude testing, polygraph lie detection, weather forecasting, information retrieval, and medical diagnosis. They strongly support the conclusions that empirical ROCs are fitted well on a binormal graph by straight lines of varying slope. Predominantly, the observed binormal slopes are between 0.7 and 1.0—some a little lower (to about 0.5) or higher (to about 1.5). The implication of the straight line is that empirical ROCs are regular, as that term is defined above. The implication of the variation in binormal slope is that a free slope parameter is required to fit data. A corollary of the observed variation in binormal slope is that any index defined in terms of a single 2×2 table will vary along empirical ROCs that have a different form (or different binormal slope) than the fixed form (and binormal slope) that is assumed by the index.

Index Variation

I illustrated earlier how much d' (and, by implication, η, LOR, and Q) could vary along an ROC of binormal slope other than 1. Now, viewing the ROCs of threshold models on a binormal graph shows that they can easily be distinguished from straight lines and that their indices vary along any empirical ROC. Figure 12a shows the ROCs for the high-threshold model and the index H_c; Figure 12b shows ROCs for the double-threshold models, corresponding to H'_C and Z, and also to PC, K, and approximately to ϕ for equal-probability alternatives ($s = .50$); it gives index values for H'_C. None of these curves would come close to meeting a chi-square criterion for a fit by a straight line.

The dashed lines in the figures bound the space of observed ROCs (binormal slope of 1.5 in Figure 12a and 0.5 in 12b) and illustrate the variation in threshold-model index values that could be assigned to a discriminator with fixed capacity to discriminate, that is, with fixed accuracy. The value of H_C assigned could vary from near 0 (chance performance) to near 1.0 (perfect performance). It varies from about 0.5 to 0.9 within a range of $f \approx .20 \pm .10$. Similarly, the indices H'_C, Z, PC, K, and ϕ could vary considerably for fixed accuracy. In the illustration, H'_C varies from about 0.8 to 0.4 in the range of f from about .1 to .5.

The use of one of the indices considered so far appears to need specific justification on conceptual and empirical grounds. An article on memory by Gillund and Shiffrin (1984) provides an example of one kind of empirical justification that might be attempted. They reported that findings and conclusions based on H'_C were unchanged by an analysis in terms of "d' measures" (p. 5). The foregoing analysis suggests that such could be the case for ROC points lying quite close to the negative diagonal of the graph, as would result from a symmetrical decision criterion—that is, one yielding equal error rates. That would probably not be the case for a nonsymmetrical criterion, for example, one set to yield a given value of f, say, .05. For an ROC point along a vertical line at that value, H'_C and d' diverge considerably from their values at the negative diagonal.

Nelson (1984) based one justification for Q on a reliability argument; specifically, he implied that Q has a smaller error variance for a given number of observations than either d' or an ROC area index of the kind defined in the next section as suitable to binormal ROCs of varying slope. However, establishing the facts in this matter may not be simple. According to an analysis suggested by C. E. Metz (personal communication, 1985), the relative error for d'_e is smaller than that for Q up to $d'_e \approx 1.4$ and $Q \approx .8$, and then is larger; in addition, the relative error for the area index A_z is always smaller than that for Q, ranging from 0.004 of the relative error for Q at $Q = .01$, up to 0.567 of the relative error for Q at $Q = .99$.[5] A fairer comparison, though, as Metz observed, would be of A_z (which ranges from .5 to 1.0) and d'_e (which ranges from 0 to infinity) in relation

---

[5]These calculations are based on the following two equations for relative error:

$$\frac{\sigma_{d'_e}}{d'_e} = \frac{\sigma_Q}{Q} \cdot \frac{Q}{1 - Q^2} \cdot \frac{1}{\ln\left(\frac{1 + Q}{1 - Q}\right)},$$

to Q after they are normalized to the range of Q from 0.0 to 1.0. Pursuing that trail indicates that the relative error in A_z is smaller than that of Q up to $Q \approx .94$, and then is larger; but it must be appreciated that certain relations involved in the derivation are accurate (within 5%) only for $Q < .90$. Normalizing d_e' relative to Q, given that d_e' ranges from 0 to infinity, is also problematic. In total, there seems to be no justification for Q in terms of a greater reliability.

Suitable Indices

Figure 13 shows ROC slopes of 1 and 0.7 on a binormal graph and indicates some quantities that may be considered in defining indices that are reasonably appropriate for nonunit slopes. The index Δm, defined in Equation 12, is the distance in z units from the origin (at $z_h = z_f = 0$) to the intersection of the ROC and the axis at $z_h = 0$. Ordinarily, one reports the slope along with Δm and together they serve more as an economical description of data than as an accuracy index. The index d_e', also mentioned earlier, equals $z_f - z_h$ at the intersection of the ROC and the negative diagonal. In Figure 13, the value of d_e' indicated is $0.6 - (-0.6) = 1.2$. Green and Swets (1966/1988) showed

$$d_e' = 2\Delta m[\text{slope}/(1 + \text{slope})]. \tag{19}$$

The quantity $z(A)$ is the perpendicular distance, in z units, from the origin of the graph to an ROC (Simpson & Fitter, 1973). It had earlier been defined (with other notation) in psychology (Schulman & Mitchell, 1966) and information retrieval (Brookes, 1968). It can be shown that

$$z(A) = \text{slope}(\Delta m)/(1 + \text{slope}^2)^{1/2}. \tag{20}$$

For ROCs of slope $= 1$,

$$d' = d_e' = 2^{1/2}z(A). \tag{21}$$

---

and

$$\frac{\sigma_{A_z}}{A_z} = \frac{\sigma_Q}{Q} \cdot \left\{ \frac{1}{4\sqrt{2}} \cdot \frac{Q}{1 - Q^2} \cdot \frac{e}{\Phi\left(\frac{\sqrt{\pi}}{4} \ln\left[\frac{1 + Q}{1 - Q}\right]\right)} \right\};$$

which, in turn, are based on the relations:

$$A_z = \Phi(d_e'/\sqrt{2}) = \Phi\left(-\frac{\sqrt{\pi}}{2} \ln\eta\right),$$

where

$$\eta = \sqrt{\frac{1 - Q}{1 + Q}}.$$

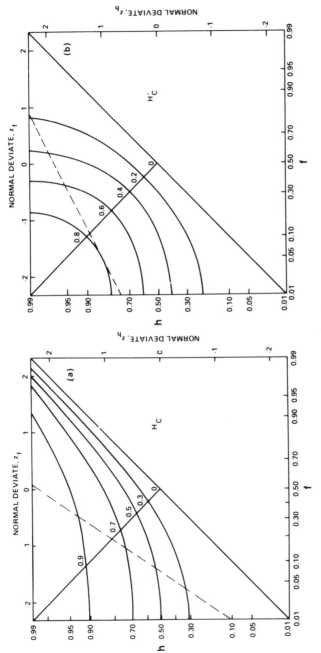

FIG. 12. a: relative operating characteristics (ROCs) for the high-threshold, two-state model on a binormal graph. b: ROCs for the double-threshold, three-state model on a binormal graph. (h: conditional probability of a hit; f: conditional probability of a false alarm; z_h and z_f: normal-deviate values of h and f; H_C: an accuracy index associated with the high-threshold model; and H'_C: an accuracy index associated with the double-threshold model.)

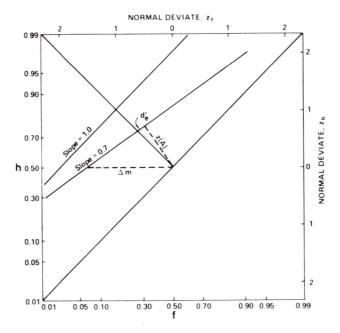

FIG. 13. Relative operating characteristics (ROCs) of two illustrative slopes on a binormal graph, and some quantities used to define acceptable indices. (*h:* conditional probability of a hit; *f:* conditional probability of a false alarm; z_h and z_f: normal-deviate values of *h* and *f*; Δm and d'_e: accuracy indices based on unequal-variance, normal distributions; and $z(A)$: an accuracy index defined as the perpendicular distance from the origin of the binormal graph to the ROC.)

The quantity $z(A)$ has a variance that is familiar in statistics and more tractable than that of d'_e (Brookes, 1968).

I would recommend the index called A_z, which is now probably the most widely used of the indices suitable to ROCs of varying slope (Swets & Pickett, 1982). In terms of the quantity just defined, it is the (tabled) area under the cumulative normal function up to the normal-deviate value equal to $z(A)$. However, A_z is better thought of as the proportion of the area of the ROC graph that lies beneath an ROC (on ordinary scales) that is assumed to be a straight line on a binormal graph. This index runs from .5, at the diagonal of the ROC graph representing chance performance, up to 1.0 for perfect performance, that is, when an ROC point is observed in the upper left-hand corner. Illustrations of the use of A_z are available (e.g., Chapter 7 in this volume).[6]

---

[6]Perhaps contrary to appearances, A_z does not assume normal distributions, but rather any form of distribution that can be transformed monotonically to the normal. A_z and, more generally, the linear

A computer program developed by Dorfman and Alf (1969) and revised by Dorfman (Swets & Pickett, 1982) provides a maximum-likelihood fit to ROC data obtained by the rating method, and estimates of the indices Δm, d'_e, $2^{1/2} z(A)$ $= d_a$, and A_z, along with their variances. A listing of this program was given by Swets and Pickett (1982), who also described the construction of ROC curves by the rating method.

Though the linearity of empirical ROCs on a binormal graph is a robust finding, one might prefer an index that is not parameterized in terms of any underlying distributions. The index here termed PA, for "proportion of area," is the proportion of area in the unit-square ROC graph (ordinary scales) beneath the observed points when they and the (0, 0) and (1, 1) corners are connected by straight lines (Green & Swets, 1966/1988). Like A_z, PA runs from .5 to 1.0. If PA is taken as the area under a continuous curve (vs. the series of linear segments), it will, of course, be slightly larger. This larger value can be shown to equal the proportion of correct choices in a two-alternative, "forced-choice" task—that is, when both Alternatives A and B are presented on each trial and the observer says which is which. This equality holds for any and all forms of assumed PDFs (Green & Swets, 1966/1988). The area index defined as A_z above, which depends on a line fitted to the observed data points (on a binormal graph), has an advantage over PA determined by linear segments (on ordinary scales) in being less dependent on the spread of the points.

I have assumed that one can usually obtain a sufficient number of data points (say, 4 or more) to define an ROC, and the force of this article is that one should do that if possible. When it is not possible, as perhaps in sensory testing of young children, the choice would seem to be among the indices of Table 3—d', η, LOR, and Q—as at least being independent of the relative frequencies, s, and implying a linear (or near-linear) binormal ROC. The use of one of those indices would be supported by a finding of nearly equal error proportions.

SUMMARY

The two-alternative single-stimulus discrimination task appears in many guises. Several indices of discrimination accuracy have been defined in terms of a single 2×2 data table. However, a discriminator under fixed conditions, and with fixed capacity or accuracy, can (and usually will) generate other 2×2 data tables that, for each of these indices, lead to different values. Similarly, two discriminators in a given setting having the same intrinsic accuracy may produce different tables, and different values on each index; in addition, two discriminators with

---

fit on a binormal graph, make a particular assumption about the (observable) functional form of the ROC, and not about the (usually unobservable) forms of underlying distributions. A_z is parameterized in terms of an effective pair of normal distributions only as a convenient convention.

unequal accuracies may produce the same table, and the same value on each index. The source of this variation is variation in the decision criterion used for choosing one alternative over the other, which the discriminator can usually select at will, and is independent of discrimination capacity. In short, indices defined in terms of a single 2 × 2 table confound discrimination capacity and decision criterion. Hence, investigators should use an index of this sort only when a very rough estimate of accuracy is adequate for the measurement problem in question.

On considering such an index, one can be informed in several ways by the ROCs that it implies. The ROC is a graph that shows how the 2 × 2 data tables can vary for any constant value of an index. It can reveal an index's violation of basic measurement purpose, such as giving the same value to performances of obviously different accuracies, for example, performances better and poorer than chance. It can point out that an index depends, inappropriately, on the relative frequencies of the two alternatives. It can disclose that two apparently different indices lead to the same result. Primarily, the ROC will reveal what an index has laid on as assumptions about the discrimination process, to the point of specifying the index's general model of the process.

Several representative indices I examined imply threshold models and produce what are defined as nonregular ROCs, and are thus inconsistent with available data, which show regular ROCs across a wide variety of discrimination tasks and settings. Other representative indices imply variable-criterion models and produce regular ROCs, but ROCs that are fixed across all conditions whereas empirical ROCs vary in a particular way. In general, discrimination accuracy is most reliably determined when several different 2 × 2 data tables are collected— or, better, one 2 × r table based on r confidence ratings—so that a full ROC is obtained, and so that an index can be calculated that depends on the locus of the full, measured ROC. Such an index is not confounded by the decision criterion, nor by the relative frequency of the two alternatives. It is consistent with the fundamental properties of the discrimination process, and accommodates the particular variation in ROCs that occurs across observers, tasks, and settings.

REFERENCES

Appleman, H. S. (1959). A fallacy in the use of skill scores. *Bulletin of the American Meteorological Society, 41,* 64–67.

Bermowitz, R. J., & Zurndorfer, E. A. (1979). Automated guidance for predicting quantitative precipitation. *Monthly Weather Review, 107,* 122–128.

Birdsall, T. G. (1966). The theory of signal detectability: ROC curves and their character. *Dissertation Abstracts International, 28,* 1B.

Birdsall, T. G., Lamphiear, D. E. (1960). *Approximations to the noncentral chi-square distribution with applications to signal detection models.* (Tech. Rep. No. 101). Ann Arbor: University of Michigan, Electronic Defense Group.

Bishop, Y. M. M., Fienberg, S. E., & Holland, P. W. (1975). *Discrete multivariate analysis: Theory and practice.* Cambridge, MA: MIT Press.

Blackwell, H. R. (1963). Neural theories of simple visual discriminations. *Journal of the Optical Society of America, 53,* 129–160.

Brier, G. W., & Allen, R. A. (1952). Verification of weather forecasts. In T. F. Malone (Ed.), *Compendium of Meteorology* (pp. 841–848). Boston: American Meteorological Society.

Brookes, B. C. (1968). The measures of information retrieval effectiveness proposed by Swets. *Journal of Documentation, 24,* 41–54.

Bush, R. R. (1963). Estimation and evaluation. In R. D. Luce, R. R. Bush, & E. Galanter (Eds.), *Handbook of mathematical psychology* (pp. 429–469). New York: Wiley.

Cohen, J. (1960). A coefficient of agreement for nominal scales. *Educational and Psychological Measurement, 20,* 37–46.

Craig, A. (1979). Nonparametric measures of sensory efficiency for sustained monitoring tasks. *Human Factors, 21,* 69–78.

Dorfman, D. D., & Alf, E., Jr. (1969). Maximum likelihood estimation of parameters of signal-detection theory and determination of confidence intervals—rating method data. *Journal of Mathematical Psychology, 6,* 487–496.

Edwards, A. W. F. (1963). The measure of association in a 2 × 2 table. *Journal of the Royal Statistical Society, Series A, 25,* 109–114.

Egan, J. P. (1975). *Signal detection theory and ROC analysis.* New York: Academic Press.

Egan, J. P., Greenberg, G. Z., & Schulman, A. I. (1961). Operating characteristics, signal detectability, and the method of free response. *Journal of the Acoustical Society of America, 33,* 993–1007.

Finley, J. P. (1884). Tornado predictions. *American Meteorological Journal, 1,* 5–88.

Fisk, A. D., & Schneider, W. (1984). Memory as a function of attention, level of processing, and automatization. *Journal of Experimental Psychology: Learning, Memory, and Cognition, 10,* 181–197.

Galen, R. S., & Gambino, S. R. (1975). *Beyond normality: The predictive value and efficiency of medical diagnoses.* New York: Wiley.

Gart, J. J. (1971). Comparison of proportions. *Review of the International Statistical Institute, 39,* 148–169.

Gilbert, G. K. (1885). Finley's tornado predictions. *American Meteorological Journal, 1,* 167–172.

Gillund, G., & Shiffrin, R. M. (1984). A retrieval model for both recognition and recall. *Psychological Review, 91,* 1–67.

Goodman, L. A. (1970). The multivariate analysis of qualitative data: Interactions among multiple classifications. *Journal of the American Statistical Association, 45,* 226–256.

Goodman, L. A., & Kruskal, W. H. (1954). Measures of association for cross classifications. *Journal of the American Statistical Association, 49,* 732–764.

Green, D. M., & Swets, J. A. (1966). *Signal detection theory and psychophysics.* New York: Wiley. (Reprinted Los Altos, CA: Peninsula, 1988).

Hanssen, A. W., & Kuipers, W. J. A. (1965). On the relationship between frequency of rain and various meteorological parameters. *Royal Netherlands Meteorological Institute, Mededelingen en Verhandelingen, 81,* 2–15.

Hays, W. L. (1973). *Statistics for the social sciences* (2nd ed). New York: Holt, Rinehart & Winston.

Heidke, P. (1926). Berechnung des Erfolges und der Guete der Windstarkevohersagen im Sturmwarnungsdienst. *Georgrafiska Annaler, 8,* 301–349.

Jeffress, L. A. (1964). Stimulus-oriented approach to detection. *Journal of the Acoustical Society of America, 36,* 766–774.

Laming, D. (1973). *Mathematical psychology.* London: Academic Press.

Landis, J. R., & Koch, G. C. (1977). The measurement of observer agreement for categorical data. *Biometrics, 33,* 159–174.

Luce, R. D. (1959). *Individual choice behavior.* New York: Wiley.

Luce, R. D. (1963). Detection and recognition. In R. D. Luce, R. R. Bush, & E. Galanter (Eds.), *Handbook of mathematical psychology* (pp. 103–189). New York: Wiley.

Macmillan, N. A., & Kaplan, H. L. (1985). Detection theory analysis of group data: Estimating sensitivity from average hit and false-alarm rates. *Psychological Bulletin, 98,* 185–199.

Mason, I. (1982). *On scores for yes/no forecasts.* Preprints of papers delivered at the Ninth Conference on Weather Forecasting and Analysis, the American Meteorological Society (pp. 169–174). Seattle, Washington.

Metz, C. E. (1978). Basic principles of ROC analysis. *Seminars in Nuclear Medicine, 8,* 283–298.

Murphy, A. H. (1977). The value of climatological, categorical, and probabilistic forecasts in the cost-loss ratio situation. *Monthly Weather Review, 105,* 803–816.

Nelson, T. O. (1984). A comparison of current measures of accuracy of feeling-of-knowing predictions. *Psychological Bulletin, 95,* 109–133.

Ogilvie, J. C., & Creelman, C. D. (1968). Maximum likelihood estimation of ROC curve parameters. *Journal of Mathematical Psychology, 5,* 377–391.

Peterson, W. W., Birdsall, T. G., & Fox, W. C. (1954). The theory of signal detectability. *Transactions of the IRE Professional Group on Information Theory, 4,* 171–212. [Reprinted in R. D. Luce, R. R. Bush, & E. Galanter [Eds.]. [1963]. *Readings in mathematical psychology* [pp. 167–211]. New York: Wiley)

Pickup, M. N. (1982). A consideration of the effect of 500 mb cyclonicity on the success of some thunderstorm forecasting techniques. *Meteorological Magazine, 111,* 87–97.

Pollack, I., & Norman, D. A. (1964). A non-parametric analysis of recognition experiments. *Psychonomic Science, 1,* 125–126.

Ramage, C. S. (1982). Have precipitation forecasts improved? *Bulletin of the American Meteorological Society, 63,* 739–743.

Rousseau, D. (1980). *A new skill score for the evaluation of yes/no forecasts.* Preprints of papers delivered at the World Meteorological Organization Symposium on Probabilistic and Statistical Methods in Weather Forecasting (pp. 167–174). Nice, France.

Schrank, W. R. (1960). A solution to the problem of evaluating forecast techniques. *Bulletin of the American Meteorological Society, 42,* 277–280.

Schulman, A. I., & Mitchell, R. R. (1966). Operating characteristics from yes-no and forced-choice procedures. *Journal of the Acoustical Society of America, 40,* 473–477.

Simpson, A. J., & Fitter, J. J. (1973). What is the best index of detectability? *Psychological Bulletin, 80,* 481–488.

Swets, J. A. (1961). Is there a sensory threshold? *Science, 134,* 168–177.

Swets, J. A. (1973). The relative operating characteristic in psychology. *Science, 182,* 990–1000. (Chapter 1 in this volume.)

Swets, J. A. (1983a). Assessment of nondestructive-testing systems—Part I: The relationship of true and false detections. *Materials Evaluation, 41,* 1294–1298.

Swets, J. A. (1983b). Assessment of nondestructive testing systems—Part II: Indices of performance. *Materials Evaluation, 41,* 1299–1303.

Swets, J. A., & Green, D. M. (1978). Applications of signal detection theory. In H. L. Pick, Jr., H. W. Leibowitz, J. E. Singer, A. Steinschneider, & H. W. Stevenson (Eds.), *Psychology: From research to practice* (pp. 311–331). New York: Plenum Press.

Swets, J. A., & Pickett, R. M. (1982). *Evaluation of diagnostic systems: Methods from signal detection theory.* New York: Academic Press.

Swets, J. A., Pickett, R. M., Whitehead, S. F., Getty, D. J., Schnur, J. A., Swets, J. B., & Freeman, B. A. (1979). Assessment of diagnostic technologies. *Science, 205,* 753–759. (Chapter 7 in this volume.)

Swets, J. A., Tanner, W. P., Jr., & Birdsall, T. G. (1961). Decision processes in perception. *Psychological Review, 68,* 301–340.

Tanner, W. P., Jr., & Swets, J. A. (1954). A decision-making theory of visual detection. *Psychological Review, 61,* 401–409.

Thurstone, L. L. (1927). A law of comparative judgment. *Psychological Review, 34,* 273–286.

Vernon, E. M. (1953). A new concept of skill score for rating quantitative forecasts. *Monthly Weather Review, 81,* 326–329.

Wald, A. (1950). *Statistical decision functions.* New York: Wiley.

Wellman, H. M. (1977). Tip of the tongue and feeling of knowing experiences: A development study of memory monitoring. *Child Development, 48,* 13–21.

Woodcock, F. (1976). The evaluation of yes/no forecasts for scientific and administrative purposes. *Monthly Weather Review, 104,* 1209–1214.

Woodworth, R. S. (1938). *Experimental psychology.* New York: Holt, Rinehart & Winston.

Youden, W. J. (1950). Index for rating diagnostic tests. *Cancer, 3,* 32–35.

Yule, G. U. (1912). On the methods of measuring association between two attributes. *Journal of the Royal Statistical Society, 75,* 579–642.

APPENDIX

HYPERBOLIC FORM OF ROCs FOR THREE INDICES

The ROCs associated with the indices η, Q, and LOR, and with equal-variance logistic PDFs in detection theory, are demonstrated here to be hyperbolas, according to a proof by C. E. Metz (personal communication, 1984).

The common functional form of these ROCs (as shown in Table 3) is

$$y = \frac{x}{x + c(1 - x)} = \frac{x}{c + (1 - c)x},$$

where c is a nonnegative constant (<1) specifying the ROC; a smaller c implies a higher ROC. These ROCs have maximum slope, $1/c$, at $(0, 0)$ and minimum slope, c, at $(1, 1)$.

If the coordinates are shifted from the x, y system to a u, v system having the center of the hyperbola at its origin, in particular, such that

$$u = x + \frac{c}{1 - c} \quad \text{and} \quad v = y - \frac{1}{1 - c},$$

so that the origin of the u, v system is $\left(\frac{c}{1 - c}\right)$ to the left of and $\left(\frac{c}{1 - c}\right)$ above the $(0, 1)$ point in the x, y system, then

$$x = u - \frac{c}{1 - c} \quad \text{and} \quad y = v + \frac{1}{1 - c}.$$

Hence, in the u, v coordinates, the equation of the ROC curve is:

$$v + \frac{1}{1-c} = \frac{\left[u - \dfrac{c}{1-c}\right]}{c + (1-c)\left[u - \dfrac{c}{1-c}\right]} = \frac{u - \dfrac{c}{1-c}}{(1-c)u},$$

or, after rearrangement,

$$uv = \frac{-c}{(1-c)^2} = \text{constant.}$$

Thus, the curve is hyperbolic, and, in particular, is a rectangular hyperbola with the u, v axes as asymptotes.

II ACCURACY AND EFFICACY OF DIAGNOSES

Chapter 4 suggests that the discrimination acuity of diagnostic systems in any field—for example, in medicine, weather forecasting, information retrieval, materials testing, polygraph lie detection, and aptitude testing—can best be measured by ROC analysis and can conveniently be referred to the same A_z scale. In all cases, one wishes to neutralize a variable decision criterion and to achieve results that are also independent of the varying prior probabilities of the events or conditions to be discriminated. This chapter shows typical values of A_z in the several diagnostic fields mentioned.

Measuring performance in practical diagnostic applications is necessarily done with less precision than in psychological tasks simplified for the laboratory. In general, the "truth data" against which responses are scored are less than perfect and the samples of cases selected for a test may be biased in some manner or simply less than fully representative of natural variation. As described in this chapter, the diagnostic fields vary widely in the extent to which test samples can be obtained that are satisfactory with respect to these and related factors.

Chapter 5 suggests that signal detection theory offers the science for choosing the best decision criterion (or "decision threshold") in diagnostic practice. If the benefits and costs of the four possible decision outcomes considered—true positives, false positives, true negatives, and false negatives—can be determined or assigned, and if the prior probabilities of the positive and negative events or conditions are known or estimated, then one can specify numerically the decision criterion that maximizes the "payoff" over many decisions—that is, maximizes the net benefit or minimizes the net cost. Other definitions of the optimal criterion are possible that require less information or judgment. Examples of the need for a rational criterion, a criterion perhaps different from one setting to another for a given diagnostic task, are drawn from testing for the human immunodeficiency virus (HIV) indicative of the acquired immunodeficiency syndrome (AIDS) and from nondestructive testing (NDT) of structural materials, for example, detecting cracks in airplane wings.

Moreover, an evaluation that goes beyond accuracy to efficacy should be based on the decision criterion that maximizes efficacy. In a medical evaluation, one considers the benefits and costs of alternative health outcomes at the ends of various possible treatment sequences, along with their frequencies or probabilities—both when the diagnostic technique in question is used and is not used (see Swets, J. A., and Pickett, R. M., *Evaluation of diagnostic systems: Methods from signal detection theory.* New York: Academic Press, 1982). Because the diagnostic technique of interest stands at the head of the decision flow diagram for further diagnostic and therapeutic choices, its decision criterion plays a large role in determining the balance among outcome probabilities, and, hence, the calculation of net costs and benefits for the technique.

The chapters in this section give an impression of the degree of diffusion and acceptance to date of ROC methods for analyzing discrimination acuity and the decision criterion in diagnostic settings. They are widely used in radiology, quite generally accepted in information retrieval, gaining credibility in weather forecasting and polygraph lie detection, unused in materials testing after much effort to make inroads in that field, newly introduced in aptitude testing, and unknown in other diagnostic fields. They have tended to reach scientists who do studies and publish results; they have not reached managers responsible for major national efforts in human health and safety. The potential value of ROC methods has, however, been noticed at the highest level of government: a report from the Office of Science and Technology Policy of the Executive Office of the President (Clinton, W. J., and Gore, A., Jr., *Science in the National Interest,* August, 1994, p. 29) describes their practical value in high-stakes diagnostics as following unexpectedly on their original development in basic research. The report describes considerations in setting a rational decision criterion and the construction of decision aids to enhance diagnostic accuracy—the aids described here in Chapter 8.

4 Measuring the Accuracy of Diagnostic Systems

Diagnostic systems are all around us. They are used to reveal diseases in people, malfunctions in nuclear power plants, flaws in manufactured products, threatening activities of foreign enemies, collision courses of aircraft, and entries of burglars. Such undesirable conditions and events usually call for corrective action. Other diagnostic systems are used to make judicious selection from many objects. Included are job or school applicants who are likely to succeed, income tax returns that are fraudulent, oil deposits in the ground, criminal suspects who lie, and relevant documents in a library. Still other diagnostic systems are used to predict future events. Examples are forecasts of the weather and of economic change.

It is immediately evident that diagnostic systems of this sort are not perfectly accurate. It is also clear that good, quantitative assessments of their degree of accuracy would be very useful. Valid and precise assessments of intrinsic accuracy could help users to know how or when to use the systems and how much faith to put in them. Such assessments could also help system managers to determine when to attempt improvements and how to evaluate the results. A full evaluation of a system's performance would go beyond its general, inherent accuracy in order to establish quantitatively its utility or efficacy in any specific setting, but good, general measures of accuracy must precede specific considerations of efficacy (1).

I suggest that although an accuracy measure is often calculated in one or another inadequate or misleading way, a good way is available for general use. The preferred way quantifies accuracy independently of the relative frequencies of the events (conditions, objects) to be diagnosed ("disease" and "no disease" or "rain" and "no rain," for instance) and also independently of the diagnostic system's decision bias, that is, its particular tendency to choose one alternative over another (be it "disease" over "no disease," or vice versa). In so doing, the preferred measure is more valid and precise than the alternatives and can place all diagnostic systems on a common scale.

On the other hand, good test data can be very difficult to obtain. Thus, the "truth" against which diagnostic decisions are scored may be less than perfectly reliable, and the sample of test cases selected may not adequately represent the population to which the system is applied in practice. Such problems occur generally across diagnostic fields, but with more or less severity depending on the field. Hence our confidence in an assessment of accuracy can be higher in some fields than in others—higher, for instance, in weather forecasting than in polygraph lie detection.

THE APPROPRIATE MEASURE OF ACCURACY

Although some diagnoses are more complex, diagnostic systems over a wide range are called upon to discriminate between just two alternatives. They are on the lookout for some single, specified class of events (objects, conditions, and so forth) and seek to distinguish that class from all other events. Thus, a general theory of signal detection is germane to measuring diagnostic accuracy. A diagnostic system looks for a particular "signal," however defined, and attempts to ignore or reject other events, which are called "noise." The discrimination is not made perfectly because noise events may mimic signal events. Specifically, observations or samples of noise-alone events and of signal (or signal-plus-noise) events produce values of a decision variable that may be assumed to vary from one occasion to another, with overlapping distributions of the values associated with the two classes of events, and modern detection theory treats the problem as one of distinguishing between two statistical hypotheses (2).

The relevant performance data.   With two alternative events and two corresponding diagnostic alternatives, the primary data are those of a two-by-two contingency table (Table 1). The event is considered to be "positive" or "negative" (where the signal event, even if undesirable, is called positive), and the diagnosis made is correspondingly positive or negative. So there are two ways in which the actual event and the diagnosis can agree, that is, two kinds of correct outcomes, called "true-positive" (cell *a* in Table 1) and "true-negative" (cell *d*). And there are two ways in which the actual event and the diagnosis can disagree, that is, two kinds of errors, called "false-positive" (cell *b*) and "false-negative" (cell *c*). Data from a test of a diagnostic system consist of the observed frequencies of those four possible outcomes.

However, if we consider proportions rather than raw frequencies of the four

TABLE 1
Two-by-Two Contingency Table

		Event		
		Positive	Negative	
Diagnosis	Positive	a True-positive	b False-positive	$a + b$
	Negative	c False-negative	d True-negative	$c + d$
		$a + c$	$b + d$	$a + b + c + d = N$

outcomes, then just two proportions contain all of the information about the
observed outcomes. Take the symbols $a, b, c,$ and d as denoting the actual
numbers of each outcome that are observed, and certain ratios, such as $a/(a + c)$,
as giving their proportions. Then, whenever the positive event occurs, the diagnosis is either positive or negative, and hence the false-negative proportion,
$c/(a + c)$, is simply the complement of the true-positive proportion, $a/(a + c)$,
with the two proportions in that column adding to one. Similarly, for the other
column, whenever the negative event occurs, the diagnosis is either positive or
negative, and so the true-negative and false-positive proportions are complements. Therefore, in a test of a diagnostic system, all of the relevant information
with regard to accuracy can be captured by recording only one member of each of
the complementary pairs of proportions (one proportion from each column). The
usual choices are those of the top row, namely, the true-positive proportion and
the false-positive proportion. The language of detection theory is often apt: those
two proportions are of "hits" and "false alarms." Any operating system, unless
perfect, will lead to false alarms as well as hits. Although other proportions can
be drawn from the table, these two proportions are the major ones and the basis
for an appropriate accuracy measure.

A measure independent of event frequencies.   Converting raw frequencies to
proportions in the way just described creates one of two fundamental attributes of
a suitable accuracy measure. If it considers only the true-positive and false-
positive proportions, an accuracy measure ignores the relative frequencies, or
prior probabilities, of positive and negative events—defined, respectively, as
$(a + c)/N$ and $(b + d)/N$, where N is the total number of events—and it does not
depend on them. This is as it should be. For example, we do not want the
accuracy score assigned a particular system for detecting cracks in metal to be
specific to the relative frequencies of cracked and sound specimens chosen for
the test sample.

A measure independent of the decision criterion.   The second fundamental attribute of a suitable accuracy measure is that it be unaffected by the system's decision bias or tendency to favor one or the other diagnostic alternative. It is convenient to think of this bias or tendency as based on the criterion used by the system to establish a positive diagnosis. This decision criterion can be thought of as the critical, or threshold, amount of evidence favoring the occurrence of the positive event that is required to issue a positive diagnosis.

The decision criterion chosen by or for the system should (and usually does) depend on the prior probabilities of the two events. Thus, in situations in which the positive event has a high prior probability, the system should have a lenient criterion for a positive diagnosis. Consider the rain forecaster in Washington (merely a hint of rain leads to a positive prediction) or the mammographer examining a high-risk or symptomatic patient (the minimal suggestion of a lesion leads to further action). Then the quantity from Table 1 that reflects the entire positive row (not column), namely, $(a + b)/N$, will be high relative to its complement in the negative row, namely, $(c + d)/N$. Conversely, a strict criterion should be used when the positive event is unlikely on prior grounds. Then the positive row's probability will be lower relative to the negative row's.

The particular decision criterion that is appropriate depends also on the benefits ascribed to the correct outcomes and the costs ascribed to the incorrect outcomes. Predicting a severe storm that does not occur (a false positive) is typically regarded as having a cost that is small relative to the cost of failing to predict a storm that does occur (a false negative), so the criterion adopted for a positive diagnosis is on the lenient side. Conversely, a strict criterion would be set when the cost of a false-positive outcome is disproportionately high; for example, the physician wants much to avoid life-threatening surgery on a patient who turns out not to have the suspected disease. Other examples exist in which one or another benefit is paramount (rather than costs as just illustrated) and hence has a major effect on the diagnostic criterion that is adopted.

When a positive diagnosis is made according to a lenient decision criterion, it will be made relatively often and both of the primary proportions in accuracy measurement, the true- and false-positive proportions, will be high. Conversely, positive diagnoses made according to a strict criterion will be made relatively infrequently, and both of these proportions will be low. A system of a fixed capacity to distinguish between positive and negative events cannot increase the true-positive proportion without also increasing the false-positive proportion. Nor can it decrease the false-positive proportion without also decreasing the true-positive proportion. A valid measure of accuracy will acknowledge that the true- and false-positive proportions will vary together, as the decision criterion changes. We desire a measure of accuracy that is valid for all the settings in which a system may operate, with any of the various decision criteria that may be appropriate for the various settings. And, within a single setting, we desire a measure of accuracy that is valid for the different decision criteria, appropriate or not, that may be set by different decision-makers. We must recognize that individuals can differ in their estimates of prior probabilities and of costs and benefits and so adopt different criteria.

Basis for calculating the suitable measure. A measure of accuracy that is independent both of the relative frequencies of the two events and of the decision criterion that is adopted for a positive diagnosis is defined in terms of the graph illustrated in Fig. 1. On this graph, one uses test data to plot the true-positive proportion against the false-positive proportion for various settings of the decision criterion. Thus, a curve on the graph shows the trading relation between true- and false-positive proportions that is characteristic of a particular system. One can see at a glance what proportion (or probability) of true positives the system will give for any particular proportion (or probability) of false positives, and vice versa. The idea then is to extract one number from a curve, which represents the entire curve, to provide a single-valued, general measure of accuracy.

Enough data points to define a curve reliably, say, five or more, are collected by either of two procedures. Under the binary or "yes-no" procedure, the system is induced to adopt a different decision criterion from one group of trials to another (*3*). Under the rating procedure, the system in effect reports which one of several different criteria is met on each trial. It does so by issuing either a rating of likelihood that a positive event occurred—for example, on a five-category scale ranging from "very likely" to "very unlikely"—or effectively a continuous quantity, for example, a probability estimate, that the analyst can convert to a rating. Then, in analysis, one considers different numbers of categories as representing a positive response (*4*). Most of the data reported in this article were obtained by the rating method.

A curve as shown in Fig. 1 is called an "ROC"—sometimes short for Receiver Operating Characteristic, especially in the field of signal detection, and sometimes short for Relative Operating Characteristic, in generalized applications. The history of the ROC and its extensive applications to discrimination tasks in experimental psychology, beginning in the early 1950s, is reviewed elsewhere (*5, 6*). It is well established that measured ROCs generally take a form much like that shown in Fig. 1 (*7*), and a detailed comparison of ROC measures of accuracy with other candidate measures is available (*8*). Methods for applying the ROC analysis to diagnostic systems have been described (*9, 10*).

The preferred measure of accuracy. A suitable, single-valued measure of accuracy is some measure of the locus of an ROC curve on its graph. The now preferred measure, specifically, is the proportion of the area of the entire graph that lies beneath the curve. The measure, denoted A in Fig. 1, is seen to vary from 0.50 to 1.0. Thus, $A = 0.50$ when no discrimination exists, that is, when the curve lies along the major diagonal (solid line), where the true- and false-

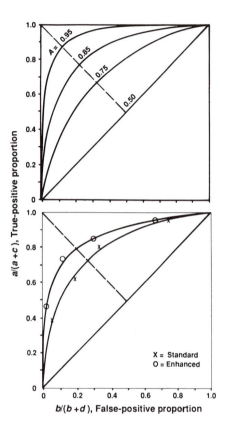

FIG. 1 (top). The ROC graph, in which the true-positive proportion is plotted against the false-positive proportion for various possible settings of the decision criterion. The idealized curves shown correspond to the indicated values of the accuracy measure *A*.

Fig. 2 (bottom). Example of empirical ROCs, showing standard and enhanced interpretations of mammograms.

positive proportions are equal. A system can achieve that performance by chance alone. And $A = 1.0$ for perfect discrimination, that is, when the curve follows the left and upper axes, such that the true-positive proportion is one (1.0) for all values of the false-positive proportion.

Three other, illustrative values of A are indicated by the three intermediate curves of Fig. 1. Observed curves usually differ slightly in shape from the idealized curves shown; they are typically not perfectly symmetrical but are a little higher on one side of the minor diagonal (dashed line) and a little lower on the other. However, the measure A suffices quite well as a single-valued measure of the locus of curves of the sort widely observed. Calculation of the measure can be accomplished graphically but is usually performed by a computer program that accepts as inputs the frequencies of positive and negative diagnoses for each alternative event that are observed for various criteria (*9–11*).

ILLUSTRATIVE CALCULATION OF THE
ACCURACY MEASURE

Techniques for obtaining an empirical ROC, making a maximum-likelihood fit of a smooth curve to its points, estimating *A*, estimating the variability in *A*, estimating components of variability in *A* due to case and observer sampling and observer inconsistency, and determining the statistical significance of a difference between two values of *A* are discussed elsewhere (*9, 10*). Here a brief illustration is given of the major aspects.

The data used for this purpose are taken from a study in which six general radiologists attempted to distinguish between malignant and benign lesions as viewed in a set of 118 mammograms (58 malignant, 60 benign), first when the mammograms were viewed in the usual manner and then when they were viewed with two aids. The radiologists came from community hospitals in the Cambridge area to BBN Laboratories where my colleagues and I had assembled an appropriate sample of mammograms from other area hospitals (*12*). The aids were (i) a checklist of perceptual features that are diagnostic of malignancy (obtained from specialists in mammography and confirmed by discriminant analysis), which elicited a scale value from the observer for each feature, and (ii) a computer system that merged the observer's scale values according to their optimal weights and estimated a probability of malignancy.

Each mammogram was rated on a five-category scale of likelihood that the lesion was malignant; the frequencies of the various ratings, as pooled over the six observers, are shown in columns 2 and 3 of Table 2. The procedure described above for converting rating data to the various pairs of true- and false-positive proportions that correspond to various decision criteria was used to generate the data in columns 4 and 5. The ROC points defined by those coordinate proportions are plotted in Fig. 2. (The points span the graph well enough to avoid much extrapolation—a five-category rating scale, which yields four points within the graph, is usually adequate; other diagnostic fields often yield more data points, for instance, weather forecasting, where 13 rating categories are the norm, and aptitude testing or information retrieval, where the analyst can often derive a dozen or so ROC points from a nearly continuous decision variable.)

A nonparametric estimate of *A* can be obtained by connecting the successive ROC points for a given condition by lines and using the trapezoidal rule, or some related formula, to measure the area beneath the connected points (*5*). In general practice, however, empirical ROCs are plotted on other scales, namely, scales that are linear for the normal-deviate values that correspond to probabilities (where probabilities are inferred from observed proportions). A robust result across diagnostic fields is that empirical ROCs are fitted well by a straight line on such a "binormal" graph, as exemplified elsewhere for the fields treated here (*7*). A computer program gives the maximum-likelihood fit of the straight line (with

TABLE 2
Data Table for Illustrative ROC Plot

Rating Category	Frequencies		Proportions	
	Malignant Cases	Benign Cases	$\dfrac{a}{a+c}$	$\dfrac{b}{b+d}$
Standard viewing				
Very likely malignant	132	19	0.38	0.05
Probably malignant	85	50	0.62	0.19
Possibly malignant	63	48	0.80	0.33
Probably benign	53	151	0.96	0.74
Very likely benign	15	92	1.0	1.0
Sum	348	360		
Enhanced viewing				
Very likely malignant	159	8	0.46	0.02
Probably malignant	102	38	0.75	0.13
Possibly malignant	36	62	0.85	0.30
Probably benign	34	131	0.95	0.66
Very likely benign	17	121	1.0	1.0
Sum	348	360		

parameters of slope and intercept) along with an estimate of A and its variance (*9, 10*). For the present purposes, the straight lines so fitted were transposed to the smooth curves on ordinary scales in Fig. 2. For the curves of Fig. 2 the χ^2 test of the goodness of fit yielded $P = 0.08$ for the standard viewing condition and $P = 0.29$ for the viewing condition enhanced by the aids, indicating satisfactory fits. The respective values of A for these curves (from pooled ratings) were 0.81 and 0.87 with standard errors of 0.017 and 0.014. (Average A values for curves fitted to individual observers are sometimes slightly different; here they were 0.83 and 0.88.) The difference between observing conditions (assessing the group values of A in either way) is significant by either a critical ratio test or t test at $P = 0.02$ (*13, 14*).

MEASURED ACCURACIES OF SOME COMMON SYSTEMS

Let us consider now measured accuracies of some common systems in six diagnostic fields. With the exception of medical imaging systems, where upwards of 100 studies have reported ROCs, I include here all of the studies in each field I know that have used (or were later subjected to) ROC analysis and can be represented by a value of A.

Weather forecasting.   ROCs for some 20 sets of weather data collected in the United States and Australia were calculated by Mason (*15*). The positive events consisted of rain, temperatures above or below a critical value or within a range, tornadoes, severe storms, and fog. I made estimates of A from his graphs. These estimates are based usually on hundreds, sometimes thousands, of forecasts, so the uncertainty in reported A values is 0.01 or so. Various values for weather events are summarized on the A scale in Fig. 3, showing ranges where available. The average or central value are approximately 0.89 for extreme cold; 0.82 for rain, 0.76 for fog, 0.74 for storms, and 0.71 for intervals of temperature (*16–18*).

Information retrieval.   Major tests of information-retrieval systems at two locations were conducted in the mid-1960s (*19*), and their analysis in ROC terms was described shortly thereafter (*20*). The task of such a system is to find the articles and books that are relevant to each of a series of queries that are addressed to it, and to reject the irrelevant documents. In a traditional, manual library system, the queries will be in terms of some indexing language; in a computer-based system, they will contain some combination of key words.

Figure 4 summarizes the results obtained with a computer-based system at Harvard University by Gerard Salton and Michael Lesk (on the right) and results obtained with a manual library system at the Cranfield libraries in England by Cyril Cleverdon and Michael Keen (on the left). The computer-based system measured the degree of relevance of every document in the file to every query addressed to the file, and I established different decision criteria by selecting in turn various values along this nearly continuous variable. Various retrieval methods used synonyms, statistical word associations, hierarchical expansions, and so forth to relate the language of the document to the key words of the query. The collections of documents were in the subject matters of documentation, aerodynamics, and computer sciences. Under each method, a few hundred documents were examined in relation to each of about 20 to 40 queries. With almost no variation among methods, the collection of documents on documentation gave a typical value of A estimated to be 0.75; the aerodynamics collection, 0.87; and two computer-science collections, 0.95 and 0.97. For the manual system, I adopted different criteria by varying the number of query terms a document had

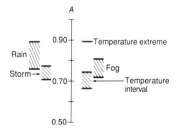

FIG. 3. Measured values of *A* for forecasts of several different weather conditions. Ranges are shown where multiple tests were made.

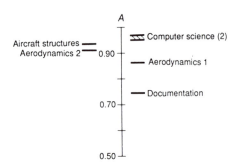

FIG. 4. Measured values of *A* for a manual information-retrieval system (on the left) and a computer-based information-retrieval system (on the right), for different collections of documents as indicated.

to satisfy in order to be retrieved. In this test, 13 retrieval methods were variations of several indexing languages. They were applied with about 200 queries to a collection of some 1500 documents on aerodynamics. Again very consistently over methods, the approximate mean value of *A* was 0.91. Six retrieval methods applied to a smaller collection on aircraft structures yielded $A = 0.93$. For both of these tests in the library setting, the numbers of observations were large enough to yield very reliable values of *A*.

Aptitude testing. The validity of aptitude tests is usually measured by a correlation coefficient, because the event predicted, as well as the diagnostic system's output, is usually represented by a continuum of many values, rather than just two. These values are typically school grades or job ratings. However, the prediction of a two-valued event is often required, as when students under individually paced instruction either complete the course or not, or when job performance is measured simply as satisfactory or not. Another example comes from current interest in how much the Scholastic Aptitude Test helps, beyond knowing rank in high school class, in predicting college graduation. For such instances I suggest that the accuracy of prediction in ROC terms is the most appropriate measure of test validity. Figure 5 shows summary results of two studies of school performance on the *A* scale. Although nearly continuous grades

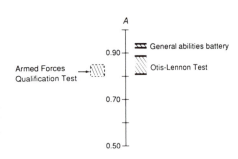

FIG. 5. Measured values of *A* for two aptitude tests (on the right) that were followed by schooling of all testees; a roughly adjusted range of *A* values for a test (on the left) that was followed by schooling only of those who achieved a criterion score on the test.

in the course happen to be available here, I simulated a binary outcome of pass-fail by selecting arbitrarily a particular level of course performance as the cutoff for passing (*21*).

The testees in the study shown on the right in Fig. 5 were approximately 450 students entering the seventh grade in four classes in each of three schools in Barquisimeto, Venezuela, all of whom would take a special course on thinking skills (*22*). The initial tests included the Otis-Lennon School Abilities Test (OLSAT) and an extensive battery of general aptitude tests (GAT). The year-end measure of performance came from an extensive test consisting of items specially written to tap the thinking abilities the course was intended to teach, called the Target Abilities Test (TAT). Actually, three values of *A* were computed for both OLSAT and GAT, one for each of three different percentile cuts on TAT performance that I took (arbitrarily) to define passing and failing. For GAT, the three corresponding *A* values ranged from 0.93 to 0.94 and for OLSAT they ranged from 0.81 to 0.89. The correlation coefficients are 0.87 for GAT and 0.71 for OLSAT. Other data so far analyzed in ROC terms are on the ability of the Armed Forces Qualification Test to predict pass-fail performance in four Navy schools (*7*) and are shown on the left in Fig. 5 (*23, 24*).

Medical imaging.   Thirty published studies of medical imaging techniques or of image interpreters, in which the ROC was used for accuracy evaluation, were reviewed several years ago (*25*). There may now be as many as five times that number in the medical literature (*5, 10*), and so the summary here must be selective. I have tended to choose studies with enough clinical cases and image readers, and with enough points per ROC, to yield relatively reliable estimates of *A*. They focus on the abilities of computed tomography, mammography, and chest x-rays to discriminate lesions indicative of disease from normal variations of organ appearance. Values of *A* are summarized in Fig. 6.

In an early study of computed tomography (CT) relative to radionuclide scanning (RN) for detecting brain lesions, images of both modalities were obtained from the same patients. With the sponsorship of the National Cancer Institute, images of 136 cases were selected from about 3000 cases collected at five medical centers. These images were interpreted retrospectively by six specialists in each modality who gave ratings of likelihood that a lesion was present

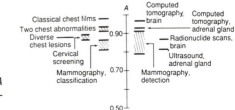

FIG. 6.   Measured values of *A* for several imaging tests in clinical medicine.

(*26*). About 60% of the cases were abnormal as proven by histology; the normal cases showed no symptoms after 8 months of follow-up. Both the pooled and average *A* values across observers were 0.97 for CT and 0.87 for RN. A study comparing CT to ultrasound in detecting adrenal disease (for the most part, with both examinations made of the same patients) was based on cases at two medical centers and on interpretations made in the course of diagnosis. Values of *A* were 0.93 for CT and 0.81 for ultrasound (*27–35*).

Materials testing.   "Materials testing" here means testing metal structures, such as aircraft wings, for cracks. There is one major study in the field, in which a set of 148 metal specimens, each regarded to be with or without cracks, was tested at 16 bases of the U.S. Air Force. The diagnostic systems consisted of ultrasound and eddy current devices used by upwards of 100 technicians in two separate tests (*36*).

Because the technicians made only binary decisions, without manipulation of their diagnostic criteria, just one point on each individual's ROC is available. To calculate *A*, I assumed that that point lay on a symmetrical ROC, as shown in Fig. 1 (not a crucial assumption here). The average *A* values across sites are 0.93 for the eddy-current technique and 0.68 for the ultrasound technique, but accuracy varied widely from one base to another, across the ranges shown in Fig. 7. Indeed, the extent of the range may be the salient result: a case could be made for analyzing the expertise at the more proficient sites in order to export it to the less proficient—along the lines of chapter 8.

Polygraph lie detection.   Studies of polygraph accuracy in lie detection are of two types. In so-called "field" studies, for various real crimes, the polygraph examiners' decisions about deception or truth are compared either to actual judicial outcomes, panel decisions about guilt, or confessions. So-called "analog" studies are of mock or role-playing crimes in a laboratory setting, for example, stealing a $20 bill from an office down the hall. The obvious differences between the two types concern the surety of the "ground truth" about the

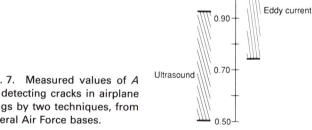

FIG. 7.   Measured values of *A* for detecting cracks in airplane wings by two techniques, from several Air Force bases.

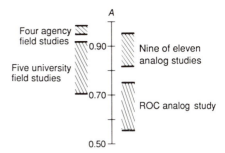

FIG. 8. Measured values of *A* for polygraph lie detection in several field studies (on the left) and several analog studies (on the right).

positive event of guilty and the negative event of not guilty, and the severity of the consequences of failing the test.

Figure 8 shows summary values for both types of study. About ten published studies exist in each category. Most of the field studies were reviewed in the context of signal detection theory and ROC analysis (*37*), and both categories were reviewed for the U.S. Congress Office of Technology Assessment (*38*). I have calculated values of *A,* again under the assumption that the single ROC points available lie on a symmetric curve as shown in Fig. 1. (The possible impact of that assumption is lessened by the fact that the studies generally gave points near the negative, dashed-line, diagonal of the ROC graph.) Of the field studies, four gave *A* values near 0.95, with one as high as 0.98; these were conducted by a commercial agency. Five field studies conducted in university settings gave *A* values between 0.70 and 0.92. Nine of eleven analog studies produced *A* values ranging from 0.81 to 0.95; *A* values for the two outlying analog studies were 0.64 and 0.98. One of the analog studies used the rating-of-likelihood procedure to yield full ROCs, based on six ROC points. In this study, six examiners yielded *A* values ranging from 0.55 to 0.75; four of them were between 0.64 and 0.68 (*39*).

QUALIFICATIONS OF MEASURED ACCURACIES

Most, if not all, of the values of *A* listed for the various fields should be qualified in one or more ways. Certain definitions, operations, and assumptions made in conducting the tests have served to bias the calculated values—often in unknown directions to unknown extents, sometimes in known directions, and, infrequently, to an extent that may be estimated. So, calculated values of *A* are neither perfectly reliable, in the sense of being repeatable across different tests of the same system, nor perfectly valid, in the sense of measuring what they are supposed to measure. There is constant, as well as variable, error. The difficulty lies not, I have argued, with the measure: as far as we can tell, there are no intrinsic limits on its reliability, beyond ordinary statistical considerations, or on its validity. The difficulty arises, rather, because the quality of test data is not everything it should be. I consider here four ideals for test data and comment on how well each of the diagnostic fields treated here matches up to these ideals.

Adequacy of truth. The tester should know certainly for every item in the test sample whether it is positive or negative. Incorrectly classifying test items will probably depress measures of accuracy.

How are truly guilty and truly innocent parties to be determined for tests of the polygraph? Judicial outcomes and panel decisions may categorize erroneously, and even confessions can be false. Hence, one may resort to the analog study, which sacrifices realism to gain sure truth.

Sure truth about cracks in metals can only be obtained destructively, by sacrificing the specimens. Destructive testing tends not to be done, because then the next diagnostic technique, or the next group of inspectors, must be tested on another, different set. A set of specimens for which fairly good truth is felt to be available is acquired only painstakingly, and a new set will not be a common ground for comparing a potential diagnostic technique with existing ones, or new inspectors with old. Just how truth is determined in this field, short of sacrifice, is not clear to me. I believe that it is based on the same diagnostic techniques one hopes to test, perhaps in the hands of experts and in combination.

The so-called "gold standard" for truth in medical imaging is usually regarded to be surgery or autopsy and analysis of tissue. It is recognized, however, that imagery and pathology are not perfectly correlated in space or time. The image interpreter and pathologist may look at different locations, and the pathological abnormality observed may not have been present when the image was taken. Moreover, the pathologist's code or language for describing lesions differs from the radiologist's. Of course, this histology standard is applied primarily to positive cases. Negative truth is usually based on months or years of follow-up without related symptoms.

For assessments of aptitude testing in terms of the measure *A* I think the problems of truth data are slight. If handing in the assigned work means passing, then we know who passed and who failed; if staying on the job constitutes success, likewise. We may assume that errors in determining who did what are infrequent.

The definition of a document's relevance to a query—or, in this context, what should constitute truth—has had a controversial history in the field of information retrieval. In the studies reviewed here, the relevance of every document in the file was judged by subject-matter experts for each query. In some instances, the degree of relevance was estimated on a four-category scale. Other studies have drawn queries directly from documents in the file, a procedure that better defines those documents as relevant than it does all others as irrelevant. In any event, the dependence of truth on judgment suggests that it will be more adequate for some subject matters, probably those with a highly technical language, than for others.

Problems in assessing truth in weather-forecasting arise primarily from logistic limitations on establishing in a fine-grained manner whether a weather event occurred throughout the area of the forecast. One knows rather surely how many millimeters of rain there are in a can at the airport, but the forecast is often made for a larger area. Similarly, tornadoes may touch down, or storms may be severe, in unobserved places. In short, it is difficult to correlate the forecast and the truth determination in space. The correlation of forecast and truth determination in time is not simple either but seems easier.

Independence of truth determination and system operation.   The truth about sample items should be determined without regard to the system's operation, that is, without regard to the system's decisions about test cases. If this condition is not met, the truth will be inappropriate for scoring the system and will probably inflate its measured accuracy.

When confessions are used to determine guilt and innocence, the likelihood of a confession depends on whether the polygraph test is judged to be positive or negative. Examiners work hard to elicit a confession from suspects who appear to test positively and believe that the existence of a positive test is often the main factor in securing a confession. (Hence, they can argue that the system's efficacy is high even if its accuracy is low.) The result for accuracy measurement is that the system is scored against a determination of truth that it helped to make. That test procedure treats the polygraph system very generously—it ought to do well. Values of A will be inflated, to an unknown, but conceivably large, extent.

If panel decisions based on all available evidence are used to establish truth in materials testing, then truth is determined in part by the operation of the system or systems under test.

In good practice in medical imaging, the truth is determined independently of system operation. Occasionally, truth is determined by all the case evidence, including the results of the systems under test. That practice can favor CT, say, over the alternative, if the CT result is dominant in calling a case positive or negative. CT is then scored against itself.

Independence of test sample and truth determination.   Procedures used to establish the truth should not affect the selection of cases. Thus, the quest for adequate truth may bias the sample of test cases, perhaps resulting in an easier sample than is realistic.

Many criminal investigations do not result in a confession. When confession is the sole basis for determining truth and hence dictates the sample, the sample will probably not represent the population of cases to which the polygraph is typically applied. As one specific, it is possible that the more positive a test appears to be, the greater the likelihood of a confession. So the sample will tend to consist of the easier cases to diagnose. Again, the possibility exists of substantial inflation of measured accuracy.

In materials testing, the use of panel decisions based on all available evidence would serve to condition the constitution of the sample of the procedure for determining truth.

In medical imaging, potential biases in the sample may result from the procedures for establishing truth. If tissue analysis is the standard, the sample will be made up of cases that achieve that advanced stage, quite possibly cases that show relatively clear lesions. For negative cases, a sample may reflect the population more or less well, depending on how long one waits for follow-up. A formula for eliminating these biases was recently proposed (40).

A problem for aptitude testing arises from the fact that testing is carried out to make selections, and ground truth is available only for those selected. How the persons scoring below the selection criterion on the aptitude test would have performed in school or on the job is usually not known. Procedures used to establish truth—observing and grading the individual in school or on the job—determine the sample completely. The sample for assessing the diagnostic system is biased relative to the population to which the system is applied.

Representativeness of the sample.   The sample of test items should fairly reflect the population of cases to which the diagnostic system is usually applied. The various types of events should occur in the sample in approximately the same proportions as they do in practice.

A representative of criminal cases could, in principle, be obtained prospectively. If all criminal cases in the country were collected for a sufficiently long time starting now, then the various types of crimes against objects and people would appear in appropriate numbers. But that would be a very long time from the standpoint of someone desirous of an accuracy measure soon. Selection of criminal cases retrospectively in the appropriate proportions would depend on a common and adequate coding of case types across the country, or a central file, and an ability to acquire full records for cases in which the polygraph was used. A reasonable deduction from sample sizes in the polygraph assessment literature, ranging typically from about 20 to 50 in field studies, is that sample items are very difficult to acquire. This is an instance of a potential bias in the accuracy measure of an unknown direction, let alone extent (41).

For reasons given earlier, it would seem to be difficult in materials testing to specify a representative sample of types and sizes of cracks and to ensure that one exists.

The problem in medical imaging of achieving representative samples with respect to type and extent of lesion mirrors the problem for criminal cases. Prospective sampling is expensive and time-consuming. Indeed, a new and advanced model of the imaging device may be available before enough cases are collected with the tested one. Retrospective sampling requires first that the data be accessible, and so far they usually have not been. Such sampling also requires great care. For example, rare cases must be present in at least minimal numbers to represent the rarity fairly, and having that number of them may distort the relative proportions.

In information retrieval, it is difficult to say whether a representative sample of documents is acquired for a general assessment of a system. Working with special subject matters seems appropriate for a given test, but most systems, as illustrated earlier, are tested with just a few of them. Across the few mentioned above, accuracy varies considerably and seems to covary with the "hardness," or technical nature, of the language used for the particular subject matter.

The ability of weather forecasters to assemble large and representative samples for certain weather events is outstanding. Prediction of precipitation at Chicago was tested against 17,000 instances, and even individual forecasters were measured on 3,000 instances. Of course, some weather events are so rare that few positive events are on record, and for such events the precision as well as the generality of the measurements will be low (*42*).

CONCLUDING REMARKS

Can we say how accurate our diagnostic systems are? According to the evidence collected here, the answer is a quite confident "yes" in the fields of medical imaging, information retrieval, and weather forecasting, and, at least for now, a "not very well" in most if not all other fields, as exemplified here by polygraph lie detection, materials testing, and (except for the few analyses mentioned above) aptitude testing for predicting a binary event. ROC measures of accuracy are widely used in medical imaging (*5, 10, 25*), have been advocated and refined within the field of information retrieval (*20, 43*), and have been effectively introduced in weather forecasting (*15, 17, 18, 44*). Although problems of bias in test data do not loom as large in information retrieval and weather forecasting as elsewhere, those fields have shown a high degree of sophisticated concern for such problems, as has medical imaging, where the problems are greater (*45*). So, in medical imaging we can be quite confident for example, about A values of 0.90 to 0.98 for prominent applications of CT and chest x-ray films and A values of 0.80 to 0.90 for mammography. Similarly, in weather forecasting, confident about A values of 0.75 to 0.90 for rain, depending largely on lead time, and 0.65 to 0.80, depending on definitions, for temperature intervals and fog; and in information retrieval, A values ranging from 0.95 to 0.75 depending on subject matter. A positive aspect of the field of polygraph lie detection is that it recognizes the need for accuracy testing and attempts to identify and cope with inherently difficult data-bias problems, and the field of materials testing is making some beginnings in these respects. Of course, for other than the special case considered here, the field of aptitude testing devotes a good deal of sophisticated effort to validity questions.

What will the future bring? A basic assumption of this chapter is that testing the accuracy of diagnostic systems is often desirable and feasible and is sometimes crucial. Although individual diagnosticians are treated here only in passing, a similar case could be made for the importance of testing them. I suggest that a wider and deeper understanding of the needs and the possibilities would be beneficial in science, technology, and society, and that it is appropriate for scientists to take the lead in enhancing that understanding. Scientists might help society overcome the resistance to careful evaluation that is often shown by diagnosticians and by designers and managers of diagnostic systems, and help to elevate the national priority given to funding for evaluation efforts. Specifically, I submit that scientists can increase general awareness that the fundamental factors in accuracy testing are the same across diagnostic fields and that a successful science of accuracy testing exists. Instead of making isolated attempts to develop methods of testing for their own fields, evaluators could adapt the proven methods to specific purposes and contribute mutually to their general refinement.

REFERENCES AND NOTES

1. The measurement of efficacy in the context of the present approach to accuracy is treated in some detail elsewhere (*9, 10*). The usefulness of empirical measures of diagnostic, and especially predictive, accuracy was further set in a societal context in a recent editorial: D. E. Koshland, Jr., *Science* **238**, 727 (1987).

2. W. W. Peterson, T. G. Birdsall, W. C. Fox, *IRE Trans. Prof. Group Inf. Theory PGIT-4*, 171 (1954).

3. With a human decision-maker, one can simply give instructions to use a more or less strict criterion for each group of trials. Alternatively, one can induce a change in the criterion by changing the prior probabilities of the two events or the pattern of costs and benefits associated with the four decision outcomes. If, on the other hand, the decision depends on the continuous output of some device, say, the intraocular pressure measured in a screening examination for glaucoma, then, in different groups of trials, one simply takes successively different values along the numerical (pressure) continuum as partitioning it into two regions of values that lead to positive and negative decisions, respectively. This example of a continuous output of a system suggests the alternative to the binary procedure, namely, the so-called "rating" procedure.

4. Thus, to represent the strictest criterion, one takes only the trials given the highest category rating and calculates the relevant proportions from them. For the next strictest criterion, the trials taken are those given either the highest or the next highest category rating—and so on to what amounts to a very lenient criterion for a positive response. The general idea is illustrated by probabilistic predictions of rain: first, estimates of 80% or higher may be taken as positive decisions, then estimates of 60% or higher, and so on, until the pairs of true- and false-positive proportions are obtained for each of several decision criteria.

5. D. M. Green and J. A. Swets, *Signal Detection Theory and Psychophysics* (Wiley, New York, 1966; reprinted with updated topical bibliographies by Krieger, New York, 1974, and Peninsula Publishing, Los Altos, CA, 1988).

6. J. A. Swets, *Science* **134**, 168 (1961); *ibid.* **182**, 990 (1973). See Chapter 1.

7. ———, *Psychol. Bull.* **99**, 181 (1986). See Chapter 2.
8. ———, *ibid.*, p. 100. See Chapter 3.
9. ——— and R. M. Pickett, *Evaluation of Diagnostic Systems: Methods from Signal Detection Theory* (Academic Press, New York, 1982).
10. C. E. Metz, *Invest. Radiol.* **21**, 720 (1986).
11. Just how much accuracy a particular value of *A* represents takes on some intuitive meaning if one examines the various combinations of true- and false-positive proportions it represents. Values of *A* between 0.50 and 0.70 or so represent a rather low accuracy—the true-positive proportion is not much greater than the false-positive proportion anywhere along the curve. Values of *A* between about 0.70 and 0.90 represent accuracies that are useful for some purposes, and higher values represent a rather high accuracy. Further intuitive meaning of any values of *A* arises from the fact that it can be viewed as the percentage of correct decisions in a "paired comparisons" task. In this task, a positive event and a negative event are always presented on each trial (side by side or one after the other), and the diagnostic system must say which is which. Although "percent correct" is usually a misleading measure for diagnostic tasks, it is a useful measure for the paired-comparisons task because here relative frequencies are not at issue and the decision criterion can be expected to be symmetrical rather than biased one way or the other (toward the left or right side or toward the first or second time interval). The value of *A* obtained in the way described above can be shown, in general, to equal the percentage correct in this special task (*5*). Thus, *A* = 0.82 for rain predictions means that if the forecaster were presented a pair of randomly sampled weather conditions on successive trials—always with one condition that led to rain and one that did not—the forecaster could say which is which 82% of the time.

    Because the slope of the ROC decreases smoothly, the numerical value of the slope at any point on the ROC is an index of the decision criterion that yields that point. Various definitions of optimal decision rules specify the optimal criterion for any specific situation (as characterized, for example, by particular prior probabilities and benefits and costs) in terms of its corresponding ROC slope (*5, 9*).
12. D. J. Getty, R. M. Pickett, C. J. D'Orsi, J. A. Swets, *Invest. Radiol.* **23**, 240 (1988).
13. A straight line on a binormal graph is predicted from theory when the distributions of samples or observations of the two diagnostic alternatives (for example, signal and noise) are Gaussian. However, almost any form of distribution, including logistic, triangular, and exponential, yields very nearly a straight line on a binormal graph, and, in particular, a form that is indistinguishable from a straight line with ordinary amounts of data (*8*). Observed slopes of the linear ROC range for the most part from about 0.70 to 1.0 (*7*). A slope of 1.0 corresponds to an ROC on ordinary scales that is symmetrical about the minor diagonal (as in Fig. 1), and slopes of less than 1.0 correspond to ROCs on ordinary scales that rise more steeply from the origin than does a symmetrical curve (*5*), as do the ROCs in Fig. 2 (whose slopes on a binormal graph are 0.92 and 0.71).

    The measure here denoted *A* (for convenience) is denoted A_z in the primary literature, where the subscript *z* serves as a reminder that the measure was obtained from a binormal graph. A_z can be estimated from the two parameters of the linear ROC by the formula $z(A) = a/(1 + b^2)^{1/2}$, where *b* is the slope and *a* is the intercept of the linear ROC, and $z(A)$ is the normal-deviate value of the cumulative standardized normal distribution that corresponds to a tabled area beneath the normal distribution equal to A_z (*9*). For some crude measurement purposes, one can estimate *A* from a single ROC point by assuming that the linear ROC has a slope of 1.0, or, equivalently, that the ROC on ordinary scales is symmetrical about the negative diagonal. A simple procedure is to use a pair of tables published elsewhere (*14*): one can take the true- and false-positive proportions to one table to obtain a quantity called *d'* (a measure of accuracy based on a linear binormal ROC of unit slope) and take that quantity to the second table to obtain *A* (there presented as the percentage of correct choices in a paired-comparisons task, as mentioned earlier).

The advantage of ROC analysis and A over other common measures of accuracy can be partially illustrated by the data of Fig. 2. Clearly, the true-positive proportion alone is inadequate as a measure: for example, for the standard condition it varies over the four observed data points from 0.38 to 0.96 although those points represent changes only in the decision criterion while accuracy remains constant. Contrary to fact, the standard condition could appear more accurate than the enhanced condition, if, for example, the third-left point were obtained in the standard condition yielding a value of 0.80 and the second-left point were obtained in the enhanced condition yielding a value of 0.75. The overall percentage of correct detections, $(a + d)/N$ in Table 1, also varies across the four points: if the relative frequencies of noise and signal trials are equal, then this measure gives 0.67, 0.72, 0.74, and 0.61 for the four points of the standard condition, and 0.72, 0.81, 0.78, and 0.65 for the enhanced condition. Were the second-left point on each curve the only one obtained, the difference between conditions would be seen as 0.09, whereas, if the third-left point were the only one obtained, the difference would be 0.04, so that the difference between conditions might be interpreted to be statistically significant in one case and insignificant in the other. Meanwhile, had the observed points been based on relative frequencies of 75 signal trials and 25 noise trials, the standard condition would yield percentages of 0.52, 0.67, 0.77, and 0.79 for the four points and the enhanced condition would yield 0.59, 0.78, 0.81, and 0.80, values quite different from those predicated on equal frequencies and either higher or lower depending on the decision criterion.

Taking both coordinate proportions from a single observed point (or from a single two-by-two contingency table) is also a common and usually inadequate practice: in medicine, the true-positive proportion is called "sensitivity" and the true-negative proportion (the complement of the false-positive proportion) is called "specificity." Such an approach is adequate only when the diagnostic tests in question have an agreed-upon and invariant decision criterion, such as a test that yields a number along a scale. A difficulty for tests that do not (for example, imaging systems with human interpreters) is that differences are often indeterminate; for example, in Fig. 2, the first-left point of the standard condition could turn out to be on the same ROC as the second-left point of the enhanced condition if the full curves were obtained, so with a single point per condition one might not know if the conditions were equally accurate or not. Taking the inverses of the two proportions just mentioned—that is, the probability of the signal event (or the noise event) given the positive (or negative) decision, which is called the positive (or negative) "predictive value" of the system—is similarly problematic: these values vary over a wide range depending both on the decision criterion and on the relative frequencies of the two kinds of events. Indeed, the positive predictive value varies from the prior probability (relative frequency) of the signal event (which may be low) when the decision criterion is lenient on up to 1.0 when the criterion is strict (9). Similar problems plague the measure called "relative risk" or "odds ratio," which is a ratio of two inverse probabilities (8, 9). In general, single-valued measures taken from a single point (or two-by-two table), such as the odds ratio and percentage correct and various measures of association in statistics, can be shown to predict ROCs of too restricted a form (for example, a binormal slope of 1.0) or of a form very different from those observed in actual practice (8).

14. J. A. Swets, Ed., *Signal Detection and Recognition by Human Observers* (Wiley, New York, 1964; reprinted by Peninsula Publishing, Los Altos, CA, 1988).
15. I. Mason, *Aust. Meteorol. Mag.* **30**, 291 (1982).
16. Several tests of rain are included, in which the likelihood of rain during the daytime hours was forecast the evening before. Their values of A are generally 0.85 to 0.90: 0.85 at the Canberra (Australia) airport, when any measurable trace of rain was defined as rain; 0.89 there when rain was defined as ≥ 2.5 mm; 0.83 at Seattle; 0.85 at Chicago; and 0.89 at Great Falls, Montana. When accuracy was measured for a fairly large area (for example, at any of 25 official rain gauges in the city of Canberra), $A = 0.74$. Recently published data on rain forecasts from the Environmental Research Laboratory at Boulder, Colorado, were based on events at different periods after issue of the forecast. The lead times and corresponding A values were: 0 to 2 hours,

0.86; 2 to 4 hours, 0.77; 4 to 6 hours, 0.75; and 6 to 8 hours, 0.75 (*17*). Similar findings were reported separately by two laboratories of Canada's Atmospheric Environment Service, showing monotonically decreasing values of *A* for two major prediction systems over six periods extending to 72 hours (*18*). Such details are also available for predictions of the other weather events.

17. G. M. Williams, in *Ninth Conference in Probability and Statistics in Atmospheric Sciences* (American Meteorological Society, Boston, 1985), p. 214.
18. N. Brunet, R. Verret, N. Yacowar, in *Tenth Conference on Probability and Statistics in Atmospheric Sciences* (American Meteorological Society, Boston, 1987); p. 12; R. Sarrazin and L. J. Wilson, *ibid.*, p. 95.
19. C. Cleverdon, *Assoc. Spec. Libr. Inf. Bur. Proc.* **19**, 6 (1967); ——— and M. Keen, *Factors Determining the Performance of Indexing Systems: Test Results*(Association of Special Libraries and Information Bureaux, Cranfield, England, 1966), vol. 2; G. Salton and M. E. Lesk, *J. Assoc. Comput. Mach.* **15**, 8 (1968).
20. J. A. Swets, *Am. Doc.* **20**, 72 (1969). See Chapter 9.
21. A problem faced in validating aptitude tests is that measures of school or job performance usually exist for only a subset of those tested, namely, those selected to matriculate or work. To alleviate this problem, the correlation coefficient is usually corrected (for example, adjusted upward), according to an accepted formula, for the restriction in the range of aptitudes considered. Similarly, one might devise a way to adjust values of *A* upward, because the discrimination task is made more difficult by considering only the more homogeneous group of testees who are selected for the school or job. I avoid the problem here, for the first study to be described, by analyzing an unrestricted set of data: all testees took the course and were graded in it.
22. R. J. Herrnstein, R. S. Nickerson, M. de Sánchez, J. A. Swets, *Am. Psychol.* **41**, 1279 (1986).
23. The approximate average value for the Navy data is *A* = 0.70, but that figure is depressed by the restriction of range (*21*). The correlations for the four schools are 0.27, 0.09, 0.31, and 0.35. I have not calculated their corrected values, but in another Navy study median uncorrected and corrected coefficients were 0.43 and 0.73 (*24*). As a very rough guess, applying some appropriate adjustment to the average *A* = 0.70 of the present data might bring it into the range 0.80 to 0.85, more like the unrestricted *A* values reported above. The Navy data are placed tentatively at that level (broken lines) on the summary scale of Fig. 5.
24. L. Swanson, *Armed Services Vocational Aptitude Battery, Forms 6 and 7, Validation Against School Performance in Navy Enlisted Schools* (Technical Report 80-1, Navy Personnel Research and Development Center, San Diego, 1979).
25. J. A. Swets, *Invest. Radiol.* **14**, 109 (1979). See Chapter 6.
26. J. A. Swets *et al., Science* **205**, 753 (1979). See Chapter 7.
27. H. L. Abrams *et al., Radiology* **142**, 121 (1982).
28. Three mammography studies treated the search for and detection of lesions then judged to be malignant. Egan's pioneering book (*29*) reported data I translate into *A* = 0.91. The remaining two studies were based on cases obtained in a national screening program in the 1970s and 1980s: one showed *A* = 0.85 for mammography alone, *A* = 0.73 for physical examination alone, and *A* = 0.91 for the two examinations combined (*30*); the other examined only "incidence" lesions (the generally smaller lesions that appeared only after the initial screening) and gave *A* = 0.79 (*31*). The study mentioned earlier of the benign-malignant classification of lesions in specified locations (*12*) is also represented in Fig. 6. A study comparing automatic computer classification of photomicrographs of cervical cells with the performance of ten cytotechnologists found that the distinction between abnormal and normal cells was made with *A* = 0.90 by the computer and *A* = 0.87 by the cytotechnologists (*32*). The classical studies of "observer error" in radiology were made for chest films in the diagnosis of tuberculosis, and were conducted by Garland and by Yerushalmy and associates in the late 1940s [L. H. Garland, *Radiology* **52**, 309 (1949); J. Yerushalmy, J. T. Harkness, J. H. Cope, B. R. Kennedy, *Am. Rev. Tuberculosis* **61**, 443 (1950)]. They were reanalyzed in ROC terms by Lusted in his book (*33*), which introduced students of medical decision-making to the ROC. Although the data points

from the two studies were in different portions of the ROC graph, for both studies $A = 0.98$. (Meanwhile, values of "percentage correct" for the two studies are 83 and 91%, indicating, spuriously, a difference in accuracy.) One recent study of chest films (*34*) gave A values of 0.94 and 0.91 for the detection of two specific abnormalities (pneumothoraces and interstitial infiltrates). Another, with diverse lesions, showed $A = 0.79$ when the observer was not prompted by the case history and 0.88 when he or she was (*35*).

29. R. L. Egan, *Mammography* (Thomas, Springfield, IL, 1964).
30. J. E. Gohagan *et al.*, *Invest. Radiol.* **19**, 587 (1984).
31. J. E. Goin, J. D. Haberman, M. K. Linder, P. A. Lambird, *Radiology* **148**, 393 (1983).
32. J. W. Bacus, *Application of Digital Image Processing Techniques to Cytology Automation* (Technical Report, Rush Presbyterian-St. Luke's Medical Center, Medical Automation Research Unit, Chicago, 1982). Some results of this study were reported by J. W. Bacus *et al.*, *Anal. Quant. Cytol. Histol.* **6**, 121 (1984).
33. L. B. Lusted, *Introduction to Medical Decision Making* (Thomas, Springfield, IL, 1968).
34. H. MacMahon *et al.*, *Radiology* **158**, 21 (1986).
35. K. S. Berbaum *et al.*, *Invest. Radiol.* **21**, 532 (1986).
36. J. A. Swets, *Mater. Eval.* **41**, 1294 (1983).
37. G. Ben-Shakhar, I. Lieblich, Y. Bar-Hillel, *J. Appl. Psychol.* **67**, 701 (1986).
38. L. Saxe, D. Dougherty, B. Scott, *Am. Psychol.* **40**, 794 (1985).
39. J. J. Szucko and B. Kleinmuntz, *ibid.* **36**, 488 (1981).
40. R. Gray, C. B. Begg, R. A. Greenes, *Med. Decis. Making* **4**, 151 (1984).
41. A review of the polygraph assessment literature, which treats the problems mentioned here and some more specific, concludes that measured accuracy values are likely to be inflated by a wide margin (*37*). That inflation is even more marked when a measurement of "percentage of correct decisions" is made rather than a measurement of A. That percentage measure sets aside cases having polygraph records that the examiner deems inconclusive—in effect, cases on which he or she chooses not to be scored.
42. I should observe in passing that accuracy measures may be biased by certain general factors other than the four treated here. The one that comes first to mind is that system tests are often conducted under laboratory, rather than field, conditions. Thus, radiologists may participate in laboratory tests under unusually good conditions: quiet, no interruptions, and no patient treatment depending on the diagnosis. Such a test may be conducted purposely, in order to test a system in a standard way and at its full potential, but the measured value may be higher than can be expected in practice.
43. Since the concern for evaluation in the field of information retrieval heightened in the 1950s, this field has used several different measures of accuracy intended to be independent of the decision criterion; see, for example, a review by J. A. Swets, *Science* **141**, 245 (1963). ROC measures have been considered extensively, for example, by B. C. Brookes, *J. Doc.* **24**, 41 (1968); M. H. Heine, *ibid.* **29**, 81 (1973); A. Bookstein, *Recall Precision* **30**, 374 (1974); M. H. Heine, *J. Doc.* **31**, 283 (1975); M. Kochen, Ed., *The Growth of Knowledge* (Wiley, New York, 1967); T. Saracevic, Ed., *Introduction to Information Science* (Bowker, New York, 1970); B. Griffith, Ed., *Key Papers in Information Science* (Knowledge Industry Publications, White Plains, NY, 1980).
44. Various scores for binary forecasts that were developed in this field were related to ROC measures by I. Mason, in *Ninth Conference on Weather Forecasting and Analysis* (American Meteorological Society, Boston, 1982), p. 169; M. C. McCoy, in *Ninth Conference on Probablity and Statistics in Atmospheric Sciences* (American Meteorological Society, Boston, 1985), p. 423; *Bull. Am. Meteorol. Soc.* **67**, 155 (1986).
45. D. F. Ransohoff and A. Feinstein, *New Engl. J. Med.* **299**, 926 (1978); G. Revesz, H. L. Kundel, M. Bonitabus, *Invest. Radiol.* **18**, 194 (1983). Recommendations for handling various bias problems are advanced by C. B. Begg and B. J. McNeil, *Radiology* **167**, 565 (1988).

5 Choosing the Right Decision Threshold in High-Stakes Diagnostics

Diagnostic tests and systems of many kinds are used in a host of practical settings to assist in making a positive or negative decision about the occurrence of a particular event or the existence of a particular condition. Will an impending storm strike? Is this aircraft unfit to fly? Is that plane intending to attack this ship? Is this nuclear power plant malfunctioning? Is this assembly-line item flawed? Does this patient have the acquired immunodeficiency syndrome (AIDS) virus? Is this person lying? Is this football player using drugs? Will this school (or job) applicant succeed? Will a document so indexed contain the information sought? Does this tax return justify an audit? Is there oil in the ground here? Will the stock market advance today? Will this prisoner vindicate a parole? Are their explosives in this luggage?

These examples are a reminder that diagnostic test results do not usually constitute compelling evidence for or against the condition or event of interest, or evidence of a sort that leads directly to either a positive or negative decision. Rather, with tests that justify the term *diagnosis,* the evidence is a matter of degree. Test results lie along a continuum or are spread across several categories. Diagnosis is probabilistic and diagnostic decisions are made with more or less confidence. Hence, making a positive or negative decision in a systematic way requires selecting a threshold along the scale of evidence, such that values above

Author's note. I received advice on acquired immunodeficiency syndrome (AIDS) testing and substantial assistance from Michael J. Barry, Bruce P. Kinosian, Albert G. Mulley, and J. Sanford Schwartz. Marilyn J. Adams, Carl J. D'Orsi, George A. Hermann, Lincoln E. Moses, Frederick Mosteller, Ronald M. Pickett, and Steven E. Seltzer commented very helpfully on drafts of this chapter.

the threshold uniformly lead to a positive decision and values below it lead to a negative decision. In principle, one can set such a *positivity criterion* anywhere along the scale and so can aspire to choose the particular criterion that is best for a given purpose and best for the specific situation at hand. In a two-alternative decision problem, two types of correct decisions and two types of errors can occur, and the "best" criterion will produce the appropriate balance among the relative proportions of these various outcomes. Although sometimes a weaker definition of the best, or optimal, criterion will be necessary, in general a criterion is optimal if it reflects appropriately the relative frequency of occurrence of the condition of interest and the benefits and costs, respectively, of correct and incorrect decisions.

Concepts and techniques of decision analysis used for decades in psychology, particularly the relative operating characteristic (ROC) of signal detection theory, enable one to specify the optimal criterion and to measure and control the criterion that is used. A recent topical bibliography of applications of detection theory cited upward of 1,000 articles in perceptual and cognitive psychology and an introductory few dozen in abnormal and clinical psychology (Green & Swets, 1966, 1988 reprint). That bibliography also included applications to practical diagnostic settings, mostly in the fields of information retrieval, military and industrial monitoring, and medical diagnosis. However, the thrust of this chapter is that the concept of setting the most appropriate criterion has yet to influence most practical arenas, including several of substantial import to individuals and society.

I demonstrate the point here with two examples of diagnostic settings that are highly visible now as vital to people's health and safety. One is clinical testing for the human immunodeficiency virus (HIV) of AIDS and the other is nondestructive testing (NDT) for metal fatigue or other structural flaws in aircraft. In the past five years, the proportion of people in this country infected by the HIV has grown tenfold, from 4 in 10,000 (Barry, Cleary, & Fineberg, 1986) to 4 in 1,000 (Angell, 1991), and it is still growing rapidly. The threat of aircraft disasters similarly grows as commercial fleets age and surpass their projected lives (Derra, 1990). Both of these diagnostic problems illustrate that diagnostic evidence may be objectively scaled—for example, a number generated by an instrument—or it maybe subjectively scaled—for example, a probability estimate made by a human observer. For these HIV and NDT examples, moreover, adequate data are available to show empirically the applicability of, and the need for, the concept of the optimal criterion.

The intent of this chapter is to promote a more general awareness of the decision problem in diagnosis, as it arises in both science and public affairs, in the interests of a more general application of the relevant concepts and techniques. Following sections describe further the decision problem in diagnosis, review the relevant decision-analytic techniques, characterize current HIV and NDT diagnostic scenarios, and present data on current HIV and NDT practices in terms of the relevant techniques. In conclusion, this chapter raises the question of how transfer of the techniques to such diagnostic settings can be facilitated.

THE DECISION PROBLEM

Assume for illustration that the continuum of test results, or *decision variable,* is a scale with 10 values, numbered 1 to 10. When the ophthalmologist's task is to determine if glaucoma exists by measurement of pressure within the eye, the 10 values represent units of pressure. When the radiologist's task is to determine if a specified disease exists by viewing a medical image, the 10 values may represent the number and strength of the diagnostically relevant features that he or she perceives in the image. Although the scale's direction will depend on the type of test, assume here that the higher values are more likely to occur when the condition of interest actually exists, whereas the lower values are more likely to occur when some other, usually less consequential or null, condition actually exists. The condition to be detected is called *positive,* and any other condition is called *negative,* without regard to their affective connotations (and so the existence of the HIV in a blood sample or a crack in an airplane wing are positive). Thus, high values of the scale give greater confidence in the existence of the positive condition, and low values give less confidence in the existence of the positive condition.

Positive and negative conditions are not completely separated by the results of an imperfect test; some, perhaps all, of the values of the decision variable can arise from either the positive or negative alternative. For this reason, some single value of the decision variable should be selected as the positivity criterion, such that values as high or higher than that criterial value always lead to a positive decision and lower values always lead to a negative decision. For any criterion, there will be four kinds of decision outcome: two types of errors, false positive and false negative, and two types of correct decisions, true positive and true negative. A fundamental point is that a compensatory relationship exists among the proportions, or probabilities, of the four outcomes. Exactly where the positivity criterion is set determines the balance among those proportions. If a low or lenient criterion is set, the proportions of both true-positive and false-positive outcomes will be relatively high and the proportions of both true-negative and false-negative outcomes will be relatively low. The converse is the case when a high or strict criterion is set.

In the following, the outcome proportions considered are the proportions of actually positive conditions that are called positive, or negative, and the proportions of actually negative conditions that are called positive, or negative. These proportions are estimates of the probabilities of a particular decision, given the existence of a particular condition (rather than the other way around). According to these definitions, the true-positive and false-negative proportions add to one, as do the false-positive and true-negative proportions, so taking one member of each pair will suffice to represent all four outcomes. I focus here on true-positive and false-positive outcomes—that is, the two outcomes that occur when values of the decision variable exceed the positivity criterion—and denote their proportions or probabilities as TP and FP.

The best balance of TP and FP will vary from one diagnostic situation to another. For instance, mammograms taken to detect breast cancer are currently interpreted with a lenient criterion (say, at 2 on the scale of 10, referred to earlier); any suspicion of malignancy is followed up in some way, in order to achieve a high TP even at the expense of a high FP. In contrast, a strict criterion (say, at 9 on the scale) will be appropriate in those instances in which one will accept a smaller TP in order to keep FP down; for example, following on the notoriety given Willie Horton in the 1988 presidential campaign, governors held responsible for prison furloughs are reported to be tending toward such conservatism. These two examples highlight the role of utilities of outcomes in determining the best positivity criterion, say, the benefit of a true-positive outcome and the cost of a false-positive outcome. Another factor in choosing the best criterion is the prior probability (or base rate) of the existence of the positive condition. A strict criterion, and few positive decisions, are suitable when that probability is low, and a lenient criterion, and many positive decisions, are suitable when that probability is high.

TRADITIONAL APPROACHES TO CRITERION SETTING

Although the positivity criterion can be set anywhere along an essentially continuous scale, three historical approaches have specified three distinct, canonical criteria—one very strict, one very lenient, and one in the middle. The strict criterion represents what may be characterized as the *industrial quality-control approach,* as applied, say, to the functioning of a manufacturing machine. The idea is to set a criterion that yields an FP on the order of 0.05 or 0.01. Then values of the decision variable falling below the criterion are regarded as representing normal or acceptable items, that is, as being the expected spread of values when the machine is functioning in its proper mode. Values exceeding the criterion are then regarded as identifying abnormal, unacceptable items. This approach is also taken in clinical laboratory tests, for example, in testing body fluids for evidence of disease, with the same rationale: Only results off at the tail of the distribution are thought to signal a problem. The approach of setting a criterion to yield a low FP is familiar to behavioral scientists from procedures for testing statistical hypotheses.

The lenient criterion, as traditionally used, is set so that TP will be very high. It derives from the *engineering fail-safe approach.* For example, automatic test devices on a sophisticated airplane that seek to detect various kinds of malfunction or other threats are designed with such a lenient criterion. Recall that a few years ago the USS *Stark* suffered extensive damage when it failed to react until actually attacked by an enemy aircraft, and that more recently the USS *Vincennes* reacted incorrectly as if it were under attack and shot down a commercial airliner; we can surmise that in the interim the navy criterion for deciding that an attack is imminent shifted from strict to lenient.

The medium criterion may be termed the *symmetrical approach* because it tends to produce as many errors of one kind as the other and as many correct decisions of one kind as the other. It is appropriate when the diagnostic task is not polarized between the positive and negative conditions, either with respect to the benefits and costs of decision outcomes or the prior probabilities of the conditions' occurrence. In those instances, the symmetrical criterion maximizes the overall percentage of correct decisions. There is a suggestion in data following that HIV screening tests tend toward this criterion.

THE RELATIVE OPERATING CHARACTERISTIC (ROC)

The most relevant decision concepts and analytical techniques in psychology for analysis of the positivity criterion are those of signal detection theory. This theory is based on statistical decision theory (Wald, 1950) and was originally developed for radar (Peterson, Birdsall, & Fox, 1954; Van Meter & Middleton, 1954). The application of the engineering and statistical theory to human judgment has been described by Tanner and Swets (1954a, 1954b), Swets, Tanner, and Birdsall (1961), Green and Swets (1966) and Swets (1973; see Chapter 1). The extension to diagnostic problems is treated by Swets and Pickett (1982). The generality of signal detection theory stems from the fact that the various conditions and events of special diagnostic interest are evidenced by signals, which tend to be confused with random interference or noise. Its analytical device called the relative operating characteristic is the primary technique.

The ROC is a convenient way to represent the placement of any given positivity criterion and also the location of the best criterion. It is a plot showing how TP and FP vary together as the criterion varies, specifically, a plot of TP versus FP, as shown in Figure 1. As mentioned, the other two proportions or probabilities (FN and TN) are, respectively, complements of TP and FP and so they can be shown on the opposite axes. Figure 1 shows an illustrative ROC as the curve extending continuously from FP = TP = 0 at lower left, for the strictest criterion (which produces no positive decisions), to FP = TP = 1.0 at upper right, for the most lenient criterion (which produces only positive decisions). Intermediate points along the curve represent the four proportions for each possible criterion. Data from a variety of diagnostic settings produce such a curve, including medical imaging, information retrieval, weather forecasting, aptitude testing, and polygraph lie detection (see Chapter 2).

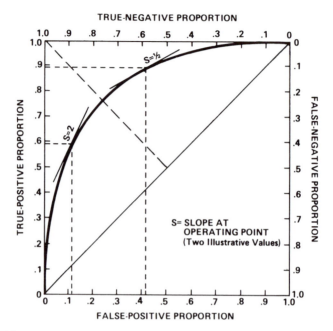

FIG. 1.   An illustrative, Idealized Relative Operating Characteristic (ROC),
Showing the Covariation in Conditional Decision-Outcome Proba-
bilities as the Positivity Criterion Varies
Note. Two illustative operating points are shown, as specified by two ROC slopes.

The ROC graph may be seen to provide measures of the two independent
aspects of diagnostic performance: A test's accuracy (discrimination capacity)
varies along the negative diagonal (dashed 45° line in Figure 1) and a test's
positivity criterion varies in the direction of the positive (solid-line) diagonal,
essentially at a right angle to accuracy. The accuracy of a test, independent of the
criterion, can be indexed by how far its ROC lies above the positive diagonal
(where the test's accuracy is at a chance level), in the direction of the upper left
corner (where its accuracy is perfect). The currently favored index of accuracy is
the proportion of the area of the unit square that lies beneath the ROC, varying
from 0.5 at chance performance to 1.0 at perfect performance (Chapter 4; Swets
& Pickett, 1982).

Because the slope of the ROC decreases smoothly from the lower left corner
to the upper right corner, the value of the slope at any given point on the curve
can be taken as an index of that point. I denote the slope index as S and speak of
it as representing an operating point on an ROC, namely, the ROC point that
corresponds to the criterion that is adopted for use. Operating points for illustrative values of S equal to $\frac{1}{2}$ and 2 are indicated by the tangent lines in Figure 1.

Dashed lines indicate the values of FP and TP that correspond, respectively, to those two points. On this symmetrical curve, the operating point for S = 1 (not shown) is the point at the negative, dashed diagonal. The ROC graph reflects the assumption that the operating point can vary continuously along the ROC, or nearly so, and need not be constrained to the three points that reflect the nominal criteria of the three traditional approaches discussed earlier.

THE OPTIMAL CRITERION

The most complete definition of the best criterion for any particular diagnostic setting and test purpose takes into account both the prior probabilities of the two alternative conditions to be distinguished and the benefits and costs of correct and incorrect decisions about these conditions. Denoting the prior probabilities P(pos) and P(neg), the benefits of correct decisions B_{TP} and B_{TN}, and the costs of incorrect decisions C_{FP} and C_{FN}, this optimal criterion may be indexed by the slope S and defined as

$$S_{opt} = \frac{P(neg)}{P(pos)} \times \frac{(B_{TN} - C_{FP})}{(B_{TP} - C_{FN})}. \tag{1}$$

Just as the negative diagnostic alternative is represented in the numerator of the probability part of the equation, so it is in the numerator of the benefit-cost part: B_{TN} and C_{FP} refer to the benefit and cost that may be realized when the negative alternative actually occurs. Similarly, both the probability denominator and the benefit-cost denominator represent the occurrence of the positive diagnostic alternative.

So, for a fixed set of benefits and costs, the optimal S will be relatively large—and the positivity criterion will be relatively strict—when P(neg) is appreciably greater than P(pos). That is, one should not make the positive decision very readily when the chances are great that the negative alternative will actually occur. Such might be the case when using a medical test broadly for screening nonsymptomatic populations. Conversely, in a medical referral center, with a higher P(pos), the optimal S is smaller and the optimal criterion is more lenient; a higher FP can be tolerated because the number of negative cases is relatively small.

On the other hand, when the prior probabilities are constant, the optimal S is large and the optimal criterion is relatively strict when the numerator of the benefit-cost part of the equation is large relative to its denominator, that is, when more importance is attached to being correct when the negative alternative occurs. Such might be the case when a surgical technique undertaken for a disease under diagnostic consideration has substantial risks and its chances of a satisfactory outcome are low. Conversely, the optimal S is small and the optimal criterion is lenient when the benefit-cost denominator is large relative to its numera-tor, that is, when it is more important to be correct when the positive alternative occurs. Such is the case in deciding whether or not to predict a severe storm.

It will usually be convenient to refer the optimal criterion from the ROC back to the decision variable, the scale on which the positivity criterion is originally set (as idealized earlier in a 10-point scale). Given the distributions of scale values for the occurrences of the positive and negative alternatives, respectively, one can determine the scale value at which the ratio of the ordinate of the positive distribution to the ordinate of the negative distribution is equal numerically to the optimal ROC slope; it can be shown that this is the value of the original scale that corresponds to the optimal criterion (Green & Swets, 1966; Swets, Tanner, & Birdsall, 1961).

ESTIMATING PROBABILITIES, BENEFITS AND COSTS

Estimates of the probabilities, benefits, and costs, as required to calculate the optimal criterion defined earlier, may, of course, be very difficult to make. Probabilities of rare events—think of the navy ships mentioned earlier as subject to attack by enemy aircraft—are estimated with little reliability. Benefits and costs are notoriously difficult to judge when human lives are at stake and are often in conflict when a balance must be struck between an individual's and society's concerns. The strong position taken by some decision theorists is that any choice of a positivity criterion implies assumptions about probabilities, benefits, and costs, and that making the assumptions explicit is preferable to leaving them tacit. As a saving grace, when the assumptions or estimates are explicit, one can make a sensitivity analysis, that is, adjust the estimates over the range of possibilities and examine the resulting changes in TP and FP, and vice versa.

A somewhat weaker approach is to consider only the cost-benefit ratio, with-out assigning absolute benefits and costs and without separating the two individ-ual cost and benefit values in each of the numerators and denominators of the formula of Equation 1. Thus, although it is no more than surmise on my part, one can imagine as a navy position before the lack of reaction by one ship to a real attack that it would rather make the correct decision in the negative instance of no actual attack, and as a new position after the attack on that ship that it would rather make the correct decision in the positive instance of an actual attack—say, five times rather, in each case. In a similar rough vein, the navy estimate of the probability of attack by a plane on course might have changed from 1 in 50 to 1 in 10. Such crude estimates are sufficient to form a rational, although not spe-ciously precise, analysis of the appropriate criterion. A still weaker, although still rational, approach is to set a criterion to satisfy a limit on false-positive outcomes. This approach might take the form, for example, of requiring a certain specified yield of positive cases from biopsies that are recommended on the basis of mammograms.

TESTING FOR THE HIV OF AIDS

Continuous Decision Variable

Commonly used tests to detect the HIV are of three general types, and all depend on a scaled decision variable. In the type of test used most, called *enzyme-linked immunoassay* (EIA or ELISA), the test result is one of a continuum of numerical values of optical density, as generated by a machine. As the main representative of the second type, regarded as more conclusive but more expensive and difficult, the *Western blot test* produces several bands along a strip that vary in visual intensity according to the degree of reaction of various proteins. These bands are interpreted visually by a technician with a subjective positivity criterion; then positive judgments about various bands and various combinations of bands are taken as more or less indicative of the HIV (Nishanian et al., 1987; Schwartz, Dans, & Kinosian, 1988). In the newest type of test popularly called a *quick test* (the latex agglutination assay) and designed for developing countries, liquids are viewed microscopically by technicians who assess subjectively the degree of their graininess or clumping (Spielberg et al., 1989).

Choice of a Positivity Criterion

EIA Test. The selection of a positivity criterion for the EIA test—a particular numerical value of optical density—is made by its manufacturer. Some data suggest an intent to select the criterion that best discriminates between positive and negative cases—but there seem to be no published rationales for the criteria chosen. As seen next, when tested on the same sample of cases, three prominent EIA tests reflect different criteria, yielding noticeably different balances of TP and FP.

An empirical evaluation of the accuracies and criteria of three EIA tests was made by Nishanian et al. (1987). This is an unusually good study in that negative as well as positive EIA results were followed by the more accurate Western blot test, so that the truth for both kinds of cases could be defined by the same rigorous procedure. These investigators broke down their results for each EIA test into six ranges or categories of optical-density values, permitting an analysis as if a positivity criterion were set successively at each category boundary, and hence five ROC points are available for each test. These points, originally plotted as ROCs by Schwartz et al. (1988), are shown in Figure 2. Theoretical curves

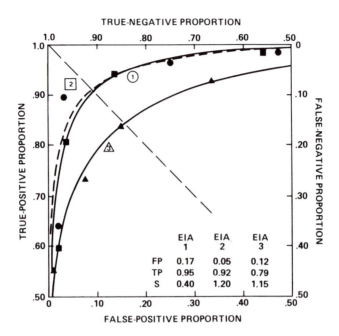

FIG. 2.   Empirical Relative Operating Characteristics (ROCs) of Three
Enzyme-Linked Immunoassay (EIA) Tests for Detecting the Human Immunodeficiency Virus (HIV)
Note. EIA 1 is represented by circles; EIA 2, by squares; and EIA 3, by triangles. The
open symbols with numerals (one for each EIA test) and the legend indicate the results
of the positivity criteria set by the three manufacturers. From 'Human Immunodeficiency. Virus Test Evaluation, Performance, and Use" by J. S. Schwartz, P. E. Dans, and
B. P. Kinosian, 1988, *Journal of the American Medical Association,* 259, p. 2574. Copyright 1988 by the American Medical Association. Adapted by permission.

were fitted to the points by a procedure designed for the purpose and supported
well across diagnostic fields (Swets, 1986; Swets & Pickett, 1982). (Note that
just the upper left quadrant of the ROC space is shown in this figure, in order to
spread out the data points).

The three open symbols in the figure (one for each test) contain numerals that
arbitrarily designate the tests and are the ROC points that correspond to the three
manufacturers' positivity criteria. As evident from the location of these points
and as represented numerically in the figure's legend, two of the tests (EIA 2 and
EIA 3) were found to have similar criteria in ROC terms (S about 1.2) and the
third (EIA 1), a noticeably different criterion on the other side of the negative
(dashed) diagonal (S about 0.4). Two of the criteria that differ are associated with
tests of very nearly the same accuracy: EIA 1 and EIA 2. It appears from

Nishanian et al.'s (1987) study that EIA 1 operates at a point relative to EIA 2, at which it gains a few more true positives—95 per 100 versus 92 per 100—at the expense of three times as many false positives—17 per 100 versus 5 per 100.[1]

Western blot test.   Several different ways of interpreting a Western blot test for degrees of positivity have been established by government agencies and by consortia and are variously in use (Schwartz et al., 1988). Data permitting an ROC evaluation of the criteria suggested by a recently convened consortium are summarized here in Table 1 and plotted in Figure 3 (Consortium for Retrovirus Serology Standardization, 1988). Reactions of the various protein bands and combinations of them judged to be positive were used to establish the test's various degrees of positivity as arranged in the eight categories of the table (with Category 1 representing the highest degree of positivity). These scaled categories were compared for two clinical groups: one in which 111 persons diagnosed clinically as having AIDS were deemed positive cases and the other in which 1,306 persons from a low-risk group were deemed negative cases.

Table 1 shows the proportions of negative and positive cases in each category and the cumulative proportions, FP and TP, across categories. The consortium chose to regard Categories 1 to 3 as *positive,* Categories 4 to 7 as *indeterminate,* and Category 8 as *negative.* By cumulating over Categories 1 to 3, the consortium's definition of *positive* is seen (from the last two columns of the table) to produce a positivity criterion that yields FP = 0.10 and TP = 0.80. If one were to include the indeterminates with the positives in order to define a more lenient criterion, the resulting values are FP = 0.16 and TP = 0.99. These points are plotted as triangles in Figure 3. (Again, just the upper left quadrant of the usual ROC graph is shown.)

One can observe that the tabled data suggest the possibility (pending more data) of a better choice for each criterion. If Categories 1 to 4 or 1 to 5 (instead of 1 to 3) are deemed positive under the strict criterion, TP increases from 0.80 to 0.94, with no increase in the FP = 0.10. Similarly, if Categories 1 to 6 (instead of 1 to 7) are deemed positive under the lenient criterion, FP decreases from 0.16 to 0.13, with no decrease in TP = 0.99. The consensus group, however, chose not to go strictly by the numbers, believing instead that a positive case under a

---

[1]As mentioned, the curves of Figure 2 show essentially the same accuracy, or discrimination capacity, for enzyme-linked immunoassay (EIA) Tests 1 and 2, whereas EIA Test 3 shows a lower accuracy; in terms of the area index of accuracy mentioned earlier, the values are 0.97 for the first two tests and 0.92 for the third. These results are not necessarily representative of the tests' absolute performances in all settings, inasmuch as the sample of cases here is a relatively high-risk group that might differ on average, in difficulty of diagnosis, from lower risk groups. The College of American Pathologists estimates FP = 0.017 and TP = 0.994 in low-prevalence populations (Bloom & Glied, 1991).

TABLE 1
Evaluation Data on the Western Blot Test for the AIDS Virus

Decision-Variable Categories	Actually Negative Cases	Actually Positive Cases	Cumulative FP	Cumulative TP
1	0.10	0.49	0.10	0.49
2	0.0	0.11	0.10	0.60
3	0.0	0.20	0.10	0.80
4	0.0	0.14	0.10	0.94
5	0.0	0.0	0.10	0.94
6	0.03	0.05	0.13	0.99
7	0.03	0.00	0.16	0.99
8	0.84	0.01	1.00	1.00
Sum	100	100	—	—

Note. FP = the probability of a false positive; TP = the probability of a true positive. Data are from "Serological Diagnosis of Human Immunodeficiency Virus Infection by Western Blot Testing" by The Consortium for Retrovirus Serology Standardization 1988, *Journal of the American Medical Association, 260.*

strict criterion should include at least two bands of different kinds (Consortium for Retrovirus Serology Standardization, 1988).[2]

Latex agglutination assay. Technicians who interpret the so-called quick tests are taught to approximate a visually defined positivity criterion. A collaborative study of six agencies evaluated five such tests in Zaire. The Western blot test was given to cases showing positive on any quick test or on the single EIA test also administered and was taken as definitive for positive cases; any case failing to exceed the positivity criteria of all five quick tests and the EIA test was taken as an actually negative case. Across the five tests, values of FP ranged from 0.01 to 0.07, while TP ranged from 0.86 to 0.99, indicating substantial differences in criteria.[3]

---

[2]In comparison with these data, the College of American Pathologists estimates a higher accuracy of the Western blot test than of the enzyme-linked immunoassay (EIA) test under ideal conditions, but a lower accuracy in actual use, namely, FP = 0.047 and TP = 0.907 (Bloom & Glied, 1991).

[3]Rough averages of the five tests are FP = 0.04, TP = 0.92 (Spielberg et al., 1989). These figures may be compared with the values of FP = 0.014 and TP = 0.986 yielded by the enzyme-linked immunoassay (EIA) test in the Zaire setting. Other reports give consistent results (Heyward & Curran, 1988). Recently described tests for detecting human immunodeficiency virus (HIV) antibodies in urine are reported to be in a slightly better range of accuracies: The averages of three tests were FP = 0.02 and TP = 0.95 (Holden, 1990).

Criterion Held as Test Purpose Changed

The EIA tests were originally developed to screen donated blood, and their positivity criteria were set in that context. However, when these tests then became routinely used in diagnosing patients, their positivity criteria were left unchanged. This, despite the fact that the cost of a false-positive decision that leads to discarding a sample of uncontaminated blood seems clearly less than the cost of a false-positive decision that leads to further, expensive, unnecessary testing of an uninfected individual and that individual's unnecessary concern.

Similarly, criteria were not reconsidered as the EIA tests were applied to different populations varying drastically in the prevalence (or prior probability) of AIDS. Schwartz et al. (1988) reported estimates of the number of infected persons per 100,000 for various populations: These estimates vary from 30 for low-risk blood donors, to 95 for high-risk blood donors, to 150 for military

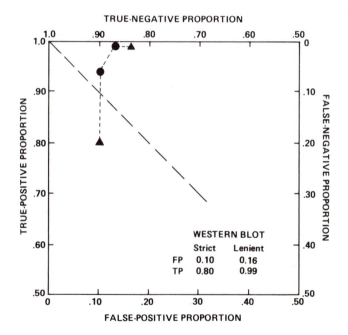

FIG. 3.   Relative Operating Characteristic (ROC) Points Obtained in an
Evaluation of the Western Blot Test
Note. The triangular points represent the two positivity criteria that correspond to the consortium's definitions; the circles represent other points consistent with the data. Data from "Serological Diagnosis of Human Immunodeficiency Virus Infection by Western Blot Testing" by The Consortium for Retrovirus Serology Standardization, 1988, *Journal of the American Medical Association, 260.*

recruits, up to 45,000 for methadone clinic attendees. When benefits and costs are constant, this amount of variation in prevalence has a massive effect on the optimal criterion; the optimal value of S defined above ranges across these populations from near 3,000 to near 1, that is, from a point very near the lower left corner of the ROC graph (Figure 1) to a point near the negative diagonal of the graph. The variation in FP and TP over that range will be very large.

Other benefit-cost factors that would affect the optimal positivity criterion include whether the test is voluntary or mandatory, and mandatory for what group of persons, for whose benefit. Thus, for example, testing is now done in connection with life-insurance and health-insurance exams, in which false-positive decisions can have significant lifetime costs, and there are other forms of mandatory testing (e.g., of certain international travelers) for which the benefits of detection are few. Still other factors ostensibly affecting the optimal criterion are whether the results are confidential; whether they are anonymous; and how effective the therapy may be (Meyer & Pauker, 1987; Schwartz et al., 1988; Weiss & Thier, 1988). Another consideration is whether the test is done as part of a survey to measure the scope of the AIDS epidemic; in this case, one might desire a symmetrical criterion to maximize the proportion of correct decisions of either kind.[4]

Multiple Tests

The medical practice followed to gain protection against the too-lenient EIA test criteria for determining infection in low-risk individuals has been to give a Western blot test to those individuals called positive by an EIA criterion.[5] The

---

[4]An indication of the large impact that variation in the criterion can have is gained by considering tests with approximately the accuracy of the latex agglutination assays (quick tests) noted earlier, as applied to low-prevalence populations, for example, with 30 actual positives in 100,000 cases. In that situation, detecting on average 27, 28, or 29 of the 30 true positives would bring along, respectively, on the order of 3,000, 5,000, and 10,000 false positives. Low-prevalence populations do tend to provide impractical numbers of false positives; a new detector for plastic explosives in luggage, considered by the Federal Aviation Administration to approach acceptable accuracy, namely, FP = 0.05 and TP = 0.95, has been estimated to produce 5 million false positives for each true positive (Speer, 1989). What is called in some fields the *positive predictive value* (PPV) is an important concept in such cases. The PPV is the inverse of the TP proportion or probability considered here, specifically, the proportion of positive decisions that represent positive conditions, or the probability of a positive condition, given a positive decision. This quantity can be so low that decision makers or operators are led to ignore positive indications from diagnostic devices, including those intended to alert them to dangerous conditions.

[5]The Western blot test has been considered confirmatory, in part because the specific proteins causing a reaction can be visualized directly as opposed to the enzyme-linked immunoassay (EIA) tests in which contaminating proteins may be influencing the optical-density results, and hence it gives greater confidence. However, I am not aware of data comparing the two types of test against the same standards of "truth" of outcome, and how much more accurate (discriminating) the Western blot test may be, to my knowledge, is not known.

use of multiple tests, in general, has two effects that should be distinguished, one on the overall positivity criterion and one on the overall diagnostic accuracy, or discrimination capacity. Multiple tests, as usually used, serve to make the overall positivity criterion stricter, because an overall positive result is declared only when all of the individual test criteria are satisfied. (In the case in which an overall positive result is declared when the criterion of any one of the individual tests is satisfied, an overall criterion more lenient than those of the individual tests is realized; Green & Swets, 1966, pp. 239–250.) However, the argument of this article suggests that when tests are used in tandem, the positivity criterion of each should be set in conjunction with the other to achieve a given overall result; the incompletely rationalized, conventional criterion of each test, when the test is used alone, should not be simply accepted as being appropriate to the tests' combined use. Although setting a lenient criterion in a screening test and a strict criterion in a confirmatory test is generally good practice, the specific quantities should be carefully considered. The relatively strict criterion presently associated with Western blot tests leaves many indeterminates, which remain problematic (A. G. Mulley, personal communication, November 13, 1990).[6]

In addition to not adjusting the EIA and Western blot criteria when the tests are used together, the common practice has been to ignore the EIA test result once a confirmatory Western blot test is given. To date, the scaled results of the two tests (or specific values of the two decision variables) have not been combined mathematically to yield a new decision variable that would permit greater discrimination than either of those of the individual tests. Approximating such a procedure is the practice used for a time by the New York Blood Center. For a highly positive EIA result, a positive Western blot result was considered definitive and a negative blot result led to still another type of test; for a slightly positive EIA result, a negative Western blot result was considered definitive (Schwartz et al., 1988).[7]

---

[6]Some screening programs have used a very rigorous regimen of four to six successive tests (including repetitions of a particular test and also tests of different kinds) in order to make the positivity criterion very strict and FP very low, for example, as conducted by the U.S. Army (Burke et al., 1988) and a Minnesota consortium (MacDonald et al., 1989). However, what happens to TP in the process is not known to date. The army study's published TP figure is based on just 15 cases; it is 0.93, with a 95% confidence lower limit of 0.80.

[7]Although multiple tests increase accuracy, two tests, even when they provide independent (completely uncorrelated) information, do not bring certainty. Given the formula that posterior odds are equal to the prior odds multiplied by the test's likelihood ratio, in which likelihood ratio = TP/FP (the probability of a true positive/the probability of a false positive), some illustrative results can be calculated. For the low-prevalence population of 30 positives in 100,000 cases, the odds against the disease before any test are about 3,000 to 1. After one positive test result from a test operated at FP = 0.05 and TP = 0.95, the odds against the disease are 175 to 1; after a second positive result from an independent, similarly accurate test, the odds are still about 10 to 1 against the disease. For tests of significantly greater accuracy, namely, FP = 0.02 and TP = 0.98, the odds against the disease after two positive tests are still better than even, about 1.5 to 1. Cleary et al. (1987) made an estimate

General Comment

Going beyond the AIDS example, one can identify several conceptual approaches to the evaluation of diagnostic tests in medicine, ranging from almost completely inadequate to the best available. In that order, the first approach is to consider only TP, without any regard to false-positive decisions (or, less often, to consider only FP, without regard to TP). A second approach is to consider TP primarily and to consider false-positive decisions qualitatively only, as perversely nettlesome errors. A third is to consider FP along with TP, but to worry about FP only if it exceeds some tolerable limit, say 0.10. A fourth is to consider FP in relation to TP, but to consider just a single pair of those values, for a single criterion that is regarded to be fixed and canonical. A fifth is to acknowledge that diagnostic evidence lies along a scale and then to see FP as on a par conceptually with TP—and covarying with TP as the positivity criterion is varied. This approach reflects a recognition that false positives come with the territory, that such is the way of nature. Unfortunately, the frequencies with which these various approaches are taken seem to be inversely correlated with their utility.[8]

INSPECTING AIRCRAFT FOR METAL FATIGUE

Continuous Decision Variable

Some techniques for nondestructive testing of aircraft structures provide a meter reading as output and others provide a visual pattern that must be interpreted by technicians, for example, eddy current and ultrasound. In both instances, the

---

specifically for the enzyme-linked immunoassay (EIA) and Western blot tests; they took into account the dependency of the two tests, used the manufacturers' claims for accuracy, and estimated for a similarly low-prevalence population that the percentage of persons with both tests positive who would actually be infected is 76%—odds of 3 to 1 in favor of the disease. This estimate is close to that of 71% made by Bloom and Glied (1991), also for a low prevalence population and independent EIA and Western blot tests, as based on the College of American Pathologists' performance estimates for the tests under ideal conditions. Using the college's performance estimates for the tests under actual conditions yields an estimate of 13%; then, after positive results on both tests, the odds are 7 to 1 against the disease.

[8]The relevant literature in medicine that awaits more general recognition begins with the book that introduced signal detection theory and the relative operating characteristic (ROC) to medical decision making (Lusted, 1968) and a following book of symposium papers (Jacquez, 1972); continues with tutorial articles by McNeil, Keeler, and Adelstein (1975), and Metz (1978) in radiology, and by Hermann and Sugiura (1984) and Hermann, Sugiura, and Krumm (1986) in clinical pathology; and includes a textbook by Weinstein et al. (1980). Although there are probably more than 200 articles on the ROC in diagnostic medicine, many of them cited by Green and Swets (1966, 1988 reprint), most are in radiology, and the ideas have not reached medicine at large. Schwartz, Dans, and

basis for a decision is again evidence that varies along a scale, and the action to be taken—accepting or rejecting a part—requires that a positivity criterion be located on the scale.

Choice of a Positivity Criterion

The costs of incorrect decisions of either kind would seem to be paramount in this diagnostic setting. A false-negative decision can lead to catastrophe and dramatic loss of lives. A false-positive decision takes a plane out of service unnecessarily at substantial dollar cost. On balance, the costs and benefits seem to tilt toward a lenient criterion for declaring a flaw, one approaching the engineering fail-safe criterion mentioned earlier. On the other hand, the prior probability of a dangerous flaw, although increasing with an aging fleet of airplanes, is still very low, and low prevalences, even with moderate to strict criteria, tend to produce an unworkable number of false positives. Setting the best criterion is clearly required, in terms of probabilities as well as costs and benefits.

Data

The available, relevant data on inspection of aircraft for metal fatigue are about as sparse, or proprietary, as they are in HIV testing. I was able to identify one major study. In this study, 148 metal specimens with and without flaws were carried to 17 bases of the U.S. Air Force, where they were inspected, in total, by 121 technicians using ultrasound and 133 technicians using an eddy-current technique. For a review, see Swets (1983).

The performance of each technician in this study is depicted by a point on an ROC graph in Figures 4 and 5. The impact of a glance at these graphs is the main result: The variation across technicians is about as large as it could be. For ultrasound, FP varies almost uniformly from 0.0 to 1.0, across the entire possible range. Some technicians adopt a very strict criterion, and others adopt a very lenient criterion. For eddy current, the variation is less but still very large: Most technicians give a FP between 0.0 and 0.20, but several range from 0.20 to 0.50.

Kinosian (1988) have recently related signal detection theory and the ROC specifically to the problem of human immunodeficiency virus (HIV) testing.

Indicative of the difficulties that will be faced in implementing optimal criteria in HIV testing are unpublished data collected by A. G. Mulley and M. J. Barry (1986). A survey they took of directors of acquired immunodeficiency syndrome (AIDS) counseling and testing centers revealed an extensive lack of consensus about the probabilities of HIV infection that should lead to certain actions. For example, 25% of the respondents said they would discuss decreased life expectancy with patients having a probability of infection greater than 0.15; about 50% would require a probability of ≥ 0.95 for that action. Meanwhile, 43% would advise against pregnancy for patients having a probability greater than 0.15, whereas 30% would require a probability of ≥ 0.95 to do so.

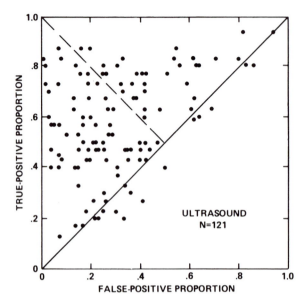

FIG. 4.   Relative Operating Characteristic (ROC) Points for 121 Technicians Inspecting Metal Specimens for Cracks With an Ultrasound Technique.
Note. Calculated from data provided by J. R. Griffin, J. A. Petru, and V. Viterbo of the
San Antonio Air Logistics Center at Kelly Air Force Base.

Analyses not shown here indicate that substantial variation in the positivity
criterion existed within a given air force base as well as across bases.[9,10]

Implementation of the Optimal Criterion

Admittedly, positivity criteria may be relatively simple to calculate by scientists
and technologists in a diagnostic field but difficult to implement as operational

---

[9]The variation in accuracy (discrimination) seen in Figures 4 and 5—ranging from chance
accuracy at the positive diagonal to very good accuracy near the upper left corner—indicates that this
aspect of performance was also not under control. In accuracy, however, technicians at a given base
were more consistent with each other than in their positivity criteria, and indeed, the averages of the
several bases varied almost uniformly across the full range of possible accuracies. This result
suggests that the inspection techniques used at the bases with high accuracy could be analyzed and
transferred to the others. An indication that the variability among technicians seen here persists in
applications of non-destructive testing is given by Harris (1991). In a study of eddy current for
examining steam generators, he found in the detection of three different faults a range in the true-
positive probability (TP) of nearly 0.40. For one representative fault, the 1 *SD* range in TP was from
0.69 to 0.93, indicating that the performance of one third of the technicians was outside that range.

[10]As in medicine, the concept of the optimal criterion appears in the literature of materials testing
(e.g., Rau, 1979). Again, however, it is not effectively used in the field. One hopeful sign for the

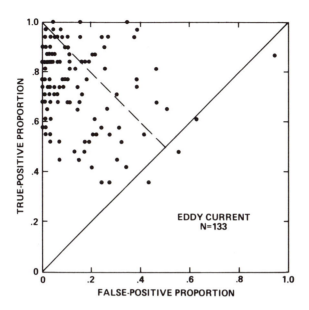

FIG. 5.   Relative Operating Characteristic (ROC) Points for 133 Techni-
cians Inspecting Metal Specimens for Cracks With an Eddy-Current
Technique.
Note. Calculated from data provided by J. R. Griffin, J. A. Petru, and V. Viterbo of the
San Antonio Air Logistics Center at Kelly Air Force Base.

standards by technicians and practitioners in that field. This discrepancy is most
problematic when the diagnostic process is largely subjective, as in visual image
interpretation. It is easy to imagine the plight of the aircraft inspector who must
contend with the rare false-negative decision leading to disaster as well as with
frequent complaints from a supervisor about false-positive decisions that drain
company profits.

   Implementing the best or optimal criterion may be facilitated by careful training of observers with immediate feedback of results or, alternatively, by separating observation and decision making. Frequently, the prior probabilities of diagnostic alternatives and the relevant benefits and costs, as well as an idea of what
level of positivity criterion they dictate, are better known to a decision maker
separate from the observation than to the observer. One thinks of the ship's
captain and radar observer; of the farmer, who must decide whether to protect
against frost, and the weather forecaster; and of the referring physician and
radiologist. A division of labor can be made, as it sometimes is in the cases of

aircraft field is that the National Aeronautics and Space Administration has begun to consider the
decision-analytic techniques reviewed here in relation to cockpit warning devices for engine malfunction, collision avoidance, ground proximity, and wind-shear effects (Swets & Getty, 1991).

these examples, by having the observer report the value of the decision variable and letting a decision maker compare it with a positivity criterion for a binary decision.

CONCLUDING REMARKS

The concept of the optimal positivity criterion has not permeated several important diagnostic fields and is effectively implemented in only a few of them. Within psychology, it has been applied to aptitude testing for personnel selection (Cronbach & Gleser, 1965). It has made practical inroads in weather forecasting for commercial interests (Miller & Thompson, 1975), and there may be a few other examples of routine and appropriate use. However, the concept has not enlightened HIV testing or materials testing of aircraft to an appropriate extent, despite the high national visibility and priority of these diagnostic problems. In HIV testing, we usually know quite precisely where the criterion is set, but are not assured that it is in the best place; in materials testing, we have almost no idea where a given inspector will set a criterion. This is not the place to attempt to detail the cost of inappropriate or unknown criterion settings to individuals and society; we can easily surmise that it is large.

Why does this situation exist? The optimality concept is not difficult, and it is not esoteric; doctors use it deliberately, if not quantitatively, when they make decisions about therapy, and airline and aircraft-manufacturing executives do so as well in their decisions. In fact, the idea is intuitively familiar to almost everyone; acting on the basis of probabilities and benefits and costs is something people do in their everyday lives. To be sure, the concept is mathematical as it would be used effectively in diagnosis, but as shown earlier, to first order it is captured neatly by a single graph and a simple equation. As mentioned earlier, it is often very difficult to estimate the prior probabilities of diagnostic alternatives and, especially, the benefits and costs of decision outcomes, and individuals may start out, at least, with widely varying estimates. However, the question that remains is why, with the computational tools available, these variables are treated only tacitly or ignored.

Can matters be improved? It is apparent that communications via conferences, journal articles, and books, although adequate to give the optimality concept scientific vetting, are not sufficient to influence currently serious practical arenas. I believe that the idea will be applied broadly in such arenas only when increasingly aware psychologists—whether primarily versed or interested in decision analysis, diagnosis, social structures, or societal problems—find ways to "give [this] psychology away." Where they have access, they might assist educational or advisory organizations in taking an initiative, or help national societies and government agencies in scientific, engineering, and health fields come officially to appreciate what is at stake. My personal impression is that most regulatory and certifying agencies are not directly approachable from outside the government with scientific ideas about their procedures, perhaps understandably in view of their pressing frontline responsibilities in relation to relatively limited resources. However, some governmental, quasi-governmental, and private agencies are chartered to examine and develop societal applications of scientific concepts, and they might be persuaded to study the issues and offer influential recommendations. Such institutions might also effectively arrange the mutual discussions between the optimality concept's advocates and its potential users that will likely be a necessary part of the transfer process.

REFERENCES

Angell, M. (1991). A dual approach to the AIDS epidemic. *The New England Journal of Medicine, 324,* 1498–1500.

Barry, M. J., Cleary, P. D., & Fineberg, H. V. (1986). Screening for HIV infection: Risks, benefits, and the burden of proof. *Law, Medicine, and Health Care, 14,* 259–267.

Bloom, D. E., & Glied, S. (1991). Benefits and costs of HIV testing. *Science, 252,* 1798–1804.

Burke, D. S., Brundage, J. F., Redfield, R. R., Damato, J. J., Schable, C. A. Putman, P., Visintine, R., & Kim, H. I. (1988). Measurement of the false positive rate in a screening program for human immunodeficiency virus infections. *The New England Journal of Medicine, 319,* 961–964.

Cleary, P. D., Barry, M. J., Mayer, K. H., Brandt, A. M., Gostin, L., & Fineberg, H. V. (1987). Compulsory premarital screening for the human immunodeficiency virus. *Journal of the American Medical Association, 258,* 1757–1762.

Consortium for Retrovirus Serology Standardization. (1988). Serological diagnosis of human immunodeficiency virus infection by Western blot testing. *Journal of the American Medical Association, 260,* 674–679.

Cronbach, L. J., & Gleser, G. C. (1965). *Psychological tests and personnel decisions.* Urbana: University of Illinois Press.

Derra, S. (1990, January). Aging airplanes: Can research make them safer? *R&D Magazine,* pp. 28–34.

Green, D. M., & Swets, J. A. (1966). *Signal detection theory and psychophysics.* New York: Wiley. (Reprinted 1988, Los Altos, CA: Peninsula)

Harris, D. H. (1991, October). *Eddy current steam generator data analysis performance.* Paper presented at the ASME International Joint Power Generation Conference, San Diego, CA.

Hermann, G. A., & Sugiura, H. T. (1984). Validity and bias in laboratory tests. *Archives of Pathological Laboratory Medicine, 108,* 769–770.

Hermann, G. A., Sugiura, H. T., & Krumm, R. T. (1986). Comparison of thyrotropin assays by relative operating characteristic analysis. *Archives of Pathological Laboratory Medicine, 110,* 21–25.

Heyward, W. L., & Curran, J. W. (1988). Rapid screening tests for HIV infection. *Journal of the American Medical Association, 260,* 542.

Holden, C. (1990). Testing for HIV in urine. *Science, 249,* 121.

Jacquez, J. A. (Ed.). (1972). *Computer diagnosis and diagnostic methods.* Springfield, IL: Charles C Thomas.

Lusted, L. B. (1968). *Introduction to medical decision making.* Springfield, IL: Charles C Thomas.

MacDonald, K. L., Jackson, J. B., Bowman, R. J., Plesky, H. F., Rhame, F. S. Balfour, H. H., Jr., & Osterholm, M. T. (1989). Performance characteristics of serologic tests for human immunodeficiency virus type 1 (HIV-1): Antibody among Minnesota blood donors. *Annals of Internal Medicine, 110,* 617–621.

McNeil, B. J., Keeler, E., & Adelstein, S. J. (1975). Primer on certain elements of medical decision making. *The New England Journal of Medicine, 293,* 211–215.

Metz, C. E. (1978). Basic principles of ROC analysis. *Seminars in Nuclear Medicine, 8,* 283–298.

Meyer, K. B., & Pauker, S. G. (1987). Screening for HIV: Can we afford the false positive rate? *The New England Journal of Medicine, 317,* 238–241.

Miller, A., & Thompson, J. C. (1975). *Elements of meteorology.* Columbus, OH: Merrill.

Mulley, A. G., & Barry, M. J. (1986). *Clinical utility of tests for HTLV-III/LAV infection* (Grant application to the Public Health Service). Boston, MA: Massachusetts General Hospital.

Nishanian, P., Taylor, J. M. G., Korns, E., Detels, R., Saah, A., & Fahey, J. L. (1987). Significance of quantitative enzyme-liked immunosorbent assay (ELISA) results in evaluation of three ELISAs and Western blot tests for detection of antibodies to human immunodeficiency virus in a high-risk population. *Journal of Clinical Microbiology, 25,* 395–400.

Peterson, W. W., Birdsall, T. G., & Fox, W. C. (1954). The theory of signal detectability. *IRE Professional Group on Information Theory, PGIT-4,* 171–212.

Rau, C. A., Jr. (1979). Proceedings of the ARPA/AFML. In *Review of Progress in Quantitative NDE* (pp. 150–161). Thousand Oaks, CA: Rockwell International Science Center.

Schwartz, J. S., Dans, P. E., & Kinosian, B. P. (1988). Human immunodeficiency virus test evaluation, performance, and use: Proposals to make good tests better. *Journal of the American Medical Association, 259,* 2574–2579.

Speer, J. R. (1989). Detection of plastic explosives. *Science, 243,* 1651.

Spielberg, F., Ryder, R. W., Harris, J., Heyward, W. L., Kabeya, C. M., Kifuani, N. K., Bender, T. R., & Quinn, T. C. (1989, March 18). Field testing and comparative evaluation of rapid visually read screening assays for antibody to human immunodeficiency virus. *The Lancet, 1*(8638), 580–584.

Sweets, J. A. (1973). The relative operating characteristic in psychology. *Science, 182,* 990–1000. (Chapter 1 in this volume.)

Swets, J. A. (1983). Assessment of NDT systems: Part I. The relationship of true and false detections, part II. Indices of performance. *Materials Evaluation, 41,* 1294–1303.

Swets, J. A. (1986). Form of empirical ROCs in discrimination and diagnostic tasks: Implications for theory and measurement of performance. *Psychological Bulletin, 99,* 181–198. (Chapter 2 in this volume.)

Swets, J. A. (1988). Measuring the accuracy of diagnostic systems. *Science, 240,* 1285–1293. (Chapter 4 in this volume.)

Swets, J. A., & Getty, D. J. (1991). *Developing methods for the establishment of sensitivity and threshold requirements for human-centered decision aids* (Report prepared for NASA, Contract No. NAS1-18788). Hampton, VA: Langley Research Center.

Swets, J. A., & Pickett, R. M. (1982). *Evaluation of diagnostic systems: Methods from signal detection theory.* San Diego, CA: Academic Press.

Swets, J. A., Tanner, W. P., & Birdsall, T. G. (1961). Decision processes in perception. *Psychological Review, 68,* 301–340.

Tanner, W. P., Jr., & Swets, J. A. (1954a). The human use of information: I. Signal detection for the case of the signal-known-exactly. *IRE Professional Group on Information Theory, PGIT-4,* 213–221.

Tanner, W. P., Jr., & Swets, J. A. (1954b). A decision-making theory of visual detection. *Psychological Review, 61,* 401–409.

Van Meter, D., & Middleton, D. (1954). Modern statistical approaches to reception in communication theory. *IRE Professional Group on Information Theory, PGIT-4,* 119–141.

Wald, A. (1950). *Statistical decision functions.* New York: Wiley.

Weinstein, M. C., Fineberg, H. V., Elstein, A. S., Frazier, H. S., Neuhauser, D., Neutra, R. R., & McNeil, B. J. (1980). *Clinical decision analysis.* Philadelphia: W. B. Saunders.

Weiss, R., & Thier, S. C. (1988). HIV testing is the answer—What's the question? *The New England Journal of Medicine, 319,* 1010–1012.

III APPLICATIONS IN VARIOUS DIAGNOSTIC FIELDS

Seven chapters here describe applications of ROC methods to evaluate the performance of diagnostic techniques in several different fields. The first three treat imaging techniques, such as X-ray and computed tomography ("CAT scans"), in clinical medicine. The third of these shows how discrimination acuity or diagnostic accuracy can be enhanced as well as evaluated.

The first medical chapter reviews some fifteen of the earliest evaluations to use ROC methods and then considers some methodological issues that arose in medicine as well as previously in the psychology laboratory. These issues include the measurement of performance from a single ROC point; going beyond lesion detection to lesion localization and/or classification of lesion type; and the use of two or more imaging techniques in combination to make a single decision. The second medical chapter describes a large-scale evaluation of computed tomography as a then new imaging modality thought likely to be a preferable alternative to the then current modality (radionuclide imaging) for the diagnosis of brain lesions.

The third medical chapter focuses on enhancing diagnostic accuracy and on the implications of enhancement for evaluation. The example used is X-ray mammography in the diagnosis of breast cancer. Various psychological and statistical procedures are used to determine which perceptual features of a mammogram are diagnostically relevant and the extent to which they are relevant (predictive of cancer). A checklist of features is then prepared for

143

the radiologist to use as he or she reads a mammogram. A scale is associated with each feature so a quantitative assessment is made. These scale values for a given case are supplied to a computer program that merges them, with individual weights based on each feature's predictive power, and reports back to the radiologist the best estimate of the probability of cancer. The combined effect of the "reading aid" (checklist with scales) and "decision aid" (computer merger of scale values) is appreciable. Either substantially more cancers are found—TPP is higher—or substantially fewer unnecessary biopsies are made—FPP is lower—or some of both kinds of enhancement may be achieved. Similar results showing large improvements are being observed in an on-going study of magnetic-resonance imaging for staging prostate cancer, where the question is whether a cancer has gone beyond the confines of the prostate gland and hence may be unoperable.

A second finding in this enhancement study is that the size of the enhancement effect depends substantially on the difficulty of diagnosis of the cases used in the study; the enhancement effect is larger as case difficulty increases. This finding is generalized to the suggestion that the comparison of any two alternative approaches to diagnosis, for example, two alternative imaging modalities for a particular organ and disease, may depend on how difficult a case set has been assembled for the test. Observed differences between two particular modalities can range from no difference in one study to a substantial difference in another, as a vagary of case-set assembly. Case-set selection may differ by design; if one wishes to represent all of the cases that undergo a particular diagnostic test, the case set will be easier than one including only cases that go on to a further, more definitive test. Analyzing subsets of cases differing in difficulty is suggested as a way of reducing such uncertainty in conclusions about diagnostic effectiveness.

Pursuing the relation of enhancement to evaluation, it seems clear that one should not make a final evaluation of a technique's potential by simply taking the technique as it comes. Rather, attempting first to enhance its accuracy gives it a fairer chance to meet requirements. A case in point is an (unpublished) evaluation by my colleagues and me of a non-invasive technique for diagnosing breast cancer called "diaphanography," in which light diffused through the breast is picked up by a video camera and processed by a computer into a displayed image. Experienced and motivated readers in a standard reading mode yielded an average $A_z = .61$, suggesting that no further consideration be given the technique. However, the same readers with the benefits of the reading and decision aids just mentioned (and described in Chapter 8) gave an $A_z = .83$. The latter figure approximates the accuracy of the long-established film mammography technique and leaves open the possibility of using diaphanography as an adjunct to mammography.

Three more chapters in this section describe applications of ROC analysis to diagnostic systems (tests or instruments) in diverse fields: information retrieval, aptitude testing, and survey research. Information-retrieval systems include conventional, manual library systems and various computer-based systems that scan documents electronically. In choosing among candidate systems, the library administrator wishes to measure purely a system's ability to segregate wanted or target documents from unwanted documents that are irrelevant to the need at hand for information. This measure needs to be independent of any subsequent user's decision criterion. Some users will desire a high yield of relevant documents, that is, a high TPP, at the expense of having to separate out of the total set of documents retrieved a large number that are irrelevant, that is, a high FPP; others will accept a lower TPP to keep FPP within smaller bounds. Users can adjust the decision criterion in different ways, including, for example, by specifying how many of a set of key words must appear in a document for it to be retrieved—the more keywords required, the stricter the criterion. One conclusion drawn from an empirical test of several systems and variants of them is that the retrieval problem is very difficult and that current variations in retrieval technique differ little in their ability to discriminate. A pervasive problem is that even a seemingly low FPP can be unacceptable in absolute terms when multiplied by the large number of irrelevant documents in most files or collections, even in collections fairly narrow in subject matter. Finding one relevant document among every dozen or so retrieved documents is not unusual.

The predictive validity of an aptitude test is usually measured by a (product-moment) correlation coefficient, suitable when both the event predicted (e.g., rank in class) and the test score vary over a wide range. The potential value of ROC methods may be considered when one wishes to predict a two-valued event, for example, pass-fail, or whether or not a student in a self-paced individualized-instruction course completes the course. A question of some current interest is how much the Scholastic Aptitude Test helps, beyond knowing rank in high-school class, in predicting the two-valued event of college graduation. The ROC measure A_z is compared empirically to the biserial correlation coefficient in Chapter 10.

Chapter 11 points up that survey interviews or questionnaires attempt often to discriminate between two factual alternatives. For example, a health interview survey may ask whether or not the respondent made a visit to a doctor in the past 6 months, or whether or not the respondent has a certain chronic illness. In this sense, a survey question is a diagnostic device. The designer may ask whether the question's wording tends to induce positive or negative responses, that is, induce a lenient or strict decision criterion. The survey respondent also has a discrimination and decision problem. Thus, a respondent may be uncertain as to whether the last visit to a doctor occurred within the past 6 months or whether an intermittent symptom qualifies as a chronic illness. And the respondent may have a bias toward or against a positive response; for example, a positive response may cause embarrassment or trigger a time-consuming series of follow-up questions. This chapter represents a preliminary, conceptual attempt to relate ROC ideas to survey design.

The final chapter is a conceptual and experimental analysis of automated diagnostic devices that detect dangerous conditions and then issue warnings to a system operator. For example, devices in the aircraft cockpit warn the pilot of potential collision, ground proximity, wind shear, and components of engine failure. As another example, various monitors of physiological conditions warn nurses of patient problems in critical-care settings. These devices have greater or less acuity in discriminating dangerous conditions from non-dangerous conditions and they have built into them a decision criterion that stipulates how strong the indication of danger must be in order to issue a warning. The pervasive problem in such settings is the occurrence of many false alarms. Many false alarms are issued because the devices' discrimination acuities are substantially less than perfect, a lenient decision criterion is set in order to avoid calamitous misses, and the prior probability of a dangerous condition is low. The problem is compounded because several devices are used in one setting and the decision criterion for each is set without regard to the others. As a consequence, the human operator or monitor tends to respond slowly, or not at all. Theoretical ROC analysis shows how the "positive predictive value" of a warning—the proportion of warnings that truly indicate danger—varies with discrimination acuity, the location of the decision criterion, and the prior probability. The bracing result of this analysis is that warning devices have to be near perfect, when the prior probability of danger is a very low—to escape a very low positive predictive value, say, crying wolf unnecessarily 19 out of 20 times—even at strict decision criteria. The same considerations apply to screening tests in clinical medicine, for example, for breast cancer, HIV, or glaucoma. Here again the probability of the condition in question can be low. In this case, however, the tendency is to respond positively very frequently and thus to trigger often a series of unnecessary further tests or therapies. The experimental portion of this chapter shows that the latency of a human operator's response to a warning varies systematically with the warning's positive predictive value. A follow-on experiment (not included here) shows a reliable impact on response latency of variation in the benefits of responding quickly and the costs of responding slowly.

6 Medical Imaging Techniques: A Review

Fundamental to the evaluation of a medical imaging technique is a reliable and valid measure of diagnostic accuracy. Ideally, an assessment of accuracy will be expressed in such terms that it can also serve as the basis for a valid description of that technique's utility, in terms of cost and benefit.

The relative operating characteristic (ROC) is the single analytic technique known to provide both the desired accuracy index and the desired basis for a description of utility. The reliability and validity of the ROC's accuracy index stem from the fact that this index reflects only the inherent discrimination factors of the diagnostic alternatives for an image reader. This index, specifically, is unaffected by decision factors, ie, by a reader's tendencies to favor or disfavor one diagnostic alternative, tendencies which will vary both between readers and within a reader. Further, the ROC analysis yields the particular balance or trade off among all image-based decision probabilities—including the probabilities of various correct and incorrect decisions—that will result from any particular decision factors that the investigator might want to specify. Therefore, in evaluating the utility of an imaging technique, by pursuing a decision flow diagram from the imaging stage to outcomes at some further stage, the investigator can begin with appropriate image based decision probabilities. The appropriate trade off among image-based decision probabilities will be the one that reflects the values, costs, and other event probabilities, that the investigator believes are inherent in that diagnostic/therapeutic technique, rather than the trade off that happens to be yielded by any test reader.

This report focuses on the use of the ROC in assessing technique accuracy. I begin with a brief review of the basic concepts of ROC analysis, emphasizing contrasts between the ROC's accuracy index and certain other indices commonly used in medical evaluation.

The main purpose of this report is to review several theoretic and methodologic questions that have arisen concerning the medical applications of ROC. Some of these questions are basic to any application of ROC techniques, such as those dealing with alternative ways to generate empirical ROC data, or with alternative forms of the ROC accuracy index. In this regard, the paper makes some specific recommendations, which are derived from extensive experience with ROC in other fields. Other questions arising in the medical setting deal with extending ROC analysis from simple detection judgments to more complex judgments, for example, to assessment of the accuracy of localization of abnormality, or to the accuracy of differential diagnosis. Also of interest are questions concerning the extension of ROC analysis into assessing the detection accuracy of a combination of imaging techniques, or a combination of readers. Several of these questions arose when ROC was applied to electronic signal detection and experimental psychology. I believe that some of these questions may be answered to some extent by work done in those fields. Answers to some long-standing questions, on the other hand, have been advanced by recent developments in the medical field, and these developments are identified. This review of issues of theory and method draws explicitly on a dozen or so of the studies that have dealt with ROC in medicine. The remaining pertinent ROC studies that I know of are briefly characterized in the concluding section of this paper, in order to indicate the range of possible applications.

A recent paper by Charles Metz[28] is complementary to this one in two ways: 1) it presents a tutorial introduction to ROC concepts for physicians; and 2) it indicates in broad outline how ROC analysis can be extended to provide a description of the medical and social utility of an imaging technique. I have therefore not attempted to cover these subjects in this report.

BACKGROUND: PSYCHOPHYSICS, SIGNAL DETECTION, AND STATISTICAL DECISION THEORY

A thorough evaluation of an imaging modality is based on an image-reading test, a form of psychophysical test that has been practiced since the inception of experimental psychology. Originally, the discipline of psychophysics sought to determine the relationship between properties of a physical stimulus and attributes of psychological (sensory or perceptual) experience, the latter as indicated by the observer's verbal report. Modern psychophysics seeks to determine the relationship between the two observables, ie, the stimulus and a report about the stimulus.[14,18] A substantial part of psychophysics is devoted to the measurement of discrimination—our present interest. In tests of discrimination the observer usually reports that some specified stimulus is or is not present, that the present stimulus is in one location or another, or that the present stimulus is of type A or type B.

The traditional concept of a physiologically determined sensory threshold left little room for non-sensory determinants of the observer's discriminative report. But the minority view, expressed throughout the history of psychophysics, was that judgmental or decision variables are necessarily involved in reports of sensory experience, particularly if the report concerns the stimulus that produced the experience rather than the experience per se. Thus, an observer's confidence threshold, or *decision criterion*, for reporting a specified stimulus as present, or for reporting a present stimulus as of a particular type, may range from lenient to strict.

Renewed interest in treating the influence of the decision criterion led to the introduction of ROC analysis into psychophysics in the early 1950's.[55] The ROC analysis, with origins in statistical decision theory,[58] conceives of the criterion as determined by two main variables: 1) the probability that the stimulus in question is present; and 2) the values and costs associated with correct and incorrect decisions. These variables relate, respectively, to the psychological processes of expectancy and motivation. The ROC isolates the effects of these variables and represents them in a separate index of the decision criterion, so that the ROC's principal index of discrimination capacity or inherent accuracy is independent of these variables. The ROC originated during the development of the theory of the detection of electromagnetic signals, historically set between the development of statistical and psychological theory.[36]

The psychophysical test supplies an objective assessment of the empirical relationship between medical images and subsequent diagnoses, or between changes in the parameters of a given imaging modality and changes in reader report. An objective test is necessary because impressions or ratings of image quality vary widely among viewers, and may have little to do with diagnostic accuracy. The psychophysical relationship must be established empirically in each instance because existing physical and psychological characterizations are inadequate to support a predictive calculation. The medical need for a bias-free, ROC-based measure of accuracy was noted in the mid-1960's.[23]

The assessment of accuracy necessitates the reader's reports being scored as correct or incorrect. This entails establishing a "truth" against which a report is scored, and this is the principal respect in which medical application of the ROC introduces problems not usually faced in psychophysics. Ordinarily, the "truth" is approximated for the patients imaged on the basis of other medical evidence, eg, histology. A far weaker form of "truth" resorted to occasionally is the consensus of expert readers.

ROC ANALYSIS

With one exception (to be discussed later), the practical application of ROC analysis is limited to two stimulus alternatives and the two corresponding response alternatives. The two alternatives of the *detection* problem are "specified stimulus present" and "specified stimulus absent," or, in the language of detection theory, "signal-plus-noise present" and "noise-alone present." The detection-theory concept is that "noise," ie, random interference both in the stimulus and the observer, may mask the presence of a weak "signal." Of course, as also recognized explicitly in detection theory, the signal may also be difficult to detect because it is not well specified. In the medical context, it is convenient to speak of the two detection alternatives as abnormal and normal, with the understanding that the class of lesions constituting abnormality will be specified for the diagnostic setting at hand.

The two alternatives of the *localization* problem are two defined areas, either of which may contain the specified signal. The two alternatives in *classification* may be any two signals of interest, eg, benign tumor and malignant tumor, or neoplastic lesion and non-neoplastic lesion. For expository purposes, consider the first situation, ie, detection, in which any one of a specified set of abnormalities is contrasted with the normal.

The two-alternative situation is completely described by a two-by-two contingency table as shown in Table 1. Lower case letters indicate the stimulus alternatives abnormal and normal as columns; upper case letters indicate the corresponding response alternatives Abnormal and Normal as rows. The entries shown are the probabilities of response, conditional on the stimulus: true-positives and true-negatives on one diagonal, and false-positives and false-negatives on the other. We shall use both sets of notation here, namely: $P(A \mid a)$, $P(A \mid n)$, $P(N \mid a)$, and $P(N \mid n)$ to represent the four possible conditional probabilities in a precise manner; and the symbols $P(TP)$, $P(FP)$, $P(FN)$ and $P(TN)$ to represent the same probabilities in an easier manner.

Note that because each column adds to unity, there are two rather than four independent entries in the matrix. By the same token, two quantities rather than one must be specified to give a complete representation of diagnostic behavior.

Indeed, the need for an ROC analysis initially arises with the recognition that the single quantity often used to index accuracy, namely, the conditional proba-

TABLE 1
Two-by-Two Contingency Table (See Text)

Response Alternative	Stimulus Alternative	
	a	*n*
A	$P(A \mid a)$ true-positive	$P(A \mid n)$ false-positive
N	$P(N \mid a)$ false-negative	$P(N \mid n)$ true-negative
	1.00	1.00

bility of a true-positive response, $P(A \mid a)$, is not only incomplete, but is likely to be biased by extraneous factors. Reader 1 will yield a higher $P(A \mid a)$ than Reader 2, even if they have the same capacity to discriminate, if Reader 1 has a more lenient criterion for deciding that stimulus "a" exists. Not all readers have the same impressions of the probabilities, values, and costs that influence the particular decision criterion. And a single reader's $P(A \mid a)$ can vary from day to day and from one setting to another, because of inadvertent and possibly unnoticed changes in the criterion employed.

A better index than just $P(A \mid a)$, a quantity often referred to as sensitivity in medical statistics, may be achieved by combining it with another quantity, namely, $P(N \mid a)$, termed specificity. The sum of the two quantities [each multiplied by the appropriate prior probability, $P(a)$ and $P(n)$] yields an over-all percent correct that is commonly taken as defining accuracy in medical statistics, engendering a confusion with the present more general use of that term.

It is a good idea to consider a second quantity from the stimulus-response matrix, particularly a quantity independent of $P(A \mid a)$, ie, one from the other column, because that second quantity will reflect changes in $P(A \mid a)$ due to changes in the criterion alone. For a constant capacity to discriminate, increases in $P(A \mid a)$ will be accompanied, for example, by decreases in $P(N \mid n)$. However, obtaining an over-all percentage correct, by adding the two quantities, obscures the effect of criterion variation: the sum of $P(a)P(A \mid a)$ and $P(n)P(N \mid n)$ can be shown to vary by as much as 40% with changes in the criterion alone.[13]

ROC analysis considers a second, independent quantity along with $P(A \mid a)$, but it is the complement of specificity, ie, $P(A \mid n)$, which is the false-positive probability. But the use of $P(A \mid n)$ rather than $P(N \mid n)$ is less significant than the fact that the ROC shows the covariation between its two quantities as the criterion changes. It is clear that, for constant capacity to discriminate, increases in $P(A \mid a)$ will be accompanied by increases in $P(A \mid n)$, but the ROC shows precisely the magnitudes of the increases.

The solid curve in Fig. 1 is an ROC curve representing a given capacity to discriminate, or a given accuracy of diagnosis. In our present context, that particular capacity to discriminate is determined jointly by the quality of the diagnostic information in the image and the skill of the reader(s) whose responses yielded that curve. The reader can choose to operate at a lenient decision criterion, say, at Point A, in which case both $P(A \mid a)$ and $P(A \mid n)$ will be relatively high; or at a strict decision criterion, say, at Point C, in which case both probabilities will be relatively low; or at a medium decision criterion (Point B). A high prior probability of alternative "a" should lead to a relatively lenient criterion for deciding that "a" is present, and the converse is also true. Also, a high cost of a false-positive response, or a high value of a true-negative response, should lead to a relatively stringent decision criterion for deciding that "a" is present; and a high cost of a false-negative response, or a high value of a true-positive response, should lead to a relatively lenient criterion for deciding that "a" is present.

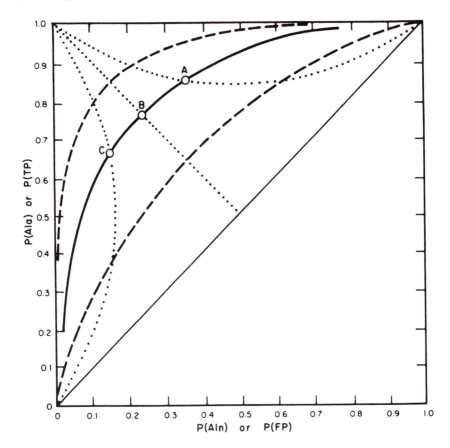

FIG. 1.   Three ROC curves (one solid, two dashed) representing different levels of discrimination. Points A, B, and C on solid curve represent
relatively lenient, medium, and strict decision criteria, respectively.
Each dotted curve represents contour of constant ROC slope.

The two dashed curves in Fig. 1 show other degrees of discrimination. Clearly, the lower curve, near the diagonal that reflects no better performance than
may be obtained by chance, exhibits low discrimination, while the higher curve,
approaching the perfection at the upper left hand corner, exhibits high discrimination.

So, it is desirable in measuring accuracy to obtain a good estimate of the
entire ROC curve. One may then extract some quantity from the curve that
reflects well the degree of discrimination or accuracy represented by the entire
curve. That quantity, presumably, will be unaffected by the placement of the
decision criterion in any instance, ie, by the choice of any particular operating
point on the curve.

We may also desire an index of the decision criterion that is independent of accuracy. It may be seen that the slope of the ROC at any point might adequately reflect the criterion yielding that point. The dotted lines in Fig. 1 represent contours of constant ROC slope. For example, the contours for ROC slopes 0.5, 1.0, and 2.0 intersect Points A, B, and C respectively.

The empirical ROC may be generated in two basic ways. With the so-called binary or "yes-no" method, the investigator induces different criteria in different test sessions, eg, by presenting the stimulus alternatives with different probabilities from one session to another, or simply by asking the test reader to vary his criterion in a specified way across sessions. In this way, a single point on the ROC is obtained from any given session, or from any given group of sessions, conducted under a constant set of stimulus probabilities or instructions. Then the number of successive conditions is chosen to generate the desired number of ROC points. Ordinarily, four or five points are adequate to define the curve reliably. Typically, each point is based on a few hundred trials.

A better way to obtain an empirical ROC curve is to ask the reader to give a rating, in one of five or six categories, of his confidence that the case before him is of the class of cases in question, eg, abnormal. The rating categories are usually presented with verbal labels, eg, almost definitely abnormal, probably abnormal, possibly abnormal, probably normal, almost definitely normal. In effect, then, the reader holds several decision criteria simultaneously, and several points along the ROC are obtained from one set of trials under a constant set of conditions and instructions. This "rating" method yields a more reliable definition of the ROC for a given number of trials.[18] A few hundred trials are ordinarily adequate to define the entire curve.

Figure 1 gives an indication of the inadequacy of using $P(A \mid a)$ alone as an index of system performance. Even if we are willing to assume a relatively stable decision criterion, eg, one yielding a $P(A \mid n)$ varying from 0.05 to 0.15, the values of $P(A \mid a)$ for the three curves of Fig. 1 will vary, respectively, from 0.20 to 0.38, from 0.43 to 0.67, and from 0.66 to 0.84. This variability in $P(A \mid a)$ is in addition to the inherent statistical variability of that quantity, and is introduced by criterion variation alone. It is quite possible that variability of that magnitude is enough to obscure true differences between imaging systems that are large enough to be of practical significance. Such variability may also produce apparent differences that do not exist.

Let us acknowledge in passing that medical assessments often make use of "backward-going," or inverse probabilities, as opposed to the "forward-going," or direct probabilities of the ROC. That is, one calculates the probability of a stimulus conditional on the response, rather than the other way around as described above. Then the quantity of primary interest is often $P(a \mid A)$—the probability of an abnormality existing given that the decision-making system (imaging modality plus reader) reported an abnormality.

The use of inverse, or posterior, probabilities to analyze and index accuracy has several drawbacks that can only be listed here; presenting support for the stated drawbacks would necessitate extensive digression. First, the quantity P(a | A) varies considerably with any changes in the decision criterion, and so is inadequate alone. Specifically, it can be shown to vary from the value of the prior probability of abnormality at a lenient decision criterion, which may be very low, to 1.0 at a strict decision criterion. Second, taking the ratio of P(a | A)-to-P(a | N)—the "relative risk" or "incidence ratio"—provides a number that will vary with variations in the prior probabilities, and is independent of the decision criterion only for empirical ROC curves of a particular form that rarely occurs. Third, using P(a | A) as one element of a kind of ROC—a response analysis characteristic (RAC) in which P(a | A) is plotted against P(a | N)[48]—doesn't help much. RAC curves are of various forms not easily described; their ranges depend on the prior probability; and the curve associated with a given prior probability *crosses* all curves associated with higher prior probabilities. So, although the inverse probability P(a | A) is of obvious practical interest, we must look to the forward-going probabilities of the ROC for analytic assistance.

The ROC, in sum, yields a pure measure of diagnostic accuracy, independent of the decision criterion. This measure is thus more reliable and valid than others available, and is fundamental to an evaluation of diagnostic technique. It characterizes the inherent accuracy of the technique as employed by a given reader or set of readers. The ROC also supplies a separate measure of the decision criterion, but this measure is less important in the evaluation of a technique; this measure comes into use when changing the decision criterion is deemed desirable. The specific measures or indices available are discussed next.

ROC Indices of Diagnostic Performance

In psychophysics, there are several alternative ways of deriving an index of accuracy, and several alternative ways of deriving an index of the decision criterion, from an empirical ROC curve. These alternative indices will be discussed and the ones that have come to be preferred will be indicated.

The several alternative accuracy indices have been devised because empirical ROCs vary somewhat in form, and measurement theorists have attempted to find the index best suited to the type of variation observed. Variations in ROC form are most easily seen on a different set of scales than those presented in Fig. 1. Specifically, ROCs are usually plotted on the probability scales shown on the left and bottom axes of Fig. 2. These scales are transformed in such a way that the normal-deviate values (or standard scores, $z = x/\sigma$) that correspond to the probabilities are spaced linearly, as shown on the right and top axes of Fig. 2. On these scales, ROCs of the particular form shown in Fig. 1 become straight lines, with a slope of unity. The line in Fig. 2 labeled s = 1.0 is the same ROC curve as the highest curve of Fig. 1.

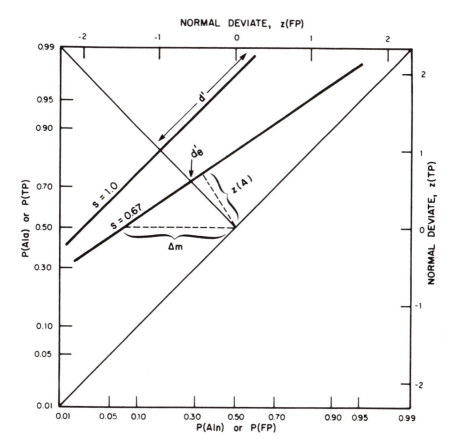

FIG. 2.   Two illustrative ROC curves on linear normal-deviate scales.
The top curve has unit slope, and the index d′ is suitable. The bottom
curve has non-unit slope, and the alternative indices d'_e, z(A), and
D(Δm,s) are more or less suitable for different purposes; a transformation of z(A) is usually preferred (see text).

In general, empirical ROCs are very close to straight lines on the scales of
Fig. 2,[11,18,52] a fact that facilitates fitting a curve to a set of data points, but the
slopes of the linear ROCs vary, usually between s = 0.50 and s = 1.50. A slope
of less than 1.0 on the scales in Fig. 2 corresponds to a curve on the scales in Fig.
1 that rises more steeply from the origin, and then flattens out more as it turns
toward the upper right corner. A slope greater than 1.0 is rarer, and rises less
steeply from the origin on the scales in Fig. 1 (see chapter 2.).

The ROC accuracy index d′ is the first-proposed and most familiar. It applies
only to ROC curves having unit slopes.[18] It is equal to the normal-deviate value

along the ordinate, z(TP), minus the normal-deviate value along the abscissa, z(FP), at any point along the ROC line. The line shown in Fig. 2 with unit slope (s = 1.0) indicates that d' = 2.0. The value of d' varies from zero at the chance diagonal of the ROC graph to about 4.0 at near perfect performance.

An alternative to d' that is suitable for ROCs of any slope has been termed d'_e. This quantity, by definition, is measured at the negative diagonal of the ROC graph, where it is equal to d'.[18] In Fig. 2, the value of d'_e indicated is 1.2, ie, $0.6 - (-0.6)$.

Another index suited to varying slopes is the quantity termed D_{YN} in psychologic literature,[40] and termed S in the literature on information retrieval.[9] Because the subscript YN connotes an unintended limitation of this measure—to ROCs based on "yes-no" responses, as compared to "rating-scale" responses—and because the symbol S is often used for variance estimates, we use here still another notation previously introduced, namely z(A).[41] The index z(A) is equal to the perpendicular distance of the ROC curve, in units of the normal deviate, from the origin of the ROC graph, ie, from z(FP) = z(TP) = 0, as indicated in Fig. 2. The quantity $\sqrt{2}$ z(A), is equal to d' and d'_e for ROCs of unit slope.

A third possible measure devised for non-unit slopes is called Δm. This quantity is equal to the (absolute) x-axis normal-deviate value of the intercept of the ROC at the y-axis normal-deviate value of zero; in Fig. 2, Δm = 1.5. Ordinarily, Δm is reported along with the ROC slope s, in the two-parameter index termed D(Δm,s). The principal virtue of the two-parameter index, of course, is that it specifies the entire ROC curve,[18] and therefore is informative when the curve itself is not portrayed. The difficulty with using D(Δm,s) as the only index is that concurrent variation of its two components precludes a simple ordering of different performances. This pair of quantities, indeed, is better viewed as a data summary than as a performance index.

The index that has recently emerged as the best of the single-parameter indices is the area underneath the ROC, ie, the proportion of the area of the unit ROC square (plotted with linear probability scales as in Fig. 1) that falls beneath the ROC. This area may be computed by connecting empirical ROC points on the scales in Fig. 1 by straight lines, and then applying the standard trapezoidal rule for calculating the amount of area contained; this index is termed P(A).[18] However, given the fact that ROCs are fitted well by straight lines on the scales in Fig. 2, one can view the ROC in terms of normal probability distributions, and use an alternative area index called A_z. A_z is better than P(A) because it is less sensitive to the location or spread of points that define an empirical ROC curve. Both A_z and P(A) vary from 0.50 at the positive, or chance, diagonal of the ROC graph, to 1.0 for an ROC representing perfect accuracy (ie, an ROC following the left and top boundaries of the ROC graph).

The measure A_z is easily calculated because its normal deviate is given by the quantity defined above as z(A).[39,41] Specifically, one can calculate z(A) = $s(\Delta m)/(1 + s^2)^{1/2}$, where s and Δm are also as defined above. Thus, one can determine Δm and s by graphical means from a plot in the form of Fig. 2, use them to calculate z(A), and go to a normal table to find A_z, the area under the normal distribution up to the normal-deviate value equal to z(A).

Alternatively, and usually preferably, one can use a computer program to obtain an objective fit to empirical ROC points, and also a maximum-likelihood estimate of A_z. One program also provides an estimate of the sampling variance of A_z so that confidence intervals may be established, as well as the statistical significance of the difference between any two values of A_z. (This program also gives estimates of Δm, s, d'_e, and $\sqrt{2}$ z(A). The quantity $\sqrt{2}$ z(A) which is elsewhere termed d_a,[41] is an essentially equivalent alternative to A_z that gives the d'-like numbers ranging from 0 to about 4, that have achieved some familiarity.)

Turning to indices of the decision criterion, the first described and best known is β, which equals the slope of a line tangent to the ROC at the data point yielded by that decision criterion[18]; contours for three values of β are illustrated in Fig. 1. Little attention was paid to alternatives to β until recently,[47] when enough proposals were made to justify a full review.[12]

One of the alternative indices of the decision criterion is called Z_k, which is the value of z(FP) corresponding to the ROC data point yielded by the decision criterion of interest, where z(FP) is as shown in Fig. 2. An available computer program supplies a maximum-likelihood estimate of Z_k and an estimate of its sampling variance. (See the Appendix.)

The choice between β and Z_k is primarily a philosophic matter. A maximum-likelihood estimate of Z_k is a refined way of representing P(FP), and is therefore appropriate when the reader is viewed as choosing the decision criteria that yields a given (maximum) value of P(FP). The index β, on the other hand, may be related to the prior probabilities of normality and of the abnormality in question, and to the values and costs associated with the four possible response probabilities. Specifically,

$$\beta = \frac{P(n)}{P(a)} \cdot \frac{V_{TN} + C_{FP}}{V_{TP} + C_{FN}} \tag{1}$$

where V and C represent the values and costs associated with the decision outcomes denoted by their subscripts. Thus, β is appropriate when the reader is viewed as choosing the decision criterion that maximizes the "expected value" of his decisions. The expected value is a maximum when P(TP) − βP(FP) is a maximum.[18] But in choosing between β and Z_k, one must decide whether a new technique yielding a greater accuracy will induce a reader to decrease the probabilities of FP and FN errors in a manner reflecting their relative costs; or, instead, to decrease only P(FN) while maintaining the same P(FP).

Measures of Accuracy Based on One Point in the ROC Space

The inadvisability of estimating the index d' from a single point in the ROC space was recognized early in the medical application of the ROC.[16,29] Given the usual case of a linear ROC of less than unit slope—and the slopes seem to be shallower for vision than for other sensory modalities[18]—the estimate of d' based on one point will be lower as that point is more to the right. Thus, in comparing two points, the value of d' associated with P_1 may be higher than the value of d' for P_2, even though P_1 may be on a curve consistently lower than the curve on which P_2 falls.

The same investigators later suggested that a reasonably good estimate of accuracy could be obtained from a single point if accuracy were indexed by the amount of information (in bits) obtained from each observation.[30] The information measure, however, implies a definite model of the relationship between accuracy and criterion change, and the characterizing features of the model don't serve particularly to recommend it. Specifically, isoinformation curves (on probability coordinates) are concave toward the upper left corner; their slope is generally less than unity for prior probabilities of signal greater than 0.5, and their slope is generally greater than unity for prior probabilities of signal less than 0.5.[30] Considering a prior probability of 0.5, the concavity is pronounced enough so that data points lying along an ROC of unit slope could vary considerably in information transmitted for constant accuracy. Maximizing transmitted information was earlier considered among the various decision rules an observer of fixed accuracy might choose to follow in order to determine the best decision criterion.[53]

Probably the best prescription for comparing two points in the ROC space was reported previously.[35] Very limited assumptions suffice to establish the regions of superiority and inferiority relative to a given point; the region of ambiguity, where no conclusion can be reached without more theory or data, is not that small, but perhaps it is small enough to permit some useful comparisons.

I believe it is best to obtain at least four or five points on an ROC for each test condition. Usually, a rating response that produces that many points can be obtained without much more time and difficulty than a yes-no (or other binary) response, and entails an incremental expense that is well compensated for by the considerable addition to the certainty of interpretation.

Localization

Occasionally, an observer correctly detects a signal, but then locates it incorrectly. This is an inherent part of the detection process, just as are noise-induced false-positive responses. Indeed, modern detection theory provides the basis for predicting the probability of correct localization from the yes-no (or rating) detection probabilities.

The earliest experiments in psychophysics conducted in the framework of modern detection theory established the predictability of discrimination capacity across yes-no, rating, and "forced-choice" procedures.[46,53,55] In the forced-choice procedure, the observer must locate a definite signal in time or space; this procedure might better have been termed "forced-location" since the yes-no and rating procedures also force a choice.[44]

Explicit concern for localization in psychophysical detection theory, other than as a test for the internal consistency of the theory, or other than as a psychophysical method relatively free of response bias, was first evidenced in audition, for the case of temporal localization.[20] The investigators showed the relationship between the percentage of correct responses and d' in a task involving both detection and localization; they provided curves and tables for various numbers of possible locations,[21] and reported data to support the predicted relationship.[19]

Localization is of considerable interest in the medical application, and the next advance was made in that context.[43] A form of ROC called the LROC was predicted from the yes-no or rating ROC and the number of possible locations of the LROC. The ordinate is the proportion of responses both correctly detected and localized, and the abscissa, as usual, is the proportion of false detections. Visual data from five observers showed very close fits to the theoretical curve.

This last result indicates that the detection response alone may be adequate in an evaluation test, even when the intent is to generalize the results to include localization. On the other hand, if the localization response is obtained, it can be treated in terms of the same theory.

A recent study of thermography as a screening tool for the early detection of breast cancer emphasizes the need to treat localization explicitly whenever it is involved.[33] The article showed some ROC data that were consistently below the 45° diagonal representing chance or guessing in the usual binary-choice ROC. The investigators concluded that thermography in the context studied is a "non-test." (They did not point out that an ROC of the usual binary-choice sort, which lies reliably below the diagonal, represents as good a level of discrimination as its mirror image about and above the diagonal: the mirror-image ROC can be obtained simply by reversing the names of the two responses.) The developers of LROC subsequently pointed out that a response in this thermography study had been scored as a true positive only if the correct breast were called positive, and so, in effect, the LROC had been plotted and presented as the ROC.[42] The LROC, of course, can legitimately be found below the 45° diagonal, inasmuch as the baseline (or chance) performance for correct detection-plus-localization is below that diagonal.

In another recent study concerning localization, it was shown that, after reading chest films in the usual manner, re-reading them with attention called to film regions containing frequently omitted findings (focused search) led to movement along the same ROC, rather than a shift to a higher ROC.[45] Thus, reduced omissions in focused search resulted from a more lenient decision criterion for a positive response, rather than from an enhanced ability to detect abnormalities.

Classification

The third general consideration in image interpretation, along with detection and localization, is the specification of lesion type. This process is termed classifica-

tion (or recognition or identification) in psychophysics, and in that context attempts to deal with recognition have much in common with approaches to localization. Recognizing which of two signals is present, like two-alternative
localization, is viewed as essentially the same process as detecting a specified
signal in noise.[54] Two medical studies have used a two-alternative *recognition*
ROC. One study showed the discrimination between segmented and band neu-
trophils in peripheral blood classification,[6] and the other showed the discrimination between malignant and benign breast lesions by both computer and expert
radiologist.[1]

Of course, both localization and recognition usually involve more than two
alternatives. Three-alternative ROC theory has been applied in experiments involving reporting signal 1, signal 2, or no signal, and in making a forced choice
among three temporal locations. With variation in the prior probabilities of the
three alternatives and in the values and costs associated with the various correct
and incorrect responses, the theory predicted the empirical response-frequency
tables, and the actual payoffs, to within a few percent. This work indicated,
however, the impracticality of treating three alternatives in a very general fashion, that is, with variation in all prior probabilities and all values and costs.[49]

It may be useful, however, to aspire to something less than a completely
general treatment of the classification of multiple alternatives, and to extend the
application of the LROC (discussed in the preceding section) from localization to
identification or classification of any sort, including the classification of lesion
type, or differential diagnosis. Preliminary experiments with non-medical images
(sound spectrograms) indicate that the predicted LROC, or what is now termed
the joint ROC, provides a good fit to classification data when the stimuli are
apparently independent (orthogonal) as assumed in the prediction, and overesti-
mates the classification data, as we might expect, when the stimuli are clearly
dependent.[50,51]

Practically speaking, one may need simply to obtain a criterion-free index of
classification accuracy, and do without a theoretical relationship between classification accuracy and detection accuracy. The joint ROC, indexed by the area
beneath it, was found useful in a recent study comparing CT and radionuclide
scanning in the diagnosis of intracranial lesions.[52]

Multiple Observations

The general question of increased accuracy through basing a decision on a
combination of observations over time, space, or observers, arises immediately
upon considering the accuracy associated with alternative imaging techniques.
One aspect of the question concerns the usefulness of combining studies sequen-
tially through a screening study and a more definitive follow-up study.[31]

Two general models for the combination of observations have been discussed elsewhere.[18] In one model, the probability information in the individual observations (eg, as made by different readers, or with different imaging modalities) is integrated across the observations (across readers or modalities), and the total weight of evidence determines the over-all decision. In the other model, a binary decision is made for each observation, and these decisions are combined into one over-all decision. Rules for combining decisions range from making a positive combined decision if any one of the individual decisions is positive (the disjunctive rule), to making a positive combined decision only if all the individual decisions are positive (the conjunctive rule). Other, more complex, rules are possible such as those involving interaction of the readers.

If the observations are statistically independent, then the integration model predicts that the accuracy index d' for the combined observations will increase as the square root of the sum of the squares of d' for the separate observations. If the independent observations are equally good (represent the same value of d') then this model reduces to the prediction that d' will increase as the square root of the number of observations. Thus, two independent observers would be predicted to yield a combined value of d' equal to $\sqrt{2}$ or 1.4 times the d' of each, for a 40% improvement. The combined-decision model, on the average, predicts about half of that increase; the conjunctive rule produces an ROC of slope greater than unity, whereas the disjunctive rule produces an ROC of slope less than unity.[18] It is important to note that the combined-decision model must be analyzed in terms of the ROC, taking both true- and false-positive decisions into account, to give a valid description of combined-decisions accuracy. The performance of combined decisions has been typically predicted and assessed by multiplying together the probabilities of false-negatives, and then subtracting the resulting probability from unity to yield the combined true-positive probability. This procedure, however, gives a highly inflated impression of the potential accuracy of combined decisions.[18]

The combined-decision model necessitates making explicit not only the rule or criterion that will be used to combine the decisions, but also the decision criteria that will be applied in making the individual decisions, eg, lenient individual criteria might be used with the conjunctive rule so that the conjunction will occur reasonably often, with the converse for the disjunctive rule. If the conjunctive rule is to be applied to two observations of different quality (different d') but equal cost, then it can be shown that a lenient criterion should be associated with the poorer observation, and a strict criterion with the better observation, for the best combined performance. However, if the observation quality is as divergent as $d' = 1$ and 3, then the combined performance is very little better than that based on the better observation, and the poorer one is unlikely to be worth its cost.[7]

It is by no means certain that combining decisions over numerous observers will yield an increase in accuracy, because several observers (readers) may be highly correlated, and thus act as essentially one observer. In the study of computed tomography and radionuclide brain scans, combining the decisions of three readers in a given modality resulted in little or no gain in accuracy.[52]

In combining diagnostic techniques, the more definitive technique will frequently cost more in terms of money, radiation exposure, or possible complications, and might be used only if the less definitive (screening) study yields a positive result. Here, an average-net-benefit approach will be useful. One application of that approach in the sequential case indicates the reverse of the result for simultaneous equal-cost observations: the optimal criterion for the less definitive study can be stricter than that for the more definitive study.[31] The study of computed tomography and radionuclide scanning, again, showed little or no gain in accuracy to result from a combination of the two techniques.[52]

In a recent nuclear medicine study, ROC was used to evaluate the detection of focal intracranial lesions both by camera scintigraphy and by the Anger multiplane tomographic scanner, singly and in combination.[57] Re-analysis of the results indicates that in this study the integration model predicts very closely the accuracy of the pair of modalities from their individual accuracies. Consider the true-positive probabilities for false-positive probabilities of 0.05, for four observers. In the order of: 1) camera only; 2) tomographic scan only; 3) both (actual); 4) both (predicted), the values are 0.35, 0.76, 0.83, and 0.85 for Observer 1; 0.26, 0.53, 0.67, and 0.64 for Observer 2; 0.35, 0.55, 0.64, and 0.70 for Observer 3; and 0.20, 0.45, 0.55, and 0.53 for Observer 4. The discrepancy between the average value obtained and the average value predicted is less than 0.01.

In another recent medical study, ROC was used to evaluate the usefulness of two types of radiographic examinations, singly and in combination, in the management of patients with hypertensive renovascular disease. The various proportions of true-positive and false-positive decisions that resulted from requiring that either test or both tests be positive were related to the cost of finding a diseased patient; to the cost of screening, definitively diagnosing, and performing corrective surgery on, the entire American population at risk; and to the life- and dollar-cost of each operative success.[26]

In another study from the same laboratory, certain historical, physical, laboratory, and radiographic findings were combined disjunctively to establish an ROC for patients with pleuritic chest pain. The true-positive proportions for pulmonary embolism increased as more findings were considered, as did the associated false-positive proportions. Considering these findings as the analog of a screening examination, the addition of a scintigraphic examination (which was read with a strict criterion) left the true-positive proportions as they were and substantially reduced the false-positive proportions.[25]

Another study of multiple observations concerned the combination of observations over space, time, and observers in the visual screening of cervical Papanicolaou smears. Empirically, the average d'_e of approximately 1.0 for one subarea of the smear, one test occasion, and one observer increased to about 2.0 for eight sub-areas; to about 2.25 for eight sub-areas and two test occasions; and to 3.50 for eight sub-areas and nine observers.[37]

ILLUSTRATIVE MEDICAL APPLICATIONS

We conclude with a brief list and synopsis of the ROC applications to image interpretation and processing not previously mentioned. These applications concern variations in observer performance as well as evaluation of various imaging techniques.

The data from the two classical studies of reader error in radiology, which were conducted around 1950,[15,59] have since been represented on ROC coordinates.[23] In one of these studies with two professional readers, the disjunctive and conjunctive rules of combination led to true-positive proportions varying from 0.57 to 0.79 while the associated false-positive proportions increased monotonically from 0.01 to 0.03. In the other study, again with professional readers, reading first with conservative and then with liberal criteria, true-positive proportions varied from 0.85 to 0.93 while the associated false-positive proportions increased monotonically from 0.05 to 0.12. Though the data from the two studies do not overlap in an ROC graph, they can be described well by the same value of $D(\Delta m,s)$, namely, (2.6, 1.13), and therefore the two studies reflect the same degree of accuracy as indexed by the ROC. As a methodologic point, we may note that the overall probability of a correct decision in these studies, often termed accuracy, as determined by sensitivity plus specificity, was 0.83 in one study and 0.91 in the other. An apparent difference of this magnitude might easily be regarded as statistically and practically significant.

Other studies of reader performance utilizing ROC compared the radiologic diagnosis of pneumoconiosis by experienced radiologists and physicians in general medicine,[32] and the interpretation of liver images by staff physicians and residents.[34] In another study, investigators examined the effects of training and experience on the reading of screen mammograms by radiologic assistants.[2,24]

To date, I know of eight additional studies that were undertaken to evaluate image-processing systems by means of the ROC. In the first, television was found to degrade detection of nodules on chest x-ray films, relative to the conventional viewbox.[22] Later studies showed a smaller difference between direct viewing and television viewing for chest radiographs,[5] and essentially no difference between the two media for a series of kidney, bladder, chest, and bone radiographs.[4] In another study, the same degree of accuracy was shown for both the direct viewing and viewing by Picturephone of radionuclide scans. This study also showed a good consistency of the yes-no and rating procedures.[3]

Results of a study of the lymphangiogram in patients with Hodgkin's disease showed ROC's obtained by a three-point rating scale to be quite similar for four senior radiologists.[27] In another study, use of a four-point rating scale in comparing tests of early pregnancy yielded the same accuracy index for days of amenorrhea, uterine size, and the ratio of the two; and a somewhat greater accuracy for ultrasound.[8] In a study of the quantitative characteristics of normal and suspicious cytologic smears, investigators used an equivalent of the ROC to evaluate screening performance for smears collected by vaginal aspiration, cervical swab, and cervical-scraping techniques,[56] and found substantial differences in accuracy between the three techniques.

The last study to be mentioned examined four radiographic screen-film systems, found good reproducibility from one observer to another, and showed average values of accuracy ranging from rather low ($d'_e = 1$) to very high ($d'_e > 4$). The investigators point out that a combination of film and screen yielding $d'_e \cong 2.2$ is about twice as fast as the combinations yielding values of d'_e of 1.3 and 3.1, resulting in about half the patient exposure,[17,30] and four times faster than the system yielding $d'_e > 4$.* In this setting, then, a good basis exists for trading accuracy and hazard.

It may be helpful to point out that the relatively well established imaging techniques used in studies of reader reliability and reader experience (mentioned early in this section), yielded values of Δm, d', or d'_e in the vicinity of 2.5. Those studies which focused on newer physical imaging techniques (with the exception of the last-mentioned studies, which covered nearly the full range of accuracy), yielded values of these accuracy indices near 1.5. One can refer to Fig. 2 to get an appreciation of the error rates associated with indices of 2.5 and 1.5. Taking points along the minor diagonal, where the probabilities of false-negatives and false-positives are equal, the probability of each error is about 0.10 for the index of 2.5 and in excess of 0.20 for the index of 1.5.

SUMMARY

An ROC measure of accuracy is appropriately used in evaluations of imaging techniques and image readers, because analysis and experiments have indicated that other available measures will confound the observer's decision bias with the variable of principal interest: either the diagnostic accuracy afforded by the imaging technique, or the perceptual capability of the observer. Several studies have demonstrated the practicality of the medical-data gathering procedure associated with the ROC. Other studies also suggest that the ROC's basis in decision theory helps to establish a link between the various decision parameters the observer can reflect and the medical and social utility of a diagnostic system.[28]

Several questions of theory and method involving the medical application of the ROC analysis have arisen earlier in the ROC's application to human sensory

---

*Personal communication.

systems, or in its application to other physical aids to those sensory systems (radar, sonar, information retrieval). To a degree, answers previously obtained supply guidelines for attaining the further answers that are desirable in the clinical setting. On the other hand, the medical application has served as a new source of motivation to extend ROC theory, thus stimulating important theoretical developments.

REFERENCES

1. Ackerman LV, Gose EE: Breast lesion classification by computer and xeroradiograph. Cancer 30: 1025, 1972.
2. Alcorn FS, O'Donnell E: The training of nonphysician personnel for use in a mammography program. Cancer 23: 879, 1969.
3. Anderson Jr TM, Mintzer RA, Hoffer PB, et al: Nuclear image transmission by picturephone. Invest Radiol 8: 244, 1973.
4. Andrus WS, Dreyfuss JR, Jaffer F, et al.: Interpretation of roentgenograms via interactive television. Radiology 116: 25, 1975.
5. Andrus WS, Hunter CH, Bird KT: Remote interpretation of chest roentgenograms. Chest 64: 463, 1975.
6. Bacus JW: The observer error in peripheral blood cell classification. Am J Clin Pathol 59: 223, 1973.
7. Birdsall TG: Unpublished memorandum, 1954.
8. Blackwell RJ, Shirley I, Farman DJ, et al.: Ultrasonic "B" scanning as a pregnancy test after less than six weeks amenorrhoea. Br J Obstet Gynecol 82: 108, 1975.
9. Brookes BC: The measures of information retrieval effectiveness proposed by Swets. J Documentation 24: 41, 1968.
10. Dorfman DD, Alf Jr E: Maximum likelihood estimation of parameters of signal-detection theory and determination of confidence intervals—rating method data. J Math Psych, 6: 487, 1969.
11. Dorfman DD, Beavers LL, Saslow C: Estimation of signal-detection theory parameters from rating-method data: a comparison of the method of scoring and direct search. Bull Psychon Soc 1: 207, 1973.
12. Dusoir AE: Treatments of bias in detection and recognition models: a review. Percept Psychophys 17: 167, 1975.
13. Egan JP, Clarke FR: Psychophysics and signal detection. In Sidowsky JB (ed): Experimental methods and Instrumentation in psychology. New York, McGraw-Hill, 1966, p 211.
14. Fechner GT: Elemente der Psychophysik. Leipzig, Breitkopf & Hartel, 1860. English translation of Volume 1. Howes DH, Boring EG (eds). New York, Holt, Rinehart & Winston, 1966. Reviewed by Swets JA, Science, 154: 1532, 1966.
15. Garland LH: Scientific evaluation of diagnostic procedures. Radiology 52: 309, 1949.
16. Goodenough DJ, Metz CE, Lusted LB: Caveat on use of the parameter d' for evaluation of observer performance. Radiology 106: 565, 1973.
17. Goodenough DJ, Rossmann K, Lusted LB: Radiographic applications of signal detection theory. Radiology 105: 199, 1972.
18. Green DM, Swets JA: Signal Detection Theory and Psychophysics. New York, John Wiley & Sons, 1966. Reprinted: Los Altos, CA, Peninsula Publishing Co., 1988.
19. Hershman RL, Levine JR, Lichtenstein M: Signal detection and localization by real observers. Percept Psychophys 6: 53, 1969.
20. Hershman RL, Lichtenstein M: Detection and localizability: an extension of the theory of signal detectability. J Acoust Soc Amer 42: 446, 1967.

21. Hershman RL, Small D: Tables of d' for detection and localization. Percept Psychophys 3: 321, 1968.
22. Kundel HL: Factors limiting roentgen interpretation—physical and psychologic. In Potchen EJ (ed): Current Concepts in Radiology. St. Louis, C V Mosby, 1972, p 1.
23. Lusted LB: Introduction to Medical Decision Making. Springfield, Charles C Thomas, 1968, p 103.
24. Lusted LB: Observer error, signal detectability and medical decision making. In Jacquez JA (ed): Computer Diagnosis and Diagnostic Methods. Springfield, Charles C Thomas, 1972, p 29.
25. McNeil BJ, Hessel SJ, Branch WT, et al: Measures of clinical efficacy, III. The value of the lung scan in the evaluation of young patients with pleuritic chest pain. J Nucl Med 17: 163, 1976.
26. McNeil, BJ, Varady, MS, Burrows BA, et al: Cost effectiveness in hypertensive renovascular disease. New Eng J Med 293: 216, 1975.
27. McNeil BJ, Weber E, Harrison D, et al: Use of signal detection theory in examining the results of a contrast examination: A case study using the lymphangiogram. Radiology 123: 613, 1977.
28. Metz CE: Basic principles of ROC analysis. Semin Nucl Med 8: 283, 1978.
29. Metz CE, Goodenough DJ: On failure to improve observer performance with scan smoothing: a rebuttal. J Nucl Med 14: 873, 1973.
30. Metz CF, Goodenough DJ, Rossmann K: Evaluation of receiver operating characteristic curve data in terms of information theory, with applications in radiography. Radiology 109: 297, 1973.
31. Metz CE, Starr SJ, Lusted LB, et al: Progress in evaluation of human observer visual detection performance using the ROC curve approach. In Raynaud C, Todd-Pokropek A (eds): Information Processing in Scintigraphy. Orsay, France, Commissariat à l'Énergie Atomique, Departement de Biologie, Service Hospitalier Frédéric Joliot, 1975, p 420.
32. Morgan RH, Donner MW, Gayler BW, et al: Decision processes and observer error in the diagnosis of pneumoconiosis by chest roentgenography. Am J Roentgenol 117: 757, 1973.
33. Moskowitz M, Milbrath J, Gartside P, et al: Lack of efficacy of thermography as a screening tool for minimal and stage 1 breast cancer. New Eng J Med 295: 249, 1976.
34. Nishiyama HJ, Lewis T, Ashare AB, et al: Interpretation of liver images: do training and experience make a difference? J Nucl Med 16: 11, 1975.
35. Norman DA: A comparison of data obtained with different false-alarm rates. Psychol Rev 71: 243, 1964.
36. Peterson WW, Birdsall TG, Fox WC: The theory of signal detectability. Trans IRE Prof Group on Inform Theory PGIT-4: 171, 1954.
37. Pickett RM: Toward more accurate and efficient visual screening of Pap smears: forced piecewise diagnosis. (Paper in preparation.)
38. Revesz G, Haas C: Television display of radiographic images with superimposed simulated lesions. Radiology 102: 197, 1972.
39. Robertson SE: The parametric description of retrieval tests. Part II: overall measures. J Doc 25: 93, 1969.
40. Schulman AI, Mitchell RR: Operating characteristics from yes-no and forced-choice procedures. J Acoust Soc Am 40: 473, 1966.
41. Simpson AJ, Fitter MJ: What is the best index of detectability? Psychol Bull 80: 481, 1973.
42. Starr SJ, Metz CE: ROC analysis of the efficacy of breast thermography when disease localization is required. Unpublished, 1976.
43. Starr SJ, Metz CE, Lusted LB, et al: Visual detection and localization of radiographic images. Radiology 116: 533, 1975.
44. Stevens SS: Is there a quantal threshold? In Rosenblith WA (ed): Sensory Communication. New York, Technology Press and Wiley, 1961, pp 806–813.
45. Swensson RG, Hessel SJ, Herman PG: Omissions in radiology: faulty search or stringent reporting criteria? Radiology 123: 563, 1977.
46. Swets JA: Indices of signal detectability obtained with various psychophysical procedures. J Acoust Soc Am 31: 511, 1959.

47. Swets JA: The relative operating characteristic in psychology. Science 182: 990, 1973. (Chapter 1 in this volume.)

48. Swets JA, Birdsall TG: Deferred decisions in human signal detection: a preliminary experiment. Percept Psychophys 2: 15, 1967.

49. Swets JA, Birdsall TG: The human use of information, III. Decision-making in signal detection and recognition situations involving multiple alternatives. Trans Inst Radiol Eng, Prof Group Inform Theory IT-2: 138, 1956.

50. Swets JA, Green DM, Getty DJ, et al: Signal detection and identification at successive stages of observation. Percept Psychophys 23: 275, 1978.

51. Swets JA, Green DM, Getty DJ, et al: Identification and scaling of complex visual patterns. Technical Report No. 3536, Bolt Beranek and Newman Inc, November 1977.

52. Swets JA, Pickett RM, Whitehead SF, et al: Accuracy of computed tomography and radionuclide scanning in detection and diagnosis of intracranial lesions: application of a general protocol for evaluation of imaging techniques in clinical medicine. Technical Report No. 3818, Bolt Beranek and Newman Inc, June 1978.

53. Swets JA, Tanner Jr WP, Birdsall TG: Decision processes in perception. Psychol Rev 68: 301, 1961.

54. Tanner Jr WP: Theory of recognition. J Acoust Soc Am 28: 882, 1956.

55. Tanner Jr WP, Swets JA: A decision-making theory of visual detection. Psychol Rev 61: 401, 1954.

56. Tolles WE, Horvath WJ, Bostrom RC: A study of the quantitative characteristics of exfoliated cells from the female genital tract: II. Suitability of quantitative cytological measurements for automatic prescreening. Cancer 14: 457, 1961.

57. Turner DA, Fordham EW, Pagano JV, et al: Brain scanning with the Anger multiplane tomographic scanner as a second examination. Radiology 121: 115, 1976.

58. Wald A: Statistical Decision Functions. New York, John Wiley & Sons, Inc. 1950.

59. Yerushalmy J, Harkness JT, Cope JH, et al: Role of dual reading in mass radiography. Am Rev Tubercol 61: 443, 1950.

7 Medical Imaging Techniques: An Illustrative Study

Many new diagnostic tests and many new, expensive imaging modalities are introduced into the health care system each year. Evaluating them can be difficult, particularly if alternative means exist to approximately the same diagnostic end. Yet, lest new techniques be introduced haphazardly, critical protocols and methods must be available so that they can be promptly assessed. We are currently completing for the National Cancer Institute a general protocol for the evaluation of diagnostic devices, with an emphasis on imaging modalities. The present study was undertaken both to refine and to illustrate this protocol (*1*).

To date, most comparative studies of imaging systems have taken one or the other of two inadequate approaches. One has been to measure fidelity—how well the system reveals the presence and detail of a standard test object, called a "phantom." The drawback of this approach is that what is measured is only the potential for mediating accurate detection and diagnosis of real lesions. The other approach, although based on using real cases and examining actual diagnostic performance, has been inadequate because of the simplistic accuracy indices that are usually obtained. Indices such as the proportion of true-positive responses, single true-positive false-positive pairs (and their ratio), single pairs of "sensitivity" and "specificity" values (and their sum), and agreement scores do not control for the influence of the reader's confidence threshold or "decision criterion," that is, the tendency to overcall or undercall disease, nor for the prevalence of disease in the study population at hand.

These two inadequacies are overcome in the approach of our general protocol. It specifies a procedure in which real cases and real diagnostic tasks are used and in which, moreover, performance is scored in relation to independent, external evidence. It further specifies a psychophysical method that generates performance data in the form of the relative (or receiver) operating characteristic (ROC). The ROC analysis provides an index of diagnostic accuracy that is independent of extra-image decision factors and of prior probabilities. It is borrowed from the general theory of signal detection (2), has been applied extensively in perceptual and cognitive studies in psychology (3, 4), and is now being increasingly applied in other fields (5), particularly in medicine (6).

The ROC is a curve showing the various trade-offs existing between proportions of true-positive and false-positive responses, as the decision criterion is systematically varied, for a given capacity to discriminate between positive and negative cases. An ROC index of accuracy reflects the location of the entire curve rather than any particular operating point on the curve. An extension of the detection ROC treats also localization and classification of abnormalities. The recommended measurements, in addition, supply the appropriate starting point for assessing the usefulness of a diagnostic system in terms of medical efficacy, risk, and cost. The basic concepts of ROC analysis have recently been explicated for a general medical audience (7).

In the present study, we applied the ROC-centered psychophysical methods to measure the accuracy of computed tomography (CT) and radionuclide scanning (RN) in a sample of patients in whom brain tumor had been suspected. Collection of the test images and other case materials, over a 3-year period, was sponsored by the National Cancer Institute in a collaborative study at five major medical centers (8). Although the images were read at the several sites and various analyses of the data made at those sites as well as at a statistical coordinating center, we were commissioned to provide a central, retrospective analysis of the data by means of a reading test conducted in accordance with the new protocol, and the images were read anew in our laboratory by radiologists recruited for that purpose. Because the protocol had not been applied before, we were asking in our study, in general, whether our psychophysical methods could be applied to complex diagnostic tasks to obtain reliable and valid estimates of accuracy or whether the complexity of real diagnostic tasks is so great as to preclude such estimates. In specific terms, we set out to measure the accuracy of CT in detecting, localizing, and diagnosing brain lesions, and also, as a point of reference, the accuracy of RN, which is CT's main competitor as a relatively noninvasive technique.

MATERIALS AND METHODS

The major characteristics of the cases, images, and other case materials were determined for the purposes of the collaborative study—a study with certain goals different from ours and, indeed, designed in advance of our study. To serve our goals, we had to impose certain restrictions which excluded from our sample a large number of the cases in the original sample. These restrictions have mainly to do with the availability of case data for establishing a reasonably credible diagnosis.

We were able to obtain imagery for 84 positive cases and 52 negative cases that met our requirements for (i) imaging in both the RN and the CT modalities, the latter with and without contrast enhancement, and (ii) credible "truth" data. For positives we required confirmation by autopsy or by histology based on cerebral biopsy or tissue from a craniotomy. The negatives were selected from a group of patients with extracerebral cancer (because the presumed normal subjects in the collaborative study were examined only by CT). They were accepted for our study if they were asymptomatic for cranial disease at the time of imaging, if the results of any other tests done then were negative, and if there was either a finding of no intracranial lesion at autopsy or live follow-up with no neurologic symptoms at least 8 months after the imaging. The diagnoses represented in our positive cases are shown in Table 1.

Twelve radiologists participated in our reading test, each spending 6 days in our laboratory over a period of 6 months. The six CT readers had an average of 3.3 years' experience in reading CT scans, about as much as was available. The six RN readers had an average of 11 years of experience. The response form, shown in slightly abbreviated form in Fig. 1, provided a basis for standardized scoring. The responses to item 1 are the basis for the conventional ROC curve.

TABLE 1
Diagnoses Represented Among the Abnormal Cases
in Our Sample

Diagnosis	Number
Primary tumors	
Glioma	31
Meningioma	13
Neurilemoma	5
Chromophobe adenocarcinoma	3
Craniopharyngioma	1
Pinealoma	1
Colloid cyst	1
Benign teratoma	1
Secondary tumors	
Metastatic	18
Direct spread/metastatic	1
Nonneoplasms	
Hematoma	3
Hemorrhage	1
Infarction	2
Arteriovenous malformation	1
Aneurysm	1
Chronic diffuse inflammation	1

1. This examination is   <u>Check One</u>

    (1) Definitely, or almost definitely, abnormal ☐

    (2) Probably abnormal ☐

    (3) Possibly abnormal ☐

    (4) Probably normal ☐

    (5) Definitely, or almost definitely, normal ☐ } [go to Item 4]

2. Site of lesion(s):

    If solitary or diffuse, indicate site(s) of <u>significant</u> anatomic involvement, or if multifocal, indicate sites of <u>major</u> anatomic lesions.

EXTRA AXIAL	LEFT	MID	RIGHT	L or M or R
(1) Skull or scalp	☐	☐	☐	
(2) Cerebral convexity or meninges	☐	☐	☐	
(3) 1 or 2 (above)	☐	☐	☐	
(4) Interhemispheric; Parasaggital	☐	☐	☐	☐
(5) Sellar region	☐	☐	☐	
(6) Cerebellopontine angle	☐		☐	

INTRA AXIAL	LEFT	MID	RIGHT	L or M or R
(7) Cerebrum	☐		☐	
(8) Frontal lobe	☐		☐	
(9) Parietal lobe	☐		☐	
(10) Temporal lobe	☐		☐	
(11) Occipital lobe	☐		☐	
(12) Corpus callosum; Thalamus/basal ganglia	☐	☐	☐	☐
(13) Brain stem; Cerebellum	☐	☐	☐	☐
(14) Lateral ventricles	☐		☐	
(15) Third ventricle		☐		
(16) Fourth ventricle		☐		

3. Differential diagnosis: Rank up to four choices

   NEOPLASM

    (1) Primary, malignant ☐

    (2) Primary, non-malignant ☐

    (3) Secondary, metastatic ☐

    (4) Secondary, direct spread ☐

   NON-NEOPLASM

    (5) Infarction ☐

    (6) Intracerebral hemorrhage (any etiology) ☐

    (7) Arteriovenous malformation (unruptured) ☐

    (8) Infectious/inflammatory process (e.g., abscess) ☐

    (9) Extracerebral collection (e.g., subdural hematoma) ☐

    (10) Encephalomalacia (e.g., atrophy, degeneration, porencephaly) ☐

    (11) Hydrocephalus (any etiology) ☐

    (12) None of the above ☐

4. Comments.

FIG. 1. Response form for readings of CT and RN images.

The five rating categories supply four points, representing four different decision criteria, on the ROC curve.

Answers for items 2 and 3 (site and type of lesion) were derived from available truth data by a neuroradiologist and a neuropathologist working independently, the latter having the final word on the few disagreements. The available data for positive cases included particulars about the type and locus of lesion in the codes of the Systematized Nomenclature of Pathology.

The CT display rested on a table which also provided space for writing on the response forms. A test administrator was seated to the right of the reader at a video terminal, from which he controlled the pace of the session. Both the display and the terminal were connected to a minicomputer that transferred images from magnetic tape to the display as required, stored the responses, and generally controlled the trial-by-trial sequence of events throughout a session.

The image-display system consisted of a COMTAL model 8000-SA image-display processor driven by the computer and in turn driving a CONRAC SNA 17-inch (43-centimeter) black-and-white video monitor. The layout of the control panel was essentially the same as that of the EMI Diagnostic Display Console, providing fast and slow controls for window level (WL) and a discrete control of window width (WW), including measure mode. An image on the monitor consisted of up to eight slices (images of the brain at different levels) presented simultaneously in a 3 x 3 matrix; the vacant cell in the lower right-hand corner contained information about current WL and WW. Each slice was approximately 70 by 70 millimeters. Each data element in the 160 by 160 EMI image matrix was represented by an independent pixel on the screen at one of 256 brightness levels.

The RN films had been taken by gamma scintillation cameras, with technetium-99m pertechnetate as the radiotracer. They were viewed on standard view boxes, two banks of four-panel GE Fluroline Illuminators. The test administrator was seated at a video terminal to the right of the view boxes. Readers were provided with both magnifying and minifying lenses. Films in our reading-test sample included a wide range of sizes and formats, namely, 11 by 14 inch individual standard views (anterior, posterior, left and right laterals, and vertex), 8 by 10 inch films containing multiple views, and 70-mm and 35-mm films of standard views. A portion of these cases included immediate views (30 minutes, minus the vertex), delayed views, and flow studies; another portion consisted of immediate and delayed views only; a third portion consisted of delayed views only. Occasional cases included special views (obliques, Waters').

Each day of the reading test was divided into four sessions of 1 to 1½ hours each. In addition, there was a preliminary session of four practice cases on the first and second visits to familiarize the readers with the procedure and equipment. For RN, the test administrator mounted all the available films for each case on the view boxes in a standard order prescribed by the reader (the readers did not handle the films). For CT, the computer first displayed the set of slices associated with one mode (either contrast or noncontrast); both modes were then available for viewing as the reader desired.

At the time the images were presented, the test administrator provided the reader with limited background information about the case—the patient's age, time of imaging relative to isotope injection (RN) and presence or absence of a contrast agent (CT). The reader was asked to vocalize his choices as he marked them on the response form to enable the test administrator to enter them into the computer disk storage. To ensure a reasonable rate of progress, a time limit of 7 minutes was set for each case. This time limit was meant to be liberal, and was, indeed, rarely approached; when it was, the test administrator provided a warning about 1 minute before the deadline.

Almost all of the 136 cases comprising our sample were viewed twice by each CT and RN reader, once on each of two different days separated generally by more than 1 month. The replication of readings was undertaken to obtain an estimate of interreader reliability, and potentially to increase the reliability of our accuracy indices, but in the present analyses we focus on the first viewing of the cases. Every reader viewed the same set of cases on a given day in the sequence of 6 days but had a different random ordering of cases, with new and formerly viewed cases randomly intermixed. In order to minimize the effect of the random sequential ordering of cases upon the CT-RN comparison, each of the six RN readers was randomly paired with one of the six CT readers, and a particular RN reader received the same case sequence on each of the 6 days as the paired CT reader did.

Our test readers judged about 45 cases per day to be a reasonable load in our setting. Relevant aspects of our setting were that interruptions were not permitted, everything we could think of to facilitate the reading process was done, only limited case background had to be considered, and treatment of the patient did not follow upon the diagnosis rendered.

DATA ANALYSES

The axes of the ROC plot—proportions of false-positive and true-positive responses—are symbolized as $P(FP)$ and $P(TP)$. We obtain four points on an ROC curve for each reader by considering the boundaries of the five categories of the rating scale (item 1, Fig. 1) as different decision criteria, or confidence thresholds, for a positive response. One point, representing a strict criterion, corresponds to $P(FP)$ and $P(TP)$ for only those cases that are placed in the highest confidence category (category 1). A second point is based on the cases placed in category 2 together with those placed in category 1, and represents a less strict criterion; both $P(TP)$ and $P(FP)$ are higher than for the first point. And so on through the fourth category, to a very lenient criterion. Four points are obtained from five categories because $P(TP) = P(FP) = 1.0$ when all five categories are combined.

Our indices of detection accuracy are based on the assumption that the empirical ROC can be viewed in terms of the normal, or Gaussian, probability distribution. Consistent with this assumption, we plot ROC data on double-probability (binormal) coordinates, on which the normal deviate is linearly spaced, and we fir the ROC points by a straight line. Our fundamental index, termed A_z, is the area beneath the fitted, binormal ROC, and ranges from a minimum of 0.50—representing chance behavior, for an ROC along the major diagonal, where $P(TP) = P(FP)$—to a maximum of 1.0—representing perfect discrimination, for an ROC showing $P(TP) = 1.0$ for all values of $P(FP)$. We report also the intercept and slope of the ROC, which provide a basis for reconstructing the ROC.

Though A_z is a quantity derived from the curve that does not correspond to any of the commonly observed response proportions, it can be related to a particular response proportion and so gain additional meaning. In a so-called forced-choice test, in which each trial presents one image from the set of positive cases and one image from the set of negative cases, and the reader is asked to say which is which, A_z is theoretically equal to the probability of a correct response (*3*, p. 47). In other words, A_z ranges from 0.50 to 1.0 in the same manner as does the proportion of correct response in a two-alternative forced-choice test.

A slightly revised version of a computer program described by Dorfman and Alf (*9*) provides chi-square measures of the goodness-of-fit of the binormal ROC to ROC data, maximum-likelihood estimates of ROC indices including A_z, and the sampling variances of those estimates.

To measure the accuracy of detection plus localization, of detection plus classification, and of detection plus localization plus classification, we use the "joint" ROC as advanced by Starr, Metz, Lusted, and Goodenough (*10*). The abscissa is the same as that of the conventional detection ROC (namely, the proportion of false-positive responses); the ordinate is the proportion of true-positive responses that are also correct with regard to another dimension or two, that is, localization or classification or both. This joint ROC is plotted without theoretical assumptions about its form, on linear probability coordinates. The joint ROC may also be indexed by the area under the empirical curve, but for convenience here we consider only the index supplied by the ordinate value at a given abscissa value.

DETECTION

In Fig. 2 individual detection ROC's are shown for the six CT readers, based on just the first reading of the cases. The four points for each reader are indicated by

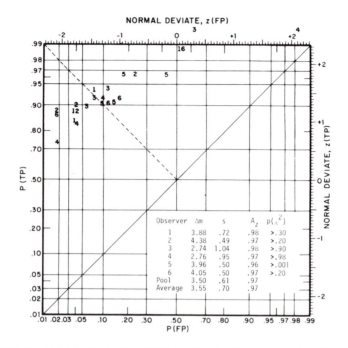

FIG. 2. Individual detection ROC's for the six CT readers, with various curve parameters.

that reader's designated number, 1 to 6. (Readers 3 and 4 each show one point outside the figure's square.) The column labeled $p(\chi^2)$ in the inset of the figure indicates that the empirical ROC's are fitted well by the assumed straight line: the probabilities associated with the chi-square measure of goodness-of-fit are, with one exception, substantially above the level that would reject linearity.

The absolute value of the intercept of the ROC with the axis at $P(TP) = 0.50$, called Δm, and the slope (s) of the linear ROC's, are given for each reader; these quantities are expressed in units of the normal deviate as given on the upper and right coordinates. As indicated, Δm and s are listed to suggest how ROC curves may be simply but completely characterized. We make no further use of Δm here, but the values of s typical of a diagnostic modality are of interest. For example, we would want to establish that there is no substantial difference in s between two modalities before comparing them in terms of the single-parameter accuracy index A_z.

The individual ROC's are seen to lie in a strikingly narrow band. The principal index, A_z, shown in the inset of the figure, varies only from 0.96 to 0.98. The CT readers further agree with one another to a considerable extent on a case-by-case basis: if we collapse the five categories of the rating scale to two (with categories 1, 2 and 3 defined as abnormal and categories 4 and 5 defined as normal), then the average percent agreement of each CT reader with the other five is 91.2. This agreement is only slightly less than the intrareader agreement over two readings of the cases, namely, 93.2 percent. We have estimated the average product-moment correlation between reader pairs to be approximately 0.65. This figure is obtained via Kendall's partial tau (*11*); reader correctness was partialed out to reduce the influence of test difficulty on the correlation estimate.

The six RN readers also show considerable uniformity on the first reading of the cases (Fig. 3), with values of A_z ranging from 0.83 to 0.89. Intrareader and interreader agreement for RN are 90.1 and 86.1 percent, respectively. The average coefficient of product-moment correlation between reader pairs was estimated to be 0.75.

The interreader correlations, within CT and within RN, were taken into account in estimating the standard errors and statistical significance levels reported in the following. That is to say, in combining readers to estimate the statistical significance of overall differences between the modalities, we did not consider the readers to be statistically independent—or, in effect, assume our sample size to be the number of cases times the number of readers—but rather used a formula

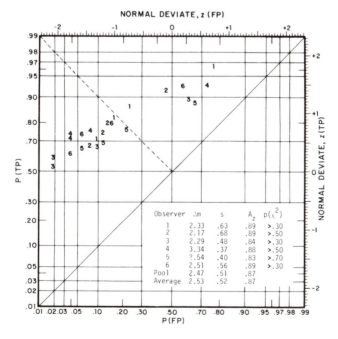

FIG. 3.   Individual detection ROC's for the six RN readers, with various curve parameters.

developed by Jarrett and Henry (*12*) to ascertain how the standard error for one (average) reader is reduced by adding other, correlated readers. We find, by the way, that our six correlated readers are the equivalent of about one and one-third independent readers, as concerns the effect of replicated readers on estimates of sample size and standard error. However, the correlation of readers across the modalities, as induced by our use of the same cases in the two modalities, was not taken into account in calculating the significance levels reported in the following, so those levels are conservative. Our significance levels are also conservative in that we have used only the first of the two readings of the cases in our calculations, and thus have not enhanced sample size to the extent allowed by the combination of the two readings.

In the insets of both Figs. 2 and 3, it can be seen that pooling the six readers' raw data, that is, treating the six readers as one reader by merging their rating responses, leads to results much like those obtained when the average (arithmetic mean) of the six individuals' derived indices is taken.

Based on pooled data, the comparison of primary interest is shown in Fig. 4. The ROC for CT is seen to be consistently above that for RN, with respective values of A_z of 0.97 and 0.87. The standard errors of those values of A_z are 0.012 and 0.027, respectively, and so the 95 percent confidence intervals are approx-

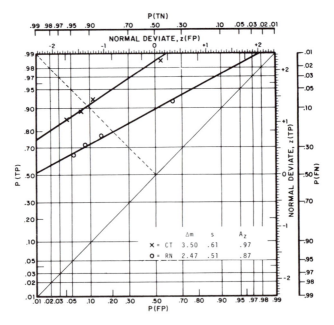

FIG. 4.   Detection ROC's for CT and RN, based on pooled data for the six readers of each modality, with various curve parameters.

imately 0.95 to 0.99 for CT and 0.82 to 0.92 for RN. The difference in A_z has associated a $p = .0007$ under the null hypothesis.

According to the ROC curves of Fig. 4, at a false-positive rate of 0.10, CT would attain a true-positive proportion of 0.91 while RN would attain a true-positive proportion of 0.73. The probability scales given at the top and right of this figure facilitate reading the graph in the other direction: at a false-negative rate of 0.10, the true-negative proportions would be 0.91 for CT and 0.49 for RN.

Let us acknowledge that in the clinic a reader will sometimes avoid both the positive and the negative response and issue an uncertain or "equivocal" response. We can deal with the use of three responses because the proportion of equivocal responses made to positive cases plus the other two proportions based on positive cases, $P(TP)$ and $P(FN)$, must add up to 1.0, and similarly the proportion of equivocal response made to negative cases and $P(TN)$ and $P(FP)$ must add up to 1.0. Thus, we can calculate the proportion of equivocal responses that would have to be made to satisfy any given limits on the two types of error. For example, according to the data of Fig. 4, CT could maintain both $P(FP)$ and $P(FN) \leq 0.10$ and produce $P(TP) = P(TN) \cong 0.90$ while sorting all the cases into positive or negative. Meanwhile, to maintain $P(FP) = P(FN) \leq 0.10$, RN would produce $P(TP) = 0.73$ and $P(TN) = 0.49$ and fail to sort definitively 17 percent of the positives and 41 percent of the negatives. Such analyses of response probabilities make clear that an observed difference of 0.10 in A_z has substantial implications for practice.

LOCALIZATION AND DIFFERENTIAL DIAGNOSIS

Various joint ROC's for CT and RN (based on pooled data for each modality) are shown in Fig. 5, along with a reproduction of the detection ROC's. They are (i) detection plus localization, (ii) detection plus "classification," or differential diagnosis, when any of the first four classification responses is scored as correct, (iii) detection plus classification when only the first choice of a differential diagnosis is scored as correct, and (iv) ROC's determined when the response must be correct with respect to detection and localization and first-choice classification in order to be scored as a true-positive response. Each curve consists of three points because localization and classification responses were given only for cases placed in categories 1 to 3 of the rating scale in item 1 of the response form.

As the true-positive response is defined in progressively more demanding fashion, the drop in $P(TP)$ is precipitous, amounting to about 0.50 for each modality. At $P(FP) = 0.10$, the advantage of CT over RN in $P(TP)$ is on the order of 0.20 to 0.25 throughout the various levels of performance measurement. On the basis of the binomial estimate of sampling variance, the probabilities under the null hypothesis across the five panels of Fig. 5, for the differences in

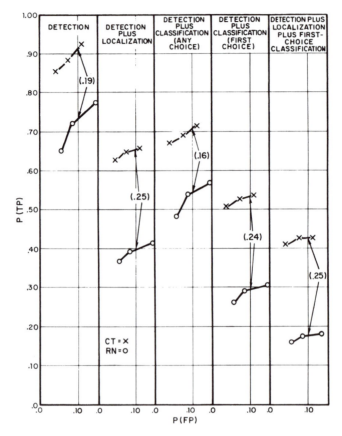

FIG. 5.   Joint ROC's for CT and RN, along with detection ROC's, based on pooled data for the six readers of each modality.

P(TP), are 0.00008, 0.0001, 0.01, 0.0002, and 0.00006. While the difference between modalities is fairly constant, the ratio of *P(TP)* for CT to *P(TP)* for RN grows as the detection ROC is extended to include localization, classification, and both—from about 1.25 to 2.5.

OTHER ANALYSES

In principle, detection ROC's may be calculated for various subsets of a broad sample of cases—in which the abnormal cases correspond to single types and sites of pathology—provided that the subsets are large enough to yield reliable measures. We calculated detection ROC's for primary tumor (56 cases), glioma (31 cases), meningioma (13 cases), and metastatic tumor (18 cases); and for lesions above (71 cases) and below (9 cases) the tentorium. The differences between CT and RN in A_z were significant at the 0.05 confidence level for the subsets with more than 30 cases and not significant for the smaller samples. None of the differences between the several types and sites within a modality reach significance in our sample. However, the pattern of results suggests that in both modalities the amount by which the detection of primary tumors exceeds that of metastatic tumors, and the amount by which the detection of supratentorial lesions exceeds that of infratentorial lesions, would be statistically significant in a slightly larger sample.

Our experimental design also permitted a comparison of CT cases read with and without contrast enhancement. In brief, detection performance between contrast and noncontrast scans differed insignificantly; however, contrast scans were significantly superior to noncontrast scans for detection plus classification.

To test whether using CT and RN together would improve detection performance over the better system alone, two decision rules were analyzed: (i) make a positive response ("abnormal") if either system's response is positive and (ii) make a positive response only if both systems are positive. For the entire sample of cases, the ROC for the combined performance resembled very closely the ROC for CT alone.

We also asked whether combining the detection reports of three readers within a modality would show an advantage over a single reader. The decision rules were to make a positive team response if (i) any one reader was positive, (ii) if any two readers were positive, and (iii) only if all three were positive. The readers' reports were independent in the sense that the readers did not communicate with each other. However, as would be expected from the high correlation among readers mentioned earlier, three readers were no better than one. The various decision rules affected the position of the points on the ROC curve, of course, but not the location of the curve.

DISCUSSION

Three factors must be considered as possible qualifications in the interpretation of our main results. Two of them stem from an extensive analysis, described elsewhere (1) in detail, of differences between our test sample and the much larger sample of the collaborative study. That analysis indicates, first, that the lesions in our test sample tended to be more apparent clinically, hence probably larger and more visible for both CT and RN, than lesions in the original collaborative sample. Second, there was a significant underrepresentation in our test sample, relative to the whole collaborative sample, of (i) cases falsely considered negative by the RN readers at the collaborative sites and (ii) cases for which the RN reader in the collaborative study failed to give the site of a lesion—that is, cases relatively difficult for RN. A third possible qualification stems from the large variability of image format in our cases as presented by RN and the opinion of our RN readers that many of those presentations were of relatively poor quality.

Concerning the first point, that our sample of cases may have been somewhat easier to diagnose than is realistic for either CT or RN, we observe again that cases in our test were read with little specific case background. Both elements considered, CT performed very well. Quite possibly RN was affected more than CT by the lack of case background.

Regarding the second and third factors mentioned as qualifications, we believe that the factor favoring RN relative to CT had at least as much effect as the factor hampering RN relative to CT and, therefore, that our comparative results may be taken at face value. These results show CT performing substantially better than RN in the detection, localization, and differential diagnosis of intracranial lesions in patients in whom tumor is suspected.

This interpretation is consistent with our analysis of a sample of some 1200 cases, as read originally by participants in the collaborative study at their respective sites, with case background available, and scored according to what was regarded as the most likely diagnosis (based on all the accumulated evidence, not just histology) at the time of our analysis. In that collaborative sample the index A_z was 0.94 for CT (compared to 0.97 in our sample) and 0.82 for RN (compared to 0.87 in our sample).

We have illustrated ROC analysis and associated study procedures in a psychophysical approach to evaluation of the accuracy of imaging techniques. Our approach obtains an ROC accuracy index that is relative to independent and credible truth, yielded by real readers, based on real cases, and measured under controlled conditions. The ROC analysis can be used to measure accuracy in detecting characteristics of a phantom test object or simulated lesions, but then it indexes the potential of the modality to affect diagnosis rather than giving a direct estimate of how the modality affects diagnosis. The ROC analysis can be used to measure the accuracy of human diagnostic judgments based on evidence in addition to, or entirely other than, image information. And it can be used to evaluate mechanized diagnostic tests that yield a single number as a result (for example, 24-hour thyroid uptake, various protein levels), with a number greater than some criterion number taken as an indication of abnormality. The present application is among the more complex of the applications mentioned, and the ROC-centered approach is seen to be practical in this application. Thus, a rigorous and objective evaluation method can be used consistently across the range of diagnostic systems.

Although our methods would apply, we did not try to develop a protocol to aid the physician in deciding whether to order CT or RN in individual cases. That development would require measures of accuracy on separate categories of cases divided according to presenting history, signs, and symptoms. It would require a larger number of cases than the number available to us that met the requirements of our test sample.

While confining our present assessment to an index of accuracy, we have mentioned that the ROC is the proper basis for an evaluation of the usefulness of a diagnostic system, which would include elements of medical efficacy, risk, and cost. In such an evaluation one proceeds from probabilities of responses based on the diagnostic system under study, through a further decision-therapeutic tree, to health outcomes. The ROC is a means of determining the response probabilities appropriate to the best available estimates of the values, costs, and event probabilities that inhere in the relevant diagnostic and therapeutic context—and not merely the response probabilities associated with whatever decision criterion might have been employed in a test of the system (*13*). Costs and benefits may, therefore, be determined for a system operating at its best. (See Chapter 5.)

REFERENCES AND NOTES

1. The materials and methods of this study are described in more detail, along with additional results and discussion, in *Technical Report No. 3818* from Bolt Beranek and Newman Inc., to the National Cancer Institute (1979).
2. W. W. Peterson *et al.*, *Trans. IRE Prof. Group Inf. Theory* **PGIT-4,** 171 (1954).
3. D. M. Green and J. A. Swets, *Signal Detection Theory and Psychophysics* (Wiley, New York, 1966; reprinted by Krieger, New York, 1974, and Peninsula, Los Altos, CA, 1988.).
4. J. A. Swets, *Science* **182,** 990 (1973).
5. ——— and D. M. Green, in *Psychology: From Research to Practice,* H. L. Pick, Jr., H. W. Leibowitz, J. E. Singer, A. Steinschneider, H. W. Stevenson, Eds. (Plenum, New York, 1978), pp. 311–331.
6. L. B. Lusted, *Introduction to Medical Decision Making* (Thomas, Springfield, Ill., 1968); B. J. McNeil, B. Keeler, Jr., S. J. Adelstein, *N. Engl. J. Med.* **293,** 211 (1975); J. A. Swets, *Invest. Radiol.* **14** (No. 2), 109 (1979); see Chapter 6.
7. C. E. Metz, *Semin. Nucl. Med.* **8,** 283 (1978).
8. Principal investigators and institutions participating in the collaborative study were H. L. Baker, Jr., Mayo Clinic; D. O. Davis, George Washington University Medical Center; S. K. Hilal, Columbia University; P. F. J. New, Massachusetts General Hospital; and D. G. Potts, Cornell University Medical Center. Data coordination for the collaborative study was supplied by C. R. Buncher, University of Cincinnati Medical Center.
9. D. D. Dorfman and E. Alf, Jr., *J. Math. Psychol.* **6,** 487 (1969).
10. S. J. Starr, C. E. Metz, L. B. Lusted, D. J. Goodenough, *Radiology* **116,** 533 (1975).
11. M. G. Kendall, *Rank Correlation Methods* (Hafner, New York, 1962).
12. R. F. Jarrett and F. M. Henry, *J. Psychol.* **31,** 175 (1951).
13. J. A. Swets and J. B. Swets, in *Proceedings of the Joint American College of Radiology—IEEE Conference on Computers in Radiology* (Newport Beach, CA, 1979, pp. 203–206).
14. Actively representing the sponsor (National Cancer Institute) to the project were R. Q. Blackwell, W. Pomerance, J. M. S. Prewitt, and B. Radovich. We are indebted to Dr. Prewitt for recognizing the need for a general protocol and for suggesting the present application. Members of an advisory panel, who contributed extensively to the protocol development and the design of this study, were S. J. Adelstein, H. L. Kundel, L. B. Lusted, B. J. McNeil, C. E. Metz, and J. E.

K. Smith. J. A. Schnur participated throughout the project; consultants for the study reported here were W. B. Kaplan and G. M. Kleinman. We are indebted also to the principal investigators in the collaborative study (8). We thank the following radiologists, who participated as readers in the tests conducted at Bolt Beranek and Newman Inc.: computed tomography—L. R. Altemus, R. A. Baker, A. Duncan, D. Kido, J. Lin, and T. P. Naidrich; radionuclide scanning—H. L. Chandler, J. P. Clements, T. C. Hill, L. Malmud, F. D. Thomas, and D. E. Tow.

8 Enhancing and Evaluating Diagnostic Accuracy

We develop two themes. The first is that diagnostic accuracy can be enhanced by decision aids. Our experimental finding that the enhancement was greater for cases more difficult to diagnose led to the second theme: an evaluation of the comparative accuracies of two diagnostic approaches, such as two alternative imaging techniques, may lead to various and contradictory conclusions depending on the spectrum of difficulty in the set of test cases.

A pair of decision aids was suggested by a conception of the diagnostic process in which pieces of evidence are individually assessed and then merged into an overall diagnosis. In our implementation, the pieces of evidence were the perceptual features of film mammograms and the diagnosis was the estimated probability of breast cancer. The first aid is a checklist of features that prompts the image reader to give a scale value for each feature, either a subjective rating of the degree to which the feature is present or a physical measurement of the extent of the feature. The second aid is a computer program that accepts the scale values from the reader, merges them with relative weights appropriate to their degrees of diagnostic relevance, and issues an advisory estimate of the probability of malignancy. In our tests, a set of approximately 150 proven cases was read twice by six radiologists, first in their usual manner and later with the decision aids.

In regard to the enhancing effect of the decision aids, this experiment extends one we reported earlier.[1] The main differences are that this experiment investigated film mammography, now more common than the xeromammography used in the earlier experiment, and it required detection of lesions as well as a benign-malignant classification. Both experiments build on an extensive literature in computer-based decision making. Dawes and Corrigan advanced the idea that simple mathematical formulas for combining pieces of evidence perform better than intuitive mergers.[2] Several applications in radiology of explicit feature assessments and formal merging were reviewed recently by Lodwick.[3]

The caution that evaluations of the accuracy and efficacy of diagnostic techniques will depend upon the spectrum of difficulty of the test cases was made by Ransohoff and Feinstein.[4] Here we demonstrate a procedure for analyzing the dependency quantitatively within a single evaluation study. Specifically, we calculate a series of accuracy indices on successive subsets of the total case set as relatively easy cases are progressively deleted from analysis. Case difficulty is seen to affect differentially the accuracies of unaided and aided reading, such that the differences between them grows systematically with case difficulty. On the grounds that case difficulty may similarly affect differentially the measured accuracies of any two alternative diagnostic techniques, we raise the possibility that two techniques may differ insignificantly for cases that represent the presenting population and, meanwhile, differ substantially for a subset of those cases that is biased in difficulty relative to the population. Common sampling schemes for assembling test sets that may introduce a difficulty bias are discussed by Begg and McNeil.[5] Such a bias would also be introduced when only cases of moderate difficulty are selected for retrospective reading in a laboratory study, a procedure designed to increase test efficiency, as discussed by Metz[6] and Begg.[7]

The Methods and Results sections that follow, along with a first Discussion section, focus on the enhancing effect of the decision aids. A second Discussion section considers the generalization of the difficulty analysis to the evaluation of other diagnostic techniques, and to the measurement in general of diagnostic performance.

METHODS

Overview

We assembled a set of some 300 cases divided about equally among normal cases, benign lesions, and malignant lesions, as proven by pathology and follow-up contact. One half of the set was used to design and implement the decision aids and a similar half was used to test them.

Our method of designing the aids consists generally of four main steps: 1) A series of interviews with several specialists in mammography is conducted to collect an exhaustive list of possibly relevant features of mammograms. 2) A perceptual test and multidimensional scaling analysis (to be described) are used to discover any latent features and to reduce the set of features to those that convey independent information. 3) Candidate features are reviewed in a consensus meeting of the investigators and mammography specialists; the features' names and descriptions are refined and numerical rating scales for them are devised. 4) The specialists view the images of one half of the available cases (the "training" set) and assign ratings to each of the designated features; a statistical analysis of these ratings, relative to the actual status of the cases rated, supplies the minimal but sufficient set of effective features along with their optimal relative weights when merged into a diagnostic judgment. The checklist (the feature-scaling aid) comprises that final set of features and their associated scales. The computer program (the feature-merging aid) is based on those same features and their weights. In the present study, only the final two steps were undertaken, inasmuch as data from the previous study were adequate again to the first two steps.

The test of the decision aids incorporated the second half of the set of available cases (the "test" set), which was read both without and, months later, with the aids by six general radiologists who had considerable experience in mammography. Analysis in terms of the relative operating characteristic (ROC) showed the gains in sensitivity and specificity of diagnoses that were produced by these feature-analytic techniques. An ROC analysis of various subsets of the full set of test cases showed how diagnostic accuracy and its enhancement depend on the diagnostic difficulty of the cases considered.

The Case Set

Film mammograms and associated case data were obtained from the University of Cincinnati Medical Center and the Dartmouth-Hitchcock Medical Center. They were taken consecutively from all symptomatic patients, referred to these centers for the evaluation of breast problems over a three-year period, who accepted light-scanning of the breast as an adjunctive examination. A study of light-scanning at the two centers (and also at the University of Massachusetts Medical Center), under a grant from the National Cancer Institute, motivated the original collection of the mammographic data we used. A small percentage of the patients referred to the two centers eliminated themselves from the experimental case set by refusing the adjunctive examination, but we have no reason to suspect a systematic effect on the representativeness of the case set finally assembled.

The lesions were proven by pathology; the normal cases were confirmed by up to four years of annual follow-up contact approximately on the anniversary of the examination. We took all of the malignant cases available, and approximately equal numbers of cases with a representative set of benign lesions (excepting cysts, which were not available to us) and normal cases matched for age with our malignant and benign cases. Both the training and test sets, in our view, reasonably represent the "inception cohort," or the population of cases that presents itself to these medical centers.

Implementation of the Decision Aids

STEP 1. INTERVIEWS TO DEVELOP A COMPREHENSIVE FEATURE LIST. The comprehensive list of features desired for film mammography in this study was derived from the list obtained in our previous study, which used xeromammography, because our mammography advisors believed that the features would be highly similar in the two techniques. In the earlier study, five mammography specialists were interviewed about the visible features they look for in detecting focal abnormalities and in classifying them as benign or malignant, and they were questioned as they read actual cases. About 50 features were identified. In the present study, this list was reviewed with three other mammography advisors (who did not participate in any other aspect of this study) and revised as deemed desirable for a comprehensive list of film-mammography features.

STEP 2. PERCEPTION EXPERIMENTS AND SCALING ANALYSIS TO EVALUATE, AND PRUNE THE FEATURE LIST. Additional relevant data from the prior study[1] came from perception experiments and associated statistical analyses that were conducted to confirm the main features identified in interviews, to help refine the descriptions of some features, to determine which of the features under consideration conveyed information independent of that contained in others, and possibly to discover relevant features not identified in the interviews. The five specialists of the earlier study made quantitative judgments about the degrees of similarity between members of all possible pairs of a set of 24 representative cases and then, to confirm their reliability, repeated the judgments for an independent, similar set of 24 cases. Multidimensional scaling analysis[8] was applied to these judgments to identify the principal, independent features they implied. Under multidimensional scaling analysis, judged degrees of similarity determine the nearness of images to one another in a multidimensional perceptual space and the analysis solves for the dimensions of the space that best account for the pattern of judgments. The dimensions are considered features. The various images were arrayed in order (successively) along each dimension and viewed by the investigators and the mammography specialists of the earlier study to help provide a description of, and a scale for, each feature.

STEP 3. CONSENSUS MEETING TO REFINE THE FEATURE LIST. The relevant independent features developed in the first two steps were discussed in a consensus group of five mammography specialists in the present study. Agreement was obtained on a list of 23 features, on how they should be described and named, and on how they could be scaled numerically by an image reader. This list of features is given in appendix A. In general, they are features of a *mass* (e.g., shape irregularity), or of *clustered calcifications* (e.g., number of elements), or of *secondary signs* (e.g., skin thickening).

STEP 4. STATISTICAL ANALYSIS OF AN EXPLORATORY READING TEST TO DEVELOP THE FINAL SET OF FEATURES AND THEIR OPTIMAL WEIGHTS. The five mammography specialists of this study rated the 23 features for each of the 150 cases in the training set. These ratings and the actual states of the cases (normal/benign vs. malignant) were subjected to linear discriminant analysis[9] to determine which features were predictive of those actual states and to what degree. Of the 23 features subjected to discriminant analysis, 12 received weights that were deemed substantial. They are identified in appendix A. The actual values of the weights are specific to the natures of their associated scales (e.g., whether physical measurements or subjective ratings), so just the ranks of the weights are given in appendix A.

These 12 features constitute a minimal but sufficient set of relatively independent features. With their scales, they made up the checklist, as reproduced in appendix B. With their weights, they were the basis for the computer program that, in the test of the decision aids, accepted the reader's feature ratings and estimated the probability of malignancy. (In the usual terminology and practice of the field, the specialists' ratings serve, via discriminant analysis, to "train" the merging algorithm, which is then applied, with ratings of an independent set of cases, to "test" it.)

Reading Test to Evaluate the Decision Aids

Six radiologists, with extensive experience in mammography, came to BBN Laboratories to read the 146 cases of test set. They were informed that this set was divided into approximate thirds as to type of case (actually 50 normal, 50 benign lesions, and 46 malignancies). For each case, they were to scan the four available images (craniad-caudad and oblique for each breast) and estimate the probability that a malignancy was present in the single breast specified by the investigators.

They read the test set twice, first essentially in their usual manner (standard reading condition). Several months later, they read the same cases with the two decision aids (enhanced reading condition). In both conditions, they read for two days. The several readers read the cases in different random orders. Viewing times were unrestricted. A regular clinical illuminator was used and a magnification lens was available.

The earlier study showed the lack of practice effect of the standard condition on the enhanced condition and hence supported a comparison of the two reading conditions.[1] Specifically, in that study, three of the six readers read the cases twice in the standard condition with essentially the same accuracy, and with less accuracy than the six readers in the enhanced condition. Incidentally, the other three read twice in the enhanced condition with essentially the same accuracy both times. (We chose not to counter learning or practice effects by conducting the enhanced condition first in half of the subjects on the grounds that any experience with enhanced reading would bring sophistication about features and scales and hence effectively prevent a standard reading.)

Prior to the enhanced reading condition, the readers were given training in making the feature ratings. Specifically, for each of about 25 cases they made the feature ratings (and probability estimate) and then were given the medians of the specialists' ratings as well as the diagnostic truth of the case. After that experience, a trainer reviewed with the reader any substantial deviations of his/her rating tendencies from those of the specialists.

For each case in the enhanced condition, the reader's feature ratings were submitted by a test administrator, as the reader made and spoke them, to the computer program. At the conclusion of the feature-rating procedure for a case, the computer immediately produced its estimate of the probability of malignancy. As seen in the response form of appendix B, the reader first recorded the computer's advisory estimate and then made his/her own estimate of the probability. (Though we would have liked to obtain the reader's estimate both before and after the computer's advisory estimate—in order to separate the effects of the checklist and those of the computer program—we chose not to elicit that initial estimate from the reader, to which he or she might feel some commitment, and then ask a few seconds later for a possible change of mind. Separating effects by running the enhanced condition twice would have exceeded the time the readers could give us and also introduced problematic practice effects.)

The reader's probability estimates were converted to best-fitting ROCs by use of Metz's LABROC computer program.[6] This program, originally intended for the essentially continuous decision-variable outputs of clinical laboratory tests, is suitable to the 100-category rating scales used by our readers in this experiment, in contrast to the more familiar five- or six-category rating scales.

Subset Analysis to Determine the Effects of Case-Set Difficulty

In our analysis of accuracy, we considered different subsets of cases as progressively more of the relatively easy cases are set aside. The relative ease/difficulty of each case was determined by the consensus of reader judgments in the standard reading condition. Specifically, for each reader, the set of cases was ranked according to the differences between his or her probability estimates and 1.0 for malignant cases, and the differences between his or her probability estimates and 0 for normal/benign cases. These rankings were averaged across readers to provide a measure of overall difficulty of each case. We considered the case set consisting of the total of 146 cases, then the subset of 96 benign and malignant cases that remain after the 50 normal cases are eliminated, then subsets consisting consecutively of five fewer cases, from 91 down to 51. With case sets of the smaller numbers, ROC analysis becomes problematic, and 51 cases were deemed to be about as small a case set as is suitable for such analysis. (We eliminated the full set of normal cases at one time because they were relatively and almost uniformly easy by definition, in appearance if not in ultimate fact: Our normal cases were selected from among those not regarded as suspicious in any way and not given a recommendation for follow-up examination or test; the results of our analysis will be seen to have confirmed this procedure. Incidentally, ties in ranks in the cutoff points were broken in a random manner to leave as nearly as possible equal numbers of malignant and benign cases.)

RESULTS

ROCS For All, and For the Most Difficult, Cases

The data are shown here on ROC graphs plotted in the usual manner, with the true-positive proportion, or sensitivity, on the (left) ordinate and the false-positive proportion, or the complement of specificity, on the (lower) abscissa. The true-negative proportion is scaled, from right to left, on the upper abscissa so that specificity can also be read directly.

Figure 1 shows empirical and fitted ROCs for both the standard and the

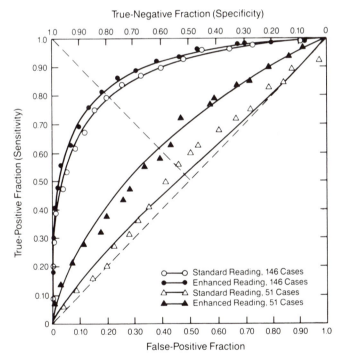

FIG. 1. Relative operating characteristics (ROCs) representing six readers in standard and enhanced reading conditions for the total of 146 cases (upper two curves) and the set of 51 cases most difficult to diagnose (lower two curves): data points and best-fitting theoretical curves.

enhanced reading conditions, both for the full set of 146 cases (top) and for the set of the 51 most difficult cases (bottom). The data points are for the six readers combined; they were obtained by pooling the rankings of the probability estimates made by each reader. It can be seen that the fits of the smooth curves to the data points are very good for the larger case set and not very good, but still adequate to our purpose, for the smaller case set. The main effects of the subset analysis are seen qualitatively: Performance in both standard and enhanced reading conditions is substantially lower, and the difference between the two conditions—the enhancement effect—is substantially greater, for the more difficult cases. Moreover, the lower pair of curves shows that the aids have a sizeable effect even when the cases are sufficiently difficult that the decisions made in the standard reading are little better than chance.

Effect of Case Difficulty on Obtained ROCS

Figure 2 shows the average of the fitted ROC functions obtained from the six readers at the 11 difficulty levels considered, for the standard reading condition. Metz's LABROC curve-fitting program gives the two parameters of the fit for each reader,[6] and the averages of those parameters were used (for a reason to be mentioned) to construct the ROC graphs shown here.

Although the set size is labelled on just three of the ROC curves in figure 2, the height of the ROC curve (relative to the positive diagonal line and the upper left corner), declines without a reversal as the set size decreases. As difficulty increases, the average values of the areas under the fitted ROC curves, denoted A_z, are 0.88, 0.82, 0.80, 0.77, 0.74, 0.71, 0.68, 0.66, 0.63, 0.60, and 0.59. We note that the smooth decline is not forced by our analysis, in that the difficulty index applied to the cases for each reader (in the analysis of fig. 2) was determined independently of that reader's performance. Specifically, in this analysis we based the difficulty index for each reader on the other five readers' judgments (in the standard condition). (For this reason, we averaged the two parameters of the ROC curve fit to obtain a group curve; a different method, namely, pooling of readers' ratings, was used for the analysis in figure 1 because we routinely use it when it is possible). The ROC curves for the enhanced reading condition (not shown) also show a monotonic decline. The effect of case difficulty on ROCs in absolute terms, for each diagnostic approach, is systematic, fine-grained, and extensive.

Differential Effects of Case Difficulty on Standard and Enhanced Readings

Figure 3 shows the average A_zs for the six readers for the 11 sets of cases that were analyzed. The standard and enhanced conditions are scaled on the left ordinate. Their difference (enhanced A_z minus standard A_z) is scaled on the right

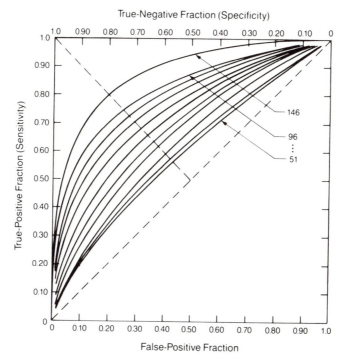

True-Negative Fraction (Specificity)

FIG. 2.   Relative operating characteristics (ROCs) fitted to the data of six readers in the standard reading condition for the 11 case sets analyzed, which varied in size from 146 to 51 and varied from all cases to those most difficult to diagnose.

ordinate. The error bars on the difference show 95% confidence limits. Here, basing the difficulty index for each reader on the other five readers' performances insured that any statistical regression toward the mean of the apparent case difficulties in a second reading—which otherwise would contribute to a shallower slope of the curve for the second (here, enhanced) reading—would now affect the standard as well as the enhanced reading.

Figure 3 shows again the smooth, fine-grained, and extensive decline in accuracy with increasing case difficulty, and, as well, the differential effects of case difficulty on the standard and enhanced reading conditions. A_z decreases less rapidly in the enhanced condition and so the enhancement effect grows with case difficulty. Whereas the A_z difference is 0.02 for the full set of cases, and 0.03 for just the 96 benign and malignant cases, it reaches approximately 0.10 for the three or four most difficult sets of cases. Probabilities associated with (one-tailed) t-tests of the observed enhanced-standard difference at each set size decrease through most of the successive sets (0.081, 0.020, 0.019, 0.012, 0.009,

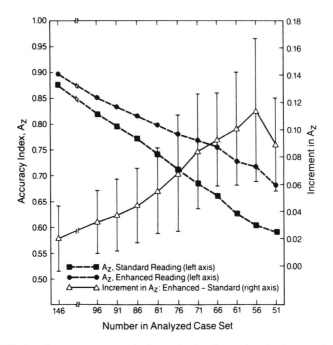

FIG. 3. Average accuracy indices, A_z, for six readers in the standard and enhanced reading conditions at 11 levels of case-set size and difficulty; the curve rising from left to right (scaled on the right-handed ordinate) shows the increment in accuracy from the standard condition to the enhanced condition—that is, the size of the enhancement effect—as the case sets analyzed become progressively more difficult.

0.012, 0.005, 0.002, 0.002, 0.004, 0.002), indicating that the differential effect holds generally for the six readers.

Colin Begg suggested to us a simpler analysis of the data in this regard, a nonparametric analysis that treats each case independently. First, all of the ratings in the standard condition were ranked as before, distinguishing diseased and normal cases. Then, for each case, the standard rating was changed to the enhanced rating and the number of cases of the other disease category that it crossed was taken as a measure of the change in accuracy induced by the enhancement. The result for the 96 benign and malignant cases, unclassified as to difficulty, was a regression line (of change in accuracy plotted against case difficulty) with a slope of 0.32, accounting for 13.7% of the variance, with a probability relative to the null hypothesis of 0.0001. To make a comparison with figure 3, where cases are grouped according to difficulty, we note that this measure of accuracy increased by an estimated 3.2 for each increase of ten cases ordered according to difficulty—thus approximating that increase of 3.2 for successive groups of ten cases. The advantage of this particular analysis for demonstrating the existence of an effect is that the cases contributing to the groupings are independent, rather than having many cases (51 cases) common to all groups. We regard it as confirming the ROC analysis, which gives quantities that are more useful.

Enhancement Effects on Sensitivity and Specificity

Figure 4 shows the ROCs obtained for the set of 146 cases and for the set of 56 cases, the latter being the set showing the maximum enhancement effect. Shown in the figure by dotted lines are the effects of the decision aids on sensitivity alone and specificity alone, when the other is held at 0.85. For the full set of 146

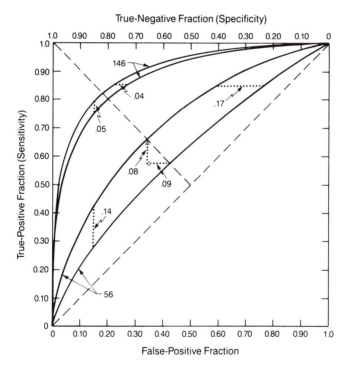

FIG. 4. Relative operating characteristics (ROCs) fitted to the data of six readers in the standard and enhanced reading conditions: 146 cases, upper two curves; 56 cases, lower two curves. The dotted lines show the increases in sensitivity and specificity that resulted from the decision aids, both when considering all cases and when considering a smaller set of cases more difficult to diagnose (as discussed in the text).

cases, the effects are about 0.04. For the set of 56 cases, the effects reach 0.14 for sensitivity and 0.17 for specificity. One may choose instead to realize the enhancement effect in both sensitivity and specificity, rather than in just one or the other. Other dotted lines in figure 4, which give results at a point on the ROC curve where these two variables are equal, show that sensitivity and specificity may be simultaneously increased by about 0.08 each.

DISCUSSION OF ENHANCEMENT RESULTS

We conclude that the two main aspects of image reading are facilitated by a pair of decision aids: a checklist of the appropriate diagnostic features with rating scales and a computer program that merges a reader's optimally weighted feature ratings into a diagnostic probability. In this study as well as a previous one,[1] these aids substantially increased the accuracy of mammographic diagnosis. Because the readers in both studies were given very little training in quantitative feature analysis (about two hours), we regard the observed gains as conservative estimates of the gains attainable.

The A_z increment of 0.03 for the 96 benign and malignant cases in this study can be contrasted with the increment of 0.07 for the benign and malignant cases (the only types used) in the previous study.[1] (The A_z values for the standard conditions in the two studies were similar, both in the low 0.80s). Although we have no basis in data to account for the difference, we note that in the previous study the aids brought general radiologists to the accuracy level of mammography specialists; in this study, the test readers were more experienced in mammography than those of the earlier study and so may have had less room for improvement. It is not feasible to make a subset analysis now of the earlier data (because the computer system in which it was stored and analyzed has been retired), but given that the earlier effect was more than twice the size of the present one, we can speculate that the earlier study would yield larger enhancements than this study did for case sets at all levels of difficulty. In any event, the indications from the data for all cases in the prior study are that: 1) of 100 patients with malignancies, on the order of ten to 15 additional malignancies can be detected with the help of the enhancement techniques; or 2) of 100 patients without malignancy, an additional ten to 15 can avoid unnecessary biopsy. In the present study, with readers highly experienced in mammography, that amount of enhancement is indicated for the most difficult third of the cases. Again, given that the number of mammograms taken annually is increasing at a very substantial rate, such that a large share of them is being read by radiologists with little experience in mammography, our present estimates of gains achievable with the decision aids are very likely to be conservative.

We suggest that these decision aids will be effective also for other image-based diagnostic problems—with other imaging techniques, organs, and diseases—

and for diagnostic problems more generally, including those that involve other perceptual components (listening, feeling, direct seeing) and also those that are predominantly cognitive rather than perceptual (for example, based on clinical workups). The feature-analytic techniques may be especially useful with new imaging technologies—to shorten appreciably the time usually taken to reach consensus on the relevant features and their weights.

Our analysis of subsets of cases according to the cases' difficulty of diagnosis showed that the enhancement effect of the decision aids is progressively larger for the more difficult cases. One aspect of this result seems obvious after the fact: cases very easy to diagnose don't need any help. The other side of the coin is not so obvious: the aids work best for the problematic cases. This result increases our confidence in the concepts underlying the aids and is practically a valuable outcome. It is good to know that considerable help can be made available for the difficult cases. As a matter of clinical efficiency, the diagnostician might prefer to use the decision aids, which do require some additional time and effort, only when the diagnosis is in some doubt. (We do not recommend this practice because a subjective judgment may not be a good indication of difficulty.) On the other hand, the diagnostician might decide to use these decision aids routinely, including with the cases apparently easy to diagnose; this practice could be especially valuable in settings in which liability is a major concern. Specifically, the feature-analytic techniques provide the basis for both a standard reading format and a standard reporting format—one that can be agreed upon and used by the diagnosticians in a particular clinical field and endorsed by professional associations and relevant government agencies. The benefits of standardized diagnostic reports for clinical communication, understanding, and efficiency are increasingly recognized.

DISCUSSION OF IMPLICATIONS FOR EVALUATION

Our subset analysis confirms and extends a concern advanced earlier that measured accuracy of diagnostic performance is dependent on the spectrum of case difficulties in the test set assembled.[4] For both diagnostic approaches evaluated, the effect of case difficulty is large, such that performances range from high to low accuracy. The analysis indicates, moreover, that comparative as well as absolute evaluations may be affected to a material extent by case difficulty. Not only will the absolute accuracy of a single diagnostic performance—for example, of a particular imaging technique—vary with the difficulty of a test's case set, but a measured difference between two diagnostic performances—for example, of two alternative imaging techniques—may depend on the difficulty of the cases selected for a test. Specifically, a case set of a difficulty represented at the left of the graph in figure 3 might yield no statistically significant difference, a case set in the middle might yield a marginally significant difference, while a case set at the right might yield a highly significant difference, of practical import.

The result of our analysis of case difficulty has general implications for technology assessment, given that various common procedures for selecting a sample of test cases will produce a set that, on the whole, is easier or more difficult to diagnose than the population to which one wishes to generalize.[5] A prime example is verification bias, in which the test sample consists only of cases that reach a level of verification regarded as a "gold standard," for example, histologic confirmation.[4,5] Such cases might have lesions that are on average larger, and easier to visualize, than those in the full set of cases in the population that undergoes a given kind of imaging. In this event, the true difference between two imaging techniques, as generally used, could be substantially underestimated.

Consider also our finding in relation to the recommended procedure in psychometric and radiologic testing of selecting a test set largely of moderately difficult cases, in order to increase the statistical power of a reading test and its efficacy in terms of reader time. As discussed by Metz[6] and Begg,[7] this procedure is appropriate only to determining the existence of a difference between two techniques and is not appropriate to the practical question of the size of a difference. Our finding points up that use of this procedure even in its limited context depends on the assumption that a diagnostic technique that is better for difficult cases is also better for easier cases. Such a homogeneity of cases would mean that the two curves of figure 3 would not touch or cross as easier cases were added to the sample. That assumption may not always, or even usually, be safe; we would hesitate to make it, for example, when comparing magnetic resonance imaging and ultrasound or when comparing mammography and breast palpation.

We suggest that the subset analysis of case difficulty will help to alleviate the general bias problem in performance evaluations. It provides a kind of sensitivity analysis, that is, an analysis of the extent to which a conclusion about a given accuracy of performance, or a given difference in accuracies, depends upon the study's assumptions about the test set of cases.

We used subset analysis here to examine the spectrum of case difficulties as defined by readers' judgments about the probability of abnormality (malignancy). However, the concept is more general: it applies to case difficulties measured in other ways and to variables other than case difficulty, including objective as well as subjective variables. An example in comparing two imaging technologies for the diagnosis of breast cancer is to vary case subsets according to the perceived density of a breast or its amount of fatty tissue; one technology may be less affected by this variable than the other.

The authors are indebted to the radiologists who participated as advisors and readers in their experimental studies: Drs. Royal Bartrum, Dale Bramen, William Castor, Kamilla Gitschlag, Marion Jabezinski, William Jobe, Lawrence Killebrew,

Daniel B. Kopans, Dean McKnight, Jack E. Meyer, Myron Moskowitz, Paul Stomper, and Clifford J. Turner. Drs. Moskowitz and Bartrum very kindly provided mammograms and associated case data from their studies at the University of Cincinnati and Dartmouth–Hitchcock Medical Centers. The authors are also indebted to Allison Hagerman for serving as reading-test administrator and technical assistant throughout the project; to Barbara Freeman for writing the computer programs required for data collection; and to A. W. F. Huggins for assisting with data analyses. This paper benefited from discussions following verbal presentations at a Conference on Visual Search sponsored by the Committee on Vision of the National Research Council, a Radiology Grand Rounds of the University of Massachusetts Medical Center, and a seminar and a workshop arranged by the Department of Health Care Policy of the Harvard Medical School. Though not responsible for the outcome, Colin B. Begg and James A. Hanley made helpful comments on a draft manuscript and Charles E. Metz advised the authors throughout the analysis.

REFERENCES

1. Getty DJ, Pickett RM, D'Orsi, CJ, Swets JA. Enhanced interpretation of diagnostic images. Invest Radiol. 1988;23:240–52.
2. Dawes RM, Corrigan B. Linear models in decision making. Psychol Bull. 1974;81:95–106.
3. Lodwick GS. Computers in radiologic diagnosis. Appl Radiol. 1986; Jan/Feb:61–5.
4. Ransohoff DJ, Feinstein AR. Problems of spectrum and bias in evaluating the efficacy of diagnostic tests. N Engl J Med. 1978;299:926–30.
5. Begg CB, McNeil BJ. Assessment of radiologic tests; control of bias and other design considerations. Radiology. 1988;167:565–9.
6. Metz CE. Some practical issues of experimental design and data analysis in radiologic ROC studies. Invest Radiol. 1989;24:234–45.
7. Begg CB. Experimental design of medical imaging trials: issues and options. Invest Radiol. 1989;24:934–6.
8. Shiffman SS, Reynolds ML, Young FW. Introduction to multidimensional scaling. New York: Academic Press, 1981.
9. Lachenbruch P. Discriminant analysis. New York: Hafner, 1975.

APPENDIX A
Feature List

The 23 features listed below were determined to be of potential importance to diagnosis in a consensus meeting that followed interviews and also perceptual-similarity tests in which data were subjected to multidimensional scaling analysis. Data obtained from subsequent scaling of these features for proven cases were subjected to discriminant analysis, which yielded the importance rankings in the righthand column. The 12 features with ranks listed were incorporated in the checklists for the enhanced readings.

Certain of the 23 features were not retained for the checklist, not because they are relatively unimportant, but because they are highly correlated with others that were retained. Which of two highly correlated features receives the larger weighting in discriminant analysis will vary with the particulars of different case sets. Some features retained here were among those dropped in the earlier study[1] and vice versa: in particular, *indistinct border* here replaced *spiculation*; *singleness of mass* was used in the earlier study and not here; *presence of focal abnormality* and *age* were used here and not in the earlier study.

(Here, three features were combinations of elemental features, as indicated in the right column: the ratio of the size in one view to the size in the other view, the product of two border indistinctness features, and the product of two features of elements of calcification clusters.)

Feature	Rank
Focal abnormality	1
Mass	
Intramammary node	
Size (cranial-caudal view)	
Size (oblique view)	} 7
Inclusion of fat	
Degree of shape irregularity	
Type of shape irreguarlity	
Spiculated border	
Indistinct border	9 }
Indistinctness due to invasion	} 4
Cluster of calcifications	
Not skin artifact	
Size of cluster (craniad-caudad view)	8
Size of cluster (oblique view)	
Number of elements	6
Shape of cluster	5
Variability of size of elements	
Irregular shape of elements	} 12
Linear or branching elements	
	11
Secondary signs	
Architectural distortion	
Asymmetric density	3
Skin thickening or retraction	
Regional calcifications	10
Other data	
Age	2

Case No. _____
Age   _____

Response Form—X-Ray Mammography

ALL RESPONSES ARE TO BE MADE WITH RESPECT TO THE SINGLE
MOST SIGNIFICANT ABNORMALITY IN THE TARGET BREAST

(A)   IS THERE A FOCAL ABNORMALITY VISIBLE IN TWO VIEWS?

      YES   NO
(IF NO, GO TO D)

(B)   IS THERE A MASS?

      YES   NO
(IF NO, GO TO C)

DESCRIPTIONS RELEVANT TO MASS

(B1)   SIZE—Largest diameter in cc view.   _____mm

(B2)   SIZE—Largest diameter in oblique view.   _____mm

(B3)   BORDER—Confidence that at least a small portion of the border
      is indistinct.

   -5 -4 -3 -2 -1 0   1   2   3   4   5
   definitely   uncertain   definitely
   not indis-   indistinct
   tinct

(B4)   BORDER—Confidence that any place where the border is indis-
      tinct, some of the indistinctness is due to incursion of the lesion
      into adjacent tissue:

   -5 -4 -3 -2 -1 0   1   2   3   4   5
   all indistinctness   uncertain   some indistinctness
   due to obscuration   due to incursion of
   of lesion by par-   lesion into adja-
   enchyma   cent tissue

(C) IS THERE A CLUSTER OF CALCIFICATIONS (WITH OR WITHOUT REGIONAL CALCIFICATIONS) *OR* REGIONAL CALCIFICATIONS ALONE?

CLUSTER   REGIONAL   NEITHER
                 ALONE

(IF REGIONAL ALONE, GO TO C4)
(IF NEITHER, GO TO D)

DESCRIPTIONS RELEVANT TO CLUSTER OF CALCIFICATIONS

(C1) SIZE—largest dimension in cc view   _____mm

(C2) NUMBER OF ELEMENTS—comprising the cluster in the cc view.

0   1   2   3   4   5   6   7   8   9   ≥10

(C3) SHAPE—suggestive of conformance to a lobule versus duct.

0   1   2   3   4   5   6   7   8   9   10
spherical shape,   tubular shape,
suggestive of   suggestive of
conformance to   conformance
a lobule   to a duct

DESCRIPTIONS RELEVANT TO ELEMENTS
(IF BOTH A CLUSTER AND REGIONAL CALCIFICATIONS ARE PRESENT, LIMIT THE FOLLOWING RATINGS TO THE ELEMENTS COMPRISING THE CLUSTER)

(C4) VARIABILITY OF SIZE

0   1   2   3   4   5   6   7   8   9   10
low variability   high variability
of size   of size

(C5) SHAPE—confidence that at least some of the elements have and irregular shape.

−5   −4   −3   −2   −1   0   1   2   3   4   5
all elements are   uncertain   at least some
round or smooth   elements are jag-
                                             ged or irregular

(C6) SHAPE—confidence that there is at least some indication of branching or curvilinearity.

punctate   or   branching/curvilinear

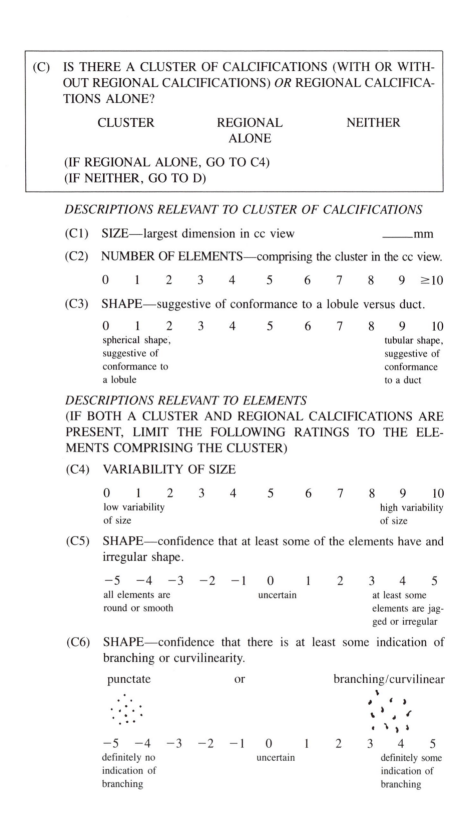

−5   −4   −3   −2   −1   0   1   2   3   4   5
definitely no   uncertain   definitely some
indication of   indication of
branching   branching

(D)   SECONDARY SIGNS

(D1)   Confidence regarding presence of architectural distortion.

-5 -4 -3 -2 -1 0 1 2 3 4 5
definitely no   uncertain   definitely some
architecutral   architectural
distortion   distortion

(D2)   Confidence regarding presence of skin thickening or retraction.

-5 -4 -3 -2 -1 0 1 2 3 4 5
definitely no   uncertain   definitely some
skin thickening   skin thickening
or retraction   or retraction

Computer Rating of Malignancy:

_____

(E)   OVERALL DIAGNOSTIC JUDGMENT

(E1)   Benign vs. Malignant—Rate the likelihood (as the number of chances in 100) that the case is malignant:

Rating (0 to 100):   _____
    0   =   certainly benign or normal
  100   =   certainly malignant

9 Information Retrieval Methods

A desirable measure of retrieval performance would have the following properties. First, it would express solely the ability of a retrieval system to distinguish between wanted and unwanted items—that is, it would be a measure of "effectiveness" only, leaving for separate consideration factors related to cost or "efficiency." Second, the desired measure would not be confounded by the relative willingness of the system to emit items—it would express discrimination power independent of any "acceptance criterion" employed, whether the criterion is characteristic of the system or adjusted by the user. Third, the measure would be a single number—in preference, for example, to a pair of numbers which may covary in a loosely specified way, or a curve representing a table of several pairs of numbers—so that it could be transmitted simply and apprehended immediately. Fourth, and finally, the measure would allow complete ordering of different performances, indicate the amount of difference separating any two performances, and assess the performance of any one system in absolute terms—that is, the metric would be a scale with a unit, a true zero, and a maximum value. Given a measure with these properties, we could be confident of having a pure and valid index of how well a retrieval system (or method) was performing the function it was primarily designed to accomplish, and we could reasonably ask questions of the form, "Shall we pay X dollars for Y units of effectiveness?"

In a previous article I reviewed 10 measures that had been suggested prior to 1963, and proposed another (*1*). None of the 10 measures, and none that has come to my attention since then, has more than two of the properties just listed. Some of them, including those most widely used, have the first two properties, and some of the others have the last two properties. The measure I proposed, one drawn from statistical decision theory, has the potential to satisfy all four desiderata. At the time it was proposed, however, the decision-theory measure had not been applied to any empirical retrieval results, so that its assumptions about the form of retrieval data had not been tested. In the present paper we examine this measure in relation to test results obtained from three experimental retrieval systems with some 50 different retrieval methods. With minor qualifications, the data are uniformly consistent with the assumptions of the decision-theory measure and quite clearly demonstrate its usefulness. A substantive outcome of the extensive analysis in terms of this measure is a clear appraisal of the current state of the retrieval art. The analysis shows in precise terms how much room for improvement is left by current retrieval techniques. The room for improvement, as we shall see, is large.

Before proceeding to a review of the decision-theory measure and to an examination of the data, let us consider briefly the domain of the measure and a disclaimer about the scope of this paper.

The measure is most clearly applicable to retrieval systems that deal in documents or messages, and it is applied here to systems of this type. Less clearly perhaps, but as well, the measure can be applied to information systems that handle facts or give answers to ordinary English questions. In both cases queries are addressed to a system and the system's responses to the queries must be evaluated. Whether the response is a set of documents or a fact selected or deduced from a collection of writings is immaterial. Appropriate text must be isolated in either case, to constitute the response or to supply the base from which the response is drawn. The data represented by the decision-theory measure are entries in a two-by-two contingency table: Just as documents suited or unsuited to a need may be retrieved or not retrieved, so facts that correctly or incorrectly answer questions may be presented or withheld. For some relatively simple fact systems, of course, such as airline-reservation systems, discrimination or correctness is not a problem; the reference here is to fact systems in which the facts to be retrieved are not all neatly isolated and in which the questions are not all anticipated in detail.

This measure, like those used most often in the past, is most directly applicable when the entire information store is known and when, in particular, the number of items appropriate as responses to each query is known. This condition is frequently satisfied in experimental systems, which usually contain no more than a few thousand items. If the measure is to be applied to stores large enough to make impractical a complete knowledge of them, three alternatives exist for estimating the required number. One is to select, by some heuristic process or by fiat, that subset of the full store likely to contain almost all of the items appropriate to a given set of queries, and to examine the subset in detail. A second alternative, used in one instance in the following, is simply to sample the large store and to extrapolate from the sample. A third alternative, used in another instance in the following, is to preselect certain items from the store and to design test queries specifically to retrieve those items.

Application of the decision-theory measure assumes that the "relevance" of any item in the store to a given query or user's need can be determined. As the reader will know, or can imagine, the definition of relevance is generally regarded in the retrieval field as a very thorny problem, and even the concept itself has at times come under attack. However that may be, the definition of relevance is an issue separate from the measure under consideration, and is not discussed here. Nor is the concept defended here; I take it for granted that it is essential to the evaluation of retrieval performance and that sooner or later we shall come to terms with it. For our present purposes, we can accept the definitions of relevance adopted by the investigators who collected the data we shall examine, just as we accept for the present purposes other experimental procedures they have followed. It will become clear, by the way, that the decision-theory measure can be applied when judges use several, rather than two, categories of relevance, and that it uses to full advantage the output of a system that ranks or otherwise scales all items in the store according to their degree of relevance to the query at hand.

DECISION-THEORY MEASURE

A good way to begin in reviewing the decision-theory measure is to consider a measure more familiar in the retrieval context and to note the differences between the two. The measure used far more than any other (2) consists of two quantities termed the "recall ratio" and the "precision ratio." Like other measures that attempt to assess only retrieval effectiveness, this measure can be described by reference to the relevance-retrieval contingency table shown in Fig. 1.

The recall ratio is defined as $a/a + c$, the number of items both relevant and retrieved divided by the number of items relevant. This ratio, then, is the proportion of relevant items retrieved, and it may be taken as an estimate of the conditional probability that an item will be retrieved given that it is relevant. The precision ratio (formerly called the "relevance ratio") is defined as $a/a + b$, the number of items both relevant and retrieved divided by the number of items retrieved. This ratio is the proportion of retrieved items deemed relevant, and an estimate of the conditional probability that an item will be relevant given that it is retrieved.

Now, if a system's effectiveness is characterized by two numbers, a value of the recall ratio and a value of the precision ratio, we know relatively little about the system, for one reason because we don't know how the two quantities relate to each other. What does it mean, for example, to say that a system yielded a recall ratio of 0.70 and a precision ratio of 0.50? If System A performs this way, and System B yields a recall ratio of 0.90 and a precision ratio of 0.40, is System B more or less discriminating than System A? That is, is a gain of 0.20 in recall and a loss of 0.10 in precision good or bad? Of course, should System B show a gain in both recall and precision over System A, we know B's effectiveness is

	r	$\bar{r}$	
R	a	b	$a + b$
$\bar{R}$	c	d	$c + d$
	$a + c$	$b + d$	$a + b + c + d$

FIG. 1. The relevance-retrieval contingency table: r and $\bar{r}$ denote, respectively, relevant and irrelevant items; R and $\bar{R}$ denote, respectively, retrieved and unretrieved items; a, b, c, and d represent frequencies of occurrence of the four conjunctions.

superior to A's, but, in general, the measure consisting of this pair of quantities will give only a partial ordering of different systems or of different methods employed by one system.

The problem here is that System A's recall of 0.70 and precision of 0.50 represents only one of the many balances between the two ratios that it can achieve. This balance might have occurred when an item had to satisfy five descriptors specified in a query in order to be retrieved. If this requirement is changed, so that now an item has only to satisfy any two of the query's five descriptors, it is very likely that more items will be retrieved, and that recall will go up and precision will go down. But we must know exactly how recall and precision will covary, along with variation in the acceptance criterion, if uncertainties are to be avoided in attempting to rank different systems or methods.

A solution to this problem, one that is sometimes adopted, is to test each system with several acceptance criteria and to present as the measure of a system's effectiveness the empirical curve so generated. Extensive tests have shown (3) that the empirical curve will resemble in form the curve shown in Fig. 2. If System A yields the curve shown while System B yields another curve everywhere above and to the right of the one shown, it is clear that B is superior to A.

However, these curves do not tell us, in general terms, by how many units B is superior to A. (We can determine that B's precision is greater than A's by some specific percentage at some specific value of recall, but this number varies widely as a function of the value of recall selected.) Nor can we tell from the curves how good either system is in absolute terms. And, of course, it is relatively awkward (We might say that a large "bandwidth" is required) to transmit and receive a full curve.

A measure that retains the basic information inherent in the recall-precision curve, and at the same time overcomes the drawbacks of using a curve as a measure, would be attained if there is a way to represent completely an empirical curve of this general sort by a single number on a scale with a unit, a true zero, and a maximum. The thrust of my earlier article was that statistical decision theory offers a way—indeed, several ways. Whether or not we can take advantage of one of them, or to what extent, depends upon the form of retrieval data when analyzed by decision-theory techniques, and that form is the concern of this paper.

Though a way might be found to completely characterize any empirical recall-precision curve by a single number on the type of scale desired, decision theory suggests using the curve that results when another variable is substituted for precision. The variable to be substituted, in the terms of Fig. 1, is $b/b + d$. This quantity is the number of items both irrelevant and retrieved divided by the number of items irrelevant, or the proportion of irrelevant items retrieved, and is an estimate of the conditional probability that an item will be retrieved given that it is irrelevant.

As in my earlier article (1), I refer to the retrieval of an irrelevant item as a "false drop." Also for consistency, the retrieval of a relevant item is termed a "hit," so instead of the term "recall ratio" I use "the conditional probability of a hit." Some of the notation used here differs from that of the previous article. Here, as seen in Fig. 1, lower-case letters, r and $\bar{r}$, designate relevant and irrelevant items, while upper-case letters, R and $\bar{R}$, designate retrieved and unretrieved items. The two conditional probabilities of principal interest are here denoted $P(R \mid r)$ and $P(R \mid \bar{r})$. In the present notation, the curve we shall consider has $a/a + c$ or $P(R \mid r)$ on the ordinate and $b/b + d$ or $P(R \mid \bar{r})$ on the abscissa. This curve is a comparison of two "operating characteristics," as the term is used in statistics, and is called here the "relative operating characteristic," or "ROC."

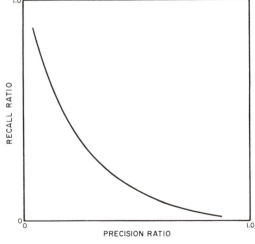

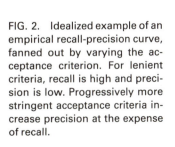

FIG. 2.   Idealized example of an empirical recall-precision curve, fanned out by varying the acceptance criterion. For lenient criteria, recall is high and precision is low. Progressively more stringent acceptance criteria increase precision at the expense of recall.

One consideration in choosing the two variables used in decision theory, which are derived from the two columns of the relevance-retrieval contingency table, is that they contain all the information in the table; the remaining quantities of the table ("misses" and "correct rejections") are, respectively, their complements. The recall and precision ratios are derived from a column and a row of the table and do not serve to specify the remainder of the table.

A related, but more salient, consideration is that using the two variables of decision theory permits us to draw upon several models of the retrieval process which stipulate different forms that empirical *ROC* curves may take. That is, each of several available models developed within decision theory precisely specifies a given form for a theoretical *ROC* curve. Or rather, each model specifies a family of *ROC* curves having an index of effectiveness as the parameter. Conveniently, the *ROC* curves of all but one of the models devised to date are straight lines or very nearly straight lines when plotted on linear normal-deviate, or "binormal," scales. A single number is adequate as an index of effectiveness, because it is sufficient to generate the entire curve, under those models that assume some fixed relationship between the degree of effectiveness and the slope of the curve. Generality is gained at the cost of a second parameter in one model that permits a variable relationship between effectiveness and slope. Still another model gives a one-parameter fit to data without regard to the slope, or, for that matter, without regard to the general form of the *ROC* curve, but this number is not sufficient to regenerate the curve from which it is taken. We turn now to a description of these alternative models, and then to the retrieval data that will enable us to choose from among them the one or ones that will be useful.

The General Decision Model

Though the assumption is not essential to their application, I shall assume in describing the alternative decision-theory models that for each query submitted to a system, the system in some manner assigns an index value (call it z) to each item in the store to represent the degree of relevance of the item to the query. Plotting separately for irrelevant and relevant items the probability of assignment of each value of z yields two probability density functions. One form the two density functions might have is depicted in Fig. 3. The left-hand and function is associated with irrelevant items, $f(z \mid \bar{r})$, and the right-hand function is associated with relevant items, $f(z \mid r)$.

If, as suggested in the figure, any given value of z might be assigned by the system to item that is relevant or to an item that is irrelevant (as judged by a user or other umpire), then, as shown, some criterion value of z, denoted z_c, should be adopted, such that items assigned values greater than z_c are retrieved while items assigned values less than z_c are not retrieved. The areas under the two density functions to the right of z_c represent the probabilities of retrieving

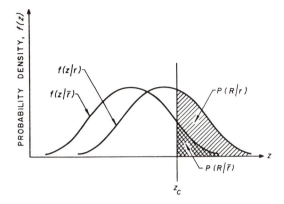

FIG. 3.   One possible representation of the density functions for relevant and irrelevant items. The abscissa is the index of relevance, z,
assigned by the system to each item. An acceptance criterion is labeled z_c.

irrelevant and relevant items. They are the coordinates of the *ROC* curve, $P(R \mid r)$
and $P(R \mid \bar{r})$.

Any given separation between the two density functions represents a stable
retrieval system, with some particular capacity to distinguish between relevant
and irrelevant items or some particular degree of effectiveness. For a fixed
separation between the density functions, variation in the acceptance criterion z_c
will result in a particular *ROC* curve. Another system or method, with greater or
lesser ability to discriminate relevant and irrelevant items, will yield a different
ROC curve as the acceptance criterion is varied.

The exact form of an *ROC* curve, it is clear, depends upon the shapes of the
density functions that underlie it. Various measurement models are generated by
hypothesizing density functions of different shapes.

Gaussian, Equal-variance Model

The density functions shown in Fig. 3 are Gaussian and of equal variance. Given
the separation shown, variation in the acceptance criterion will trace the *ROC*
curve labeled $E = 1$ in Fig. 4. The measure E is defined as the difference
between the means of the two density functions divided by their common standard deviation. If the separation is increased so that the difference between the
means is twice as great as that shown in Fig. 3, then criterion variation will
produce the *ROC* curve labeled $E = 2$ in Fig. 4.

We see that empirical data obtained from a test of a retrieval system could be
plotted in the space of Fig. 4. If the data points followed the contour of one of the
curves shown, or one of the intermediate curves not shown, the label on that

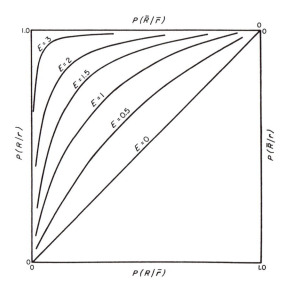

FIG. 4. A family of relative-operating-characteristic curves, based on Gaussian density functions of equal variance, with values of the parameter *E*. Labels on the upper and right-hand scales indicate that the full relevance-retrieval contingency table can be recovered from the plot.

curve would completely describe the effectiveness of the system: Knowing the single number permits reconstruction of the entire curve.

It is more convenient to plot data fitted by the *ROC* curves of Fig. 4 on binormal scales, that is, on axes scaled linearly for the normal deviate, for then these *ROC* curves are straight lines with unit slope, as shown in Fig. 5. The measure *E* for any curve can be read from the normal-deviate scales; one simply subtracts the value on the right-hand scale from the value on the top scale corresponding to any point on the curve. In Fig. 5, *E* is also scaled along the negative diagonal.

It can be seen that for practical purposes *E* has a maximum of approximately 5.0; though the axes could be extended to show higher values of *E*, effectiveness is not really at issue for retrieval systems yielding a hit probability greater than 0.99 and, simultaneously, a false-drop probability less than 0.01. There is the additional fact that reliable estimation of such extreme probabilities demands a sample of excessive size.

Gaussian, Unequal-variance Model

If the density functions are Gaussian, but of unequal variance, the *ROC* curves on the scales of Fig. 5 will be linear with slopes other than unity. In particular, the slope of the *ROC* curve is equal to the ratio of the standard deviation of $f(z \mid \bar{r})$ to the standard deviation of $f(z \mid r)$.

For density functions of unequal variance, E must be redefined, for it was previously defined in terms of a standard deviation common to the two functions. Note that for *ROC* curves of non-unit slope, the value of E obtained by subtracting a normal-deviate value on the right scale from one on the top scale is not constant along the curve. The definition adopted here consists in normalizing the difference between the means of the two density functions by their average standard deviation; this definition is reflected by measuring E at the intersection of the *ROC* curve and the negative diagonal of the *ROC* space.

Now, at least two alternatives are open to us. If we find that the slopes of empirical *ROC* curves vary without regard to E (measured at the intercept of the negative diagonal), two parameters will be needed to fit the curve. Reconstruction of the curve will require reporting the value of the slope, s, in addition to the value of E. It could turn out, on the other hand, that s bears some fixed relation to E, for example, that s increases regularly as E increases. This would be the case if the ratio of the increment in the mean of $f(z \mid r)$ to a decrement in its standard deviation were a constant. If this constant were a stable property of a given retrieval system, it could be reported once, and then the single value of E would

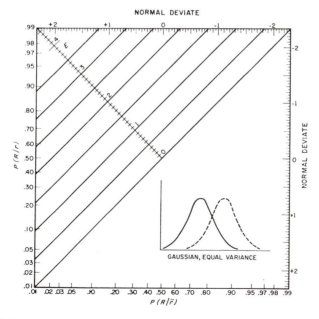

FIG. 5.   The relative-operating-characteristic curves of Fig. 4 on binormal scales, that is, on axes scaled linearly for the normal deviate. Density functions inserted at lower right identify the basis of these *ROC* curves in Gaussian, equal-variance density functions.

be sufficient to describe the various curves the system produces as a result of changes in one or another independent variable.

Exponential Model

Simply as an illustration of further modelling possibilities, consider hypothesizing that the density functions are exponential in form, as shown at the lower right in Fig. 6. Then, again, the *ROC* curve is essentially linear on probability scales and can be described by a single parameter. The parameter $K = \sqrt{k}$ is defined in the figure; for $k > 1.0$, the *ROC* curves have the property that s decreases regularly as the effectiveness (K) increases.

Distribution-free Model

If, after looking at data, hypothesizing some particular form of the density functions, and hence of the *ROC* curve, seems too strong a procedure, we can resort to a measurement scheme that leaves these forms unspecified and free to vary. We can take as the measure of effectiveness the percentage of the area of the *ROC* space that falls beneath any empirical *ROC* curve, when plotted on linear scales (as in Fig. 4). This measure, call it *A*, will vary from 50% for a curve that follows the positive diagonal, representing equal hit and false-drop proportions

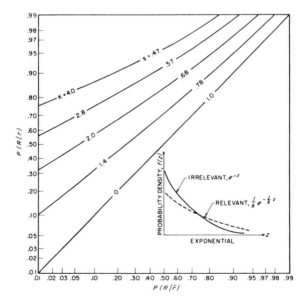

FIG. 6. A family of *ROC* curves based on exponential density functions, plotted on probability scales.

or no discrimination, to 100% for a curve that follows the extreme left and top coordinates of the graph, representing a hit proportion of 1.0 at a false-drop proportion of 0.0 or perfect discrimination. The measure A, though a simple summary measure of effectiveness, does not permit reconstruction of the empirical curve from which it is drawn. It has the property useful for conceptual purposes that the value of A is equal to the percentage of correct choices a system will make when attempting to select from a pair of items, one drawn at random from the irrelevant set and one drawn at random from the relevant set, the item that is relevant. As demonstrated elsewhere (4) this equality holds for *ROC* curves of any form.

DATA

The three sets of data we shall examine were collected, respectively, at the Computation Laboratory of Harvard University by Gerard Salton (now at Cornell University) and Michael Lesk; under the Aslib project at Cranfield, England, by Cyril Cleverdon and Michael Keen; and at Arthur D. Little, Inc., by Vincent E. Giuliano and Paul E. Jones. These data were originally presented in technical reports published in late 1966 (*3, 5, 6*).

Salton and Lesk and Giuliano and Jones kindly made their raw data available to me so that I could calculate the hit and false-drop proportions. Cleverdon and Keen presented these quantities in their report. Though they are not responsible for the outcome, one or more of the authors of each report discussed with me the problem of measurement and commented on a draft of this paper. Their cooperation was essential, and I am pleased to acknowledge their very helpful advice and criticism.

Plots of data following are identified by the various terms for independent variables used in the original reports, to make possible cross references, but the terms are not defined here. Similarly, our present purposes do not require a description of the procedures of the three sets of experiments. However, a brief characterization of the scopes of the studies will be helpful in evaluating the general conclusions drawn here.

At Harvard, the questions asked experimentally include these: "Can automatic text processing methods be used effectively to replace a manual content analysis; if so, what parts of the documents [titles, abstracts, full text] are most appropriate for incorporation into the analysis? Is it necessary to provide vocabulary normalization methods to eliminate linguistic ambiguities; should such normalization be handled by means of specially constructed dictionaries, or is it possible to replace thesauruses by statistical word association methods? What dictionaries can be used most effectively for vocabulary normalization? Is it important to provide hierarchical subject arrangements, as is done in library classification systems; alternatively, should syntactical relations between subject identifiers be preserved? Does the user have an important role to fulfill in controlling the search procedure?" (5, pp. I-3, I-4). The experimental retrieval system, which operated on an IBM 7094 computer, was fully automatic in most applications; content-analysis procedures incorporated into the system processed documents and queries in natural language with no prior manual analysis. Stores of items used consisted of four collections of documents in three subject fields: documentation, aerodynamics, and computer sciences.

Experiments at Cranfield were based on manual analysis of documents. They were conducted to examine several different index languages (some languages using single terms, others based on concepts, and others based on a thesaurus); the exhaustivity of indexing; the level of specificity of index terms; a gradation of relevance assessments; and the amount of intelligence applied in formulating search rules. Two collections used consisted of documents in aerodynamics and aircraft structures.

The experiments at Arthur D. Little, Inc., evaluated manual and automatic indexing; length of the query; coordinate retrieval methods; and retrieval methods based on statistical word associations, with and without human intervention. The system operated on an IBM 1401 computer, with fully automatic indexing in most applications. All items in the file were abstracts of reports in the aerospace field.

Data from the three sources lead to the same conclusions about the usefulness of a decision-theory measure, so the analyses of the three sets of data will be presented with little evaluative comment prior to a general discussion of results. Each of the *ROC* plots is made on probability scales. Most of the plots summarize the results of one method of retrieval used with a given system; a few of them summarize the results of a single query used with a given method. The first question we ask is whether or not the plots of data are adequately fitted by straight lines. If they are, then we are interested in the slopes of the lines.

Harvard-Cornell Data

All of the data I obtained from the Harvard-Cornell project are presented here; this set includes almost all of the data collected under the project before June of 1966, the major exception being some collected toward the end of that time in tests permitting iterative searches under the user's control.

The system at Harvard, called "SMART," assesses the relevance of each item in the store to each query addressed to the system. Print-outs of data containing the relevance index for each item are, of course, extensive, and are not usually obtained; therefore we can not examine directly the shapes of the density functions. The standard print-out lists, for each query, the code number of every item relevant to it and the rank value of each of these items in a list ordered (by the system) according to degree of relevance. Data in this form permit adopting, for purposes of analysis, each of several arbitrary acceptance criteria according to the total number of items considered as retrieved. That is, $P(R \mid r)$ and $P(R \mid \bar{r})$ are calculated in turn, for example, for the 5 items ranked highest, the 10 items ranked highest, the 15 items ranked highest, and so forth, terminating at an arbitrary point.

To gain a relatively stable sample, results are combined for all queries used with a single method. One can pool results before calculating $P(R \mid r)$ and $P(R \mid \bar{r})$, or alternatively, can calculate these quantities for each query and take their average. The first of these procedures was followed in the analyses reported here.

Figure 7 shows the results for the collection of items in the subject field of documentation (called the ADI collection), under each of six retrieval methods. As in subsequent figures, in order to conserve space, only a portion of the *ROC* space is shown for each plot; the last panel in the figure reproduces the lines of the previous panels on the full *ROC* space. These lines, in all cases, were fitted to the data by eye.

The data are quite adequately fitted by straight lines in every instance. Indeed, according to standards acquired through experience in other fields (for example, human signal detection and recognition memory) where the decision-theory measure has proved to be useful (*4*), the fits are very good.

A small staircase effect can be discerned in the data. This effect may be the result of having a relatively small sample (containing an average of five relevant items for 35 questions); the procedure used in analysis for defining acceptance criteria forces each successive point a certain distance to the right, and a low density of relevant items would produce irregular upward movement. In any case, the effect is not large enough to be of much concern. We can see also some variation in the slopes of the lines; we shall consider the significance of this variation after all the data have been examined.

Figure 8 shows the results of seven retrieval methods applied to a collection of items on aerodynamics borrowed by the Harvard-Cornell group from the Cranfield project. Again, the straight-line fits exceed reasonable aspirations, and a variation in slopes appears.

Figure 9 represents one of two collections in the subject area of computer science, called IRE 1, and six retrieval methods. Figure 10 shows the second IRE collection and 10 methods. Figure 11 shows the second IRE collection with a different set of 10 methods.

With the IRE collection we notice a tendency, at higher values of E, for the slopes to be greater than unity. The slopes in Fig. 9 range from 0.95 to 1.12, in Fig. 10 from 0.98 to 1.40, and in Fig. 11 from 1.20 to 1.56. With the ADI collection (Fig. 7) the slopes range from 0.83 to 0.99, and with the Cranfield collection (Fig. 8), from 0.76 to 1.00.

We can't help but observe the substantive result of this analysis that the differences in effectiveness among the various methods are small relative to the differences among collections. The range in E for the six methods applied to the ADI collection is 0.20 (from 0.90 to 1.10); for the seven methods used with the Cranfield collection, 0.35 (from 1.45 to 1.80); for the six methods used with the IRE 1 collection, 0.40 (from 2.00 to 2.40); for the first 10 methods used

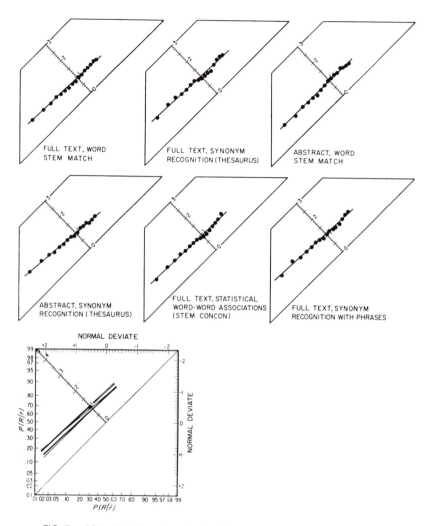

FIG. 7. ADI collection: 6 methods. 82 items, 35 queries. 170 relevant + 2,700 irrelevant = 2,870 total. Criteria: 3, 6, 9, . . . , 47 retrievals. Harvard-Cornell: Salton and Lesk.

with the IRE 2 collection, 0.55 (from 1.95 to 2.50); and for the second group of 10 methods used with the IRE 2 collection, 0.30 (from 2.10 to 2.40). These ranges, on the order of 0.50 or less, can be compared with the range over all collections of 1.60, keeping in mind the scale range of about 5.00 from chance performance to very good performance. The Harvard-Cornell and Cranfield investigators are inclined to believe that the dependency of effectiveness on the collection results both from differences in the "hardness" of the vocabularies of

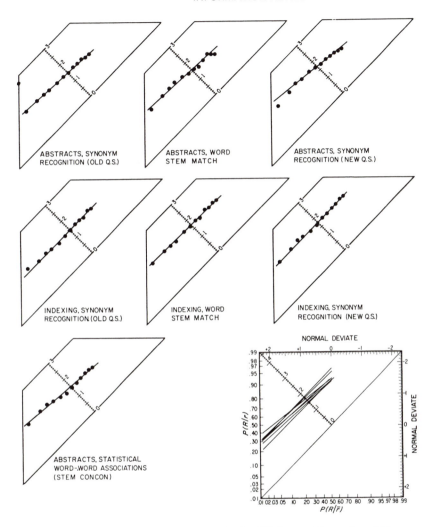

FIG. 8.   Cranfield collection: 7 methods. 200 items, 42 queries. 198 relevant + 8,202 irrelevant = 8,400 total. Criteria: 5, 10, 15, 20, 30, 40, . . . , 100 retrievals. Harvard-Cornell: Salton and Lesk.

the three subject fields and from the use of different procedures with the three collections for establishing relevance (7).

Cranfield Data

The study at Cranfield has been actively pursued for several years, and the last report contains an enormous amount of data. I have plotted only a fraction of the

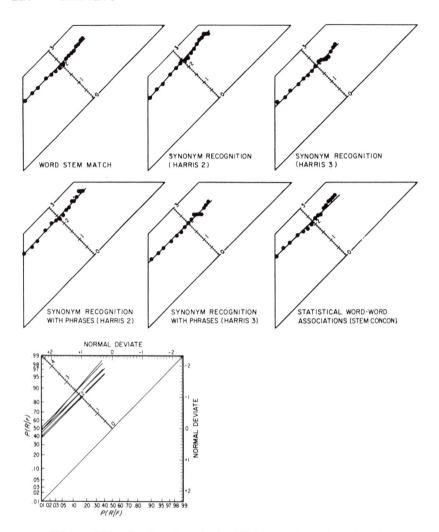

FIG. 9.   IRE1 collection: 6 methods. 405 items, 17 queries. 186 relevant + 6,699 irrelevant = 6,885 total. Criteria: 10, 15, 20, 30, 40, . . . ,
150 retrievals. Harvard-Cornell: Salton and Lesk.

results; however, I am not aware of any particular bias in my casual sampling,
and all the plots prepared are included here.

The Cranfield data are distinguished from the Harvard data in being based on
a larger file (in most cases 1,400 items, as compared with the largest Harvard
collection of about 400 items), and on more questions (approximately 220, as
compared with the Harvard maximum of about 40). One consequence is the
appearance of lower false-drop proportions, proportions that fall off the graph
paper (Codex Graph Sheet No. 41,453) used in the preceding figures. So we use

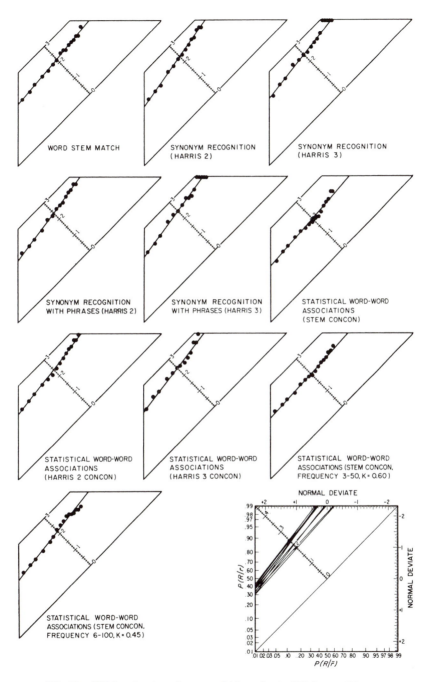

FIG. 10.   IRE 2 collection: first set of 10 methods. 380 items, 17 queries. 181 relevant + 6,279 irrelevant = 6,460 total. Criteria: 10, 15, 20, 30, 40, . . . , 150 retrievals. Harvard-Cornell: Salton and Lesk.

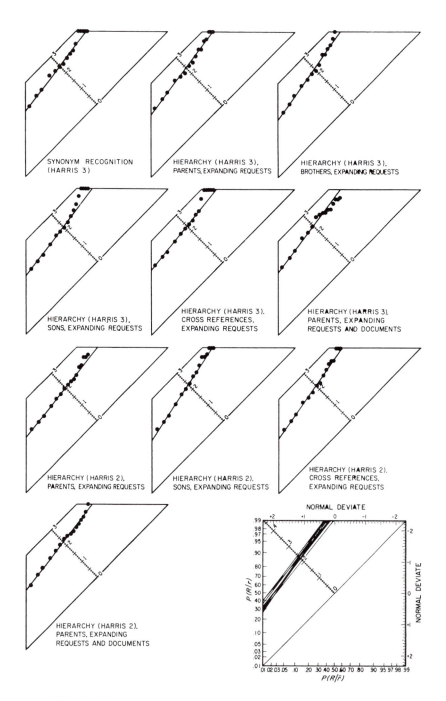

FIG. 11. IRE 2 collection, second set of 10 methods. 380 items, 17 queries. 178 relevant + 6,282 irrelevant = 6,460 total. Criteria: 10, 15, 20, 30, 40, . . . , 150 retrievals. Harvard-Cornell: Salton and Lesk.

another graph paper (Keuffel and Esser Co. No. 47 8062) that ranges down to a proportion of 0.0001. Though the graphs have on them scales of the normal deviate, these scales, unfortunately, are not given on the Keuffel and Esser paper available commercially.

In the Cranfield system, a manual one, the relevance of every item to every query is determined by judges, but the system itself does not rank items according to their degree of relevance to the query. Various acceptance criteria are obtained by establishing different "levels of coordination," that is, by varying the requirements on the number of query terms an item must satisfy in order to be retrieved.

Figure 12 shows the results of five retrieval methods that vary in the "recall

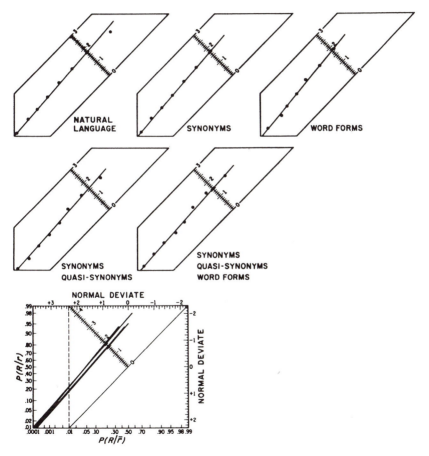

FIG. 12. Recall devices, single-term index language: 5 methods. 1,400 items, 221 queries. 1,590 relevant + 307,810 irrelevant = 309,400 total. Criteria: levels of coordination. Cranfield: Cleverdon and Keen.

device" they employ. The slopes are quite uniform, slightly greater than unity, and not many of the points fall off the fitted lines. Essentially the same comments apply to Fig. 13, which shows two levels of indexing exhaustivity for two sets of recall devices. Likewise for Fig. 14, which illustrates the effects of requiring different degrees of relevance for retrieval to be effected. The left panel results when all four categories of judged relevance satisfy the retrieval criterion; moving to the right, the relevance requirement is strengthened, so that in the last panel we have the results when only those items with the highest degree of relevance are retrieved. Figure 15 shows some results obtained with a smaller collection when retrieval is based on only titles and abstracts, or on titles only, and the fits are about as good as before.

In Fig. 15 values of E range from 1.33 to 1.70, and values of the slope range from 0.80 to 0.95. In the three figures preceding, E ranges from 1.58 to 1.86, and s lies between 1.08 and 1.18.

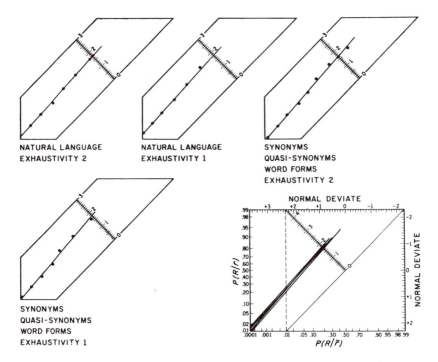

FIG. 13.   Indexing exhaustivity, single-term index language: 4 methods. 1,400 items, 221 queries. 1,590 relevant + 307,810 irrelevant = 309,400 total. Criteria: levels of coordination. Cranfield: Cleverdon and Keen.

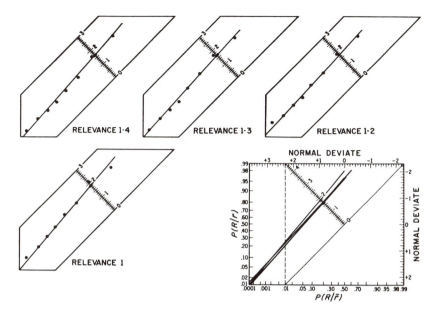

FIG. 14. Document relevance, single-term index language, natural language: 4 methods. 1,400 items, 50 queries. Relevance 1–4: 361 relevant + 69,639 irrelevant = 70,000 total. Relevance 1–3: 297 relevant + 69,703 irrelevant = 70,000 total. Relevance 1–2: 155 relevant + 69,845 irrelevant = 70,000 total. Relevance 1: 95 relevant + 69,905 irrelevant = 70,000 total. Criteria: levels of coordination. Cranfield: Cleverdon and Keen.

Arthur D. Little, Inc., Data

Like the Harvard system, the system constructed at Arthur D. Little, Inc. (ADL) assigns an index value to each item according to its relevance for each query. Again, however, the system did not produce a print-out of data in full enough form to enable us to look directly at the density functions supposed to underlie the *ROC* curves.

The ADL system was used with a still larger store, effectively 4,000 items. I have based arbitrary acceptance criteria, again, on the number of items considered as retrieved. The terminal criterion, in this case, was determined by the ADL investigators; they proceeded through the items according to their rank to judge the relevance of each, and stopped when it seemed that relevant items were turning up on a random basis. In order to determine the recall ratio or hit proportion, the total number of relevant items for each query had to be established. These numbers were estimated at ADL from a sample of 400 items drawn from the store of 4,000 items.

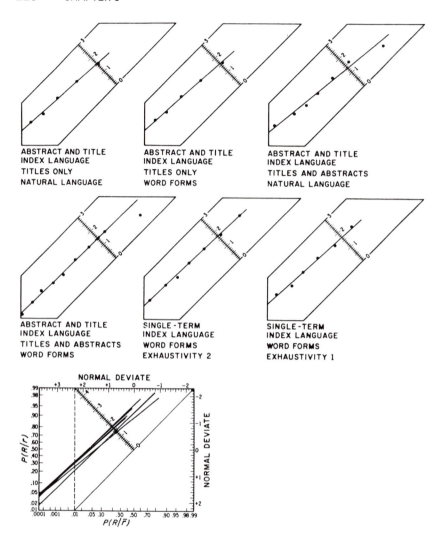

FIG. 15. Abstracts and titles: 6 methods. 200 items, 42 queries. 198 relevant + 8,202 irrelevant = 8,400 total. Criteria: levels of coordination. Cranfield: Cleverdon and Keen.

Included in the following figures are almost all the data, and all the major data, collected at Arthur D. Little, Inc. A difference between these and foregoing is that most of these are based on single queries. The data points, surprisingly, do not show much greater scatter about a line, but substantially greater variation in the slopes is evident.

Figure 16 shows the associative retrieval method applied to four queries

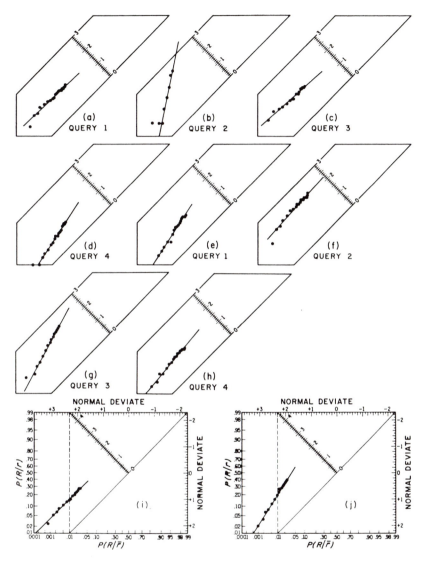

FIG. 16. (a)–(d): Fully automatic associative, 4 full-text queries. (e)–(h): Fully automatic associative, 4 CBU queries. 4,000 items. Number relevant: Query 1, 80; Query 2, 30; Query 3, 70; Query 4, 100. (i), (j): Average of Queries 1, 3, and 4. (i): full-text queries; (j): CBU queries. Criteria: 5, 10, 15, 20, 30, 40, . . . , retrievals. Arthur D. Little, Inc.: Giuliano and Jones.

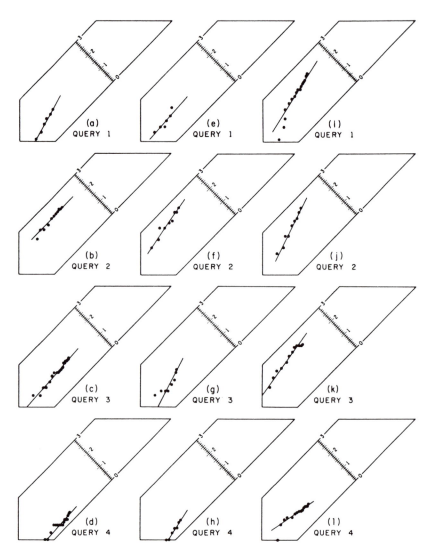

FIG. 17.   CBU queries: 3 methods. (a)–(d): Modified coordinate. (e)–
(h): Frequency-weighted coordinate. (i)–(l): Selected associations.
Number of items, number relevant per query, and criteria as in Fig. 16.
Arthur D. Little, Inc.: Giuliano and Jones.

which consisted of abstracts ("full text queries"). Also shown is the same method
applied to briefer forms of the same queries. In the latter case ("CBU queries")
the queries consisted of critical word strings selected from the abstracts, designated as "content-bearing units." The full *ROC* plots show the pooled results for
queries *1*, *3*, and *4* for each type of query. Query 2 was excluded from the pooled
results because the range of acceptance criteria available for it was relatively

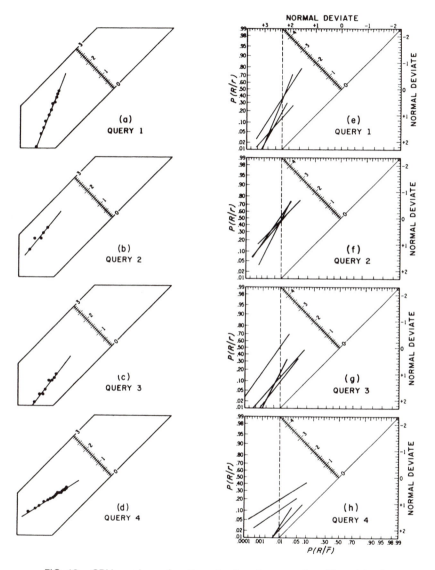

FIG. 18. CBU queries: a fourth method, and summaries of it and the 3 methods of Fig. 17. (a)–(d): Reweighted associative. (e)–(h): results of 4 methods for each query. Number of items, number relevant per query, and criteria as in Fig. 16. Arthur D. Little, Inc.: Giuliano and Jones.

limited, and various means of pooling queries with different ranges of acceptance criteria proved unsatisfactory. If the curves of the last two plots are extrapolated to the negative diagonal, values of E are obtained (approximately 1.30 and 2.20) that lie in the range of empirical values noted earlier. The slopes of the lines (approximately 1.00 and 1.50) are also in the range of empirical values noted earlier.

Figure 17 shows three different retrieval methods used with the short queries. Figure 18 shows another method and reproduces the fitted lines for the four methods of Figs. 17 and 18 for each query. There is a tendency for the slopes to depend more upon the query than the method. Averaging over methods, the slopes range from about 1.00 for query 4, through approximately 1.45 for queries 2 and 3, to about 1.75 for query 1. Average slopes for the four methods lie between 1.28 and 1.52. The average values of E associated with the four methods, by extrapolation, range from 1.60 to 2.10.

We may note that the highest value of E, 2.10, is obtained with the method called "selected associations," shown in panels (i) through (l) of Fig. 17. It can be seen that, in fitting straight lines to the data obtained with that method, data points falling below the line at the lower false-drop probabilities were virtually ignored in the case of two queries (queries 1 and 4). Clearly, if we were to restrict our interest to low false-drop probabilities—say, if we were to consider only the left-most half-dozen or so points—then the slopes for that method would be steeper, and the values of E estimated would be higher. In fact, if the four queries are pooled with only the left-most nine points included, the resulting value of E is close to 3.0 (and the resulting slope is about 1.8). The "selected-associations" method is one of two methods tried at ADL with user intervention between iterative searches. The other method in which adjustments were made between iterations is the one called "reweighted associative," shown in Fig. 18; in that case all the data points are quite well taken into account in fitting lines, and an E = 1.90 is obtained.

CONCLUSIONS

The consistent linearity of the empirical relative-operating-characteristic curves confirms that a decision-theory measure can be used to reflect solely the effectiveness of a retrieval system, and effectiveness unconfounded by variation in the acceptance criterion. The apparently irregular variation in the slopes of the curves presents a slight complication relative to achieving a measure that is a single number, but not enough of a complication to impair seriously the usefulness of a decision-theory measure.

Two numbers—E measured at the negative diagonal of the ROC space, and the slope, s—give an accurate description of the curve representing constant retrieval effectiveness over varying acceptance criteria. Two numbers are not as convenient as one, but these particular two give a considerably more economical description of the performance curve than available previously and can be reported in cases where conveying information about the full curve is desirable.

The data at hand indicate, however, that for most purposes conclusions about effectiveness can be drawn from the value of E alone, without regard to s. In short, there is little point in concern over small differences in s when differences in E are small. We have seen that when values of s are based on more than a few queries they do not vary enough to obscure a substantial difference in E.

What constitutes a "substantial difference" in E, or a difference of practical significance? An approximate answer derived from the present data is that a difference in E in the neighborhood of 0.30 to 0.50 is a reasonably significant one. Thus, for example, in the Harvard data based on the IRE collections (Figs. 9, 10, 11), a difference between two methods of that magnitude corresponds to a factor of about two in the false-drop probability. (By way of illustration, it can be seen in Fig. 9 that at a hit probability of 0.90 the extreme methods show false-drop probabilities of approximately 0.25 and 0.13; at a hit probability of 0.70 the extreme false-drop probabilities are about 0.13 and 0.07; at a hit probability of 0.50 the extreme false-drop probabilities are about 0.02 and 0.01.) It seems unlikely that a smaller experimental difference would have much practical import.

As discussed earlier, if it should seem worthwhile to have a measure that is both a single number and sensitive to variation in slope, the distribution-free measure A could be used. Let us use the measure A now to get a different view of the observed differences among methods in the present sample, a view that will help us judge how small a difference in E is practically significant. A, it will be recalled, is the proportion of the area of the ROC space that lies beneath an ROC curve plotted on linear scales (as in Fig. 4), and is equal to the probability of choosing between two items, one drawn at random from the relevant set and the other drawn at random from the irrelevant set, the item that is relevant. Assume for the purpose at hand that all of the ROC curves in our sample are of unit slope; this approximation introduces a distortion that is negligible relative to the point of interest here, and permits a conversion from E to A by means of published tables (8). For the Harvard data, values of A, or values of the probability of a correct choice in a two-alternative forced-choice test, denoted $P_2(C)$, range from 0.74 to 0.78 for the ADI collection (Fig. 7), from 0.85 to 0.90 for the Cranfield collection (Fig. 8), and from 0.92 to 0.96 for the IRE collections (Figs. 9, 10, 11). For the Cranfield data, $P_2(C)$ ranges from 0.87 to 0.91 for the large collection (Figs. 12, 13, 14) and from 0.83 to 0.89 for the small collection (Fig. 15). For the data collected at Arthur D. Little, Inc., the range of the four "CBU" methods (Figs. 17, 18), averaged over the four queries, is from 0.87 to 0.93. It might be argued, again, that the differences between extreme methods for any collection, of 0.04 to 0.06, are real differences, but it seems unlikely that differences of less than 0.04 in $P_2(C)$ have material implications.

These values of $P_2(C)$ lying between 0.74 and 0.96 indicate that present retrieval methods leave considerable room for improvement. (Said otherwise, these values of $P_2(C)$, considered along with the competence and diligence with which the experiments here represented were pursued, indicate that information retrieval is a very difficult problem.) On the face of it, choosing the single relevant item from a collection of two items is not a demanding task, and we should hope that our retrieval systems would make the correct choice almost every time, say, with a probability of 0.99 or greater. A more compelling impression, however, of the current state of the retrieval art is gained by taking pairs of hit and false-drop probabilities from the empirical ROC curves and converting these probabilities to raw numbers.

Consider an ROC curve with $E = 2.5$ and $s = 1.3$. This curve is close to the best of the curves seen in the foregoing, and exceeded by none of them. It passes through the points $P(R \mid \bar{r})$ and $P(R \mid r)$ having coordinate values of $(0.001; 0.12)$, $(0.01, 0.42)$, and $(0.10, 0.88)$. Assume a file of 3,000 items and a group of queries to each of which 10 of the 3,000 items are relevant. Now, if we will settle for retrieving, on the average, only 1 of the 10 relevant items per query, we will also receive 3 false drops each time. If we desire 4 of 10 relevant items, we will have to winnow the 4 from 30 irrelevant items. If we should aspire to 9 of 10 relevant items, we would have to examine more than 300 items in response to each query to find the 9.

These noise-to-signal ratios are dramatically large. The ratio mounts rapidly even for a file as small as 3,000 items: from 3 to 7 to 33 for the three acceptance criteria of the example. For a file of 10,000 items the corresponding noise-to-signal ratios are 10, 25, and 100 plus. It is with these ratios in mind that I earlier suggested dismissing small differences in E and ignoring small variations in s.

The decision-theory analysis can be seen to set the stage clearly for identifying an important advance in retrieval technique. The best of the performances sampled here, in the vicinity of $E = 2.5$ and $s = 1.3$, gives a false-drop probability of approximately 0.10 for a hit probability of 0.90. Assuming the same slope, and taking the same hit probability, an $E = 3.0$ corresponds to a false-drop probability of 0.05, and an $E = 3.8$ corresponds to a false-drop probability of 0.01. An $E = 4.0$ means a false-drop probability of 0.005, or reception of 15 unwanted items along with 9 of the 10 wanted items from a file of 3,000. An $E = 4.5$ means a false-drop probability of 0.001, or reception of 3 unwanted items along with 9 of the 10 wanted items from a file of 3,000.

A belief of several people working in the retrieval field is that a very significant advance in retrieval effectiveness will be achieved in the near future by "on-line" systems, in which the user is given immediate feedback and enabled to progressively refine the search prescription over successive trial searches. It will be informative to apply the decision-theory analysis in experiments on on-line procedures. Will we see values of E in the vicinity of 3.0, or 3.5? Might we even find values of E about 4.0—or will present knowledge of language forms impose a barrier at a lower level of effectiveness?

REFERENCES

1. Swets, J. A., Information Retrieval Systems, *Science,* 141:245–250 (1963).
2. Bourne, C. P., *Annual Review of Information Science and Technology,* Interscience, New York, 1966, Chapter 7, pp. 176–179.
3. Cleverdon, C., and M. Keen, *Factors Determining the Performance of Indexing Systems,* vol. 2, *Test Results,* Association of Special Libraries and Information Bureaux, Cranfield, England, 1966.
4. Green, D. M., and J. A. Swets, *Signal Detection Theory and Psychophysics,* John Wiley, New York, 1966, pp. 45–51. Reprinted by Peninsula Publishing, Los Altos, CA, 1988.
5. Salton, G., M. Lesk, et al., *Information Storage and Retrieval,* Scientific Report No. ISR-11, Department of Computer Science, Cornell University, 1966.
6. Giuliano, V. E., and P. E. Jones, *Study and Test of a Methodology for Laboratory Evaluation of Message Retrieval Systems,* Interim Report, Arthur D. Little, Inc., Cambridge, Mass., 1966.
7. Lesk, M., and M. Keen, Personal communications, 1967.
8. Swets, J. A. (Ed.), *Signal Detection and Recognition by Human Observers,* John Wiley, New York, 1964, pp. 682–683. Reprinted by Peninsula Publishing, Los Altos, CA, 1988.

10 Predictive Validities of Aptitude Tests

Signal detection theory and its relative operating characteristic (ROC) are firmly established in psychophysics. Interested readers can readily find systematic accounts of the theory and methodology (see, e.g., Green & Swets, 1988). For most psychologists, in all probability, there is no other known area of application. A recent review, however, has extended application of the theory and methodology to measuring the accuracy of diagnostic and predictive systems in widely different areas of research (Swets, 1988, Chapter 4 in this volume).

Applications require that the predictor variable be continuously or quasi continuously distributed and that the criterion be a dichotomy or convertible to a dichotomy. The ratio of signal to noise changes monotonically with the level of the continuous predictor, and a prediction or decision is made concerning the presence or absence of the signal at each of multiple levels of the predictor. The accuracy of the predictions or decisions at each level of the predictor determines the ROC curve. The A_z statistic is defined by the area under the curve and describes the degree of accuracy in detecting the signal. The zero point of the A_z scale is .50, which is the chance level of the yes/no decision, and the maximum value is 1.00.

SOME NUMERICAL EXAMPLES

Chapter 4 applied the ROC and the index A_z to weather forecasting and reported an A_z of .89 for a forecast of extreme cold and .71 for intervals of temperature. In an information-retrieval application, the accuracy with which retrieval systems could select books and articles relevant to a selected topic and reject the irrelevant ones was tested. Accuracy depends on subject matter. In medical imaging, the accuracy with which human diagnosticians could detect pathology from records obtained with tomography, mammography, and chest x-rays was the objective. For example, an A_z of .97 was found for tomography.

Other applications did not achieve the level of accuracy, by and large, of the decisions in the first three. Materials testing on several Air Force bases involved the detection of cracks in aircraft wings. Wide variability from base to base was observed. Bases with higher accuracy either had better trained personnel or had interpreted the records in ways not generally used at other bases. Chapter 4 discussed polygraph lie detection and aptitude testing applications. An example of the latter involved dichotomizing an examination administered late in the academic year and using earlier tests as predictors. A_z values were in the .80s and low .90s. In four Navy schools, pass/fail predictions for the Armed Forces Qualifying Test were less accurate.

OUR MODIFIED OBJECTIVE

Chapter 4's discussion of these applications gave primary attention to the accuracy attained. Here we take a closer look at the relation of the A_z statistic to the commonly used biserial correlation (r_{bis}). We selected for this purpose a very large sample of published data obtained in an actual selection situation. The size of the sample provides a severe test of the fit of the model that, if the model is successful, should encourage additional applications in personnel-selection research.

SITUATIONS AND DATA SELECTED
FOR COMPARISON

Pilot Training in World War II

Three primary training classes for United States pilots in World War II were selected: Classes 43-H, 44-I, and 45-B. Data from these classes were attractive for several reasons. For one thing, sample sizes were large, and the elimination rate in primary training was substantial. Given a difference between theory and observation in the population, sample chi-squares increase linearly with the number of observations. Small chi-squares in these classes would be impressive evidence for the fit of the ROC model. Second, when the validity of the tests became established by experience in early classes in which tests were used only for classification, cut-off scores were imposed for pilot trainees by the U.S. Army Air Forces. This aspect of the data allowed us to study the effects of restriction in range of talent on A_z and r_{bis}. A third attractive feature of the data was that the criterion for minimally satisfactory pilot performance changed as the war progressed, which allowed us to test the robustness of the ROC curves and r_{bis} to different definitions of pass/fail.

Organization of pilot training.   Designations of pilot training classes provided information about the expected date of graduation (when pilot's wings and a commission as second lieutenant were awarded). Students spent two months each in preflight, primary, basic, and advanced training, with only a few days between each phase. Preflight training was physical and academic. The three flight training phases were conducted in successively more advanced aircraft. The pilot stanine, a normalized transformation in nine steps of a weighted raw-score composite of several different tests, was about equally valid at each stage of flight training after necessary corrections for restrictions in range of talent had been applied. The larger number of eliminations and the fewer sources of restriction of range of talent made the primary phase of flight training attractive for this research.

Approximately 40 civilian contract schools were involved in primary flight training and were organized, within the training command, into three regional commands. The schools were scattered from California to Florida, a few being north of the Sun Belt. Four students were typically assigned to an instructor so that, in round numbers, 10,000 students would have been evaluated by 2,500 instructors. In primary training, instructors were civilians, but their pass/fail recommendations were checked by military pilots.[1]

Changes in the predictor.   The tests and their weights entering the pilot stanine were changed from time to time as research information was accumulated. These changes took place quite rapidly in 1942, and the increases in predictive validity were substantial. The earliest class selected for the present research, 43-H, was tested on the pilot stanine of December 1942. This stanine was short of the level of predictive validity reached later but was much closer to that level than it was to the stanine of February 1942. The two later classes, 44-I and 45-B, were tested on the stanine of November 1943, which represented the second small increment in validity since 43-H and which had validity just short of the level of two subsequent changes.

Population sampled.   Even though there were fewer sources of restriction of range for the primary flight training phase, aviation students were highly selected

---

[1]In addition to information about the World War II Aviation Psychology Research Program in the two volumes referred to in this chapter (Davis, 1947; Dubois, 1947), an interested reader can consult the remaining 15 volumes. Of these, the four edited by Flanagan (1947), Melton (1947), Guilford and Lacey (1947), and Miller (1947) are most relevant to the present discussion. The titles of these four volumes are a sufficient guide to their contents.

when they entered preflight training (despite the absence of an educational requirement). The mean score on the Army General Classification Test (AGCT) of an experimental group accepted in pilot training without meeting any test requirement was 114 (DuBois, 1947). The passing score on the qualification test required of all other applicants prior to preflight training was approximately the equivalent of an AGCT score of 119 (Davis, 1947). In comparison, the normative mean and standard deviation for the AGCT were 100 and 20, respectively.

Data to Be Analyzed

Pass/fail data (taken from DuBois, 1947) for the three classes selected are presented in Table 1 as a function of the pilot stanine. Also included are the traditional correlations. The biserial correlations estimate what the product-moment correlation would have been if one of the variables in a bivariate normal distribution had not been dichotomized. The corrected biserials were obtained from the Pearson formula in which a standard deviation of 2.10 represented the range of talent in the standardization sample after augmentation by the typical frequency of credit for previous flying experience.

Change in predictor cut-off and standards in training. Between 43-H and 44-I, the decision was made to use a minimum cut-off of 4 on the pilot stanine for entry to pilot training. This cut-off was followed with few exceptions in 44-I and 45-B. A comparison of percentages eliminated across the rows defined by a given level of the stanine indicates that the definition of satisfactory performance in primary training also changed from one class to another. Instructors and check pilots in 44-I were more lenient than their counterparts in 43-H. The instructors may have been overly influenced by the knowledge that current classes were more highly selected than earlier ones. (They did not have access to the scores of individual trainees, however.) They may also have been influenced by early reverses followed by painfully slow gains in the progress of the war and the severe losses experienced by air crews in the early months of the war. The substantial increase in standards from 44-I to 45-B had a known cause: A shortage of pilots had become a surplus. The commander of the training command, almost certainly with the support of higher authority, instructed trainers to increase minimum standards for graduation.

Problems with biserial correlations. If the traditional correlations were completely satisfactory, the fit of signal detection theory to these data would be a matter of little direct concern to selection psychologists. Both uncorrected and corrected correlations are problematic. Although the assumption that a continuous normal distribution underlies the pass/fail decision is reasonable, the accuracy with which the product-moment correlation in the bivariate normal distribu-

TABLE 1
Pass/Fail Classification in Three Pilot Training Classes in World War II, Broken Down by Stanine Level

Stanine	43-H			44-I			45-B		
	No. passed	No. failed	% failed	No. passed	No. failed	% failed	No. passed	No. failed	% failed
9	663	45	6.4	683	17	2.4	1,061	86	7.5
8	565	101	15.2	718	76	9.6	464	96	17.1
7	988	249	20.1	1,166	159	12.0	801	229	22.2
6	1,184	486	29.1	1,306	327	20.0	834	425	33.8
5	1,127	708	38.6	962	405	29.6	513	357	41.0
4	841	827	49.6	359	282	44.0	144	301	55.2
3	401	620	60.7	2	3	—	0	3	—
2	148	397	71.5	1	0	—	0	1	—
1	43	214	83.3	0	0	—	0	1	—
Total	5,970	3,647	37.9	5,197	1,269	19.6	3,917	1,499	27.7
r_{bis}	.497			.409			.441		
Corrected r_{bis}[a]	.518			.540			.540		
SD	1.991			1.468			1.625		

Note. The data are from *The classification program* (Research Report No. 2, Army Air Forces Aviation Psychology Program) by P. H. DuBois, 1947, Washington, DC: U.S. Government Printing Office. In the public domain.
[a]Based on a standard deviation of 2.10 in the unrestricted range of talent. The corrected r_{bis} was the expected value after the standard deviation of the pilot stanine in the standardization sample (1.96) was augmented by the typical number of bonuses for previous flying experience.

tion is estimated depends on having a continuous predictor measure that is normally distributed in the sample.

Biserial correlations corrected for restriction in range of talent always fail to meet assumptions. If restriction in the predictor is imposed in a bivariate normal distribution by truncation, the linear regression of the criterion on the predictor is unaffected. Under these circumstances, the Pearson correction is accurate. The regression of the pass/fail dichotomy on the continuous measure is distinctly nonlinear, however, and the correlations corrected for restriction in range consistently underestimate the biserial correlation in the original range of talent. The gain in validity between 43-H and the two later classes is probably underestimated by the corrections in Table 1.

RESULTS AND EVALUATION

Basic Comparisons

The type of program for the fitting of ROCs in this exploration of the methodology is discussed by Swets and Pickett (1982), and a modification is discussed by Metz (1986).[2] ROCs for the three classes are presented in Figures 1, 2, and 3. Important numerical data generated by the program also appear. These are the slope of the linear fit on a binormal plot (as in the lower panel of each figure), denoted B_{sip}, and the area under the curve transposed to ordinary scales (as in the upper panel of each figure), taken as an accuracy or validity index and denoted A_z (the z connotes the binormal assumption). Also included are the chi-squares for the three classes after eliminating the small frequencies at Stanines 1–3 for 44-I and 45-B.

Goodness of fit. The chi-squares, like all such, are a function of the degrees of freedom. Also, as mentioned earlier, when the model is not precisely true, they are a function of sample size as well. Given the size of the sample in 43-H, the fit is remarkably good. Chi-squares for the other two classes also indicate satisfactory fits, although p values are smaller. Discrepancies between model and observation at Stanine 9 are perhaps attributable to the bonus for previous flying experience, which was an ad hoc solution to a complex problem. It is striking, however, that the curves for the two classes subjected to similar truncation at the lower end of the distribution of scores but to quite different decision biases are almost identical. If the two curves are plotted on the same graph, they can hardly be distinguished from each other with the naked eye.

---

[2]We used a version of Metz's program, not generally available, written by D. Tani of BBN Laboratories to supply graphic output on the Macintosh computer.

Best-fit ROC curve, P-Scale

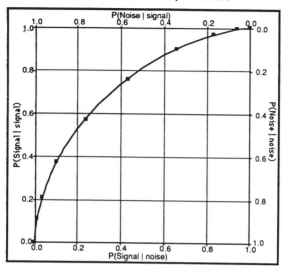

Best-fit ROC line, Z-Scale

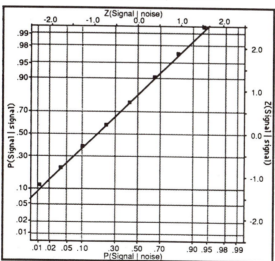

FIG. 1.   Fit of the ROC model to pass/fail data in Class 43-H (B_{slp} = .971; A_z = .734; χ^2 = 4.73 with 6 df, p > .50).

Best-fit ROC curve, P-Scale

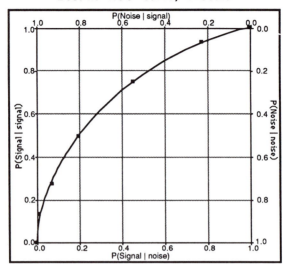

Best-fit ROC line, Z-Scale

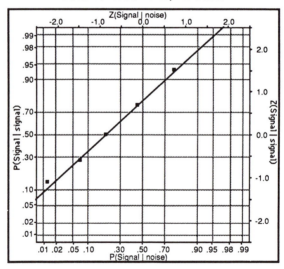

FIG. 2. Fit of the ROC model to pass/fail data in Class 44-I (B_{slp} = .914; A_z = .714; χ^2 = 7.69 with 3 df, p > .05).

Best-fit ROC curve, P-Scale

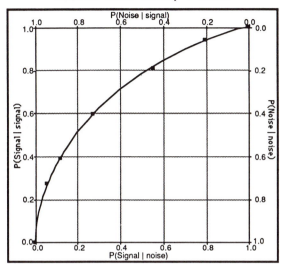

Best-fit ROC line, Z-Scale

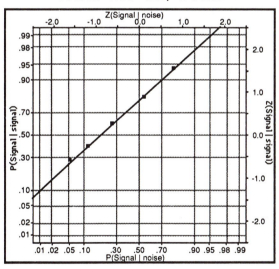

FIG. 3. Fit of the ROC model to pass/fail data in Class 45-B (B_{slp} = .902; A_z = .717; χ^2 = 3.88 with 3 df, $p >$ .25).

Influences on predictive accuracy. As described earlier, A_z represents the accuracy with which the signal can be detected in the presence of noise. In this application, more is involved than the noise in the predictor arising from measurement error and from less than perfect validity. The pass/fail decision that is the analogue to physical reality was itself made fallibly, so that a true measure of the signal is not available. In the present data, 43-H has more area under the curve than the two later classes in spite of the presumptively lower validity of the stanine. Thus, A_z is affected by restriction in range of talent, as is the biserial correlation. The slope statistic, B_{slp}, is also smaller in the two classes that were selected on a more accurate predictor. Like A_z, B_{slp} changes little from 44-I to 45-B. Both of the ROC statistics seem to be highly insensitive to differences in the definition of pass/fail and to be affected by restriction in range of talent.

An Investigation of Restriction of Range

Class 43-H had been relatively little affected by restriction in range occurring at the classification centers and had samples of a suitable size available at each level of the stanine scale. We decided, therefore, to conduct a range of talent investigation using that class. ROCs and biserial correlations were computed for six different bivariate distributions by making successively higher cuts on the stanine.

Table 2 contains the biserial correlations, A_z, B_{slp}, and chi-squares for each set of data. Also included are the same statistics for 44-I and 45-B for comparison with 43-H at comparable levels of restriction of range. All sample descriptive statistics show a monotonic decline with increasing restriction of range. Chi-squares for the six sets of data from 43-H all show excellent fits of the ROC curves. When 43-H is restricted by the truncation of Stanines 1, 2, and 3 (representing 23% of the standardization sample), which approximates the restriction that occurred in the two later classes, A_z is smaller than it is in 44-I and 45-B. A_z in the later classes is approximately equivalent to the value obtained in 43-H when frequencies for Stanines 1 and 2 only (11% of the standardization sample) are truncated. The later pilot stanines were expected to be more valid, and this greater validity is now demonstrated without the correction of a biserial correlation for restriction of range.

Relation of A_z *and* B_{slp}. The ROCs underlying the data of Rows 2 to 6 in Table 2 (not shown) clarify the relation between the A_z and B_{slp} statistics. Note in the first place that pass/fail frequencies and proportions of Stanines 6 through 9 are constant in the successive truncations of the distribution of 43-H. The true-positive intercept, which is adjacent to the leftmost points representing the high end of the stanine scale, remains very nearly constant at .07 for all of the successive ROCs of 43-H. In contrast, as the rightmost points of these ROCs, representing the low end of the stanine scale, are "stretched out" to fill in for the

TABLE 2
Effects of Restriction of Range on the Biserial Correlations
and ROC Statistics in Class 43-H and a Further Comparison
With Classes 44-I and 45-B

Range	SD	r_{bis}	A_z	B_{slp}	χ^2	df	p
		Restriction-of-range effect					
1–9	1.991	.497	.734	.971	4.73	6	.58
2–9	1.889	.467	.722	.936	2.40	5	.79
3–9	1.736	.429	.706	.906	1.88	4	.76
4–9	1.552	.382	.686	.883	1.60	3	.66
5–9	1.338	.328	.664	.861	1.47	2	.48
6–9	1.095	.284	.647	.847	1.47	1	.69
		Comparison with other classes					
Class 44-I	1.468	.409	.714	.914	7.69	3	.05
Class 45-B	1.625	.441	.717	.902	3.88	3	.27

stanines eliminated by the successive truncations, the false-positive intercept moves monotonically toward 1.00, as reflected in the monotonically decreasing B_{slp}. Search for a possible correction of the effects of restriction of range on ROCs may need to focus on B_{slp}.

Relation of A_z and R_{bis}. The plot of the biserial correlations against the A_z values for the same pair of distributions in Figure 4 is linear. When a given continuous distribution is successively truncated, the biserial correlation and A_z, each in its own way describing degree of accuracy, do measure the same thing. In the different distributions of 44-I and 45-B, however, the two statistics are pulled apart. That is, the A_z statistics for these two classes are almost identical, but the r_{bis} statistics differ. The difference in the latter statistics, furthermore, is expected from the difference in variances. Both r_{bis} and A_z are affected by the virtual absence of Stanines 1, 2, and 3 in these classes, but A_z is not affected by the difference in variance.

Evaluation and Implications

In an important sense, both r_{bis} and A_z are statistics for theoretical purposes. Neither provides information about the accuracy of predicting X from Y or Y from X in data in which X is dichotomous. Both statistics are measures of intrinsic validity, but with a difference. The biserial correlation estimates what the product-moment correlation would be in a bivariate normal distribution. It assumes that there is a continuous normal distribution underlying the dichotomy and that the continuous distribution is normal in the sample. Any substantial

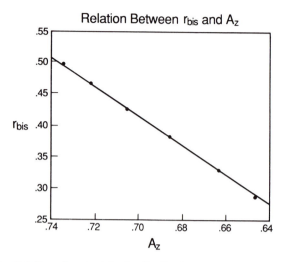

FIG. 4.   Relation of r_{bis} to A_z in the distributions of Class 43-H resulting from successive truncations.

departure from normality of the latter distribution produces an inaccurate estimate. Thus r_{bis} can be greater than 1.00 in samples from nonnormal populations. In contrast, A_z assumes that the theoretical processes underlying the distributions are bivariate normal. It is robust to departures from normality of the continuous distribution in the sample.

Robustness to change in criterion standards.   The difference in elimination rates at each stanine score for 44-I and 45-B allowed a comparison of the robustness of r_{bis} and A_z to changes in bias (criteria for passing). A_z is almost identical in the two training classes because it is independent of the differences in frequencies of the marginal distribution from one stanine score to another, whereas r_{bis} is dependent on such frequencies. These frequency differences produced an increase in variance of the marginal distribution from 44-I to 45-B even though the truncation due to selection for training occurred at the same point in both distributions.

Robustness to restriction in range.   Both r_{bis} and A_z are reduced by restriction in range of talent. For the biserial correlation there is available a correction that is known to be inadequate even when the distributional assumption of the correlation is met. Presumably it becomes more inadequate with departures from the assumption of normality of the continuous distribution. There is no correction for restriction of range available for A_z, but the ROC statistic shrank in our data toward its null value of .50 more slowly than r_{bis} shrank toward its null value of zero. If the straight line in Figure 4 is extrapolated, it does not run through zero and .50 at the low end of 1.00 and 1.00 at the high end. The two statistics provide identical information only under restrictive circumstances. A_z is sensitive to the scatter of data points representing successive signal-to-noise ratios but not to the variance of the marginal distribution for a given set of data points.

Given the robustness of A_z to the distribution of the predictor in the sample, that statistic is a more accurate way of measuring intrinsic validity in a constant range of talent. It may also be a more accurate way of estimating intrinsic validity in the population from which a given sample was selected when the selection did not take place by truncation. If there are sufficiently large frequencies in the lower tail of the marginal distribution to estimate signal-to-noise ratios following selection, A_z should be more robust than a corrected r_{bis}.

Testing construct validity of the predictor. The failure of ROC analysis to fit pass/fail criterion data in a particular instance is also an important consideration in evaluating the potential applications of the methodology. A possible explanation for failure of the model to fit would be that the predictor measures different traits or characteristics in different parts of the distribution of scores. The plot should reveal the locus of the problem. When using a biserial correlation, one can inspect the proportions of passing and failing at each score level and evaluate the departures from expectations based on the same trait or combination of traits. However, r_{bis} is not accompanied by a chi-square that alerts the investigator to the problem. In this application it is necessary to evaluate a large chi-square relative to the power in the study. Sufficient power can lead to rejection of the model in cases in which the departure from expectation is trivial in size.

Testing predictive bias. There are also implications for the evaluation of predictive bias in minority groups. This application is particularly useful when there is only a dichotomous criterion, because the standard regression comparisons are not applicable. If the ROC model can be rejected only in the minority group, there is a problem with the construct validity of the predictor for that group. If, when applied to the same range of data points, the model cannot be rejected in either group but there is a significant difference in A_z (standard errors are available), the intrinsic predictive validities for the two groups differ. If both of the first two group comparisons produce null results, one can proceed to an evaluation of a possible intercept difference by examining pass/fail proportions at equivalent levels of the predictor measure. From this point of view, there was an intercept difference for classes 44-I and 45-B. The intercept on the normal distribution underlying the dichotomy was higher for 45-B than for 44-I.

All in all, we believe that selection psychologists should be alert to possible applications of ROC analysis. It is clearly more useful than r_{bis} for certain applications. ROC analysis is contraindicated when there is need to correct for substantial restriction in range of talent produced by truncation.

REFERENCES

Davis, F. B. (1947). *The AAF qualifying examination* (Report 6, Army Air Forces Aviation Psychology Program Research Reports). Washington, DC: U.S. Government Printing Office.

DuBois, P. H. (1947). *The classification program* (Report 2, Army Air Forces Aviation Psychology Program Research Reports). Washington, DC: U.S. Government Printing Office.

Flanagan, J. C. (1947). *The aviation psychology program in the Army Air Forces* (Report 1, Army Air Forces Aviation Psychology Program Research Reports). Washington, DC: U.S. Government Printing Office.

Green, D. M., & Swets, J. A. (1988). *Signal detection theory and psychophysics.* Los Altos, CA: Peninsula.

Guilford, J. P., & Lacey, J. I. (1947). *Printed tests* (Report 5, Army Air Forces Aviation Psychology Program Research Reports). Washington, DC: U.S. Government Printing Office.

Melton, A. W. (1947). *Apparatus tests* (Report 4, Army Air Forces Aviation Psychology Program Research Reports). Washington, DC: U.S. Government Printing Office.

Metz, C. E. (1986). ROC methodology in radiologic imaging. *Investigative Radiology, 21,* 720–733.

Miller, N. E. (1947). *Psychological research on pilot training* (Report 8, Army Air Forces Aviation Psychology Research Reports). Washington, DC: U.S. Government Printing Office.

Swets, J. A. (1988). Measuring the accuracy of diagnostic systems. *Science, 240,* 1285–1293. (Chapter 4 in this volume.)

Swets, J. A., & Pickett, R. M. (1982). *Evaluation of diagnostic systems.* San Diego, CA: Academic Press.

11 Accuracy and Response Bias in Survey Research

An important kind of survey question attempts, for each respondent, to discriminate between two factual alternatives, often between the occurrence or nonoccurrence of a given event or between the existence or nonexistence of a given condition. For example, the Health Interview Survey may ask whether or not the respondent made a visit to a doctor in the past six months and whether or not the respondent has a certain chronic illness.

Such survey questions may be seen as members of a broad class of "diagnostic" devices that attempt to discern, though admittedly in an imperfect manner, some underlying truth about binary events or conditions. Other devices in this class attempt to reveal whether or not there is a lesion in a patient, a flaw in a metal structure, a malfunction in a processing plant, a lie in a suspect's statements, or a relevant document in a library. Some diagnostic devices look to the future and attempt to predict whether or not rain will fall, an applicant will perform satisfactorily, the market will go up, or a tax return should be audited. In the most general sense, these devices attempt to detect signals (e.g., a lesion, a malfunction, a relevant document) in a background of random events that mimic signals (e.g., a fuzzy radiograph, the multiple processes of an operating manufacturing plant, the many potentially relevant documents in the library) or to discriminate between two confusable alternatives that may be termed "noise-alone" and "signal-plus-noise." Modern signal detection theory (SDT) has been advanced as the best way of analyzing and assessing their performance (Swets and Pickett, 1982).

Specifically, SDT provides an analytical technique that separates two fundamental and independent aspects of performance in tasks of the sort exemplified and quantifies each aspect in a numerical index. The two aspects are: (1) *discrim-*

ination capacity or *accuracy* and (2) *decision criterion* or *response bias*. The former is a matter of how well the two alternatives are discriminated: one desires a pure measure of the ability of the device, or person working with the device, to distinguish between the presence or absence of a signal. The latter comprises the decision factors that come into play when the typically probabilistic output of a discrimination process must be translated into a binary (yes or no) response: it can be viewed, for a person, as how certain the person must be that a signal was present to respond "yes." The person or device may have a bias toward or against a positive response—depending upon, for example, whether the signal-plus-noise alternative has a high or low prior probability of occurrence or upon whether a false-negative error is more or less serious than a false-positive error. Other existing indices of discrimination accuracy (including "percentage correct" and various coefficients of statistical association) confound the two aspects of performance, with the consequences of unreliability and invalidity.

This chapter describes SDT and examines its applicability in the survey context. Note that the theory may apply doubly in this context. As indicated, a survey *question* of the sort defined is a device to distinguish between two alternatives relative to each respondent—or between two kinds of respondents, those who have and those who have not. And the question's wording, for example, may tend advertently or inadvertently to induce positive or negative responses. Moreover, the survey *respondent* faces a similar discrimination and decision problem. Thus, a respondent may be uncertain as to whether the last visit to the doctor was within the past six months or whether an intermittent symptom qualifies as a chronic illness. And the respondent may have a bias toward or against a positive response, depending, for example, on the subjective cost of making that response (e.g., in terms of a time-consuming series of follow-up questions, or in terms of embarrassment).

The next section describes SDT as a general model for discrimination and decision. A following section relates this model to some issues in survey interpretation and design, including the estimation of survey biases (particularly the overreporting and underreporting of events and conditions), and tradeoffs of cost and benefits. The fourth section illustrates some ways in which SDT might be applied to the Health Interview Survey (conducted by the Census Bureau for the National Center for Health Statistics). The fifth section is an attempt to delineate the scope and the limitations of SDT applicability to surveys and considers the possibility of applications beyond the health field, for example, to population variables. The final section states conclusions and makes some recommendations for experimental applications of SDT in survey research.

SIGNAL DETECTION THEORY

The ROC

SDT separates the two basic aspects of discrimination and decision performance by means of the so-called Relative Operating Characteristic (Peterson, Birdsall, and Fox, 1954; Swets, 1964; Green and Swets, 1966; Swets, 1973, Chapter 1 in this volume). The "ROC" is derived from the standard two-by-two table that shows the two possible event (or condition) alternatives as columns and two permitted responses (yes and no) as rows; see Table 1. Specifically, it is based on two quantities that contain all of the information in that table, namely the true-positive ratio (TPR), defined as $a/(a + c)$, and the false-positive ratio (FPR), defined as $b/(b + d)$. (The false-negative ratio and true-negative ratio are, respectively, their complements.) In particular, the ROC is a graph of TPR versus FPR showing how those two quantities covary as the decision criterion (or response bias) varies.

We pause to acknowledge that the concept of a "bias" toward or against a positive response may be more immediately understood than the concept of a "criterion" for making a positive response, which is formally equivalent, although carrying a different connotation. However, the second concept is useful here, as the SDT model is further explicated. As discussed later, the idea is that a diagnostic device bases each decision on the value of a variable that represents the probability that the signal-plus-noise alternative is true relative to the probability that the noise-alone alternative is true—a form of "likelihood ratio." A criterion, or cut value, is placed on that decision variable such that values greater than the criterion lead to a positive response while lesser values lead to a negative response. We speak of the criterion as varying from very strict (only the highest values of the decision variable exceed it) to very lax (almost all of the values exceed it.) Thus, the weather forecaster may have a more lenient criterion for predicting a hurricane than light rain, since the cost of a false negative is so much greater in the former case. Application of the ROC to surveys is based on the assumption that the criterion associated with a canonical question may vary—

TABLE 1
Two-by-Two Table

		Event	
		Signal-plus-Noise	*Noise-Alone*
Response	Yes	a	b
	No	c	d
		a + c	b + d

251

perhaps from one wording to another, from one population subgroup to another, from one time to another, from one data user to another, and so on. (In addition, different questions, sequences of questions, or modes of administration may affect discrimination; for example, probes that help a respondent to remember probably have their effects via enhanced discrimination.)

Figure 1 shows the ROC traced, for a given level of discrimination capacity or accuracy, as the decision criterion for a positive response varies from one group of trials to another, that is, from one two-by-two data table to another. With a strict criterion, there will be fewer positive responses overall, and both TPR and FPR will be low; a point on the ROC near the lower left corner is obtained. With a lenient criterion, both TPR and FPR will be high; a point on the ROC near the upper right corner is obtained. Intermediate criteria produce points in between. Note that the ROC is independent of any particular decision criterion because it is the locus of points obtained with all possible criteria.

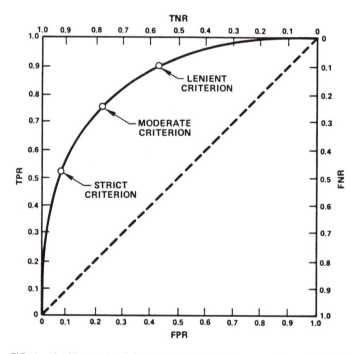

FIG. 1. An illustrative ROC, as a plot of the true-positive ratio (TPR) vs. the false-positive ratio (FPR), for a given discrimination capacity or accuracy, as the decision criterion varies. Nominally strict, moderate, and lenient criteria are indicated. (The right and top axes indicate that the false-negative and true-negative ratios are complements, respectively, of TPR and FPR.)

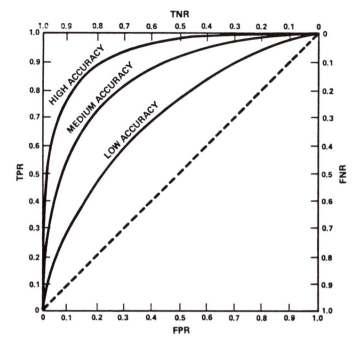

FIG. 2.   ROCs representing three degrees of discrimination capacity or accuracy.

Index of Accuracy

The degree of accuracy represented by any ROC is quantified by some measure of its position in the unit square: the lower bound is the positive diagonal, which represents chance accuracy (TPR no higher than FPR), and the upper bound is a function running along the left and top sides of the graph, which represents perfect accuracy (TPR = 1.0 for any value of FPR including 0). Three intermediate degrees of accuracy are illustrated in Figure 2. Figure 3 indicates that the proportion of the square's area that lies under the ROC (termed A_z) can serve as an index of accuracy; it varies from 0.50 at the chance diagonal to 1.0 for perfect performance.

Index of Decision Criterion or Response Bias

Figure 4 indicates that the slope of an ROC at any point (termed β) can index the decision criterion that produced that point. The three dotted lines illustrate "iso-criterion" contours, moving from left to right, of ROC slopes of 2.0, 1.0, and 0.5, respectively.

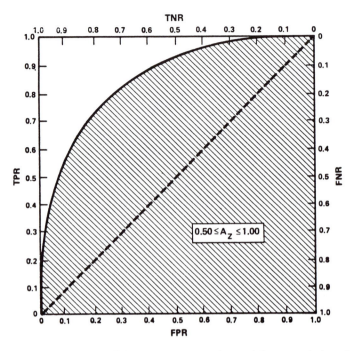

FIG. 3.   Illustration of the area measure, denoted A_z, as an index of discrimination accuracy. This index is the proportion of the area in the unit square that lies beneath the ROC. It varies from 0.50 for an ROC lying on the (dashed) diagonal, representing chance performance, to 1.00 for an ROC showing TPR = 1.0 for all values of FPR.

The optimal value of β can be stated for any of several definitions of optimum. For example, the value of β that *maximizes the expected value* of a decision is the one that maximizes the quantity

$$\text{TPR} - \beta \cdot \text{FPR}$$

where

$$\beta = \frac{P(n)}{P(sn)} \cdot \frac{B_{TN} + C_{FP}}{B_{TP} + C_{FN}},$$

and where P(n) and P(sn) are the prior probabilities of the two (noise-alone and signal-plus-noise) alternatives and the Bs and Cs stand for the benefits and costs of the four possible outcomes of a decision: true positive, true negative, false positive, and false negative (Swets and Swets, 1979). As discussed below, this formulation allows for the explicit integration of costs and benefits into comparisons of the "accuracies" of different ways of collecting data.

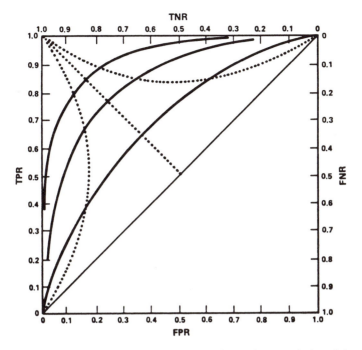

FIG. 4.   Illustration of the slope measure, denoted β, as an index of the decision criterion. This index is the slope of (a line tangent to) the ROC at the point yielded by a given criterion. It varies from plus infinity to zero as the criterion varies from the most strict to the most lenient extreme. The dotted lines show constant ROC slopes (and values of β) of 2.0, 1.0, and 0.5, respectively, from left to right.

Statistical Model of the ROC

Note that the ROC can be modelled in terms of the distributions of the decision variable that arise from each of the two alternatives to be discriminated; see Figure 5. Each decision is based on a variable quantity, denoted x. The left distribution represents the values of x that arise from nonoccurrence of the event in question (denoted n for noise-alone) and the right distribution, with a higher mean, represents values of x stemming from the occurrence of the event (denoted sn for signal-plus-noise). Higher values of x represent higher likelihoods of occurrence of sn, and conversely. A critical value of x is selected as the decision criterion, x_c : values of $x > x_c$ lead to "yes" responses and values of $x < x_c$ lead to "no" responses. High values of x_c, at the right, correspond to strict criteria and produce low values both of TPR (equal to the area under the sn distribution to the right of x_c) and FPR (equal to the area under the n distribution to the right of x_c). As x_c is set progressively lower, the ROC fans out from (0,0) to 1.0, 1.0).

In theory, the decision variable x may be regarded as a value of the appropri-

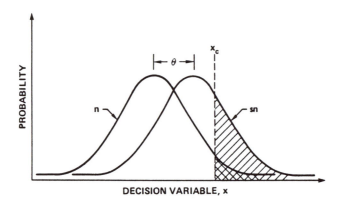

FIG. 5. Statistical model of SDT, showing values of a unidimensional decision variable x that arise from each of two alternatives in question, denoted n and sn. A decision criterion x_c, as a cutoff value of x, determines which values of x lead to sn ("yes") and n ("no") responses. The accuracy of discrimination depends on the difference between (the means of) the distributions, denoted θ.

ate *likelihood ratio*—the ratio of the ordinate of the sn distribution to the ordinate of the n distribution—or as any monotonic transformation of that likelihood ratio, including the posterior probability of occurrence of the sn alternative. The quantity β discussed above as an index of the criterion can be shown to be equal to x_c when x is expressed as a value of the likelihood ratio. Thus, β quantifies an actual or optimal decision criterion, both as a value of the likelihood ratio on the decision axis and as the slope of an ROC at the point produced by that criterion.

It can be seen in Figure 5 that the accuracy of the decisions, under this model, is determined by the degree of overlap of the two distributions, as reflected, for example, in the difference between the means of n and sn, shown as θ. Higher θs produce ROCs higher in the unit-square space of the ROC graph.

The distributions are shown here as normal (Gaussian) and of equal variance and the ROCs in Figures 1–4 are based on those assumptions. The first assumption is robust, the second less so, and, hence, the form of the ROC varies somewhat across tasks. Technical details of fitting empirical ROCs and estimating their parameters are given elsewhere (Green & Swets, 1966).

Obtaining Empirical ROCs

One technical point that bears mention here is that empirical ROCs are not usually obtained from a series of two-by-two data tables, each reflecting a different decision criterion, as described above for didactic purposes. Rather, they are obtained from r-category *rating scales,* which produce single data tables having r rows, and yield at once several points on an ROC. Thus, for example, a respondent would state how certain s/he is that an event occurred (or condition exists) according to, say, five categories of certainty—ranging from "very certain of occurrence" (category or row 1) to "very certain of nonoccurrence" (category or row 5). Then the boundaries of the categories are treated in analysis as different decision criteria for a positive response: the entries in the first row are taken as exceeding the strictest criterion; the sums of entries in the first two rows are taken as exceeding the next strictest criterion; and so on until r categories yield r-1 ROC points, the rth point being (1.0, 1.0). Note that this technique reflects the interpretation of a response as based on a process within the respondent that essentially computes the probability of signal occurrence.

An illustration of rating-scale analysis is given in Table 2, based on hypothetical data. The five rows give decreasing levels of confidence that respondents had a hospital stay in the past year, ranging from "1 = yes, with high confidence" to "5 = no, with high confidence." The left column shows the distribution of responses of those whom the records showed to have had a hospital stay in the specified period and the right column, those who have no record of such a stay. The first entry in each cell is the tally (raw frequency) of responses. Thus, 35 stayers and 5 nonstayers were highly confident they had stayed; their responses are regarded in analysis as exceeding a strict criterion for a positive response (located, in effect, at the boundary between confidence-categories or rows 1 and 2). Next, combining rows 1 and 2, relative to a less strict criterion (one between rows 2 and 3), gives $35 + 30 = 65$ stayers and $5 + 10 = 15$ nonstayers who are now treated as having made a positive response. And so on.

The second entry in each cell, in parentheses, gives the proportion or ratio of responses, relative to the sum of each column, *cumulatively* from the first through the fifth row. Those ratios are, respectively, the TPR and FPR defining

TABLE 2
Illustrative Rating Data

	Record of Hospital Stay	No Record of Hospital Stay
1. Yes, high confidence	35 (.35)	5 .05)
2. Yes, low confidence	30 (.65)	10 (.15)
3. Doubtful	20 (.85)	20 (.35)
4. No, low confidence	10 (.95)	30 (.65)
5. No, high confidence	5 (1.00)	35 (1.00)
	100	100

(effectively) four ROC points, which progress from lower left to upper right on the ROC graph—from (.05, .35) to (.15, .65) to (.35, .85) to (.65, .95).

SURVEY INTERPRETATION AND DESIGN

Two points of contact between the ROC and issues in survey design and interpretation are identified in this section. One, the ROC relates to the estimation of certain survey biases, namely the overreporting and underreporting biases as obtained in record-check studies. Two, it facilitates cost-benefit analyses for survey design and implementation.

Underreporting and Overreporting Biases

Marquis (1983) showed how two common methods in health-related record-check studies each provide incomplete data and give an estimate of underreporting or overreporting but not both. Under one method, the investigator first checks the records to select cases with the characteristic of interest present and then interviews the people selected to see if they report that characteristic. The underreporting rate, $c/(a + c)$ of Figure 1 or the false-negative ratio (FNR), is measured and $b/(b + d)$ or the FPR (overreporting) is ignored. In short, a measure is taken from just one column of the two-by-two table—namely, FNR (the complement of the ROC's TPR)—and some of the information in the table necessary to represent performance fully, from the second column, is ignored. Under the second method, the investigator conducts the survey first and then checks the records of people reporting the characteristic of interest. Here, the measure of survey bias is taken as $b/(a + b)$ and called the overreporting rate. Just one row of the table is considered (to yield a different kind of FPR, akin to an inverse, response-dependent, conditional probability) and c-cell information (underreporting) is ignored.

Upon comparing the bias estimates from these two incomplete record-check designs to the bias estimate from a full method—in which both the population and the records are sampled independently of the presence of the characteristic of interest—it can be demonstrated (Marquis, 1983) that the incomplete methods tend to overestimate the size of a response bias and can misestimate the direction of the bias. The type of design reliably predicts the direction of the bias it discovers. In these circumstances, incorrect inferences are drawn about underreporting (often characterized as resulting from "forgetting") and overreporting (often assumed to result from "telescoping" longer reference periods into the shorter reference period that is stipulated) and about changes in the tendencies to make these errors as the time since the event in question increases. Moreover, the incomplete methods systematically convert random classification errors made by data analysts into one or the other kind of bias, again depending on the nature of the design.

Our general observation is that whereas a bias, say, of underreporting, may seem undesirable and may be interpreted as a lack of accuracy, some bias in that direction may actually be desirable, depending on circumstances. Steps taken to reduce the underreporting bias may serve also to increase the overreporting bias—perhaps with a gain in overall accuracy, or no gain, or a loss. The full method of record checking is needed, along with ROC analysis, so that the two directions of bias may be considered in relation to one another and in relation to accuracy.

Cost-Benefit Analyses

Concerning cost-benefit analyses, two points may be made. The first is that the ROC isolates a pure measure of accuracy; its accuracy index is not inadvertently contaminated by unmeasured variation in the decision criterion and it does not give a performance index in which an accuracy variable is deliberately combined with benefit and cost variables into an omnibus figure of merit. Thus, upon comparing the experimental results of alternative survey designs, one can relate potential gains in pure accuracy to the additional costs they may entail, generating literally unbiased data to use to answer questions like: "Should we spend d more dollars on a more extensive and expensive survey design in order to gain u more units of accuracy?" These u units of accuracy can be converted quantitatively into probabilities of TP and FP errors, via the ROC, and so one can relate increased dollars to decreased sizes of error probabilities. This approach, for example, provides an explicit way of comparing telephone and face-to-face modes of interview as to cost-effectiveness. Again, different question modes or questioning strategies can be compared.

A slightly different issue can also be addressed: "How can we allocate the fixed amount of respondent time to maximize accuracy of information across our information needs?" Survey designers must specify the costs and benefits of different levels of accuracy across different questions; the SDT framework then allows benefit to be maximized for a fixed cost. Note that this approach also allows the survey designer to maximize the information value across an entire questionnaire (of a fixed length). The designer must specify the costs and benefits of differing levels of accuracy on different questions. When data on alternatives for these questions have been obtained, the SDT framework makes it possible to optimize information value of the questionnaire. Thus, tradeoffs between devoting additional interview time to alternative pieces of information can be made explicit and embedded in a uniform formal framework.

The second point is that the decision criteria used by survey respondents can be adjusted to maximize the value of the data to the survey user. As indicated above, different criteria produce different balances of reporting errors: the FPR and the complement of the TPR, namely, the FNR. Also indicated above, given the relative seriousness of the two errors to the user, the best (optimal) balance for the user can be calculated.

Of course, SDT does not specify how the desired criterion is to be achieved. However, the survey designer can manipulate the criterion in a variety of ways. For example, with a yes-no question about existence of a chronic health condition, the designer might effect a lenient criterion by instructions such as "say yes if you think you might have had this condition" or a strict criterion by instructions such as "say yes only if you are quite sure that you had this particular condition." When a rating-scale question is used instead of a yes-no question, no special instructions are necessary; under this method the data are at once related to several criteria and the analyst can select the (yes-no) decision criterion corresponding to any of the four or so criterion levels that the rating scale represents.

HEALTH INTERVIEW SURVEY

The application of ROC analysis to record-check studies based on the Health Interview Survey (HIS) is considered here as illustrative of some possibilities. The two indices of the ROC—of accuracy (e.g., A_z) and of decision criterion or response bias (e.g., β)—can be determined as dependent variables for any of several independent variables. Five independent variables, whose effects should be interpreted in terms of both of those dependent variables, are: (1) nature of the question, (2) wording of the question, (3) mode of administering the survey, (4) population subgroups, and (5) length of reference period. All five could have effects on accuracy or decision criterion (response bias) or both.

Concerning the nature of the question, certain events or conditions will be more salient than others and better remembered, so accuracy (i.e., discrimination) will be higher. For example, a question about the occurrence of a hospital stay may be answered more accurately than a question about the occurrence of a visit to a doctor. A question about a serious health condition, similarly, may be answered more accurately than one about a minor condition. But the different questions may also be answered with different criteria or biases: more salient events and conditions, for example, may more likely be telescoped from a time prior to the stipulated reference period into that period, and reporting a health condition may depend on how embarrassing it is to have that condition. For example, abortions should be well remembered (have high discrimination) but respondents might be reluctant to report them (show a high criterion or, in this case, bias).

A clearly worded question should promote greater accuracy than an ambiguously worded question. But question wording can also affect the criterion of reporting an event or condition, for example, if it encourages a respondent to make a positive response only when she/he can make it confidently or if it seems instead to encourage positive responses that can be made with less confidence. The introduction to and wording of a question often implicitly help to define a criterion for the respondent.

Face-to-face interviews might well show greater accuracy than telephone interviews, but it is possible that persons will be more or less likely to report sensitive health events or conditions in one or the other mode.

Again, different population subgroups may have different accuracies and criteria. Higher socio-economic status could be correlated with better memories and, depending on specifics, with more or fewer sensibilities or more or less desire for privacy.

Lastly, increasing the length of the reference period could produce dimmer memories, and, in addition, more lenient criteria for reporting, perhaps resulting from reduced sensitivity to a once-embarrassing condition. One theory (Sudman and Bradburn, 1974) is that forgetting increases with time while telescoping decreases with time. Depending on their exact relationship, however, one could observe only a criterion effect or an accuracy effect as well. The data suggest, rather, that both errors increase with time, leading predominantly to an accuracy effect (Marquis, 1983).

OTHER APPLICATIONS

In this section, we discuss some additional possible applications of SDT to survey research. These are of two distinct types, and are treated in separate subsections. The first considers some of the possible applications of SDT to other surveys and survey problems. We should stress that this discussion is illustrative, and is constrained by our limited familiarity with the full range of federally-supported regular surveys. We consider the Current Population Survey and then deal with the issue of income reporting, which we have not tied to a particular survey.

In the second subsection, we return our focus primarily to the HIS, but take a more speculative stance: we briefly consider a possible application of SDT that might require some elaboration of the theory or, at a minimum, of the technical means that have hitherto been used to apply it. We believe that there are a number of additional important issues in survey design and interpretation that might be fruitfully approached using SDT, the investigation of which could help to enrich SDT itself.

Applications to Other Surveys

The Current Population Survey (hereafter, CPS) is used to estimate unemployment rates; as such, it is of considerable practical importance. For example, changes in state unemployment rates by a few tenths of a percentage point affect the amount of unemployment compensation paid by the federal government to the states.

We take it as given that separation of discrimination and criterion effects in reporting would be potentially useful, and will suggest several ways in which they might be distinguished. A critical question in the CPS asks how many hours the target respondent worked last week, at all jobs. The respondent is asked for a numerical answer, to the nearest hour. In most uses of the data, 35 hours per week is used as the cutoff for full-time work.

It might be possible to ask a respondent for an approximate answer—e.g., the question could begin: "About how many hours. . . " Follow-up questions could then probe for how certain the respondent was, thus getting at possibly different levels of the criterion, via the rating-scale methodology described earlier. Note that the content and sequence of such follow-up questions could vary, depending on the initial answer. Thus, an answer of "32 hours" could be followed-up by: "How sure are you that it was more than 30 hours?" "How sure are you that it was less than 35 hours?" An answer of 36 hours would get different follow-up questions.

Such an approach might be useful since, especially when the respondent is supplying figures for someone else, the respondent may be giving an uncertain estimate rather than reporting a known fact. SDT makes it possible to use this uncertainty as part of the analysis, rather than leaving it implicit, as noise in the data. As we understand it, periodic verification studies are done of the CPS, where pay stubs are collected from respondents and employers, social program participation records are checked, and the like. Such studies could provide the truth data for the application of SDT. We note that it should be possible to apply SDT to the CPS with little change in the sequence or wording of questions; all that is required is a mechanism for respondents to give confidence judgements for their numerical estimates.

Alternatively, it might be possible to use SDT methods without objective truth data. This use would require that the sorts of questions we suggest—asking for an approximate answer and then confidence estimates on boundaries of the answer—be appended to the CPS, and asked after the interview has been completed. (We note that this may require some explanatory material for the respondent.) This would make it possible to treat the original answer as the ground truth, which is what the CPS normally does. Although it would not permit the calculation of objective discrimination and criterion scores, it would make possible several useful analyses.

First, the sensitivity of results to changes in the "pseudo-criterion," as it might be called, could be estimated. If ultimate survey results seem highly sensitive to variations in this criterion, then further methodological research might be desired to determine the optimal level of this criterion and to attempt to design ways to induce respondents to employ it. Second, the pseudo-criterion might be found to vary systematically with socio-economic or demographic factors, perhaps even with those that correlate with unemployment. This finding, too, could have implications for survey design, since it would help in assessing the "exposure" of the CPS figures to response error, as a function of the composition of the sample.

A second important concern of the CPS is to determine, for those who are not now working, whether they have been looking for work in the past four weeks and when they last looked for work. These data are used to calculate the number of discouraged workers, those who drop from the labor force and are no longer part of the base used to calculate the percentage unemployed, and, thus, by extension, the unemployment rate itself. We hypothesize that what counts as "looking for work" can vary considerably across individuals, and, thus, that there might well be substantial criterion effects operating. If different criteria are being used across people, perhaps varying systematically by population subgroups, that fact will bias the results of the survey. Rewording questions and/or changing their introductions or probes could help to reduce such sources of error.

The most direct approach to using SDT in this connection would be via a verification study. Thus, the question could be reworded to ask for confidence estimates that the target respondent was looking for work; the data from these would be categorized into a table based on the results of the verification study, and a ROC could be constructed. (Such ROCs could be constructed for different population subgroups as well, assuming sufficient sample sizes.) It seems possible, however, that it would be rather difficult to obtain reliable truth data, even in a verification study.

An alternative approach would be to use available or currently collected data. There are several questions that ask for more detail on work-seeking: one asks what activities the target respondent has engaged in to look for work, one asks how long the target respondent has been seeking work, and one asks if the target respondent wants a job. Such items could be used to construct a scale of work-seeking; thus, for example, engaging in several activities to look for work would result in higher scale values than engaging in only one. Different scale values could then be treated as different levels of the criterion. We should note that this would be a novel application of SDT, and, thus, would require some exploration and development.

Many federal programs set income (and asset) criteria for participation. Government expenditures on such "means-tested" programs are sensitive to changes in either the financial criteria applied or to the methods used to assess and verify income. However, in some cases, the cost to the program of obtaining more accurate income data may exceed any savings that results from eliminating some unqualified applicants and from discouraging others (as well as, inevitably, some who are qualified). This is an area where SDT seems particularly appropriate, since issues of costs and benefits are directly relevant, in addition to issues of accuracy.

In this discussion, we assume that an income-verification study will be the vehicle used, so that there will be truth data available; our concern will be how to maximize the utility of data collected in such a survey. We should note that there might well be both criterion and discrimination factors affecting income reporting. In general, respondents may well be biased to underreport income, both for reasons of program participation and concerns about the Internal Revenue Service. But there may also be discrimination (in particular, memory and classification) problems, for example, for odd jobs worked or for small bonuses (particularly when either of these occurred some time ago).

The basic method of asking for confidence ratings of income reports can be used to collect the data necessary for construction of an ROC. As in the previous example, it might be useful to get a confidence limit that income falls within a range, since the task of assigning confidence to a point estimate of income may seem strange to respondents. The midpoint of the range can then be used as the imputed point estimate.

There is another way that an ROC can be constructed, which involves asking respondents for only a point estimate. That is to treat different discrepancies between reported and verified income as different criteria. Thus, under a stringent criterion, any discrepancy greater than, say, $500 might be treated as an incorrect response, while the most lenient criterion might treat any difference of less than $3000 as a correct response.

A refinement to these analyses can be introduced by considering income sources as a classification variable. (We are indebted to Steven Fienberg for this suggestion.) Thus, discrimination and criteria could be computed for each such income source, and possible systematic differences could emerge. (Note that there is a scaling issue, since different income sources can be expected to provide substantially different amounts of income.) This analysis could only be made if income verification is tied to sources, which is typically the case.

Respondents themselves could be classified depending on income sources, and separate ROCs could be calculated for each such respondent group. Each respondent would be classified based on the particular combination of income sources reported (above some cutoff in amount or percentage of the respondent's income). Thus, for example, a respondent who reported some regular employment income, unemployment compensation, and food stamps, would be in a different classification from a respondent who reported only some regular employment income and food stamps. There would, in general, be more respondent groups than income sources, reflecting the fact that many respondents will have multiple sources. Classification by respondents would make it possible to do such analyses without income-source information from the verification. In addition, focusing on respondents rather than sources might be of greater utility in survey design and analysis, because it might be useful in developing the sampling plan.

Finally, if source information were available in the verification study, an ROC could be constructed for each source. Since a respondent either does or does not report each source, and either does or does not have income from it, the two-by-two table fundamental to the ROC can be obtained. A series of such tables can be constructed by considering different amounts of source income as different levels of the criterion.

Further Extensions

Consideration of the problems of survey research suggest that there are several ways in which SDT can be applied in a relatively straightforward manner, without requiring substantial developments of the theory. In addition, however, some of the issues that arise in survey research might be powerful stimuli to developments in the theory of SDT and in the ways in which it is operationalized. One such issue—applying SDT to data with a similarity structure—is briefly discussed in this portion of our report.

The subsequent discussion is frankly speculative, in two senses: first, the ideas are not fully developed, and some of them might prove unworkable from the point of view of the theory. Second, even if they can be worked out and developed, they might not have sufficient payoffs for survey methodologists to devote resources to their development. They could still be of theoretical interest in such a case, of course, and could prove to be of practical utility as well, in other applications. To give this discussion a specific focus, our example will be taken from the HIS.

A major concern of the HIS is collecting data on chronic conditions. Data collected from the HIS are used to develop prevalence figures for a number of such conditions. However, a persistent source of response error appears to be the fact that respondents do not know or cannot remember the precise name of their condition; this failure may result in no report for a given condition or a "classification error," where one condition is reported when another was actually present. For some uses of the condition data, such classification errors are presumed not to matter, since medically similar conditions are aggregated for such uses. The assumption here, of course, is that such classification errors by respondents are generally along the dimensions of medical similarity.

The problem of how chronic conditions are organized conceptually for respondents is related to issues in cognitive psychology, specifically, research on classification and categorization (Smith and Medin, 1981). The basic assumption made in such research is that the entities to be classified or categorized have a similarity structure: that is, for any two items, it makes sense to ask how similar they are to each other; such similarities are symmetrical; and they form a ratio scale. Thus, for example, eczema is quite similar to psoriasis and not very similar to arthritis. A number of studies have looked at such similarity structures for sets of concepts, and several statistical techniques are generally applied (such as clustering and factor analysis). An additional type of structure is hierarchical; in the simple example given, eczema and psoriasis are both instances of "dry, flaky skin diseases," or a similar higher-level category. They might both, with, say, "skin allergy," be examples of "localized skin eruptions," which arthritis is not. Clearly, the structure can be extended, through higher-order nodes of "chronic conditions," "diseases," and the like. The HIS questionnaire, in fact, does not distinguish between eczema and psoriasis; for some summary statistics, it aggregates at higher levels. (Techniques exist for imputing distances, and, thus, similarities, to concepts organized in a hierarchy.)

Analytical techniques for looking at hierarchies in particular and similarity structures in general have been rather well-developed, and some might be fruitfully applied to the "conceptual space" of chronic diseases. However, as far as we know, SDT has never been applied to such data or, indeed, to aggregation or structuring problems in general, and the HIS might offer an opportunity to do so.

We assume that two kinds of data are available: record-check data for the HIS, and a matrix of similarities for the chronic conditions. (Such a matrix can be obtained from another group of respondents via any of several techniques used in cognitive psychology.) The application of SDT can then be explored by allowing different degrees of similarity to be different levels of the criterion. For example, at the strictest criterion, a similarity of 1.0 would be required; that is, only responses that correctly identified the condition would be scored as correct. At a lower criterion, say of .8, highly similar but non-identical conditions would be counted. Thus, if a respondent said "eczema," when the condition on the medical record was "skin allergy," that might count as a correct response on the more lenient criterion. Note that such a response would generate imputed positive responses to all conditions within the similarity cutoff; thus, both true positives and false positives would be generated.

Whether or not this approach would generate a curve that approximates an ROC is an empirical issue. If it did, then consideration of the uses to which the data could be put would enable the survey designer to assign costs and benefits to different degrees of accuracy; these, in turn, could be used to determine the level of the criterion—that is, in this case, the similarity—that maximizes the benefit-cost ratio (Chapter 5). Note that this approach would allow the questions to continue to be asked in their detailed form, by specific conditions; the enhancement it would provide would be in the aggregation step, where it would ensure that the benefit-cost ratio was maximized.

A similar general approach could possibly be used with hierarchical data. Here, proxies for the different levels of the criterion would be how "high-level" the nodes in the hierarchy were. Thus, "flaky skin diseases" might be the immediate superordinate to eczema and skin allergy, while "skin-diseases" might be super-ordinate to that. Again, consideration of the uses to which the data are to be put would make it possible for survey designers to assign costs and benefits, and these could be used, with the empirically derived ROC, to select the method of aggregation that maximizes the benefit-cost ratio. We should point out that the application to non-hierarchical similarity data seems to offer more potential for payoff, since it is quite likely that hierarchical data are aggregated along hierarchical lines; thus, if the data proved to have a strongly hierarchical organization, it is unlikely that the application of SDT that we envision could substantially increase the benefit-cost ratio obtained in aggregating information.

CONCLUSIONS

This section briefly summarizes three major conclusions about the potential applications of SDT to survey research.

1. *The separation of a pure measure of accuracy and the decision criterion made possible by SDT can be quite useful in survey research.* Each of these can be a distinct source of response error; different approaches are appropriate to address those two sources of error. The application of SDT required to make this separation is quite straightforward for a number of methodological questions in survey research, and involves the use of techniques that are well-understood in SDT.

2. *SDT can be integrated into existing approaches for methodological studies in survey research.* For example, relatively minor changes or additions would need to be made to planned (full-design) record-check studies in health, or verification studies of income reporting, to apply SDT to the resulting data. Thus, some of the benefits of using SDT can be obtained at relatively low incremental cost to methodological studies now in the planning or design stages.

3. *Additional applications of SDT to survey research seem possible, some of which would require advances in the theory or, at a minimum, in the techniques for applying SDT.* Such applications might well be fruitful and cost-effective for survey researchers; however, their development will require further effort.

REFERENCES

1. Green, D. M., and Swets, J. A. *Signal Detection Theory and Psychophysics.* New York: John Wiley and Sons, Inc., 1966. Reprinted by Robert E. Krieger Publishing Co., Inc., Huntington, New York, 1974, and Peninsula Publishing Co., Los Altos, CA, 1988.
2. Marquis, K. H. Record checks for sample surveys. Prepared for the Advanced Research Seminar on Cognitive Aspects of Survey Methodology, unpublished, 1983.
3. Peterson, W. W., Birdsall, T. G., and Fox, W. C. "The theory of signal detectability." *Transactions IRE Professional Group on Information Theory,* 1954, *PGIT-4,* 171–212. Reprinted in R. D. Luce, R. R. Bush, and E. Galanter (Eds.), *Readings in Mathematical Psychology.* New York: John Wiley and Sons, Inc., 1963.
4. Smith, E. E., and Medin, D. *Categories and Concepts.* Cambridge, MA: Harvard University Press, 1981.
5. Sudman, S., and Bradburn, N. M. *Response Effects in Surveys: A Review and Synthesis.* Chicago: Aldine Press, 1974.
6. Swets, J. A. *Signal Detection and Recognition by Human Observers,* (Ed.). New York: John Wiley and Sons, Inc., 1964. Reprinted by Peninsula Publishing Co., Los Altos, CA, 1988.

7. Swets, J. A. "The relative operating characteristic in psychology." *Science,* Dec. 7, 1973, *182*(4116), 990–1000. (Chapter 1 in this volume.)

8. Swets, J. A., and Pickett, R. M. *Evaluation of Diagnostic Systems: Methods from Signal Detection Theory.* New York: Academic Press, Inc., 1982.

9. Swets, J. A., and Swets, J. B. "ROC Approach to Cost-Benefit analysis." *IEEE Proceedings of the Sixth Conference on Computer Applications in Radiology,* Newport Beach, California, June 1979, 203–206. Reprinted in K. L. Ripley and A. Murray (Eds.), *Introduction to Automated Arrhythmia Detection.* New York: IEEE Computer Society Press, 1980, 57–60.

12 System Operator Response to Warnings of Danger

There are many instances in which system operators tend to respond slowly or not at all to warnings of danger and some instances in which the operators disable the warning devices. A primary reason is that the warnings have "cried wolf" too often to be credible (e.g., Sorkin, 1988). Moreover, the penalties of leaving the operational task to respond to false alarms may be considerable; thus, for example, the Federal Aviation Administration not long ago ordered a shutdown of collision-warning devices on commercial airliners because of serious distractions they presented both to pilots and air traffic controllers.

In this chapter, I treat quantitative aspects of crying wolf in terms of the positive predictive value (PPV) of a warning; that is, the probability that a warning will truly indicate some specified dangerous condition. I consider first theory and quantification of the PPV and then present a laboratory experiment in which participants were exposed to different values of PPV. The participants performed a continuous, manual tracking task at a computer workstation, during which randomly occurring warnings required them to leave the tracking task to make a specified response to the warning. With a bonus scheme, premiums were placed on carefully setting an automated tracker before leaving the tracking task and on responding quickly to the warning. Over five conditions, the PPV of the warning was set variously at 0.25, 0.39, 0.50, 0.61, and 0.75.

A practical concern is that values of PPV sufficient to ensure a reliable response are difficult to attain. The reason is that even very sensitive detectors will have a low PPV because the prior probability (*base rate*) of a dangerous condition is usually very low. The problem is exacerbated by the tendency of system engineers to set detector thresholds for issuing a warning leniently enough to achieve a very low probability that the detector will miss a dangerous condition; even slight changes in the threshold in the direction of leniency serve to decrease the PPV sharply. I take up this practical concern in the concluding discussion.

THEORY

PPV can be analyzed quantitatively in terms of signal detection theory (Green & Swets, 1966; Swets & Pickett, 1982). That is, the detector that issues the warnings will have an inherent sensitivity that is reflected in its relative operating characteristic (ROC): a trading relationship between the true-positive proportion (TPP), sometimes called the *hit* proportion, and the false-positive proportion (FPP), sometimes called the *false-alarm* proportion, that is traced out as the amount of evidence required to issue a warning, or the decision threshold, varies from strict to lenient. At very strict thresholds, both TPP and FPP are low, near 0; at very lenient thresholds, both are high, near 1.0.

The main quantities are defined in terms of the 2×2 table of Figure 1, showing "truth" relative to the existence or nonexistence of the dangerous condition and the "response" (i.e., warning or no warning) of the detector. The quantity TPP is equal to $a/(a + c)$ and FPP is equal to $b/(b + d)$. (Note that TPP and FPP are estimates of conditional probabilities: the probability of a positive response conditional on the occurrence or nonoccurrence of a specified event.) Both quantities increase when the number of positive responses $(a + b)$ increases (i.e., as the decision threshold becomes more lenient). The PPV, an inverse true-positive proportion, is defined as $a/(a + b)$, the proportion of positive responses

Truth

		Positive	Negative	
	Positive	a	b	a+b
Response				
	Negative	c	d	c+d
		a+c	b+d	a+b+c+d

FIG. 1. The 2×2 table of truth relative to the existence or not of a dangerous condition and of the detector's response (i.e., warning or not).

that truly indicate a dangerous condition. So TPP is conditional on the column sum and PPV on the row sum.

It is sometimes convenient to calculate PPV when the full 2×2 table is not available. Denote the probabilities of positive and negative truth as $P(T+)$ and $P(T-)$ and consider them to be known. Consider the ROC and decision threshold to be established so that the values of TPP and FPP are specified. Then (taking proportions as estimates of conditional probabilities) the PPV can be calculated from Bayes's theorem:

$$ \text{PPV} = \frac{\text{TPP} \times P(T+)}{[\text{TPP} \times P(T+)] + [(\text{FPP} \times P(T-)]} . $$

In an alternative form of Bayes's theorem, PPV is calculated from prior odds and the likelihood ratio. Specifically, define prior odds as $P(T+)/P(T)$ and the likelihood ratio as TPP/FPP; then multiply them to obtain the posterior odds. To convert odds to probability, note that the PPV equals the posterior odds divided by the posterior odds $+1$.

The critical interactions of these several variables—particularly $P(T+)$, the relation of TPP and FPP, and the decision threshold—in determining PPV are illustrated in Figure 2. The top of the figure shows the ROC of a detector that is quite sensitive. To indicate how sensitive by way of customary ROC indexes, I note that on a binormal graph (i.e., one having the normal deviates of TPP and FPP spaced linearly and hence showing a linear ROC; Swets, 1986), this ROC's y intercept is 3.5 units on the normal-deviate scale, and its slope is 0.8, a typical value (chapter 2). Alternatively, represented by underlying normal distributions, the difference between the means of the T+ and T− distributions, in terms of the standard deviation of the T+ distribution, is 3.5, and the ratio of the standard deviation of T− to that of T+ is 0.8. Thus, for calibration by a familiar index, this ROC has a d' of approximately 3.5 (Green & Swets, 1966). In terms of the preferable index that is the proportion of the graph's area that lies beneath the ROC, A_z, which is equivalent to percentage correct in a paired-comparisons task, the sensitivity indicated by this ROC is 0.995 (see chapters 3 and 4).

For this particular ROC, the remainder of Figure 2 shows three curves of PPV representing the three values of prior probability of .1, .01, and .001, respectively. Consider the bottom curve for .001 as likely the most realistic of the three for warning situations. Here, it is seen that at a quite strict decision threshold, yielding FPP = .0025 and TPP = .90 on the ROC, the PPV is about .25; hence, 1 of 4 warnings is a true warning. It is likely, however, that TPP = .90 will be regarded by system engineers and managers as too low. Note that if the threshold is relaxed to achieve TPP = .97, meanwhile increasing FPP to about .02, then PPV = .05, such that 1 in 20 warnings is valid.

The range of typical prior probabilities of dangerous conditions for system operation is difficult to characterize in general, as is the sensitivity of detectors in

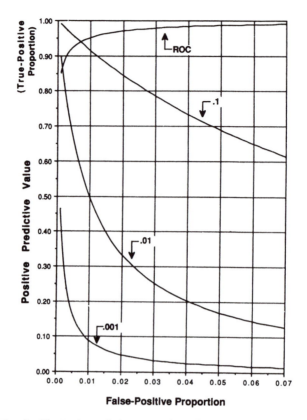

FIG. 2. An illustrative relative operating characteristic (ROC: true-positive proportion vs. false-positive proportion) and the corresponding curves of positive predictive value for each of three values of prior probability.

general use. Harvey (1992) and Harvey, Hammond, Lusk, and Mross (1992) have considered signal detection theory and PPV extensively in theory and in certain practical settings (e.g., the detection of severe weather at an airport). They mentioned some higher prior probabilities than the .001 I illustrated but generally consider detectors of lower sensitivity than the one I illustrated. In any case, we see that easily conceivable combinations of the relevant variables—of low priors, of detector sensitivity short of perfect, and of relatively lenient thresholds chosen to give high hit rates—will conspire to yield low values of PPV. Human reactions to various values of PPV are, therefore, of interest, and our experiment is a preliminary attempt to explore some qualitative and quantitative aspects of human performance. Moreover, although not capturing all aspects of warnings in real life operational tasks, the experimental setting gives a concrete view of a typical situation and so helps to set the stage for some practical analysis and suggestions in the concluding discussion.

METHOD

Tasks

The background tracking task and the warning response task were presented in the context of an adaptation of a Multi-Attribute Task Battery developed at the Langley Research Center of the National Aeronautics and Space Administration (Comstock & Arnegard, 1992). The screen displayed to the experimental participants is shown in Figure 3.

At the upper center of the screen, the tracking task requires participants to manipulate a joystick with compensatory movements to keep a randomly moving dot (cursor) as close as possible to a fixed, marked, central position. Before leaving the tracking task to respond to a warning, the participant must hold down a button to set an automated tracker. The accuracy of the automated tracker is indicated by a circle superimposed on the tracking display with a diameter that

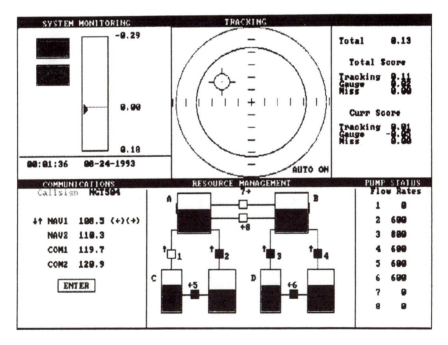

FIG. 3. Workstation display screen to present participant's tracking and warning-response tasks.

decreases linearly with the length of time the button is held down. The tracking cursor is constrained to stay within the autotracking circle. Because the accuracy of the automated tracker is a direct function of the time the button is held down, participants must decide how accurately they want to set the automated tracker before leaving the tracking task.

At the upper left of the screen, the warning task is initiated by a randomly occurring yellow light. After the appearance of the warning light and after the participant sets and releases the button that sets the automated tracker, a gauge is revealed with an indicator that moves along the gauge to show how far the dangerous condition has developed. The indicator will be at the bottom of its range for a false alarm, higher for a true alarm, and still higher if the participant has responded slowly to the warning. (The indicator rose at a constant speed and required 11 s to reach the top of the scale.) In addition, a red light comes on with the gauge if the alarm is true. The participant then presses the keyboard's space bar to bring the indicator back to the normal operating level. For a false alarm, a minimal time is required for the warning system to reset itself before the participant can move back to the tracking task; for a true alarm, added time is required that depends linearly on how far along the gauge the indicator has moved. If the participant fails to respond to a warning within 15 s, the warning is terminated and the warning system is reset. (The lower half of the screen, part of the Multi-Attribute Task Battery, was present but not used in our experiment.)

Participants

Four participants were selected from undergraduate applicants at the University of Massachusetts at Lowell on the basis of a screening interview and a pretest. They were all right-handed men and native English speakers. The pretest consisted of performing the manual tracking task for 10 to 15 min to demonstrate adequate visuomotor skills. Three of 4 participants completed the experiment. They spent 2 hr in initial training and then 6 hr in each of the five conditions of PPV.

Bonus Scheme

In addition to a base rate of $6.00 per hour, the participants could earn up to an additional $6.00 per hr conditional on the quality of their performance. They could earn bonuses for good tracking and for rapid response to true alarms. They could lose their bonus accumulated within a session for poor performance on either task. The two tasks were in competition, and so the participants had to learn the relative importance of the two in order to maximize their bonuses. In both tasks, the relation of bonus earned to a measure of performance was linear. For tracking, the performance measure was the root-mean-square (rms) error in

5-s intervals, and for the warning task the performance measure was total time from alarm onset to the keypress response to the (true) alarm. No bonuses or penalties were assigned to responses to false alarms. A penalty was assessed for failure to respond to an alarm within 15 s.

Independent Variable: PPV

Even the smallest of the experiment's five values of PPV (.25, .39, .50, .61, and .75) may be large compared with many that might be expected in real life situations. These particular values were selected because they were expected to bracket a major change in the participants' average speed of response to warnings.

The five conditions of PPV were each divided into three equal parts, and the $5 \times 3 = 15$ segments were represented in a different order to each participant. Each segment ran for two consecutive (not contiguous) 1-hr sessions, with the same PPV. Each hour was divided into 20-min periods separated by a short break. Each participant knew that the same PPV would hold for a given 2-hr segment but was unaware of the new value of PPV in effect for each successive 2-hr segment. In each segment, the first 20 trials—while the participant was adjusting to a new PPV—were omitted from data analyses. The decision to eliminate the first 20 trials was based on examination of the trial-by-trial latency plots. For most segments, the pattern of latencies appeared to stabilize within the first 20 trials.

The warning occurred on average every 34 s, distributed rectangularly between 30 and 38 s. So there were 216 warnings in a 2-hr segment of fixed PPV and 648 warnings in all for each PPV. Note that such a high event rate allowed use of a visual warning, as used primarily in cockpits, rather than an auditory warning, as might be appropriate to a lower event rate.

Dependent Variables: Accuracy of Tracking, Latency of Response to the Warning, and Bonuses Earned

There were three dependent variables. Accuracy of tracking was measured by rms error in 5-s intervals. Latency of response to the warning was measured in three components as well as their total: (a) from onset of light to pressing of the button to set the autotracker, (b) the duration of pressing the autotracker-setting button, and (c) the reaction time from releasing the autotracker-setting button to hitting the space bar to reset the warning system. Bonuses earned were calculated and displayed on a continuous basis: In the tracking task, a total earned was given for the preceding 5 s along with an update of the total for a 20-min period; for the warning task, at each response the bonus or penalty for that response was displayed along with the cumulative bonus and penalty. A cumulative total was also given for the two tasks combined and updated when either of the single-task bonuses was updated. The bonus information was given at the upper right of the display screen (see Figure 3).

RESULTS

The experimental results are given next for each participant in terms of (a) histograms showing the frequencies of the various (warning-response) latencies for each PPV, (b) graphs showing several percentiles of the latency distribution as a function of PPV, (c) a sampling of trial-by-trial warning-response latencies to show fine-grained patterns of behavior across PPVs and participants, (d) a graph showing mean latency as a function of the length of the preceding run of true or false alarms, and (e) graphs of expected bonus as a function of warning-response latency for each PPV and each participant.

Histograms of the Latency Distribution

The response-frequency distributions over latency are shown for each participant and each PPV in Figures 4, 5, and 6. The main effect is that shorter latencies are much more frequent at higher PPVs, and longer latencies are much more frequent at lower PPVs.

Participant 1 treated the highest two PPVs (.75 and .61) essentially alike, giving predominantly short latencies; gives many medium latencies for PPV = .50 and .39 while maintaining the preference for short latencies; and then shows a tendency toward longer latencies at PPV = .25. The longer latencies appear to form a bimodal distribution, with the two modes at about 6.7 and 8.1 s. Participants 2 and 3 were relatively similar to each other primarily in avoiding medium latencies. The short latencies dominate for both from PPV = .75 down through .39, whereas some longer latencies appear at .50 and .39; and a crossover to long-latency domination is made between .39 and .25, although some substantial number of short latencies remain even at the lowest PPV = .25. Throughout the lowest three PPVs, Participant 2 yielded slightly more medium latencies than did Participant 3.

In summary, Participant 3 gave evidence of pure or extreme strategies, as did Participant 2, although a little less so, and Participant 1 tended toward a more diffuse pattern. In individual interviews after the experiment, all 3 participants reported that they deliberately adopted an approximation to an all-or-none strategy. They said that when they were in doubt as to the dominance of true or false alarms, they tended to respond as if the alarm were true. Participant 1 acknowledged adopting occasionally a 50-50 strategy when neither true nor false alarms seemed to predominate. As shown later, all-or-none responding, yielding either minimally short or maximally long latencies, is an optimal strategy, depending on the PPV condition. Whatever the individual differences, and they are instructive, the strong effect of PPV on latency is clear for all 3 participants.

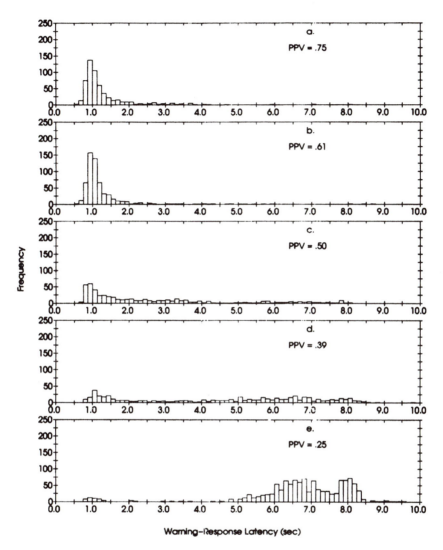

FIG. 4. Histograms of warning-response latencies for five positive predictive values (PPV): Participant 1.

Percentiles of the Latency Distribution as a Function of PPV

As an alternative presentation of latency-distribution data, Figure 7 shows five percentiles (90, 70, 50, 30, and 10) of the distribution of warning-response latencies for each participant at each of the five values of PPV. These plots present somewhat more succinctly than the preceding histograms the effects of

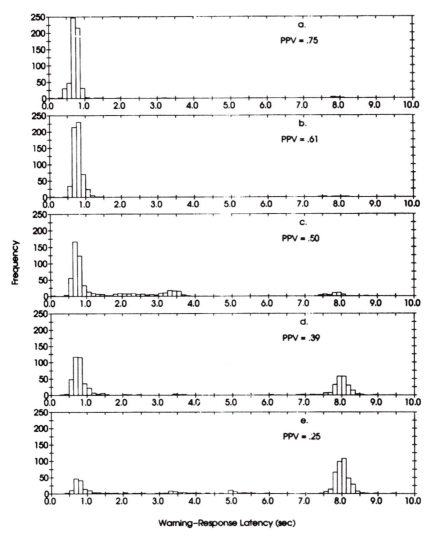

FIG. 5. Histograms of warning-response latencies for five positive predictive values (PPV): Participant 2.

PPV on latency, showing both central tendency and spread as a function of PPV. Again, Participants 2 and 3 tended toward pure or extreme strategies, Participant 2 less than Participant 3, and Participant 1's pattern is diffuse. Thus, for example, at PPV = .39, 70% of Participant 3's responses are in a narrow range less than 2 s, whereas approximately 20% of Participant 1's responses are in that range, and the remainder of them are widely distributed up to the maximum latency of about 8 s.

Average Latency as a Function of PPV

Regarding median latencies (the 50th percentile), Participants 2 and 3 maintained short latencies (median about 1 s) as PPV decreased from .75 to .39 and then shifted abruptly to long latencies (median about 8 s); Participant 1 shifted more gradually in median latency as PPV decreases.

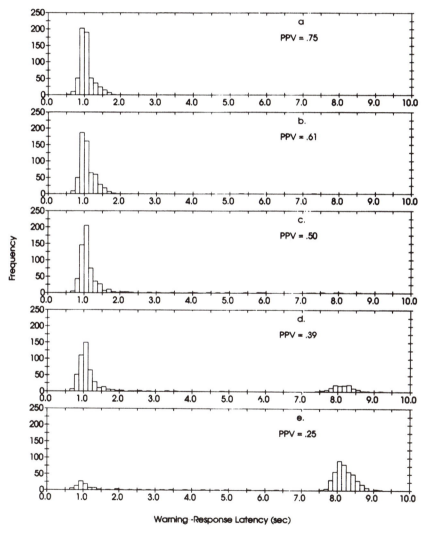

FIG. 6. Histograms of warning-response latencies for five positive predictive values (PPV): Participant 3.

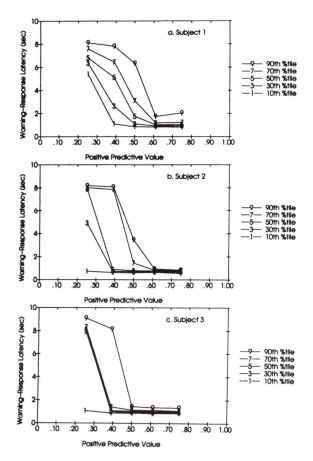

FIG. 7. Percentiles of the warning-response latency distributions for the five positive predictive values: (a) Participant 1; (b) Participant 2; (c) Participant 3.

Decomposition of Warning-Response Latency

I mentioned earlier the three components of warning-response latency. There was essentially no effect of PPV on the first component—the reaction time after the alarm onset until the first press of the button to set the autotracker—but a consistent difference between Participant 2 and the others. The median reaction time averaged across PPVs was 415 ms for Participant 2 and 657 and 664 ms for Participants 1 and 3, respectively. Across PPVs, there was little variation in this first component of reaction time. Note that it was in the participants' best interest to keep this time minimal; extending it could have only a negative effect on bonus. The second component of latency—the amount of time the button is held down to set the autotracker—showed approximately the same effect as seen in the total latency (see Figure 7), which implicates this component as the main contributor to total latency.

The third component of latency—the movement time from release of the autotracker-setting button to the press of the space bar to reset the warning system—showed essentially no effect of PPV. The median reaction times, averaged across PPVs, were 110, 109, and 131 ms for Participants 1, 2, and 3, respectively. The larger value for Participant 3 is due to an increased reaction time for PPV = .25; when this condition is omitted the median reaction time averaged over the remaining four conditions is 109 ms. Presumably, the 3rd participant observed that taking a longer time to press the space bar on false alarm trials cost him nothing.

Trial-by-Trial Warning—Response Latencies

Trial-by-trial latencies provide our closest approximation to raw data, and examinations of them were suggestive of some of the summaries of this report. Nine samples from a total of 90 plots are shown in Figures 8, 9, and 10 to represent different strategies observed within and across participants. All come from the three PPVs of .25, .39, and .75, the two extremes and also the value closest to the point of indifference relative to cost and benefit, as discussed later. Figure 8, in which PPV = .25, shows all 3 participants to begin a new PPV condition, as they typically do, by responding quickly, although for different numbers of trials from 1 participant to another. After switching to long latencies, Participant 1 gave an indication, as is typical of him, of gradual changes in latency, here first decreasing and then increasing. By contrast, Participants 2 and 3 showed abrupt and large changes, largely between minimally short and maximally long latencies. Participant 2 showed many oscillations as well as a period of intermediate latencies and several long blocks of long latencies. Participant 3 made one transition from short to long, where he stayed.

At PPV = .39 in Figure 9, Participant 1 again exhibited gradual changes in mean latency over time. Participant 2 again showed many oscillations as well as blocks of trials at one or the other extreme. Participant 3's behavior was similar, although with a lower frequency of oscillation and longer blocks of extreme latencies.

At PPV = .75 in Figure 10, Participants 1 and 3 were pretty much pinned at the short latencies, whereas Participant 2 showed occasional long latencies as if attempting to confirm that they are still paying less bonus and as if less convinced of the stability of PPV across a session.

Does Run Length Affect Warning-Response Latency?

That is, are participants more likely, as evidenced by warning-response latency, to regard a particular warning as true when it has been preceded by a string of true warnings and as false when preceded by a string of false warnings? The

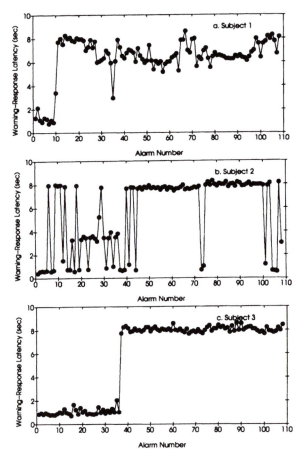

FIG. 8. Sample of trial-by-trial latencies from 3 participants for positive predictive value of .25: (a) Participant 1; (b) Participant 2; (c) Participant 3.

answer is no, as seen in Figure 11 for Participant 3; graphs for the other two participants are very similar.

These graphs again show warning-response latency to increase with decreasing PPV, latency to remain rather constant over different run lengths (except for variability caused by increasingly small sample sizes with increasing run length), and no distinction in latency between response after runs of true alarms and runs of false alarms. The appropriate conclusion seems to be that the participants are aware of the inherent PPV during a condition in which it is fixed and are not influenced by random, local variations over time within a condition.

Expected Bonus as a Function of Latency

The ultimate goal of a cost-benefit analysis undertaken here is to show the expected net benefit as a function of warning-response latency for each PPV and each participant. One arrives at that estimate by determining the actual benefit received by each participant as a function of the warning-response latency, separately for true and false alarms.

Figure 12 shows a pooling of trials from all five PPV conditions, separately for each participant. Net benefit on the ordinate was defined as the total benefit over the interval between the onset of one alarm event and the next. It can be

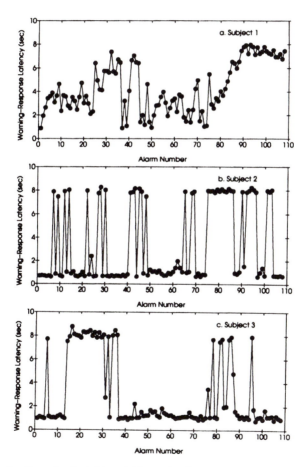

FIG. 9.   Sample of trial-by-trial latencies from 3 participants for positive predictive value of .39: (a) Participant 1; (b) Participant 2; (c) Participant 3.

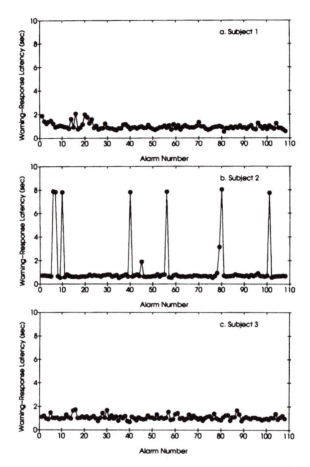

FIG. 10.   Sample of trial-by-trial latencies from 3 participants for positive predictive value of .75: (a) Participant 1; (b) Participant 2; (c) Participant 3.

seen that the participant, on true alarms, makes more money for shorter latencies, consistent with the structure of the bonus scheme. Conversely, on false alarms the participants make more money for longer latencies.

One can note again the typically different behaviors of the 3 participants: Participants 2 and 3 showed latencies clustered at the extremes (Participant 2 less than Participant 3), whereas Participant 1 showed a more uniform distribution of latencies.

The vertical spread at a particular latency, for a particular type of alarm, is due to variability in trial-by-trial tracking performance. As an approximation to the true relationship, one can fit a second-order polynomial to the data, shown by the solid lines. These two lines represent the expected benefit to be realized from hypothetical conditions consisting of 0% and 100% true alarms, respectively. Optimal behavior for such an extreme condition consists of either all long latencies (for 0% true alarms) or all short latencies (for 100% true alarms).

However, we want to predict expected net benefits for conditions containing different mixtures of true and false alarms. Figure 13 shows intermediate curves obtained by taking a weighted average of the two extreme curves for the five values of PPV used, the weight reflecting the PPV. From each curve, one can predict the optimal behavior, that which produces the maximal net benefit, for each participant. For example, at PPV = .25, all 3 participants showed a curve of positive slope and would benefit maximally from long latencies. Conversely,

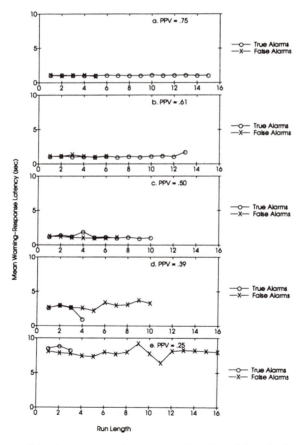

FIG. 11. Warning-response latency as a function of length of run of true or false alarms for the five positive predictive values (PPV).

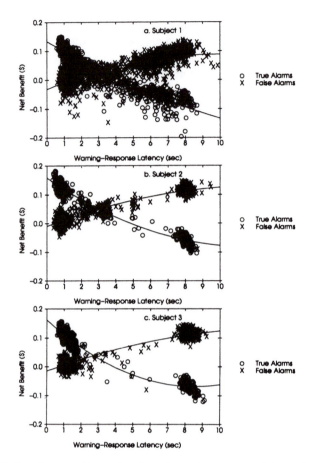

FIG. 12.   Net benefit as a function of warning-response latency for all five positive predictive values combined: (a) Participant 1; (b) Participant 2; (c) Participant 3.

for all participants at PPV = .75, the curves have a negative slope, so that shorter latencies are best. Intermediate curves differ slightly among participants, as does the PPV for the curve of zero average slope; at zero slope, latency has no effect on benefit. The curve of zero slope is near PPV = .39 for all 3 participants. Recall from the histograms in Figures 4 to 6 that Participant 1 showed a broad distribution of latencies at that PPV; at that PPV, the other 2 participants showed a bimodal distribution.

The behaviors of the participants demonstrate their sensitivity to the PPV variable in that the central tendencies of their latency distributions are close to the optimal for each value of the PPV. Further research should examine participants'

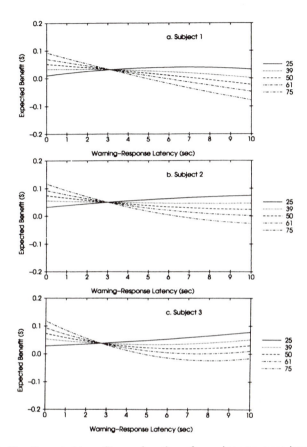

FIG. 13. Expected benefit as a function of warning-response latency for the five positive predictive values: (a) Participant 1; (b) Participant 2; (c) Participant 3.

sensitivity to changes in benefits and penalties by varying them while holding PPV constant.

DISCUSSION

Why do system operators ignore warnings? The answer, now generally appreciated, is that the warnings "cry wolf" too often. In present terms, their PPV is low. Typically, operators have better things to do than to respond to what is likely to be a false alarm. Moreover, frequent responses to false warnings can endanger a system's performance.

Signal detection theory provides a way of analyzing a warning system with respect to PPV—including as variables the detector's sensitivity and its threshold for issuing an alarm, and the decision problem of the human operator—and also with respect to the context in which the system is being used, including as variables the probability of a dangerous condition, the benefits and penalties of responding or not responding to a warning, and the penalties and benefits of leaving a primary task or not in order to respond.

Reported here is a laboratory experiment in which the PPV of a warning was varied from relatively low to high. The PPV quantity represents the combined contributions of a detector's sensitivity and threshold and the prior probability of the dangerous condition to be detected. For fixed benefits and penalties associated both with accuracy of performance in the background task and speed of response to a warning, the study examined in some detail the effects of PPV on a human operator's behavior relative to both tasks.

What does this experiment reveal? The participants, while showing some individual differences, behaved in a rational manner as specified by signal detection theory. In brief, they responded slowly to low PPVs and quickly to high PPVs to maximize the net gain from the benefits and penalties imposed. For this particular benefit-penalty structure, they responded slowly to a PPV of .25 and quickly to PPVs of .50 and greater and were less decisive at a PPV of approximately .40.

The benefit-penalty structure used was indeed particular, and so the exact quantitative performances observed in relation to the PPV variable are not general. However, the participants behaved qualitatively as signal detection theory would have it and in a manner that is quantitatively optimal for the specific benefit-penalty conditions we set. This experiment is a demonstration experiment, and it supports the idea that signal detection theory is a comprehensive tool for analyzing responses to warning signals. An extension of this demonstration is provided by another experiment in which the cost-benefit structure is varied for constant values of PPV; an article reporting the second experiment is being prepared.

A laboratory experiment, of course, does not faithfully represent the real world in several respects. Clearly, the costs assessed are not as severe as in real situations, and monetary costs and benefits probably did not capture the full range of motivating forces in real life settings. Moreover, the experiment was artificial in presenting many warnings in a short period of time, thus minimizing the roles of boredom and fatigue and their effects on attention. The participants were college students, not, for example, aircraft pilots.

There are two other respects in which the present experiment is only a beginning. First, this experiment provided the participant with a good deal of information, with its concentrated periods and high rate of warnings, as well as definite feedback regarding the truth or falsity of a warning, so that clearer realizations of optimal strategies were likely to emerge than in practical settings. Second, participants appear to vary in sensing and responding to the desirability of changing their strategies. The number of participants was small, so that individual differences in strategy could not be adequately explored.

Why is the PPV of a warning often low? A large part of the answer, perhaps not widely enough appreciated, is that the PPV is usually low because the prior probability of a dangerous condition is characteristically very low. That probability dominates PPV and produces low PPVs even for highly sensitive detectors with strict thresholds for issuing a warning. A second part of the answer is that system designers typically wish to minimize the probability of missing a dangerous condition and hence permit a decision threshold that is lenient enough (a false-positive proportion that is high enough) to further decrease the PPV.

Incidentally, Figure 2 can be used to calibrate the five specific PPV values used in the experiment. At the first ROC point mentioned in the discussion of that figure (FPP = .0025, TPP = .90), the PPVs, which ranged from .25 to .75, are seen to span the range of prior probabilities between .001 and .01. Alternatively, for a prior probability of .01, the PPV values span a range of FPP from .0025 to .03 and, simultaneously, a range of TPP of .90 to .98. For a prior probability of .001, the five experimental PPV values have values of FPP less than .0025, and have values of TPP less than .90; for such a low prior probability, a very strict decision threshold is required to yield PPVs as high as .25 to .75.

What PPV is required to ensure the desired, reliable response to a warning? This is a question that systems engineers are tempted to ask. I understand anecdotally that they may go on to ask what is considered to be a psychological question, namely, "What PPV is generally adequate?" For example, "Is a ratio of one false alarm to one true alarm (PPV = .50) acceptable?" Two comments are appropriate. First, the present analysis, as in Figure 2, indicates that a 1:1 ratio of false alarms to true alarms would be difficult to achieve, particularly if a low miss rate is desired, as it usually is. Second, the PPV required for a reliable response surely depends on the particular benefits and penalties associated with the system operation task and the warning-response task in a given system. Even in a given system, these benefits and penalties can vary over time as the operating conditions change (e.g., the penalty of leaving the system operation task will depend on how well or poorly the system happens to be operating at a given time). So there is no single adequate PPV that is general to all systems, or even to systems of a particular class, and no single adequate PPV that will hold across different conditions for a given system. Further research is needed to illuminate and exemplify the dependency of warning-response time on benefits and penalties.

The explicit introduction of systems engineers above highlights the fact that the general warning-system problem is one in which there are two decision makers in sequence: one is an automatic device designed to detect a dangerous condition, and the other is a human who sees the device's warning only as probabilistic input for his or her own decision analysis. This sequential problem has been addressed in detection theory models for a task similar to the present one, as developed by Murrell (1977), Sorkin and Woods (1985), and Robinson and Sorkin (1985). They modeled a task in which the operator made an observation and then a detection decision about the existence of a dangerous condition after being alerted by a warning. The concern here has been for how the PPV of the first detector affects observed behavior of the human who is expected to respond immediately to a warning. To the extent that the human responds unreliably at some values of PPV, attention should be focused on the performance of the automatic detector, as well as on the performance of the human.

What needs to be done? From my perspective, two systems issues have received less deliberate attention than they deserve. First, who is taking what kinds of considerations into account in setting the automatic detector's thresholds for issuing a warning? The engineer attempts continually to develop detectors of greater sensitivity but must work with what is available at a given time, and he or she must also accept the prior probabilities of a dangerous condition as being what they are. However, the decision threshold is a powerful variable that requires and rewards very explicit concern. We saw, for example, in Figure 2 that PPV can vary from near 1.0 to as little as .1 for a realistic prior probability, .001, as the FPP varies below .01. The tendency observed and remarked on, to set the threshold to achieve a very high TPP without sensitive awareness of the corresponding values of FPP and PPV, can undermine warning effectiveness to a large extent and perhaps completely.

The second question is a repeat of the first in a setting (e.g., the aircraft cockpit) in which there are multiple automatic detectors (e.g., a dozen or more). When the thresholds of several automatic detectors are each set primarily to avoid a miss, the overall PPV of the system can be very low indeed. A procurement process in which several independent manufacturers set thresholds to meet a specified, very high TPP for their own detector—with an unspecified effect on its FPP and, hence, on the total system's PPV—is clearly not going to be adequate.

The science exists for choosing the best decision thresholds in high-stakes detection and diagnostic settings (Chapter 5). These quantitative procedures focus attention, in any given setting, on the data that need to be gathered on prior probabilities and on the judgments that need to be made about costs and benefits of relevant behaviors—and they show how to combine this information optimally in selecting one or more thresholds. The discipline and assistance these procedures provide in designing and operating detection systems remain to be applied to systems in which warnings of danger are critical.

REFERENCES

Comstock, J. R., & Arnegard, R. J. (1992). *The multi-attribute task battery for human operator workload and strategic behavior research* (NASA Technical Memorandum No. 104174). Hampton, VA: National Aeronautics and Space Administration, Langley Research Center.

Green, D. M., & Swets, J. A. (1966/1988). *Signal detection theory and psychophysics*. New York: Wiley. (Reprinted by Peninsula Publishing, Los Altos, CA).

Harvey, L. O., Jr. (1992). The critical operating characteristic and the evaluation of expert judgment. *Organizational Behavior and Human Decision Processes, 53*, 229–251.

Harvey, L. O., Jr., Hammond, K. R., Lusk, C. M., & Mross, E. F. (1992). The application of signal detection theory to weather forecasting behavior. *Monthly Weather Review, 120*, 863–883.

Murrell, G. W. (1977). Combination of evidence in perceptual judgment. In M. F. Kaplan & S. Schwartz (Eds.), *Human judgment and decision processes in applied settings* (pp. 169–201). New York: Academic Press.

Robinson, D. E., & Sorkin, R. D. (1985). A contingent criterion model of computer assisted detection. In R. Eberts & C. G. Eberts (Eds.), *Trends in ergonomics/human factors* (Vol. II, pp. 75–82). Amsterdam: North-Holland.

Sorkin, R. D. (1988). Why are people turning off our alarms? *Journal of the Acoustical Society of America, 84*, 1107–1108.

Sorkin, R. D., & Woods, D. D. (1985). Systems with human monitors: A signal detection analysis. *Human-Computer Interaction, 1*, 49–75.

Swets, J. A. (1986). Form of empirical ROCs in discrimination and diagnostic tasks: Implications for theory and measurement of performance. *Psychological Bulletin, 99*, 181–198. (Chapter 2).

Swets, J. A. (1988). Measuring the accuracy of diagnostic systems. *Science, 240*, 1285–1293. (Chapter 4).

Swets, J. A. (1992). The science of choosing the right decision threshold in high-stakes diagnostics. *American Psychologist, 47*, 522–532. (Chapter 5).

Swets, J. A., & Pickett, R. M. (1982). *Evaluation of diagnostic systems: Methods from signal detection theory*. New York: Academic Press.

Appendix: Computer Programs for Fitting ROCs

Described here are five computer programs (or sets of programs) for fitting ROCs. They are ordered according to the time of their appearance; the later programs give increasing coverage of types of experimental conditions. They all give estimates of one or more measures of discrimination acuity and decision criterion along with variance information.

1. DORFMAN, ALF. An improved version of the 1969 RSCORE program published by Donald Dorfman and E. Alf, Jr., called RSCORE II, was listed in the book Evaluation of Diagnostic Systems: Methods from Signal Detection Theory by J. A. Swets and R. M. Pickett; New York: Academic Press, 1982. For rating data, it gives the binormal ROC area index A_z, some variants of d' for binormal ROCs of non-unit slope, and the variances of the estimates. In addition, it gives z-values for decision criteria. The program prints out the variance-covariance matrix of the binormal-model parameter estimates.

2. CENTOR. Robert M. Centor has made available The ROC Analyzer. Again from rating data, this program gives both the "nonparametric" and parametric (Gaussian) ROC area measure, along with other parameters. A new version is Windows based and gives a graphical representation of the ROC. One can contact Robert M. Centor, M.D., via email at RCENTOR@GIM.MEB.UAB.EDU.

3. METZ. Charles E. Metz provides a set of four programs. ROCFIT is an enhanced version of the Dorfman-Alf program that provides a more flexible input format, checks input data for "degeneracy," uses somewhat more robust numerical methods, and provides additional output such as a list of the coordinates of representative points on the fitted binormal ROC. LABROC accommodates data collected on a continuous (rather than discrete categorical) scale and, thus, is useful for ROC analyses that involve probability judgments and results of

quantitative laboratory tests. CORROC2 uses a bivariate binormal model to analyze paired confidence ratings (e.g., from two imaging techniques applied to the same cases) that are collected on discrete categorical scales; the primary purpose of this program is to evaluate the statistical significance of differences between two correlated ROC estimates. CLABROC is similar to CORROC2 but is designed for paired confidence ratings collected on continuous scales. All four programs are available in versions for MS-DOS machines, Apple Macintoshes, and VMS and Unix workstations. A new integrated software package, entitled ROCKIT, that performs the functions of all four existing programs and adds several new features is scheduled for release in late 1995 or early 1996. Dr. Metz can be reached at the Department of Radiology, The University of Chicago, Chicago, Ill 60637; via email at C-METZ@UCHICAGO.EDU.

4. DORFMAN, BERBAUM, METZ. These authors recently presented a program based on the jackknife method that permits generalization to both the population of test cases obtained with a given diagnostic technique and the population of test diagnosticians ("readers"). It extends Metz's CORROC analysis from one test reader to multiple readers. Called "MRMC" for multi-reader/multi-case, it focuses on the index A_z, but applies to other models and measures. The program is available free of charge from Dr. Donald Dorfman, Department of Psychology, The University of Iowa, Iowa City, IA 52242. His email address is donald-dorfman@uiowa.edu.

5. DORFMAN, BERBAUM. These authors have recently developed an enhanced version of RSCORE II, entitled RSCORE 4. The program provides a solution to the problem of degenerate data sets sometimes obtained with sparse discrete rating data, as well as providing the usual maximum-likelihood binormal model estimates and corresponding variances and covariances. A series of computer simulations showed that it outperformed ROCFIT as well as the Wilcoxon statistic on a variety of standard measures of diagnostic accuracy. The program is available from Dr. Dorfman.

Author Index

Numbers in italics *denote pages with complete bibilographic information.*

Y

Yacowar, N., *119*
Yager, D., *30*
Yerushalmy, J., *119, 167*
Youden, W. J., 65, *95*

Young, F. W., *199*
Yule, G. U., 5, 33, *58,* 66, 72, *95*

Z

Zurndorfer, E. A., 66, *92*

Subject Index

Speech, 28
Standard Deviation, 11, 36, 69, 211–213
Statistical Decision Theory, 2, 15–19, 67, 149–150, 210–215
Statistical Hypotheses, 2, 9, 13, 16–19, 67, 100
Statistical Power, 2, 17–19, 198
Stimulus, xiii–xiv
  Error, 14
  Null, 9, 12, 14, 15
Subliminal Perception, 26
Subset Analysis (of test cases), 180–181, Chapter 8
Survey Question, 250, 260–264
Survey Research, 145, Chapter 11
Survey Respondent, 250, 259, 262–264
Systems Considerations (for danger signals), 289–290

T

2AFC (two-alternative forced-choice), *see* Forced-Choice Method
Test Set (of cases to be diagnosed) 187, 189
Thermography, 159
Threshold
  Decision Threshold, *see* Decision Criterion
  Models, 34, 79–87
    Double-Threshold, 34, 81, 86, 89
    High-Threshold, 34, 81, 84, 89
  Physiological, 9, 10, 13, 14, 55
  Sensory, 1, 2, 9, 10, 25
  Stimulus, 10, 14, 15
  Theory, xiv
Training Set (of cases to be diagnosed), 187, 189
True-Negative Response/Probability, xiv–xv, 21
True-Positive Response/Probability, xiv–xv, 2, 4, 21, 123–124, 153, 271–272
Truth Data, 97, 100, 112–113, 182, 187, 198, 206, 262–263

Two-by-Two Table, 4, 21, 22, 37, 62–63, 67, 77, 86, 91–92, 100–101, 151, 207–208, 251, 270–271
Type I Error, 2, 17–19
Type II Error, 17–19

U

Utility/Utilities, *see also* Costs and Benefits, Cost-Benefit Analysis, xv, 56, 99, 147, 258

V

Variability, Sensory, 8, 9
Variance (of Distributions), 11–12, 22, 24, 33, 36, 53, 68–71
Vigilance, 3, 25, 26, 56

W

Warning Systems, 146, Chapter 12
Weather Forecasting, 3, 48, 49, 79, 107, 112–115, 118–119 (Notes 16, 44)
Western Blot Test for AIDS, 129–136

Y

Yes-No Method/Task, 1, 3, 25, 37, 103, 153

Z

Z (index of discrimination acuity), 64, 66, 81, 83–84, 87
z(A) (index of discrimination acuity), 88, 90–91, 117 (Note 13), 156–157